MIND GAME

By the Writers of Baseball Prospectus

Jim Baker

Will Carroll

James Click

Clifford J. Corcoran

Clay Davenport

Steven Goldman

Jay Jaffe

Rany Jazayerli

Chris Kahrl

Jason Karegeannes

Jonah Keri

Ben Murphy

Doug Pappas

Dave Pease

Dayn Perry

Joe Sheehan

Nate Silver

Paul A. Swydan

Keith Woolner

Derek Zumsteg

Steven Goldman, Editor

Workman Publishing • New York

Library of Congress Cataloging-in-Publication Data

Mind game : how the Boston Red Sox got smart and finally won a World
    Series / by the writers of Baseball prospectus, Steven Goldman, editor.
        p. cm.
    Includes index.
    ISBN-13: 978-0-7611-4018-4 (alk. paper)
    ISBN-10: 0-7611-4018-2 (alk. paper)
        1. Boston Red Sox (Baseball team) 2. World Series (Baseball) 2004.
    I. Goldman, Steven, 1970– II. Baseball prospectus.

GV875.B62M56 2004
796.357'64'0974461--dc22

                                                            2005051433

Cover design by Paul Gamarello

Workman Publishing Company, Inc.
708 Broadway
New York, NY 10003-9555
www.workman.com

Printed in U.S.A.
First printing September 2005

10 9 8 7 6 5 4 3 2 1

I don't think that exists, and we look forward to proving it.
—RED SOX GENERAL MANAGER THEO EPSTEIN on *"The Curse."*
baseballprospectus.com interview, February 10, 2004

I can show you a trick or two which I don't teach to everybody,
I can tell you! . . . Bring along lots of dry statistics—it is the very
best sauce a humorous book can have. Ingeniously used,
they just make a reader smack his chops in gratitude.
—MARK TWAIN, *letter to a potential collaborator, 1875*

CONTENTS

ACKNOWLEDGMENTS

In April 2005, the novelist Neil Gaiman gave a speech in which he quoted a bit of advice from the fantasy writer Gene Wolfe. In response to Gaiman's assertion that with his latest book he had finally "figured out how to write a novel," Wolfe said, "You never learn how to write a novel. You merely learn how to write the novel you're on." *Mind Game* is not a novel, but Wolfe's observation still applies. Though I have written books of my own and participated in the making of a few more, this volume presented a new set of challenges to which only a little of my previous experience applied. As such, I am indebted to many for supplying me with assistance and insight at crucial moments:

Not only did Jonah Keri contribute three chapters, despite having just finished his own grueling work as co-editor of *Baseball Prospectus 2005*, but he acted as Horatio to my Hamlet (or maybe that's Jester to my Lear), offering assistance, guidance, sagacity, and even some tough love at key moments. Whenever I questioned one of my own judgments, Jonah was there to affirm or deny the decision with unimpeachable logic. If you can imagine a vacillating Jimmy Stewart being schooled by a Jewish John Wayne in *The Man Who Shot Liberty Youkilis*, you'll understand what Jonah meant to this project.

My BP mentor, Chris Kahrl, wrote several chapters under stressful circumstances, among them the completion of *her* work as co-editor of the BP annual. The instructiveness of Chris's vast experience in preparing books for publication and in dealing with other professionals cannot be overstated.

Keith Woolner and James Click were always ready to answer even my most mundane statistical questions and to supply whole hard drives of data for inclusion in the book. Derek Zumsteg leapt into the breach to supply a great deal of fine material at a moment's notice, and also graciously endured my occasional ill-humor and impatience while I waited for him to save my bacon. Jay Jaffe also stepped in on short notice and executed with his usual style and good humor (even though I was getting between him and planning a wedding). Jim Baker received some of the toughest assignments in the book and handled each of them with aplomb. Paul Swydan, Dave Haller, Dave Metz, and Caleb Peiffer pored over years of box scores without grumbling—or at least not so I could hear it. BP contributor Chaim Bloom also spent some of his valuable time securing information for the project.

Very special thanks go to Jason Karegeannes, who acted as my research assistant on this project, finding answers to my every question, no matter how esoteric.

Baseball Prospectus's executive board, headed by Nate Silver, selected me for this project and I thank them (and Nate in particular) for their faith. Indeed, I must thank all the members of Baseball Prospectus, who were challenging to deal with in the best of ways, forcing me to *think* on a daily basis. It is my honor to be taught by you.

Outside of Baseball Prospectus, I owe debts of gratitude to Cliff Corcoran, who gave me the benefit of his experience in publishing despite being busy editing a certain future bestseller himself; the always canny and supportive Andrew Baharlias; the wise and charming Angèle Fauchier, who kept me laughing (and challenged me to do yet more critical thinking!) with conversation during the many nights I was up late minding *Mind Game*. Will Weiss and Fred Harner at YES were both supportive and patient given the many disruptions to my *Pinstriped Bible* publication schedule.

My serenely patient wife, Stefanie, endured my many hours of isolation, despite traveling most of the way through pregnancy while my eyes were fixed on the computer screen. I have been blessed with a wife who believes in me and wholeheartedly supports me in the projects I take on, no matter how quixotic they may seem at times. Gentlemen, if you don't have someone like this in your life, I advise you to go find her and never look back. Stefanie, otherwise known as Dr. Goldman, scientist, also contributed a key piece of analysis that solved a vexing problem in the book.

My daughter, Sarah, the most good-humored four-year-old it has been my pleasure to know, was good enough to understand that "Daddy is in trouble" meant that he could only spare the time for a quick hug and a kiss before getting back to work. Without her patience, no doubt inherited from her mother, this project would have been impossible.

Finally, many thanks to Workman's Richard Rosen, who embraced this project and was most generous with me personally, despite my frequent absences to go off and have a two-week case of the flu or have a potentially fatal tumor subjected to laser thermography. Richard is exacting but fair, and I am certain that this book would not be as good as it is without his tireless examination of every thought herein for the faintest flaw. Given a choice between Richard's intensity and some workaday Perry White whose only worry is when you're going to hand in the text, I'll take Richard every time.

Baseball Prospectus would also like to thank Theo Epstein, Nelson de la Rosa, Peter Gammons, Gary Gillette, Bill Morgan, Pete Palmer, Ryen Russillo, Curt Schilling, Cory Schwartz, Steve Silva, David Vincent, Dave Wallace, Jared Weiss, and, of course, our most excellent agent Sydelle Kramer.

—STEVEN GOLDMAN
EAST BRUNSWICK, NEW JERSEY
JULY, 2005

A COMFORTING NOTE
ABOUT STATISTICS

Although Baseball Prospectus is well known for its penetrating, insightful, and admittedly sometimes arcane baseball statistics, you can thoroughly enjoy *Mind Game* without a degree in advanced mathematics—or even the ability to multiply 4 times 17 in your head. For those new to the whole concept of advanced baseball statistics, which are really just the old baseball statistics remixed to make them more meaningful, there is an extensive glossary and leader list appendix. It's not mandatory to read it—that's why it's an appendix.

However, there are two statistical references that the typical reader may not have encountered before that appear frequently throughout the book. The "slash stats"—typically rendered as, for example, .310/.428/.510—stand for the triple-headed goddess of baseball statistics: batting average (the number of hits per at-bat), on-base percentage (essentially the number of hits plus walks per plate appearance), and slugging percentage (the number of *bases* per at-bat, a statistic that favors extra-base hits). In 1927, the year he hit 60 home runs, Babe Ruth batted .356/.486/.772. That's pretty good. In 1999, the year he sank the Mets in the National League playoffs, Rey Ordonez hit .258/.319/.317. That's pretty bad. Baseball analysts differ over whether power or patience is the most important skill for a player to have, but the essence of the game is getting on base, so a high number in between those slashes trumps all.

The other reference that frequently comes up is VORP, which stands for Value Over Replacement Player. VORP was invented by Baseball Prospectus's Keith Woolner, and it's an all-in-one stat that answers the question "How many more runs does this guy generate than the freely available Triple A minor leaguer or utility veteran who would most likely replace him at his position?" If you're a Red Sox, Rangers, or Diamondbacks fan, you're probably thinking about Donnie Sadler just now (career VORP is –38.9). In 1927, Babe Ruth's VORP was 127.8, the all-time twelfth-best season in this category. Since 10 runs over replacement adds about one win to a team's record, Ruth was worth roughly 13 wins to the Yankees over his theoretical replacement. In 1999, Rey Ordonez's VORP was 4.3, which meant he was barely better than whoever the Mets could've come up with to replace him if he were injured—or too embarrassed to continue playing.

That's all you need to know.

INTRODUCTION:
A BRAIN SURGEON
WALKS INTO A BAR . . .

A brain surgeon walks into a bar after a hard day in the OR. He sits down at the counter, orders himself a cold one, and takes note of the big-screen television. It's tuned to one of the popular forensic crime dramas that rule network television schedules. A medical examiner leans over a mutilated body in an alleyway.

"Take a close look at this entry wound, Detective," the examiner is saying. "The bullet penetrated here, then turned his left parietal lobe into hamburger. Must've hurt like the dickens."

The brain surgeon winces. "That's completely inaccurate. He's pointing to the wrong part of the brain. The bullet hit the right temporal lobe, not the left parietal lobe."

"No way, man!" shouts a man in a faded Detroit Tigers jersey two barstools away. "That ain't no right temporal! They made the right call! I've been a brain fan since I was seven years old and I know! Up yours, buddy!"

Baseball may not be brain surgery, but that doesn't mean that everyone is an expert on the national pastime any more than we expect the man on the street to know neurophysiology. Yet virtually everyone who follows baseball acts as if he knows what he's talking about. This book is your insurance policy against being one of those people.

A century of sportswriters, broadcasters, guys in bars, and baseball men themselves have burdened our understanding of the game with half-truths and outright inventions. To take a few examples:

- Leadoff hitters have to have speed.
- Character is more important than talent.
- The more RBIs a player has, the greater his contribution to his team.
- Some players hit better in the clutch.
- Teams that hit a lot of home runs don't win as many big games as those that bunt and steal bases.
- Bullpen pitchers fall into two categories: regular relievers and those who can close.
- The closer is the most important man in the bullpen.
- A player who can't hit but is an above-average fielder is just as valuable as a good hitter who is an average defender.

One of the greatest myths of all was the Boston Red Sox curse. There *was* no curse. There was just a tradition of incompetence and mismanagement going back to 1919. Believing their own evasions, the Red Sox continued to assemble one team after another without ever using their brains or their common sense to address their actual flaws.

Since its founding in 1996, Baseball Prospectus has developed a reputation through its annual guide and magazine-style Web site as the nation's foremost independent group of baseball analysts and pundits, breaking new ground in areas the game has long neglected: intelligent team design, objective player evaluation, injury-preventative pitcher usage, as well as dozens of other insights, many of which are now commonly utilized in the game, or soon will be. In the pages that follow, the writers and performance analysts of the Baseball Prospectus group dissect and explain the process that enabled the 2004 Red Sox to win their first championship since 1918. Week by week and in some cases day by day, BP considers the problems encountered along the way, both on and off the field, and reveals that winning a World Series is not just a matter of getting the big hits at the right time, but of having a plan and a rational worldview.

In short, the Red Sox finally got smart and won themselves a championship. Of course, getting smart doesn't guarantee a World Series championship, but it sure beats staying dumb and hoping one will find you by accident.

—STEVEN GOLDMAN

PROLOGUE

O ctober 17, 2004, the American League Championship Series, New York Yankees at Boston Red Sox. It is the bottom of the ninth inning of Game Four, and it is all over, again, over like 1949 with Vic Raschi and Joe Page and Joe DiMaggio, over like 1978 with Bucky Dent, over like 2003 with, of all people, Aaron Boone. The Yankees won 101 games during the regular season. They have won six straight playoff games, including the first three games of this series. In the previous game they put 19 runs on the board. This one is closer, just 4–3, but the Yankees have a future Hall of Famer in closer Mariano Rivera, whose steadfastness in the crucible of the postseason is legendary. For the eighty-sixth time going on infinity, the Red Sox are cooked.

Dave Roberts dances off first base, having entered the game as a pinch runner for Kevin Millar, who worked Rivera for a five-pitch walk to open the inning. By all rights Roberts shouldn't even be on the team. He had been with the Los Angeles Dodgers since 2002, using his exceptional speed to establish himself as the team's center fielder and leadoff hitter. This was quite an accomplishment for a player who was drafted in 1993 at age twenty-one and didn't make the majors to stay until he was thirty. It was the speed that did it. It was his calling card, his only calling card. Roberts didn't hit for great average or any kind of power, and he wasn't all that good at getting on base, but boy, could he run, and the old school baseball types loved that.

Too bad, then, that the Dodgers weren't being run by an old-school baseball type, but by one of those pencil-necked refugees from Billy Beane's radical Oakland commune. Paul DePodesta had become the general manager in February 2004, and he had learned to think of the running game as a distraction from the important business of taking walks and hitting home runs.

DePo, as he is called, had about four outfielders he'd rather try ahead of Roberts, so it wasn't surprising that on July 31, the trading deadline, Roberts was traded away from Los Angeles. What was surprising was where he was headed: Boston, home of general manager Theo Epstein, a kindred spirit to DePodesta and Beane, the youngest of a new generation of baseball executives who believed that the pure base stealer should go the way of the ice wagon and flannel uniforms. Indeed, the Red Sox ran and bunted only under extreme duress. The 1985 Cardinals this was not.

Once Roberts got to Boston, he mostly sat. And sat. The manager kept an eye on him but didn't call his name very often. It was as if Roberts had changed from a ballplayer into some kind of glass-front box with the words *break in case of need for stolen base* stenciled on the front. But Epstein's orthodoxy, reinforced by special adviser, Bill James, the creator of the whole analytical business that had debunked stolen bases in the first place, held that if you built the right kind of team, Roberts's skills set would be largely extraneous. Except—and this was the key part of it, the flexible part of it that most people didn't get—except when it *was* necessary.

And so here Roberts was, glass broken, standing on first base with Bill Mueller at the plate, the only potential run of the year that mattered anymore. It was a desperate moment, but nonetheless *a moment that had been planned for.* That was the difference between this time around and 1949, 1978, 2003, and all the other disappointments of the last century. God was in the details, and so were playoff victories. And the Red Sox were finally looking after the details.

Rivera threw over to first. Once. Twice. Roberts got back to the bag. Every problem is a lock looking for a key. The Red Sox had spent decades half-asleep, oblivious to the locks, never mind looking for the keys.

Rivera returned his focus to the man at the plate. Roberts took his lead—not an inch shorter than before, maybe half an inch longer now. Rivera got set in the stretch, looked once more at Roberts, then committed to home plate with a barely perceptible transfer of weight to his right foot, his left foot now rising off the mound.

But Roberts was already gone, digging toward second, erasing the past with every step.

1

THE BANALITY OF INCOMPETENCE
1919–2002

I marvel they never spoke of these matters; or, verily, I marvel not, seeing that the least rumor of the sort would have driven them from New England. We are a people of prayer, and good works to boot, and abide no such wickedness.
—NATHANIEL HAWTHORNE, *"Young Goodman Brown," 1846*

The Cubs have waited longer. The White Sox have not only waited longer, but carry a burden of a tragedy worthy of Shakespeare, that of the manipulated, manipulating Black Sox of 1919. The Cleveland Indians have suffered more pathetically. The Phillies have a history of greater neglect, enduring decades with owners who invested nothing in the franchise. A's fans had to wait forty years, through the senescence of Connie Mack, the double-dealings of Arnold Johnson with the Yankees, and Charlie Finley's learning curve, and they had to wait in three different cities. The Giants are fifty years and three thousand miles removed from their last championship.

All of these teams have gone years without competent leadership. Yet only the Red Sox had a curse—the Curse of the Bambino that was supposed to have descended on the franchise on January 3, 1920, when pitcher/outfielder George Herman "Babe" Ruth was traded to the Yankees by Red Sox owner Harry Frazee in exchange for $125,000 and the $300,000 personal loan secured by the mortgage on Fenway Park.

Boston Red Sox owner Tom Yawkey and his wife, Jean, 1938

Superstition is avoidance, a way of explaining things we don't understand and relieving feelings of helplessness. By consigning these things to a higher sphere, we are left with nothing to do but, as the prayer goes, find the courage to accept what we cannot change. Then, as humans have done throughout history, we take a knee. The truth is that for nearly a century the Red Sox never found the courage, or the competence, to change things that could have been changed. Boston has been victimized by some of the worst owners and administrators in sports history. There is no Curse of the Bambino, unless the curse is construed to visit on its victims astonishing incompetence, complacency, and bigotry.

The last is the most important. In his oft-revised book *The Curse of the Bambino*, Dan Shaughnessy called the sale of Ruth to the Yankees "Baseball's original sin." That's a dramatic overstatement: Frazee's sale of Ruth to the Yankees was at worst a misjudgment, nothing more—the kind that every team has made, although the subsequent and persistent mediocrity of the Red Sox has made it seem like the granddaddy of all mistakes. Baseball's real original sin was racial segregation, and Boston had more to do with perpetuating that sin than any other team. In 1630, Boston's founding father, John Winthrop, said that the new settlement would be a "city on a hill," a beacon to all nations. Although Boston may have been a hotbed of abolitionist sentiment in the nineteenth century, its American League franchise was, until the last possible moment, a hotbed of racial hate. You can't build a shining contender on a hill when you're standing in a hole.

Until 1918 they were the team of the teens; between 1912 and 1918, Boston won four league championships and four World Series. The last of these teams featured stars like left fielder Duffy Lewis, shortstop Everett Scott, catcher Wally Schang, pitchers Carl Mays, Bullet Joe Bush, Ernie Shore, Dutch Leonard, Sad Sam Jones, Herb Pennock, and Babe Ruth. Then the trouble began and there was nothing supernatural about it. For decades, the story of the fall of the Red Sox has been told this way:

In a flush moment, Broadway producer Harry Frazee bought the Sox—on credit. Now he was flat broke. In 1918, Frazee was attempting to mount a new musical, *No! No! Nannette!* featuring songs by the composer Vincent Youmans. He had also just been hit with an expensive divorce settlement, and the former owners of the Red Sox were pressing him for payment. His sole salable asset was his ballclub. Rather than sell the whole team, the usual last resort of wayward owners, Frazee opted to make his money by selling off his best players in piecemeal fashion. He took a championship team and traded it to the New York Yankees, permanently reversing the relationship between the two clubs.

Frazee's theater headquarters on 42nd Street (he commuted to Boston) was only a couple of doors down from the Yankees' Manhattan office, and it was only natural that, in his moment of need, he should turn to Yankee owners Jacob Ruppert and Til Houston, with whom he had become friends. Between 1918 and 1923, Frazee sent his best Red Sox to New York, including Carl Mays, Duffy Lewis, Dutch Leonard, Everett Scott, Wally Schang, Ernie Shore, Sad Sam Jones, Joe Bush, Herb Pennock, pitching prospect George Pipgras, manager Ed Barrow, Babe Ruth—and the mortgage on Fenway Park.

That's the story—and almost none of it is true. Vincent Youmans had just turned twenty-one when Ruth was traded and didn't publish his first song until the following year. *No! No! Nanette!* didn't reach Broadway until 1925. To believe that Frazee needed money for *No! No! Nanette!* means you have to believe that the musical had a six-year gestation period at a time when Victor Herbert had five Broadway shows come and go between February 1919 and June 1921. Jerome Kern had five during roughly the same period.

As Glen Stout and Richard A. Johnson write in the book *Red Sox Century,* Frazee never did run out of money: "The press reported that Frazee turned a profit on the Red Sox in 1919. And Frazee's grandson recalls that no financial trouble was ever mentioned by his father when he was growing up, nor has he ever uncovered any evidence of it in family papers."

The correct context for understanding the Ruth trade—just one of ten with the Yankees during a four-year period—is not the need for money to finance a musical, but the desire to reorganize the team following the First World War. In light of the economic conditions both in baseball and the nation at the time—113,000 dead in the war, 3.5 million newly laid-off workers, the worst influenza pandemic in history—it was inevitable that the Red Sox would trade Ruth. Frazee was not broke but, as evidenced by the loan component of the Ruth deal, lacked liquidity. Ruth was demanding compensation commensurate with the game's biggest stars, but his drawing power in the face of these crises was questionable. Red Sox attendance had declined for five straight years, going from 539,885 in 1915 to 249,513 in 1918 (due in part to the truncated season caused by the government's "work or fight" directive to baseball). Attendance rebounded to 417,291 in 1919, but the increase is misleading: The American League as a whole saw attendance jump by over 100 percent, so Boston ranked only fifth in the league, compared to third in 1918. Relative to the rest of the league, Boston declined from 14.6 percent of league attendance to 11.4 percent. The short-term outlook for baseball in Boston was not good.[1]

Money was a factor in the Ruth sale, but at Ruth's instigation. After 1918 he had agreed to a three-year contract calling for $10,000 a year. After his superb 1919 season, he was threatening to hold out for $20,000. This exacerbated the already substantial resentment about Ruth's behavior. Like the trade of Nomar Garciaparra in 2004, the Ruth deal was driven as much by personality issues as by greed or need. After the trade, Frazee said that "the Boston club could no longer put up with his eccentricities . . . Twice before he has jumped the club and revolted. . . . Ruth is taking on weight tremendously. . . ."[2] Ruth retorted: "I have never been a disturbing element on the Red Sox. . . . I am thinking very seriously of taking the matter to court to prove these statements untrue and show Boston fans that they are being tricked by the so-called sportsman Frazee." History would prove Frazee the more accurate observer of human nature.

THE FRAZEE TRADES, 1917–1923		
Date	Red Sox Receive	Yankees Receive
12/18/18	OF Frank Gilhooley P Slim Love P Ray Caldwell C Roxy Walters $15,000	P Ernie Shore P Dutch Leonard OF Duffy Lewis
5/19/19	OF Bill Lamar	Cash
7/29/19	P Allan Russell P Bob McGraw $40,000	P Carl Mays
1/3/20	$125,000 $300,000 loan	OF Babe Ruth
12/15/20	C Muddy Ruel 2B Del Pratt OF Sammy Vick P Hank Thormahlen	P Waite Hoyt P Harry Harper C Wally Schang IF Mike McNally
12/20/21	SS Roger Peckinpaugh P Jack Quinn P Rip Collins P Bill Piercy	SS Everett Scott P Bullet Joe Bush P Sad Sam Jones
2/24/22	P Alex Ferguson	Waiver price
7/23/22	OF Chick Fewster OF Elmer Miller SS Johnny Mitchell P Lefty O'Doul $50,000	3B Jumping Joe Dugan OF Elmer Smith
1/3/23	C Al Devormer Cash	P George Pipgras OF Harvey Hendrick
1/30/23	OF Camp Skinner IF Norm McMillan P George Murray $50,000	P Herb Pennock

4

The Red Sox club was at the end of its age. At that time, before the advent of the farm system, a team could only improve itself through trades, the purchase of players from the minor leagues, or scouting and signing of minor leaguers. The latter two required cash, the one thing Frazee and the Red Sox did not have. Frazee claimed that cash from the trades would be plowed back into the team, and, indeed, some of it was. The loan portion went toward purchasing a theater in New York.

The remaining Frazee-Yankees trades, with the exception of the last two, which were made to spite the American League after Frazee knew he would be selling out, were made in an effort to burn down the roster and start over. The 1918 team was old. It possessed an offense that scraped the bottom side of average (.255 EqA),* with only two players, Ruth and Harry Hooper, who were more than ten runs above average at their position. The only other asset was their four fine starting pitchers. When the team crashed to sixth place in 1919, it was clear that it had to be rebuilt, with Ruth or without him.

Frazee finally sold the Red Sox in August 1923, turning the team over to a group of investors led by the experienced but ineffectual baseball man J. A. Robert Quinn. Quinn had already peaked, credited with being the architect of a surprisingly good 1922 St. Louis Browns team that nearly beat the Yankees to the pennant—an accomplishment on which Quinn dined out for the next twenty-five years. By all accounts an honest, hard-working man, Quinn lacked discernment in identifying talent, in business partners, even in choosing which franchises to invest his hard-earned money in. Over the course of his long career in baseball, Quinn would be involved with three of baseball's most financially bereft franchises—the Red Sox, the Dodgers, and the Braves. In general, Quinn lacked both the capital and the imagination to resuscitate a drowning franchise, and his tenure in Boston was no exception. From 1924 to 1932, the Red Sox had an aggregate record of 483–897 (.350). The team lost more than 100 games five times, climaxing with a historic 111 losses in 1932. They finished sixth once, seventh once, and eighth seven times, six of them consecutive.

Quinn's few attempts to improve the team usually backfired. In 1927, to complete a deal with Washington Senators owner Clark Griffith, Quinn insisted on a Senator infielder named Bobby Reeves, although Griffith

*See the Glossary for an explanation of EqA.

offered another shortstop named Joe Cronin. Quinn prevailed, Reeves couldn't hit and was out of the majors in three years, and the acquisition of future Hall of Famer Cronin would have to wait for Tom Yawkey. Quinn's other most notable transaction involved the

QUINN-ERA ALL-STARS BY TOTAL WARP (Wins Above Replacement Player) 1924–1932		
Name	Pos	WARP
Dale Alexander	1B	6.2
Bill Regan	2B	7.3
Buddy Myer	3B	9.5
Topper Rigney	SS	7.9
Earl Webb	OF	10.6
Ike Boone	OF	7.3
Ira Flagstead	OF	22.8
Charlie Berry	C	8.7
Red Ruffing	P	20.4

transfer of right-handed pitcher Charles "Red" Ruffing from the Fens to the Bronx in exchange for outfielder Cedric Durst and $50,000. The Red Sox met the payroll; the Yankees got four consecutive twenty-win seasons and another player who wore their cap to the Hall of Fame.

The management skills of Frazee and Quinn were a sufficient plague on the team, but it was nothing compared to the curse—not of the Bambino, a self-centered but basically genial fellow—but of the next man to own the team, Thomas A. Yawkey. After struggling to find a buyer at the nadir of the Great Depression, Quinn finally sold out in late 1932 to Yawkey, a New Yorker by way of Detroit. From 1933 until 2002, the Red Sox would be run by Yawkey or people associated with Yawkey, including his widow and the foundation that bears his name. For the vast majority of that time, leadership by Yawkey meant well-meaning incompetence, although the qualifier *well-meaning* credits Yawkey with more generosity than he actually displayed. Yawkey was famous for liberally compensating his players, the good and bad alike, on one condition: They were white. To African Americans he would not give a dime. When Yawkey took over the Red Sox, he was but one of sixteen segregationists in baseball. By the time a black man played for Boston, Yawkey would be the sole holdout, the last devotee of apartheid in the national pastime.

Yawkey was born in Detroit on February 21, 1903, the same year his uncle William Hoover Yawkey bought the Detroit Tigers with money from a fortune acquired through timber and mining interests. When his mother died in 1917, the young Yawkey was adopted by his uncle. His youthful exposure to the Tigers set the course for the rest of his life. He liked the idea of palling around with ballplayers. Ty Cobb was an early friend, though seventeen years his senior. Another friendship was formed in 1928, when Cobb introduced Yawkey to future Hall of Fame second baseman Eddie "Cocky" Collins.

When Yawkey turned thirty, he came into an inheritance (somewhere between $20 and $40 million) that had been held in trust. Yawkey decided to buy himself a baseball team as a birthday present and, loyal to the American League, he persuaded Eddie Collins to come with him to Boston and be his general business manager. Four days after coming into his inheritance, Yawkey owned the Red Sox. His goal, he said, was to build a "First-class, high-spirited ballclub" . . . and to beat the Yankees.[3]

An orgy of acquisitions followed. Much as the Yankees had benefited from Frazee's decision to rebuild the Red Sox, Yawkey's Red Sox benefited from the dismantling of another great team, the Philadelphia A's. Yawkey spent more money than any team owner had before. In addition to buying the team and renovating Fenway Park—a $166 million project (in today's money) that briefly made Yawkey the biggest employer in Boston—Collins made seventeen trades during his first thirty-six months in office, nearly all of them sweetened with unprecedented amounts of cash. The 1934 purchase of shortstop Joe Cronin from the Washington Senators for $225,000 remains one of the most expensive player acquisitions ever, worth over $37 million in current dollars.

The Red Sox were soon popularly rechristened "The Millionaires," but failed to net any pennants. In 1935 the Sox enjoyed their first winning season since 1918, but fell back quickly to the second division. In 1938, the last year before the arrival of Ted Williams, they had their best season in two decades, going 88–61 (.591) and finishing in second place—but it was a distant second in a race Boston showed no signs of winning after July. "It soon became apparent," Yawkey observed, "that most of the men we had bought were merely helping us mark time until we could develop our own young players who would put us in the pennant fight."[4]

The concept of the farm system had been around for years by 1936, when Yawkey hired former umpire and Cleveland GM Billy Evans to try and slap together a farm system of the Sox's own. In 1920, Branch Rickey, then general manager of the St. Louis Cardinals, began acquiring minor league teams as a way of avoiding having to purchase players on the open market. Almost from the beginning, these arrangements were controversial within baseball, and arguments about whether the farm was good for the minors raged throughout the twenties and into the thirties. Gradually, other clubs saw how Rickey now had such a steady influx of talent that he was able to field a consistent winner in the majors and sell the excess personnel for cash. Even the Yankees, who had little incentive to economize on player acquisition costs, had started acquiring minor league teams in 1932. Boston never recovered from spotting New York such a head start; when the Sox system peaked with fifteen affiliates in 1948, the Yankees had twenty-four. At no time between 1936 and 1969 did the Red Sox field more minor league teams than the Yankees.[5] The talent shortfall, particularly in pitching, would soon become crippling.

For the moment, though, things looked fine. The prewar years would be good ones for Boston. The arrival of Californians Bobby Doerr and Ted Williams signaled a new era of talent acquisition, albeit one still largely built on buying players rather than developing them. Neither Doerr nor Williams would be products of the Red Sox farm system, having already played at a high level for San Diego of the stubbornly independent Pacific Coast League. In five seasons, from 1938 to 1942, at which point military call-ups took away most of the team's best players, the Red Sox would finish second four times.

Despite this improvement, the team was hamstrung by Yawkey's management style, which could be described as delegating everything, then disclaiming all responsibility for the results. Yawkey apparently did not think it was in his province to offer any direction at all, especially if it meant coming into conflict with any of the player/manager/drinking buddies who increasingly populated the team. Yawkey and his coterie were often sidetracked by personalities and petty feuds. When he hired his first manager, Bucky Harris, who had won the 1924 and 1925 pennants for the Senators, he failed to consult Collins about the move and therefore did not realize that the two were mortal enemies. Then, rather than address the problem, he allowed Collins to maneuver Harris out. Winning took a backseat that year to cleaning up the mess Yawkey's mismanagement had made.

By contrast, the Yankees, despite four changes of ownership during Yawkey's first fifteen years in baseball, remained relentlessly focused on the finish line. The people who ran the Yankees were not nice men. Jacob Ruppert, Ed Barrow, Joe McCarthy, and later George Weiss and

Casey Stengel were each in their own way haughty men lacking in human empathy. They helped to drive Babe Ruth out of baseball when he no longer suited their purposes. Lou Gehrig got sick, and they were sincerely sad, but they didn't offer him a dime. They still won the pennant that year. Bob Shawkey, who had been with the organization for more than fifteen years, didn't work out as manager in 1930; they let him go without even telling him he was fired. Phil Rizzuto was the team's biggest booster for a dozen seasons. In 1956, Stengel and Weiss sat him down and told him he was the least valuable Yankee and let him fire himself. Joe Page, the relief specialist, was once asked about the circumstances of his release by Stengel. "Shake my hand?" Page replied. "He wasn't even there to say good-bye." The Yankees were a brutally cold bunch.

When Yawkey hired Joe Cronin in 1934 and made him shortstop/manager, he acquired more trouble. As a manager, Cronin was nervous and indecisive. On the field, his jitters translated into run-of-the-mill fielding—and worse. Cronin developed a mental block about fielding grounders and had to go down to one knee to get them. Shortstops who play on their knees lack both range and dignity. "For Pete's sake, Joe," Cronin's double-play partner Ski Mellillo said, "if you're going to miss 'em, you might as well stand up and miss 'em like a big leaguer."

Cronin's refusal to yield his position to shortstop Eric McNair, acquired from the A's with Doc Cramer, drove pitchers crazy—no one more than right-hander Wes Ferrell. "If we had a shortstop, we'd win the pennant," he said. "Cronin has lost me four games already." Upset by errors, in August 1936 the temperamental Ferrell walked off the mound and out of the ballpark during consecutive starts (ironically, Cronin was out with a broken finger for both games). The response from Yawkey was further evidence of his tenuous grasp of baseball reality: "Instead of a better shortstop helping the pitchers, don't you think better pitchers would help the shortstop?" As Yawkey was getting to be a problem drinker at this time, it is possible this proposed "solution" came out of a bottle.[6]

THE PITCHERS CRY MERCY: WORST DEFENSIVE SEASONS BY RED SOX SHORTSTOPS BY FIELDING RUNS ABOVE AVERAGE		
	YEAR	FRAA
Freddy Parent	1905	−19
Joe Cronin	1935	−20
Don Buddin	1959	−20
Jackie Gutierrez	1984	−28

Nonetheless, Yawkey had purchased a part interest in the Louisville franchise of the American Association so the Red Sox could have first dibs on a young shortstop in their possession, twenty-year-old Harold Reese, better known as Pee Wee. Here was the solution to Boston's problems: Cronin and his superior bat could move to third base, the slick-fielding Reese could take over at shortstop, and Red Sox pitchers, who were threatening to lynch Cronin, could calm down. It didn't happen. Cronin saw himself as a shortstop, downplayed Reese's abilities, and refused to admit he was a prospect. In 1939, he quietly arranged for Reese to be sold to the Brooklyn Dodgers. With characteristic obtuseness, Yawkey let the sale happen—in the same way that he would allow Cronin to dump Ben Chapman, Wes Ferrell, and Buck Newsom, talented but temperamental players with whom Cronin did not get along.

As great as Yawkey's managerial and personnel sins were, they were nothing compared to the consequences of his refusal to follow Branch Rickey into the new world of racial integration (as he had refused to follow him into the age of farm systems). The Red Sox segregationist stand survived for almost *two decades* after Jackie Robinson broke the color line— and Yawkey was never made to answer for it. Under pressure, the team did agree to audition three black players on April 16, 1945. Jackie Robinson, Sam Jethroe, and Marvin Williams appeared at Fenway to work out for venerable coach Hugh Duffy. (Duffy, seventy-eight, had a big-league career that stretched back to 1888, long enough to have been a contemporary of Moses Fleetwood Walker, the last African American to have been allowed, however briefly, to play with whites. No one noticed the irony.) Duffy worked out the three players while manager Cronin and GM Collins watched from the stands. The players acquitted themselves well and Duffy was complimentary. The occasion was marred only by a voice that shouted from somewhere in the rear of the stands, so that all heard it clearly: "Get those niggers off the field!" The voice was never positively identified, but a reporter present at the time was certain it had belonged to Yawkey.[7] The Red Sox executives told the African Americans "We'll call you," and never did.

As the color line was being broken, Yawkey entered a reclusive phase, perhaps because of his drinking habits. This left Cronin, who succeeded Collins as GM in 1947, to offer increasingly lame excuses for the Red Sox failure to sign an African American ballplayer along the lines of Collins' earlier "None have ever asked."[8] Cronin's version was, "The Red Sox care nothing about a man's color, they only want good ballplayers."[9] There were also mealymouthed excuses about how blacks would not/could not sign with the Red Sox because their top farm team was located in medieval Louisville, Kentucky. (The Sox changed their top minor league affiliation to San Francisco in 1956, three years before Pumpsie Green was signed.) When the Sox actually signed their first black player in 1950, a Negro League middle infielder named Piper Davis, they sent him to Scranton in the Eastern League, where he opened the season batting .333 with power. The Red Sox cut him for "economic reasons."[10]

Yawkey had a knack for attracting influential defenders who offered increasingly dubious explanations for the owner's bigotry. In his book *Yaz: Baseball, the Wall, and Me,* Carl Yastrzemski offers this disingenuous passage about Yawkey and race:

I was aware of another rap that the ball club had—a bad rap. It was that the Red Sox—and Mr. Yawkey in particular—were anti-black. We talked about that a lot. All I knew was that I was on one side of [Yawkey's] locker and that Joe Foy and then Reggie Smith, who were both black, had seats on the other side of him. He spent more time talking with us than with any of the other players. . . . Whenever he read a story that claimed we didn't have enough black ballplayers, he'd come to me and say, "Yaz, don't you think I'd rather have signed a Willie Mays instead of a Gary Geiger?"[11]

Yastrzemski failed to note both that the earliest a conversation between Foy, Smith, and Yawkey could have taken place was in September 1966, nearly twenty years after Jackie Robinson, and that Yawkey's organization had first crack at signing Willie Mays, and had passed.

In 1960, as Yawkey was pressuring Boston politicos for a government-financed baseball stadium (there was nothing yet "sacred" about Fenway Park, at least not to Yawkey), Boston sportswriters turned on him. Yawkey reacted with petulance. "There is such a thing as human dignity, and the American way of life in which I believe," he said, "but when [the writers] go beyond that, I don't like it. They better not push me too far or

I'll take this team out of Boston. I am not bluffing."[12] A few years before this tirade, hearings by Massachusetts civil rights agencies had failed to uncover a single African American working at Fenway Park. Even the janitorial staff was lily white.[13]

The Red Sox became the last team to integrate by more than a year when, on July 21, 1959, they haltingly, grudgingly promoted infielder Pumpsie Green to the majors. "The Red Sox will bring up a Negro when he meets our standards," Yawkey had said earlier that season. By then, of course, Hank Aaron, Willie Mays, Larry Doby, Satchel Paige, Roy Campanella, Ernie Banks, Elston Howard, and others were playing in the majors. Jackie Robinson had come and gone. It wasn't until general manager Dick O'Connell's first season, 1966, that the team began to even approach the kind of race-blind meritocracy that sports teams are supposed to be. Though Earl Wilson, the team's first black pitcher, was traded after a spring training incident in a bar that refused to serve "his kind," Joe Foy, George Scott, Reggie Smith, and others were now on the club. "I don't care what color a player is as long as he can play," O'Connell said. "If he is any good I want to sign him."[14] For the first time, the words meant something, but by that time the Red Sox had handicapped themselves in nearly two decades' worth of pennant races.

During this period, Yawkey had found the perfect id to his ego in denial. Beginning in 1947, Yawkey engaged his former third baseman and hunting partner Mike "Pinky" Higgins for a variety of jobs. Higgins managed Boston's affiliate in the Piedmont League, then gradually worked himself up to Louisville, and finally reached Boston in 1955, taking over as manager from Lou Boudreau. From 1960 through 1965, the Texas native also served as general manager. Higgins was a drunk (later jailed for negligent homicide after killing a highway worker in a drunk-driving incident) and an unabashed racist who once dumped a plate of beef Stroganoff into the lap of a sportswriter who pressed him on the racial issue, and told another, "There'll be no niggers on this ballclub as long as I have anything to say about it."[15] In 1959, Higgins tried to sandbag Green's promotion at the last minute but was finally overruled in the face of a media outcry. (When Higgins suffered his fatal heart attack in 1969, two days after being released from prison, Earl Wilson, the first black pitcher on the Red Sox, said, somewhat enigmatically, "Good things happen to some people.")[16]

Yawkey nearly always picked bad managers and general managers. Much that happened on the field flowed naturally from these choices: The poor pitching selections, from Bob Klinger in 1946 to Denny Galehouse in 1948 to Tex Hughson in 1949 (Boston was behind the curve in bullpen innovation, too); the powerhouse teams that led the majors in scoring from 1946 to 1951 yet seemed never to hit when it mattered because Fenway Park vastly overstated their power; the youth movement

COLORADO OF THE EAST: RED SOX HOME/ROAD SPLIT, 1946–1951[18]					
1946	**AVG**	**OBP**	**SLG**	**RA**	**H/9**
Home	.298	.382	.447	3.98	9.88
Away	.241	.327	.352	3.74	7.92
1947	**AVG**	**OBP**	**SLG**	**RA**	**H/9**
Home	.285	.367	.415	4.31	9.58
Away	.242	.323	.341	4.33	8.18
1948	**AVG**	**OBP**	**SLG**	**RA**	**H/9**
Home	.287	.389	.431	4.31	9.27
Away	.263	.360	.389	5.20	9.42
1949	**AVG**	**OBP**	**SLG**	**RA**	**H/9**
Home	.310	.407	.472	4.00	8.69
Away	.261	.360	.372	4.75	8.73
1950	**AVG**	**OBP**	**SLG**	**RA**	**H/9**
Home	.335	.420	.519	5.49	9.62
Away	.268	.346	.396	5.11	9.00
1951	**AVG**	**OBP**	**SLG**	**RA**	**H/9**
Home	.292	.379	.446	4.22	8.54
Away	.241	.334	.336	5.02	9.39
Total Home	.301	.391	.455	4.38	9.25
Total Away	.253	.342	.365	4.69	8.87

18. Compiled by Baseball Prospectus.

of the mid-fifties that went forward without the benefit of youth, and so on. Even after Yawkey's death in 1976, he left his imprint in the form of managers, executives, and sometimes players who were incapable of making winning a priority. John McNamara kept Bill Buckner on the field in Game Six of the 1986 World Series so he could celebrate a championship that hadn't yet been won. Roger Clemens threw a temper tantrum at an umpire and got himself booted from Game Four of the 1990 American League Championship Series rather than deal with the pressure of having to win the game. The reliably self-defeating manager Jimy Williams started Pete Schourek instead of Pedro Martinez in the elimination game of the 1998 American League Division Series. Even John Harrington, the last ruler of the Red Sox before the Yawkey Trust finally sold out, called the team a small-market ballclub whose efforts to compete were handicapped by their small ballpark.[17] There were no magic spells at work, only failures of intelligence, concentration, and imagination.

The purchase of the Red Sox by John Henry literally wiped the slate clean. The Yawkey era had finally been consigned to the dustbin of history. Even venerable Fenway Park, long considered by Yawkey and his successors a detriment to the franchise's financial well-being, has undergone almost continual renovation as the new administration has sought to find ways to turn its many charming nooks and crannies into additional sources of revenue.

There would still be human error, of course, in the form of Grady Little and his reluctance to point to the bullpen, but such faults would not merely be winked at. Complacency was out, competitiveness was in. For the first time since 1918, the team was ready to play the mind game.

—STEVEN GOLDMAN

EXTRA INNINGS

HOW IMPORTANT IS A TEAM'S BEST PLAYER? THE NONCURSE OF THE GREY EAGLE: A CASE STUDY

From 1912 to 1918, the Red Sox won four championships. The team had many great stars, including Babe Ruth, who joined the team in 1914, but by far the best player on those teams was Tris Speaker—"The Grey Eagle" or "Spoke"—who played center field and batted third. With .337/.414/.482 averages during that time, he was a reliable top-three finisher in the batting race; on defense he was the premier outfielder of the age. His great range and instincts allowed him to play such a shallow center field that he sometimes functioned as a fifth infielder. He averaged twenty-six assists a season, in part because of his strong arm, in part because his positioning sometimes enabled him to throw out runners at first base on would-be base hits. In 1912, he was named the league's Most Valuable Player.

TOP PLAYERS BY WINS ABOVE REPLACEMENT 1909–1915			
1. Walter Johnson	Washington	RHP	86.8
2. Eddie Collins	Phil-A	2B	81.7
3. Ty Cobb	Detroit	CF	75.1
4. Tris Speaker	Bos-A	CF	72.7
5. Honus Wagner	Pittsburgh	SS	60.7

In 1914, Major League Baseball came under attack from the Federal League, a new circuit that was attempting to claim major league status and trying its best to entice as many established American and National League stars as possible to jump to the new league. The Major Leagues bribed their stars to stay with higher salaries. Speaker saw his salary double from $9,000 to $18,000. The Federal League gave up the fight after two years of play and some fruitless litigation. Despite having done his usual fine job, Speaker, twenty-eight, was asked to return to his former salary for the 1916 season. He held out, working out with the club during spring training as he attempted to negotiate. His bottom line was $15,000. Shortly before the regular season began, owner Joseph Lannin informed him that he had won the salary battle, then promptly traded him to Cleveland for $55,000, pitcher Sam Jones, and infielder Fred Thomas.

At the moment of the trade, Speaker was one of the top three position players in baseball and remained so into his late thirties. His offensive and leadership skills

TOP PLAYERS BY WINS ABOVE REPLACEMENT 1916–1928			
1. Babe Ruth	NY-A	OF	160.7
2. Rogers Hornsby	St. Louis	2B	128.9
3. Tris Speaker	Cleveland	CF	113.3
4. Walter Johnson	Washington	RHP	96.7
5. Ty Cobb	Detroit	OF	96.4

were amply demonstrated in 1920, when, as player/manager, he batted .388/.483/.562 and took the Cleveland Indians to a rare World Series, even as Babe Ruth was rewriting the record books in Manhattan. Speaker's reputation as the preeminent defensive center fielder in baseball went unchallenged for decades.

Deprived of their superstar, the Red Sox could have expected to suffer a severe collapse in the standings from their rarified 101–50, World Series–winning finish of 1915. Speaker's replacement, Tilly Walker, proved to be less than half the offensive player Speaker had been, and a poor outfielder to boot. Indeed, the Red Sox did decline. They lost thirteen more games in 1916 than they had in 1915. They declined from first place right back into . . . first place and another World Series title. After a strong second-place showing in 1917, the Red Sox again won the American League pennant and the World Series in 1918.

The loss of any one player, no matter how great, is not enough to derail a competently run franchise for one year, let alone eighty. The Red Sox themselves showed this in 1916–1918. Fortunately for them, the popular memory was as short then as it is now, and they and their apologists could spend the rest of the century smiling blandly whenever their permanent undoing at the hands of Babe Ruth and Harry Frazee came up.

—STEVEN GOLDMAN

2

SHOPPING FOR WINNERS
NOVEMBER 25, 2003

There's a learning curve to every job, especially the job of general manager of a baseball team that hadn't learned much over the years about how to win championships. In the case of Theo Epstein, who wasn't even supposed to *have* the job of general manager, the spirit was willing and the mind was strong. God knows he came from intelligent stock. His father, Leslie Epstein, is a novelist, professor, and man of letters whose *Life and Death in the American Novel* remains a critical classic four decades after it was published. His grandfather and great uncle co-wrote the screenplay for *Casablanca*. That the scion of such a profoundly literary family could end up as GM of a team that has long been the darling of the intelligentsia was something right out of the movies. If the Boston Red Sox's World Series victory of 2004 could be traced to a single event, it would have to be the almost accidental hiring of this highly intelligent, baseball-mad Epstein prodigy.

Epstein's road to the Boston GM job was paved by John Henry. A commodities trader who mastered the intricacies of the futures market to build a vast personal fortune, Henry took over ownership and operation of the Red Sox in February 2002. The shopping spree mentality one might expect of a new owner was conspicuously absent: Henry could hardly be called "new," of course, as he had owned baseball clubs for twenty years. That, combined with the good judgment sharpened by many years in the financial trenches, had helped him evolve a prudent, measured approach. Henry started off small in the late 1980s, experimenting with the ill-fated Senior Professional Baseball League, and later, a minor league team

(Tucson). In 1992 he joined the Yankees as a limited partner, which turned out to be a stepping-stone for bigger things, rather than merely an excuse for Big Apple bragging rights.

In the fall of 1997, Florida Marlins owner Wayne Huizenga decided to sell out, despite his club's having just won a World Series. No one in Florida was too sorry to see him go. The 1990s had seen numerous MLB team owners attempt to blackmail and bully local politicos and voters into giving their own franchise a publicly financed stadium. "Pony up the bucks," the party line went, "or I'll move the team to Washington, D.C." (or Portland, Oregon, the Carolinas, Las Vegas, San Jose, or wherever the empty-bluff location du jour happened to be at the time). Huizenga was one of the loudest lobbying owners, arguing that South Florida couldn't sustain an MLB club unless its citizens forked over the several hundred million dollars needed to erect a palatial new ballpark. If building a park was such a moneymaking gold mine, one might have wondered, why didn't the owners lay out the money themselves, knowing they could enjoy the benefits down the road? Because the rich know one thing above all: Always use other people's money.

The taxpayers of South Florida stood up to Huizenga. Still, for Major League Baseball, the issue lived on, with or without Huizenga. For the Marlins to remain in Miami—and no team had been moved in over twenty-five years—the new ballpark drive would have to be revived. To regain some measure of credibility upon which to build a later exercise in ballpark brinkmanship, the industry needed a steady hand to step in. Through this new figure, the franchise would shed the mercenary image it had acquired on Huizenga's watch. In what would become a pattern in the Selig era, the industry turned to an insider, Henry.

In his three years in Florida, Henry put a good public face on his ownership of the Marlins, making the right kinds of sounds about building trust, connecting with the community, and all of the other blandishments needed when your goal is to induce the taxpayers to build you a stadium instead of buying themselves some new schools or a light-rail system. With Commissioner Bud Selig and individual team owners still pleading their case for publicly financed parks from coast to coast, Henry needed to make the same proposal to the state as the one pitched by Huizenga. The hope was that the people would finally relent if the question was asked in a nicer way, by someone not associated with the destruction of the 1997 Marlins team. Instead, the populace held its ground again.

Then fate intervened to give Henry his chance to do what any successful Wall Street trader would do: trade up. The Red Sox had gone up for sale as the longtime Yawkey Trust ownership prepared to dispose of the team. Meanwhile, the Montreal Expos were slipping further into financial ruin and were ready to be euthanized. Selig crafted a syndicalist solution to the twin problems of the Expos and Sox, both of which were systematically being devalued by their present, uninspired ownership. Major League Baseball traded the Yawkey Trust's problematic stewardship of the Red Sox for the burden of having to operate the Expos until new, stable ownership could be found—art dealer Jeffrey Loria traded in the Expos for the Marlins, and Henry, backed by an equally well-heeled group of collaborators, assumed control of the Red Sox.

Henry stepped into a favorable situation. The Red Sox were one of the game's most storied franchises, with a healthy revenue stream and rabid fan base. Moreover, Henry would team up with two partners who could fill some of the gaps in his own game. Tom Werner may have seemed a dubious accomplice, based on his unfortunate stretch as Padres owner in the early 1990s, when he presided over his own Huizenga-like dispersal of a winning team, but at least the man had baseball experience. And his immensely successful career as television producer (*Roseanne*, *Cosby*, *Third Rock from the Sun*, etc.) made Werner an ideal choice to oversee the New England Sports Network, which had been included in the purchase price. New Red Sox president and CEO Larry Lucchino figured to fill another key role. A hard-driving executive who'd done heavy lifting for two franchises, Lucchino led the drive to get Oriole Park at Camden Yards built in Baltimore while running the Orioles. After moving to the Padres, where he worked alongside both Werner and then new owner John Moores, Lucchino helped spearhead the Padres' successful drive to build a new ballpark in downtown San Diego. His experience would come in handy since plans were afoot to upgrade venerable Fenway Park. Lucchino also had a strong reputation for regional marketing, an important consideration for the team's far-flung New England fan base. Henry's financial background, Werner's media savvy and creativity, and Lucchino's fifteen-hour workday, bulldog approach to marketing, management, and

stadium construction constituted more expertise than most other ownership groups in the game—and a massive upgrade over the increasingly
absentminded ownership of the Yawkey Trust.

New ownership groups often bring in new general managers, and this
would be no exception. Long criticized for his impersonal management style
and his exotic taste in statheads, Dan Duquette had overseen a decline in
the Red Sox's fortunes and been vociferously criticized in the media.
Duquette may have lured Pedro Martinez from the Expos back in 1997 and
acquired Manny Ramirez from the Indians in 2001, but he was more closely
identified with recent disappointments—the failure to re-sign Mo Vaughn,
the ill-considered decision to sign Jose Offerman and bill him as the centerpiece of the offense, and the team's lousy starting pitching, to name just a
few. Not all of these were Duquette's fault—and not signing Vaughn, for
one, proved a happy non-event for the Sox—but Duquette's negative image
had sealed his fate. More to the point, he wasn't Henry's guy, or Lucchino's.

Having quickly purged the most visible member of previous management, Henry's management crew was in no rush to pick a successor. In
part, this was because they wanted to see if they could woo one of the rising GM stars in the industry—Billy Beane from Oakland, J. P. Ricciardi
from Toronto, or perhaps Beane's assistant, Paul DePodesta. Besides,
when Henry finally took over the Red Sox, it was halfway through spring
training, a little late to start pressing the owners of the A's and Blue Jays
about the availability of their general managers. Ownership made industry lifer Mike Port the front man for the 2002 season.

Meanwhile, Lucchino had an ace up his sleeve. In San Diego, he'd discovered a young, shrewd baseball mind in Theo Epstein. When Lucchino
would hole up in his office well past eight and nine P.M. on an off-season
night, the only other light on in the Padres' management offices belonged
to Epstein, who, rather than going home to sleep, would often press on
into the wee hours of the night to finish a project. That stamina, combined
with a precocious mind and a calculating demeanor that in many ways mir-
rored Lucchino's own, earned him the role of Padres' director of baseball
operations. Now Lucchino pressed Epstein to follow him to Boston as Red
Sox assistant general manager. And he did.

The new crew did not produce an instant on-field success. Although
the team's star shortstop, Nomar Garciaparra, had a great season and

newcomer Johnny Damon filled the lead-off spot, the offense was erratic. Regulars Jason Varitek and Trot Nixon were good, not great; Ramirez missed a quarter of the season with a broken finger, then struggled after his return; and after a hot start, third baseman Shea Hillenbrand failed to contribute. The real sore spots were first base, second base, and designated hitter, positions the team had patched with worn-out veterans. On the mound, they had Pedro Martinez and sinkerballer Derek Lowe, who had made a remarkable return to the rotation after four years in the bullpen and had turned in a completely unexpected Cy Young–worthy season. Elsewhere, however, free-agent starters Frank Castillo and John Burkett were disappointments, and the bullpen was pedestrian. The Sox finished 93–69, an eleven-game improvement over the team's 2001 record. Still, they had ended up ten games behind the Yankees—Boston's fifth straight bridesmaid finish.

In the 2002–2003 off-season, Epstein was put in the unenviable position of searching for his future boss. Although Massachusetts native Ricciardi seemed an easy fit, he liked his GM job in Toronto and the Jays liked him. Sensing Boston's interest, the Blue Jays gave Ricciardi a five-year contract extension, taking him off the table.

However, it was Billy Beane, the man who had made as disciplined and successful a general manager as he'd been an undisciplined washout of a player, that Epstein really wanted. Beane was interested, and better still, Oakland's owners gave him permission to talk to Boston. He came to terms with the Sox, an event that conjured up images of a sabermetric golden age in Beantown. But Beane had a last-minute change of heart and stayed in California out of consideration for his family.

Now it was November 2002, and the executive troika and Epstein were in a bind. They didn't want to spend a second season with a cipher going through the motions of running the ballclub. Suddenly, Theo himself began to look pretty good. He was twenty-eight and younger than most of the players, but the owners soon agreed that it made more sense to promote him than to scrounge around for an outsider who, at best, would be their third or fourth choice. Epstein also had the advantage of already being indoctrinated into the organization's new management culture. Epstein was college-educated; weaned on the works of Bill James, Pete Palmer, and Craig Wright; at home with applied performance analysis; and willing to reconsider just about every aspect of the team's operation. He was a believer in change. He also had another virtue: immediate availability. There was an off-season's worth of player acquisitions to get to, and the front office needed to stop fidgeting and get on with its business.

After moving into the office for which he had just been trying to find an occupant, Epstein was given free rein to aggressively solve the team's roster problems. The cure for the lineup seemed simple enough: He signed second baseman Todd Walker to give the club a solid bat at the position, then turned to a sabermetric favorite, Jeremy Giambi (Jason's younger brother), to fill the club's designated hitter vacuum. Bench players like Damian Jackson and Adrian Brown were brought in to provide depth. The bullpen received free-agent reinforcements: Ramiro Mendoza, signed away from the Yankees; Mike Timlin, picked up from the Phillies; and the occasionally healthy, occasionally dominating Chad Fox, signed away from the Brewers. The stated purpose of these multiple expenses was that rather than spend a ton of money on a single high-profile reliever, the Sox were going to assemble a bullpen loaded with interchangeably effective parts.

To shore up the rotation, Epstein was given the go-ahead to try to land purported Cuban ace Jose Contreras, who'd recently defected. The rotation needed better balance, a third wheel to decrease dependence on Pedro's questionable durability and insure against a disappointing second season from Lowe. It was not to be. After a tough bit of wrangling, the Yankees won the bidding, handing the unknown Contreras a four-year, $32 million deal based on little more than rumor.

These pickups would not turn out to be enough. Walker wasn't and isn't Jeff Kent; he's a useful hitter, not a great one, and had a miserable season with the glove, even by his own middling standards. Mendoza was a disaster, as regrettable as Frank Castillo had been for the previous administration. Despite a minor league track record that impressed statheads, Jeremy Giambi stumbled due to problems both on field and off.

Fortunately, the new Sox management style was no longer to run an unsuccessful plan into the ground. When Duquette had snagged outfielder Troy O'Leary off waivers in 1995, he overcommitted to him. O'Leary floundered in 2000–2001 after putting up good numbers at a relatively low price for much of 1995 to 1999, costing the Sox runs, wins, and $8.6 million during two seasons where they were expected to contend. Rather than cut bait and go fishing in Pawtucket, where the Triple-A PawSox were almost always stocked with useful minor league veteran hitters, Duquette settled for what he'd signed, and he lost with it. By contrast, when Epstein signed Giambi, he didn't assume he had automatically solved his DH problem. In January 2003, when David Ortiz became available because of the Twins' failure to appreciate his virtues (see Chapter 8), Epstein snapped him up. He then followed with the controversial acquisition of Kevin Millar. Millar had agreed in early January to a $6.2 million, two-year contract with the Chunichi Dragons of Japan's Central League, and the Marlins released him in exchange for a $1.2 million payment from the Dragons. But Millar had second thoughts, especially after the Sox jumped in, making overtures to Millar and then to the Dragons in an effort to lure him to Boston. After weeks of negotiating, the Dragons released him and returned him to the Marlins, who sold him to the Sox, who signed him to a two-year, $5.3 million contract.

During the 2003 season the Red Sox beat their opponents to a bloody pulp with their bats, scoring a MLB-leading 961 runs, leading the league in on-base percentage and breaking the 1927 Yankees single-season team record for slugging percentage with .491. The Sox won the wild card and rallied to beat the A's in the Divisional Series. Unfortunately, Boston's opponents also got to bat, and the regular season was riddled with poor pitching performances. Lowe didn't perform nearly as well as he had in his superb 2002 campaign and Wakefield had lost some prowess, leaving the Red Sox with only Martinez as a top-flight starter. Picking up Byung-Hyun Kim from the Diamondbacks didn't solve the rotation's problems. And midseason pickup Jeff Suppan turned out to be just another mid-rotation sort of guy.

All this, of course, was felt in the bullpen, which, although bolstered by Epstein's off-season shopping spree, still fell short of wonderful. Oft-injured Chad Fox got hurt again and Ramiro Mendoza was so ineffective against Boston's evil empire that, in a bit of Gulf War II humor, Boston wags referred to him as the "embedded Yankee." Epstein and company had aspired to assemble a pen of dependable, interchangeable pitchers that would lead the team to postseason glory while rewriting the rules for using a traditional closer. With no proven closer to protect ninth-inning leads, Little was supposed to use his relievers according to their relative strengths, playing matchups and going to different arms to close out games depending on everything from the hand with which they threw, recent usage, and the team in the opposing dugout. This tactical innovation reflected the understanding that a game's most critical moments weren't concentrated in the ninth inning. The outcome of a given game might depend on escaping a bases-loaded jam in the fifth, or inducing a two-out ground ball in the seventh, and in neither instance did you want to use your fourth-best pitcher. Saving your best reliever to protect a ninth-inning lead that never comes—thanks to poor middle-relief—is a waste of a valuable resource.

What the team got was an impossible situation in which Little was supposed to juggle a bunch of generic relievers, none of whom ever quite understood their role. And in Little, the new-age Sox organization did not exactly have the ideal avatar. He had been lukewarm to the idea of the headless bullpen in spring training, never stopped complaining about it, and proved unable to muster the courage, creativity, and smarts it took to make the idea work, if indeed it could have been made to work, given the talent on hand.

After two months of trying things management's way, Little was openly pining for a closer. Fox had broken down and the temptation to return Kim to his former position of closer, in which he had thrived in Arizona, was overpowering. Kim logged only five starts before Epstein gave in and Kim marched off to the bullpen. The move paid off: After posting poor peripheral stats in his brief stint as a Sox starter, Kim doubled his strikeout rate and shrunk his walk, home run, and hit rates as a reliever.

Having torn up the committee bullpen plan to cater to Little, and then losing in the playoffs through another exercise of Little's judgment (the infamous decision to keep Pedro Martinez in the final game beyond his usual one-hundred-pitch limit), it was entirely understandable that Epstein fired him. Some in the media rallied to Little's side with the credible defense that winning 188 games over two seasons wasn't exactly shabby, but that missed the bigger picture: Little had been handed a good ballclub, and in the places where his discretion was decisive, it had been decisively wrong.

As the New England leaves turned color and fell, Epstein needed three things: a top starter, a manager, and a closer. Within a mere six weeks after the Marlins' World Series victory over the Yankees, he had landed all three.

In 2003, Epstein had learned some lessons that elude many GMs for a lifetime. Pitchers like Kim, Burkett, and Suppan come cheaply because they are inconsistent. At their best they can be winning pitchers, but neither the teams signing them nor the pitchers themselves can reliably know on any given day if they've brought their best stuff to the ballpark. Success would require them all to perform at or near the top of their game almost all the time, something that almost never happens. The Sox needed a sure thing. Happily, Arizona's unwieldy payroll had made one available. Struggling to pay the bills left over from their successful drive to a championship in 2001, the Diamondbacks were looking for creative solutions. To create financial freedom to retool and return to contention, GM Joe Garagiola Jr. asked co-ace Curt Schilling (who, with Randy Johnson, had been essential to their World Series victory) to waive his no-trade clause so Arizona could create enough space on their payroll to accommodate Milwaukee Brewers' slugger Richie Sexson. Schilling, under contract only through 2004, was in a position to demand an extension or a new deal as his price for waiving it. Effectively, that made Schilling too expensive for most teams. Boston and New York were really the only prospective buyers, so they reprised their fight over a pitching ace from a year before, with Schilling standing in for Jose Contreras.

The Yankees were the early favorites, but in three weeks of dickering, Steinbrenner & Company couldn't produce the package of prospects and big-league talent that the Diamondbacks wanted in return. Steinbrenner's starry-eyed priorities had turned New York's farm system into a dustbowl. Just before Thanksgiving, Epstein and Lucchino flew to Arizona to talk turkey with Schilling in the comfort of his home. While they couldn't deliver all the talent the D'backs wanted—in the end, Arizona had to settle for three live arms and a player to be named later—the Red Sox offered a $25.5 million extension that would secure Schilling through 2006, with a $13 million option for 2007. Perhaps it was the personal, hat-in-hand approach. Maybe it was a chance to pitch for the sport's most history-minded fan base, something that the history-obsessed Schilling would appreciate. Or maybe it was the money. In any case, Schilling agreed to waive his no-trade clause and come to Boston. The Red Sox had flexed financial muscle, beaten the Yankees at their own game, and now they had a tandem of aces. It was a turning point for both teams.

For better or worse, Schilling brought more than mere talent to the table. He seemed to have been born with an excess of personality. Just as Pedro Martinez presented a special problem for managers because of the need to carefully monitor his workload, so the hardworking Schilling was famous for his stubbornness about being yanked before he was ready to leave a game. He was notoriously glib off the field, happy to share his thoughts on what his ballclub ought to do. His potential indiscretion presented an additional worry for a front office already catering to the various personality quirks of Martinez, Nomar Garciaparra, and Manny Ramirez.

Schilling's arrival influenced the search for a new manager by introducing the desirability of someone already familiar with Schilling's idiosyncrasies. Terry Francona, his former manager in Philadelphia, was conveniently available. Although the Red Sox deny that Schilling had any input, Francona appeared to be the only candidate the Sox took seriously, and it surprised no one when Francona was handed the job just days after Schilling had been acquired.

The son of big-league outfielder Tito Francona, Terry had been a star outfielder at the University of Arizona, where he was a lefty line-drive machine, although not especially gifted with power, patience, or speed. Today he would be a second-tier prospect, but in the days before the statistics revolution changed the way properties like power and patience were weighed, he was considered a blue-chipper. In 1980, he won the Golden Spikes Award as the best player at the collegiate level, was named the *Sporting News* College Player of the Year, and earned the College World Series MVP Award. Picked in the first round by the Expos that same summer, he went straight to Double-A, and split 1981 between Double-A and Triple-A, before ascending to the majors in September for a spot on the Expos bench in the strike-generated round-robin playoffs. The following June, Francona tore up his knee. Sports medicine was nowhere near what it is today, and Francona's skill set wasn't broad enough to make a limping line-drive hitter who couldn't play center a useful everyday player, so he settled for an eight-year run mostly playing the role of reserve and pinch hitter.

In the middle of a 1991 season that had been spent marooned in the minors, Francona hung up his spikes and turned to coaching in the White Sox organization. From that point forward, he did all of the things you should to prepare for a job as major league manager. After finishing 1991 as a hitting instructor in the short-season Gulf Coast League, Francona nabbed the managing job at the lowest full-season rung in the White Sox's farm system, South Bend in the Midwest League. He took on assignments managing in the Arizona Fall League, a good way to get noticed by other organizations, since AFL managers handle prospects from multiple organizations. Having passed these tests, Francona was bumped up to Double-A Birmingham, where he reached the playoffs in his first season. He got a handy background in celebrity babysitting the following year, in a Birmingham ballclub burdened with the conceit that Michael Jordan could play baseball. By all accounts he got along famously with Jordan—while not hesitating to confront the superstar when he failed to run out ground balls and pop-ups—a factor that helped him land the Philadelphia Phillies job in 1997. Francona was a people person, a soothing presence with a reputation for handling potentially prickly clubhouse situations.

To this point in his career, Schilling's lifetime record included 52 wins and 187 days on the disabled list, including annual stays of longer than a month in 1994 through 1996. Though he had excelled in the 1993 post-season and was voted the National League Championship Series MVP, he had never been named to an All-Star team or received a single vote in the Cy Young balloting.

Francona's major league managerial career nearly ended before it had begun. The Phillies lost 72 of their first 106 games, putting them on a pace for 110 losses and Francona on the fast track to termination. In a mid-season closed door meeting, Francona blasted his team—and they promptly won 38 of their last 50 games. Francona was applauded for his handling of the situation and his ability to motivate a team that had little viable pitching after Schilling and a mismatched roster that featured a starting outfield of the midget infielder Gregg Jefferies, the five-year veteran "prospect" Midre Cummings, and the ancient catcher, Darren Daulton.

In Francona's second season, 1998, the Phillies fooled themselves into thinking they were contenders with a 55–50 start, after which they crash-landed in slo-mo with a 20–37 record the rest of the way. The team went into 1999 with unrealistic expectations. Francona went to the whip early and worked his entire rotation hard; the season came apart when Schilling's shoulder gave out in June. Francona also overworked young starters Robert Person and Carlton Loewer, and the breakdowns of the rotation contributed to burning out his bullpen in August. It was a primer on how not to handle a pitching staff, and before it was over Francona had adversely affected the careers of Loewer, Person, and Randy Wolf, not to mention Schilling—all pitchers the Phillies were supposed to be able to count on for their rebuilding.

When the Phillies fell to last place in 2000, Francona made for an easy scapegoat. He wasn't solely responsible; it wasn't Francona who had brought in weak hitters like Doug Glanville or Mark Lewis to fill out a lineup stocked with All-Stars like Bobby Abreu, Scott Rolen, and Mike Lieberthal. At the same time, he didn't suggest many alternatives. Francona seemed only too happy to play the hand he was dealt. The downside of amiability proved to be pliability.

A four-year exercise in failure is usually enough to finish off most aspiring big-league managers. To his credit, Francona didn't give up. He latched on with the Indians as a special assistant to GM John Hart in 2001 and also managed Team USA to a silver medal in the baseball World Cup. The next year he went to Texas to serve as manager Jerry Narron's bench coach, then took the same position with Oakland, working for Ken Macha. He nearly didn't live to take the job; blood clots, the result of surgery on his still troublesome knees, traveled to his lungs and nearly killed him. After four months in the hospital, Francona finally joined the A's.

Not only had Francona been given a second lease on life, but his exposure to the offensive philosophy of the Athletics was a kind of rebirth as well. At Billy Beane's direction, the A's have generally sworn off the running game and its perils, and have heeded the wisdom of Hall of Fame manager Earl Weaver by ditching the sacrifice bunt as a needless waste of a valuable out. At the plate, the focus is on getting on base or getting your pitch; on the mound, the organization

FRANCONA: EVOLVING TACTICIAN 1997–2000 AND 2004					
	Rank Among Major League Managers				
	1997	1998	1999	2000	2004
# Lineups used	20/26	25/28	24/29	18/30	1/26
Sac attempts	7/26	10/28	11/29	6/30	26/26
Def subs	10/26	19/28	8/29	19/30	3/26
High pitch outings	4/26	6/28	9/29	3/30	23/30

makes a point of charting everything, including warm-up pitches and off-day workouts. It exposed Francona to a different ideology, and it was a significant factor in his favor with the Red Sox. Having struggled with Little's resistance to his newfangled ideas, Epstein wanted a manager who had already been indoctrinated in sabermetric teachings. Francona's pliability, a flaw in Philadelphia, would be an asset in Boston, where it was reframed as a willingness to learn and grow.

Having found his ace and his manager, Epstein could finally turn to getting a closer. Rather than stubbornly stick to the innovative committee bullpen plan, he did what any self-respecting GM with money would do: he went out and bought himself a real major league closer. There was really only one on the market: free agent Keith Foulke.

If the Sox couldn't have a bullpen-by-committee, they would have something better: a bona fide closer who would allow them to use their other strong relievers in the sixth or seventh innings, and achieve much the same effect. Foulke agreed to a back-loaded three-year plus option deal for $21 million. If that would seem in retrospect a bit of a bargain for an elite reliever, Foulke's market value was suppressed at the time. There were still some people who remembered how he had briefly struggled with the White Sox (after several years of dominance there) before being run off to Oakland, but they forgot that Foulke's struggles were largely the product of mismanagement. Others felt that Foulke lacked the overpowering assortment of the classic closer, without recognizing that, however he did it, the man beat people. Other teams' hang-ups enabled Epstein to get his last, key ingredient, at a slight discount to boot.

By mid-December, Epstein had put three gifts under the Red Sox Nation Christmas tree: an ace starter, an ace reliever, and a manager who was familiar with both players. He'd arranged for all three with ease, even subtlety. Now Epstein would go in the opposite direction, shocking baseball by attempting one of the biggest, most unexpected trades in the history of the game.

—CHRIS KAHRL AND JONAH KERI

DAN DUQUETTE:
FAILED EPSTEIN PROTOTYPE

Dan Duquette and Theo Epstein stepped into similar situations as the new general manager of the Boston Red Sox. Both became GM a year after a change in ownership[1]—Duquette in 1993, a year after club administration shifted from the deceased Jean Yawkey (Tom's widow) to club steward John Harrington; Epstein a year after Harrington sold the club to John Henry's group. Each took over a team that had not made the playoffs in three seasons. Both GMs were once the youngest in baseball; Duquette was only thirty-four when named the Expos GM,[2] and Epstein was only twenty-eight when tapped by the Red Sox. As lifelong Red Sox fans and Massachusetts natives, each man grew up dreaming that he might one day hold the reins to the Red Sox carriage. Both started in player development but became known for being statistically oriented. Lastly, both quickly led the Sox to the playoffs.

Duquette, the so-called first Rotisserie general manager, lasted seven years in Boston, guiding the team to a winning percentage of .533,[3] fourth among modern Sox GMs.[4,5] The Sox had the sixth-best record in baseball for that period. The club made three playoff appearances, including the team's first consecutive playoff appearances in over eighty years.[6] Duquette's success was predicated on buttressing his core talent with low-cost acquisitions, whether through trades, waiver claims, or inventive signings. Unfortunately, Duquette's constant tinkering ceased to be effective, and this, combined with his sour relationship with the fans and media, led to his undoing.

In 1995, Duquette made five key moves. He brought in former Texas Rangers skipper Kevin Kennedy, a "player's manager," to run the team on the field, acquired second basemen Luis Alicea from St. Louis over the winter, then really scored in mid-April, netting free-agent pitchers Erik Hanson for $1.5 million[7] and Tim Wakefield for $175,000, and claimed Troy O'Leary off waivers for $125,000.[8] Alicea started at second base and turned in a .367 OBP. O'Leary became the starting right fielder and finished at .308/.355/.491. Hanson and Wakefield won thirty-one games and carried the staff when Roger Clemens could not. These four additions cost $2.6 million, and their efforts helped the Sox win the AL East for the first time since 1990, Duquette's second year at the helm.[9] O'Leary and

Wakefield were vital members of the team for many years. Together they were two of Duquette's most cost-effective transactions:

MOST COST-EFFECTIVE ACQUISITIONS

PLAYER	CAREER	W/BOSTON	BOSTON VORP	BOSTON $	BOSTON $/VORP
Doug Mirabelli	'96–Pr.	'01–Pr.	14.81	147,500	9,959.49
Brian Daubach	'98–Pr.	'99–'02, '04	67.57	910,000	13,467.71
Derek Lowe	'97–Pr.	'97–'04	138.25	3,167,000	22,907.94
Rich Garces	'90–'02	'96–'02	84.92	2,779,500	32,731.58
Jason Varitek	'97–Pr.	'97–Pr.	66.96	2,582,500	38,568.38
Erik Hanson	'88–'98	'95	37.78	1,500,000	39,707.75
Rheal Cormier	'91–Pr.	'95, '99–'00	46.92	3,450,000	73,527.84
Reggie Jefferson	'91–'99	'95–'99	109.92	9,757,500	88,769.91
Tim Wakefield	'92–Pr.	'95–Pr.	178.68	18,125,000	101,441.16
Troy O'Leary	'93–'03	'95–'01	128.01	15,965,000	124,720.72

Due to his success with low-cost/high-performance players, Duquette often had money left over to grab the big fish. Stars Manny Ramirez, Johnny Damon, and Pedro Martinez, while not as cost-effective, were vital cogs to Duquette's Red Sox.

Duquette's bargain-basement shopping turned out to be his downfall. Duquette could not resist tinkering with his roster, and this led to time poorly spent on fruitless fantasies such as outfielders Izzy Alcantara, Rudy Pemberton, Tuffy Rhodes, and pitcher Robinson Checo. These were the equivalent of athletic get-rich-quick schemes. To compound this problem, Duquette was well known for his impatience with players. Excluding draft picks, the average tenure of a Duquette acquisition was just under 355 days. His expectations for players were often too lofty, and when they were not met, he moved quickly to correct his "mistake." Too frequently he succeeded only in giving the problem a new face.

WORST ACQUISITIONS

POSITION PLAYER	CAREER	W/RED SOX	BOSTON VORP	BOSTON $	BOSTON $/VORP
Dante Bichette	'88–'01	'00–'01	23.53	7,000,000	297,517.85
Dustin Hermanson	'95–Pr.	'02	14.81	5,833,333	393,877.99
Bryce Florie	'94–'01	'99	5.58	2,800,000	501,882.06
Sang-Hoon Lee	'00	'00	4.83	5,000,000	1,036,269.43

(continued)

POSITION PLAYER	CAREER	W/RED SOX	BOSTON VORP	BOSTON $	BOSTON $/VORP
Steve Avery	'90–'03	'97–'98	2.44	8,750,000	3,586,065.57
Hector Carrasco	'94–'03	'00	–2.99	137,500	–45,971.25
Ed Sprague	'91–'01	'00	–4.43	400,000	–90,334.24
Rico Brogna	'92–'01	'00	–4.83	1,400,000	–289,975.14
Tony Clark	'95–Pr.	'02	–13.60	5,000,000	–367,647.06
Mike Lansing	'93–'01	'00–'01	–7.16	8,333,333	–1,163,548.36

Notice that some players had negative VORP, which means they cost the teams more runs than a replacement-level player, in addition to costing the team his salary. Most of these players lasted only one season with the Olde Towne Team. They weren't just costly in a salary sense, they were also costly in the sense that the Sox had to go through the process of finding a replacement.

Due to his impetuousness, most Duquette draft picks reached the majors with other ballclubs. Lew Ford, Adam Everett, Mike Maroth, Mark Teixeira, David Eckstein, Chris Reitsma, Pat Burrell, and Carl Pavano[10] could have been Red Sox, but Duquette either traded them away or failed to sign them following the draft. While Pavano helped net Pedro Martinez, the others brought many of the players listed in the "worst" chart above.[11,12,13] Complicating this further was Duquette's questionable drafting strategy. His administration produced only three players who have had a significant role with the Red Sox: Nomar Garciaparra, Shea Hillenbrand, and Kevin Youkilis.

Duquette's behavior alienated his peers. His trade record shows that only a few teams dealt with him, diminishing his potential returns. Of the seventy trades Duquette completed as Red Sox GM, over half were conducted with just eight teams.[14]

This was symptomatic of Duquette's entire regime. Duquette did little to mask the disregard he felt for players and personnel whose goodwill he needed to retain in order to function. He had several run-ins with players, managers, and the media. His public, inept evaluation of Roger Clemens's status following the 1996 season haunted him. He feuded with Mo Vaughn following the first baseman's car accident while returning home from a gentleman's club.[15] Vaughn claimed Duquette and the Sox tried to smear his reputation over the incident, citing Vaughn's refusal to submit to a team-requested "alcohol evaluation" shortly after the accident. Other incidents included his furtive, sometimes dishonest approach to player health,[16] trying to bully Mark

Teixeira's father into an unfair contract,[17] and the shameful handling of the volatile conflict between Carl Everett and Jimy Williams, which in turn begat a conflict between Williams and Duquette when the GM publicly deserted his manager.[18]

Though Duquette's Red Sox peaked in 1998 and 1999, his teams were consistently in contention. He wasn't at the helm for the Red Sox's recent championship, but he deserves credit for helping to provide its underpinnings. Ultimately, though, Duquette's "GMitis," along with his bad personal relationships, got the best of him. In many ways Duquette was a modern litmus test for how to handle the "soft" aspects of being a sports executive in Boston. Theo Epstein, a more refined, mentally flexible, and affable version of the Duquette model, has been able to do what Duquette could not. Duquette could identify the team's needs, but he was so eager to find solutions that he short-circuited many of his own plans before they could come to fruition.

—PAUL A. SWYDAN AND BEN MURPHY

3

THE A-ROD ADVANTAGE
NOVEMBER–DECEMBER 2003

One of the biggest stories of the Yankees–Red Sox rivalry in 2004 occurred four months before the season began. Throughout November and December of 2003, the Red Sox were trying furiously to trade their best hitter, Manny Ramirez, for the American League's best player, Alex Rodriguez, shuffling huge amounts of money in the process. The deal was billed as the biggest in baseball history, and, indeed, it was hard to recall a time when such talented ballplayers had been traded in the middle of their careers. Certainly, the scope of the money involved was unprecedented—Rodriguez and Ramirez had a collective $280 million remaining on their long-term contracts. What's more, the deal was packaged with an aftershock that was major news in its own right: With A-Rod on hand to play shortstop, the Red Sox were going to send the displaced incumbent, Nomar Garciaparra, to the White Sox for outfielder Magglio Ordonez.

The scope of the deal was so large, in fact, that the commissioner's office and the players' union would soon become involved. The proposed trade would have restructured the terms of the $252 million deal that Rodriguez had signed with the Texas Rangers before the 2001 season, reducing his salary in some places and deferring it in others, lessening its present-day value; in exchange, Rodriguez would be guaranteed additional marketing rights and would be allowed to become a free agent after the 2005 season.[1] The union, reluctant to set a precedent for decreasing the value of the largest player contract in baseball history, opposed the restructuring, arguing that it had the right under the Collective Bargaining Agreement to unilaterally reject any renegotiation that would have reduced the value of an existing contract.[2] Commissioner Bud Selig, meanwhile, perceived a chance to put the union in its place while facilitating a deal that, his concerns about competitive balance aside, would have aligned one of baseball's best players with one of its biggest markets, stealing a lot of headlines in the process. Indeed, Selig had already gone out of his way to facilitate the deal, allowing contract negotiations to occur between the Red Sox and Rodriguez before the deal had been consummated.[3]

The trade soon collapsed under its own weight. On December 17, union lawyer Gene Orza announced that the Players Association would exercise its veto power over the deal, killing the initial agreement between the Red Sox, the Rangers, and Rodriguez. That evening, as the sides continued to engage in emergency talks to resurrect the deal by finding a restructuring more palatable to the union, Red Sox CEO Larry Lucchino launched a tirade against the union's interventionism:

It is a sad day when the Players Association thwarts the will of its members. The Players Association asserts that it supports individual negotiations, freedom of choice, and player mobility. However, in this high-profile instance, their action contradicts this and is contrary to the desires of the player.[4]

And then, the following day, with the parties still working behind the scenes to strike a deal and repair the damage caused by Lucchino's prior statement, the CEO issued another press release, proclaiming the trade talks DOA:

The proposed trade between the Boston Red Sox and the Texas Rangers is dead. The Players Association's intransigence and the arbitrary nature of its action are responsible for the deal's demise today. Reports that negotiations are continuing and shall continue are inaccurate.[5]

Whether they were some sort of negotiation ploy or simply venting, Lucchino's statements infuriated Rangers' owner Tom Hicks. Hicks continued negotiations with Red Sox chairman Tom Werner and owner John Henry for some time afterward, while Lucchino was exiled to Pittsburgh for "vacation," but his self-imposed deadline of December 23 came and went without a trade.

Rodriguez, Ramirez, and, especially, Garciaparra were upset. Lucchino had cost himself and his organization credibility, Theo Epstein's golden-boy image had been tarnished, and the union and commissioner had another conflict to add to their long list of grievances. Coming on the heels of Aaron Boone's left field shot in the 2003 ALCS, it was hard to imagine things getting much worse.

Just seven weeks later, they did. Yankees GM Brian Cashman announced that his team had acquired Rodriguez for second baseman Alfonso Soriano and a minor league infielder. The deal had come together with remarkable efficiency, with neither public blowups nor premature leaks to the media. Because the Yankees' deal with Rodriguez did not require a substantial restructuring of his contract, the union did not get heavily involved, and Selig approved the trade quickly. The money had not been a problem, not with George Steinbrenner involved. In contrast to the atmosphere of urgency and disorganization surrounding the failed Red Sox deal, the Yankees' acquisition of Rodriguez seemed almost cavalier: *We've got the players, we've got the cash—why the hell not?* Not only had the Yankees one-upped their rivals, but the Red Sox had been made to seem impotent in the process.

It is easy to forget now that A-Rod is as entrenched a part of the "evil empire" as the center field monuments, but there was a tremendous amount of momentum in favor of the trade in December 2003. The Red Sox's baseball people, including Epstein, wanted the trade. The Rangers wanted the trade. Rodriguez and his agent, Scott Boras, wanted the trade. The commissioner's office wanted the trade. The deal fell apart for two interrelated reasons:

1. The Red Sox's reluctance to accept the deal without receiving a substantial discount on the back end of Rodriguez's contract, in spite of the union's opposition, and
2. The poisoned negotiating environment created by Lucchino's public statements.

It was the second factor that was ultimately responsible for the demise of the trade. The union did not oppose the trade on principle, so much as it saw an opportunity to leverage the eagerness of others involved in the deal.[6] The Red Sox were not operating under a particularly tight budget, especially with Ramirez's contract to come off the books, and almost certainly could have and would have picked up a larger fraction of Rodriguez's contractual burden had the negotiations been allowed to take their natural course. But Lucchino's statements, amplified by media noise, gave the discussions a tone of brinkmanship and irrationality, upsetting the delicate balance in what was effectively a five- or six-way negotiation.

Baseball—if not life itself—is an endless series of decisions and forks-in-the-road and serendipitous circumstances, most of it not worth our replaying and wondering What if . . . ? In baseball, however, unlike most other venues of life, we have a welter of statistics to help us play a somewhat more meaningful version of that game. What if the Rodriguez-to-Fenway deal had been consummated? Would things have proceeded just about the same? Would Boston have found the going easier, beating the Yankees in five games instead, with Rodriguez leading the victory rally at Government Center? Or might they have missed the playoffs? By answering the question as best we can, with some informed suppositions based both on statistical tools and some commonsensical inferences about how the clubs might have reacted as events unfolded, perhaps we can get a little closer to the heart of what *did* happen in 2004.

To start with, we'll lay down a ground rule, and assume that the players would have provided the same amount of value regardless of the uniform they were wearing. That is, we'll assume that their offensive and defensive performances would have been the same as they actually were in 2004: If A-Rod hit 36 home runs as a Yankee, then he'd also have hit 36 home runs as a Red Sock, give or take a couple because of what we call ballpark effects. We'll also make the more dubious assumption that Magglio Ordonez's knee injury, which caused him to miss two thirds of the season with the White Sox, would have occurred if he were playing in Boston.

With these parameters in mind, we can establish a parallel timeline of events:

- December 19, 2003: The Red Sox announce that they have brokered a deal with the players' union. Manny Ramirez is sent to the Rangers in exchange for Alex Rodriguez.
- December 28: ESPN's Peter Gammons reports that the Red Sox have traded Nomar Garciaparra to the White Sox in exchange for

Magglio Ordonez. Theo Epstein confirms the deal at a press conference the next day.

- March 30, 2004: The Yankees open the regular season with a two-game series against Tampa Bay in Japan. Enrique Wilson and Miguel Cairo are expected to share time at third base, with Wilson starting on Opening Day.
- May 15: Dissatisfied with the production they're getting from the third base position, the Yankees acquire Joe Randa, who is hitting .286 for the struggling Royals, in exchange for a minor league prospect.
- May 25: Magglio Ordonez leaves a game against the Oakland A's with what is reported as a strained left calf. The injury turns out to be more serious and Ordonez misses six weeks. David McCarty becomes the regular right fielder in Ordonez's place.
- July 10: Ordonez, struggling since returning to action the previous week, plays in his last game of the season as his injury problems worsen.
- July 17: The Red Sox, wary of Ordonez's diagnosis, acquire Jeromy Burnitz from the Colorado Rockies for minor league pitcher Manny Delcarmen. Burnitz displaces McCarty in right field.

This chain of events results in changes at just two positions apiece for the Yankees and the Red Sox. The Red Sox would have replaced Ramirez's playing time in the outfield with a combination of Ordonez, Burnitz, and additional at-bats for David McCarty. A-Rod would have taken over at shortstop, eliminating the playing time that Garciaparra amassed for the team, and making the acquisitions of Pokey Reese and Orlando Cabrera unnecessary. In terms of plate appearances, we get something like this:

HYPOTHESIZED RED SOX PLATE APPEARANCES
AFTER A-ROD-TO-BOSTON DEAL

	Actual	PA	Hypothetical	PA
OF	Manny Ramirez	663	Magglio Ordonez	222
			Dave McCarty	200
			Jeromy Burnitz	241
SS	Nomar Garciaparra	169	Alex Rodriguez	685
	Pokey Reese	268		
	Orlando Cabrera	248		

Meanwhile, the Yankees would have had a combination of Wilson, Cairo, and Randa at third base rather than Rodriguez, and Soriano at second base rather than Cairo and Wilson:

HYPOTHESIZED YANKEES PLATE APPEARANCES
AFTER A-ROD-TO-BOSTON DEAL

	Actual	PA	Hypothetical	PA
3B	Alex Rodriguez	698	Enrique Wilson	175
			Miguel Cairo	125
			Joe Randa	398
2B	Miguel Cairo	408	Alfonso Soriano	658
	Enrique Wilson	250		

It's reasonable to assume that all other players would have remained the same. Both the Red Sox and Yankees were on track to enter the season as relatively complete entities, with or without Alex Rodriguez, so there is no reason to posit some sort of domino effect on other positions.

We can evaluate the impact of this alternate reality by using a metric called Wins Above Replacement Player, or WARP. WARP is a player evaluation tool devised by Baseball Prospectus's Clay Davenport. It accounts for virtually all aspects of a player's contributions both on offense *and* defense—the latter crucial since the players who were impacted by the deals ranged from Gold Glove winner Rodriguez to defensively challenged players like Ramirez. A WARP score of zero represents the value of about the very worst player who could hold down a major league job—that is, someone who could have been picked up without any acquisition cost, such as a waiver wire grab or an organizational player sitting in a team's farm system.[7] WARP also has the convenient property of being denominated in wins; a player with a WARP score of 8 can be said to have produced three more wins for his team than a player with a WARP score of 5.

The 2004 WARP scores for the players impacted by the real and hypothesized A-Rod trades are listed on the next page. It is worth noting that Rodriguez, in spite of having his worst year in several seasons, was still the best player involved in the potential trades by a large margin.

ACTUAL 2004 WARP AND PLATE APPEARANCES

Player	PA	WARP	Player	PA	WARP
Jeromy Burnitz	606	5.4	Manny Ramirez	663	8.0
Orlando Cabrera*	248	1.7	Joe Randa	539	4.4
Miguel Cairo	408	3.2	Pokey Reese	268	1.3
Nomar Garciaparra*	160	1.5	Alex Rodriguez	698	9.9
David McCarty†	168	0.8	Alfonso Soriano	658	4.4
Magglio Ordonez	222	1.9	Enrique Wilson	262	−0.2

*Playing time with Red Sox only

†Value as a position player only; McCarty also appeared in three games as a pitcher.

Using these figures, we can construct "balance sheets" for the Red Sox and the Yankees that describe the impact of the roster changes on the team's respective bottom lines. Where necessary, we will prorate a player's WARP score upward or downward in order to match a change in his playing time. For example, if McCarty was worth 0.8 wins in 168 PA, we'll assume that he would have been worth 1.6 wins, or exactly twice as much, if he had 336 PA, or exactly twice as many.

This is how things might have looked for the Red Sox had they pulled the trigger on the A-Rod deal:

RED SOX BALANCE SHEET, AFTER A-ROD-TO-BOSTON DEAL

Red Sox	PA	WARP
Manny Ramirez	−663	−8.0
Nomar Garciaparra	−169	−1.5
Pokey Reese	−268	−1.3
Orlando Cabrera	−248	−1.7
Magglio Ordonez	+222	+1.9
Dave McCarty	+200	+1.8
Jeromy Burnitz	+241	+2.1
Alex Rodriguez	+685	+9.7
Net	0	**+3.0**

The Red Sox lose the contributions of Ramirez, Garciaparra, Reese, and Cabrera but gain those of Rodriguez, Ordonez, Burnitz, and McCarty. The key entry is in the last row of the table—the Red Sox would have won three additional regular season games if the Rodriguez deal had been completed.

The Yankees can be evaluated in the same fashion:

YANKEES BALANCE SHEET, AFTER A-ROD-TO-BOSTON DEAL

Yankees	PA	WINS
Alex Rodriguez	−698	−9.9
Miguel Cairo	−283	−2.2
Enrique Wilson	−75	+0.1
Joe Randa	+398	+3.2
Alfonso Soriano	+658	+4.4
Net	**0**	**−4.4**

The Yankees would have swapped A-Rod's 9.9 WARP for Soriano's 4.4, while Randa would have displaced some playing time from Cairo and Wilson. Had they not been able to acquire A-Rod, we estimate that the Yankees would have finished with between four and five wins fewer than they actually did. And so, instead of having this:

A-Rod to Yanks	W	L	GB
New York	101	61	—
Boston	98	64	3

We might have ended up with something like this:

A-Rod to Sox	W	L	GB
Boston	101	61	—
New York	97	65	4

In other words, a net swing of seven or eight wins in Boston's favor. The Red Sox would have had home field advantage throughout the playoffs, and played the Twins rather than the Angels in the Division Series.

How things would have played out from there is beyond our capacity to know, but at the very least, it seems ridiculous to suggest, as some commentators have, that the failure to trade for A-Rod somehow facilitated the Red Sox's championship. Rodriguez has a reputation as a selfish player who falters in the clutch, but he led the Yankees to a 101-win season, and is a career .330 hitter in 26 playoff games, including a .320 performance in the 2004 postseason. In fact, the failure to obtain A-Rod meant the team had incrementally less talent on the field, which made a World Series victory incrementally less likely.

Even if we use performance prior to the 2004 season as the benchmark, we have to conclude that the Red Sox would have been a better team in 2004 with Rodriguez and Ordonez. In 2002, Ramirez and Garciaparra combined for 17.5 WARP, while Rodriguez and Ordonez combined for 21.6 WARP. In 2003, Ramirez and Garciaparra combined for 16.8 WARP, but Rodriguez and Ordonez combined for 21.8 WARP. In essence, the Red Sox would have been trading two very good players for one very good player and one world-class, once-in-a-generation player. That sort of deal would have come out as a net positive under any credible analysis, at least in terms of on-the-field performance.

The longer-term impact of the Trade That Wasn't was not felt on the field; it was felt in the way Theo Epstein and the rest of the Red Sox front office conducted its business. If nothing else, it was a learning experience:

Lesson #1. Keep a unified front.

Regardless of the merits of Lucchino's point of view, he should not have been allowed to make public statements that did not represent the consensus of the Red Sox's internal opinion, especially with negotiations still ongoing.

Lesson #2. Don't burn your bridges.

The public nature of the A-Rod negotiations caused significant strains on the Red Sox's relationships with Manny Ramirez and Nomar Garciaparra. Ramirez, who had also been placed on waivers prior to the start of the negotiations, turned out to be fine, taking care to improve his public image and having a characteristically productive season. But Garciaparra pouted, publicly and privately, compromising his trade value while he was also underperforming on the field.

Lesson #3. Don't do your negotiating in the media.

Frenzied media environments like Boston and New York require special handling. The Yankees' brass does its share of grandstanding, but it also knows how to insulate itself when it needs to get a deal done, as evidenced by the comparative air of quiet surrounding their eventual acquisition of A-Rod.

These are the sorts of lessons that any young executive needs to learn, whether he is in baseball or in widgets, and he's usually going to learn them the hard way. Epstein and the Red Sox would put them into practice from virtually the very moment of the Rodriguez deal's collapse. Consider this press release, dated December 23, 2003:

> *[The] Boston Red Sox issued the following statement on behalf of John Henry, Tom Werner, Larry Lucchino, and Theo Epstein:*
> *"There is nothing further to report relating to the consummation of a transaction between the Boston Red Sox and the Texas Rangers involving Alex Rodriguez. No further discussions regarding this transaction are planned."* [8]

In contrast to Lucchino's maverick statements of the previous week, the Red Sox's brain trust had spoken as one. Just as important, they had accepted their fate politely without pouring more fuel on the fire.

In February 2004, after the initial outcry from the A-Rod deal had died down, the Red Sox announced that longtime media relations director Kevin Shea had left the organization to pursue other opportunities. In July, the Garciaparra–for–Orlando Cabrera trade occurred in an atmosphere of discretion and diplomacy. The move took observers by surprise in part because the Red Sox had taken steps to downplay Garciaparra's level of dissatisfaction in Boston; media accounts pointed out how Terry Francona was appointed to serve as the fall guy for perceived and real clubhouse dissention. And in the winter following their championship season, the Red Sox would take a decidedly lower profile in their negotiations with the 2004-2005 free-agent class. There would be no Thanksgiving dinner with Carl Pavano or David Wells, as there had been with Curt

Schilling, and there would be no dramatic meeting in the Dominican Republic between Epstein and Pedro Martinez, as Martinez's most ardent suitor, the Mets' Omar Minaya, had arranged for.

In a sense, the failure of the Rodriguez deal would negatively affect the Red Sox for several years—the years he would not be a member of the Red Sox. However, the failure had a powerful positive effect as well: A-Rod's non-arrival proved to the club that the front office had built a team robust enough to withstand the loss, to its sworn enemy no less, of the league's very best player.

—NATE SILVER

4

SQUEEZING THE MERCHANDISE
MARCH 7 AND MARCH 24, 2004

"God, that's sick," said Joe Torre, observing the vendors selling commemorative pins marking the resumption of "the rivalry," the never-ending clash for supremacy between the Boston Red Sox and the New York Yankees. Torre wasn't naïve; it wasn't the idea of exploitative merchandise that turned his stomach. All he had to do was take a walk outside Yankee Stadium or Fenway Park before any regular season game between the two teams to see opportunistic capitalism in action. Rather, what was disturbing was that this wasn't New York or Boston, but Fort Myers, Florida, and the game in question was a spring training exhibition.

Throughout the New York and Boston areas that week, jaded journalists beat the drums of overhype. The headline on the *New York Post* said, "Welcome to the Rivalry, A-Rod." There were a dozen columns in the tristate area alone proclaiming, in one manner or another, "Red Sox! Yankees! This Time It's for Real!" Except, no, it wasn't real. Dave McCarty played first base for the Red Sox. Pokey Reese was the shortstop. Alex Rodriguez spent less time at third base than did Erick Almonte. Neither manager's job hung on the outcome. Red Sox fans were passive during this game, largely sitting on their hands once the Yankees went ahead.

Granted, the coverage of the game was a cynical attempt to drum up interest and controversy at a slow time of year for the sports pages, but there *was* an element of truth in the contest's billing—a scintilla of a reason to camp out for standing-room-only tickets, or, as some did, pay $200 to a

Former Boston Red Sox great Johnny Pesky
with current great Curt Schilling in spring training

scalper. From 1998 to 2003 the American League East standings had looked like a still life: the Yankees finished first, the Red Sox second, the Blue Jays third, the Orioles fourth, and the Devil Rays fifth. Things at the bottom were not likely to change. The Blue Jays were in a perpetual rebuilding program that had all the hallmarks of one of those graft-ridden rural highway projects that are never completed. The Orioles, who had signed Javy Lopez and Miguel Tejada, were in their umpteenth year of investing money in their team, but only in places where it wouldn't change their outlook. As for the Devil Rays, back in 1998 the team had hopped off the franchise incarnation wheel at a point somewhere between Sisyphus Stadium and Slough of Despond Park.

For Boston, then, the path to the division title, the first step to the World Series, would be through New York, and the reverse was true as well. It was a bilateral world of two superpowers in which the only moves that really mattered were the ones that bestowed even an incremental advantage over the other bully on the block. That the Yankees ultimately beat the Red Sox out in the race to acquire Alex Rodriguez made many think they had already won the winter. In reality, the talent gap of 2003 had narrowed considerably. Boston had won the off-season arms race. While the Yankees' politburo-style leadership had paralyzed the team's ability to confront its growing list of problem areas, the more streamlined management of the Red Sox aggressively pursued every opportunity to improve their team. The Yankees faced problems, like their fallow farm system, that had festered for so long they resisted easy solutions. They also had the daunting task of replacing four fifths of their 2003 starting rotation. Roger Clemens, Andy Pettitte, and David Wells had departed due to "retirement" and free agency. These were not the 3-4-5 starters for the Milwaukee Brewers, but three of the top pitchers in the game; losing all three at once would have been a devastating blow to any organization.

The Bombers traded for right-handed pitcher Javier Vazquez of the Expos, then dealt for Kevin Brown, a great but aging and injury-prone right-hander. They hoped that, after a year of rehabilitation following Tommy John surgery, Jon Lieber could approximate his twenty-game-winning form of 2001. They prayed they could decipher the inner workings of Cuban escapee Jose Contreras, a pitcher they had snatched from under the Red Sox's noses the year before; it had proved to be a Pyrrhic victory since Contreras approached each start as if he were being compelled to undergo sexual reassignment surgery. In the bullpen, there was no reliable lefty; erratic journeyman Felix Heredia was signed to a two-year deal on the basis of a few mediocre innings the previous fall. The starting rotation would also be without a left-hander, an unusual state for the Yankees given the configuration of Yankee Stadium.

The team's attempts to deal with their misshapen core of regulars were even more dubious. The lineup had become a patchwork of expensive secondhand toys:

- When Jason Giambi had proved to be a first baseman who couldn't play first, the team signed journeymen Tony Clark and Travis Lee. The former was a past-his-prime free swinger who never saw a pitch he couldn't miss, the latter a formerly overhyped hitting prospect who had proved to have the bat of an anemic middle infielder.
- Because center fielder Bernie Williams, thirty-five, seemed to be in a state of rapid decline, the team signed the even more ancient Kenny Lofton, thirty-seven, part of an ad hoc plan to make Williams the designated hitter, although Giambi had been ticketed for that slot.
- After swing-and-miss specialist/third baseman Aaron Boone crippled himself in an ill-advised pickup basketball game, the Yankees traded second baseman Alfonso Soriano for Alex Rodriguez. Regardless of the vast benefits Rodriguez would provide, he was no second baseman. The Yankees signed Miguel Cairo with the intention of using him as a back up to Enrique Wilson, the incumbent utility man now promoted to starter. Neither player could be counted on to produce even league-average offense at the position.

The Yankees temporized because they had been caged by their own aggressiveness. With their budget-setting new records each year, the team had finally run out of financial maneuvering room. Significantly, they would not admit this until after the season.

While New York had compromised, Boston had solved major problems with major solutions, adding a second ace in Curt Schilling, shoring up their bullpen with elite closer Keith Foulke, and fixing their second base problems with an offensive-defensive combination of Mark Bellhorn and

Pokey Reese. As Opening Day approached, here's how the two lineups looked in head-to-head competition.

FIRST BASE[1]

Yankees: Jason Giambi	
Projected AVG/OBP/SLG	.282/.414/.557
Projected VORP	59.6

Red Sox: Kevin Millar	
Projected AVG/OBP/SLG	.289/.357/.492
Projected VORP	24.6

Giambi had suffered through a so-called off year in 2003. Patellar tendonitis in his left knee and an eye infection depressed his batting average to .250, but he had still hit 41 home runs and taken 129 walks. A player with that kind of power and patience can hit .210 and still be valuable. Millar was a right-handed hitter who posted above-average to strong numbers powered mostly by batting average, as his .290/.362/.495 career line attested. Fenway Park was friendly to him, the Green Monster helping him pad his average and doubles totals.[2] A good deal of his value was in his versatility. Millar could play both outfield and infield corners without embarrassing himself. Conversely, Giambi's glove had all the flexibility of gypsum. Still, if Giambi was only healthy enough to repeat his 2003 batting numbers, he would put at least twice as many runs on the board as his Boston counterpart. There is no substitute for getting on base, and the Yankees held a big edge.

SECOND BASE

Yankees: Enrique Wilson	
Projected AVG/OBP/SLG	.238/.287/.351
Projected VORP	1.3

Red Sox: Mark Bellhorn	
Projected AVG/OBP/SLG	.248/.350/.427
Projected VORP	13.3

The Yankees abdicated the second-base competition to the Red Sox. Wilson, a career backup who had recently been discovered to have been born in 1973 rather than his listed year of 1975, had hit .253/.296/.358 in 384 career games. He had earned just 3.1 wins above replacement *for his career*, coming perilously close to negative returns. A strong argument could have been made that a veteran Triple-A infielder, chosen at random, could have outperformed Wilson.

The Yankees, apparently not grasping the perils of small sample size, sold themselves on Enrique Wilson as their starting second baseman, based largely on the fact that Wilson had hit over .400 against Pedro Martinez. However, Wilson had turned the trick in fewer than twenty at-bats, rendering his mastery of Martinez all but meaningless. Boston's interest in Bellhorn was based on his far broader, although frustratingly inconsistent, record of success. Bellhorn was a "three true outcomes" player, meaning that most of his at-bats resulted in either a walk, a strike-out, or a home run. The problem was that he ran into stretches where he was a one-outcome player, and that outcome was a strikeout. His defense was not good enough to keep him in the lineup if he wasn't going to hit.

Bellhorn was a product of the A's system, but even that team, which cherishes players with high on-base and slugging percentages, had been reluctant to invest heavily in him. After being traded to the Cubs for infield prospect Adam Morrissey in November 2001, Bellhorn flourished as an everyday player in 2002 (albeit at five positions), batting .258/.374/.512 with 27 home runs, 76 walks, and 144 strikeouts. Bellhorn's numbers that year equated to a .301 EqA. He was the third-most productive second baseman in the game. Had Bruce Kimm remained Chicago's manager, 2003 would have marked Bellhorn's first spring training as an incumbent starter. Instead, Kimm was fired, replaced by Dusty Baker, and Bellhorn's career was again in jeopardy. Disdaining players who take walks as base-cloggers, Baker insisted Bellhorn needed to be more aggressive at the plate to win a job. With Bill Mueller gone to the Red Sox and a possible trade for that team's strikeout-conscious Shea Hillenbrand dead, Baker unenthusiasti-cally marked Bellhorn down as his starting third baseman. When Bellhorn opened the season in a 1-for-22 slump (followed by a marginally more impressive 10-for-54), Baker benched him, then buried him. In June he was traded to the Rockies. Even in that hitter's paradise, Bellhorn was unable to regain his confidence, in part because of an injured shoulder.

Like the A's, even the performance analysis-influenced Red Sox were reluctant to entrust Bellhorn with an everyday role, signing good-field/no-hit infielder Pokey Reese to play second base. Late in the spring, Theo Epstein seriously contemplated a deal that would have sent Bellhorn to the White Sox for left-handed reliever Kelly Wunsch.[3] Reese, projected to bat .242/.300/.349, was still likely to outplay Enrique Wilson, but not by enough to hold a job. Nor was he durable. Given past history, it seemed likely that neither Bellhorn, Reese, nor Wilson would play anything resembling a full campaign. With New York's only alternative being utility infielder Miguel Cairo (projected .263/.315/.400), the Red Sox held the edge regardless.

THIRD BASE

Yankees: Alex Rodriguez	
Projected AVG/OBP/SLG	.295/.398/.594
Projected VORP	86.6

Red Sox: Bill Mueller	
Projected AVG/OBP/SLG	.275/.352/.423
Projected VORP	22.1

At third, the Yankees possessed the incumbent MVP, the Red Sox the defending batting champion. A .286/.370/.399 career hitter prior to batting .326/.398/.540 in 2003, Mueller was almost certain to regress in 2004. Even so, his ability to get on base would have value. Regardless, he would likely pale in comparison to Alex Rodriguez, who had every chance to become the most productive third baseman ever for a team whose list of outstanding offensive performers at third base is surprisingly small. The question of whether relocating the famous shortstop to third made sense for a team whose regular shortstop's defensive record was one of the poorest in the game went unaddressed.

SHORTSTOP

Yankees: Derek Jeter	
Projected AVG/OBP/SLG	.292/.364/.433
Projected VORP	41.4

Red Sox: Nomar Garciaparra	
Projected AVG/OBP/SLG	.310/.360/.505
Projected VORP	52.1

Jeter and Garciaparra were two of the most celebrated players of their day, but as 2004 approached, both were seriously overvalued by fans and management alike. Garciaparra had turned thirty the previous July, while Jeter would exit his twenties in June. Despite productive seasons for each in 2003, both seemed likely candidates for an early decline. As measured by every defensive metric known to man, Jeter's defense had been dismal—perhaps even untenable—for years. From 1999 to 2003, Jeter had posted

DEREK JETER REBEL WITHOUT A GLOVE		
YEAR	G	FRAA
1999	158	-18
2000	148	-20
2001	150	-18
2002	156	-18
2003	118	-20
5 Yrs.	730	-94

five of the most damaging defensive seasons by a modern shortstop (post-1901) in the history of the game (these metrics include Baseball Prospectus's Davenport Fielding Translations and Bill James's Win Shares). In the chart on the prevous page, FRAA stands for Fielding Runs Above Average, a Baseball Prospectus metric measuring how many runs a player saved over the average fielder at his position. Only one other shortstop in history was permitted to post as many as three such devastating seasons without being benched, demoted, or moved to another position—Larry Kopf, who played for the Cincinnati Reds in the late teens.

In fact, of the players who put their teams through seasons in which they allowed eighteen or more runs on defense more than the average shortstop, few kept their jobs. More than half of the defensively challenged shortstops were no longer in possession of their position within a year (in itself a validation of statistical evaluations of defense that have since come into use). With the demonstrably better-fielding Alex Rodriguez on board, the Yankees were free to transfer Jeter to any of the positions where they had openings—third base, second base, or center field. Instead, as a concession to Jeter's ego, they moved Rodriguez to third.

The Garciaparra dilemma was more straightforward. Since missing most of 2001 with an injury to his right wrist (see Chapter 12), his offensive production, though still hearty, was not nearly what it had been. Other physical problems had begun to curtail his defense. If Garciaparra missed significant time with injury, it would be a long drop to reserve Pokey Reese. Garciaparra was in the final year of his contract, and the Red Sox were in no hurry to negotiate a new contract with him. As the season began, there were intimations that this could become a distraction to Garciaparra or possibly to the team as a whole.

CATCHER

Yankees: Jorge Posada	
Projected AVG/OBP/SLG	.261/.368/.460
Projected VORP	35.3

Red Sox: Jason Varitek	
Projected AVG/OBP/SLG	.268/.343/.456
Projected VORP	21.0

Jorge Posada finished third in the 2003 MVP voting, finally gaining some recognition after long holding the status of one of the most underappreciated players in the game. As a defender, he left much to be desired. He was merely adequate at throwing out base runners, permitted an inordinate number of passed balls for a catcher who never dealt with knuckleballers, and visibly shied away from blocking home plate. But he more than made up for these deficiencies with his tremendous bat. Critics sometimes focused on Posada's relatively low batting averages and high number of strikeouts, oblivious to his power, walk total, and all-around offense at a position at which good bats are nearly impossible to find. From 2000 to 2004, Posada posted on-base and slugging percentages of .391 and .494, far above the American League's average figures of .337 and .431.

By contrast, Jason Varitek was generally not thought of as an important part of the Red Sox offense, getting much more credit in the areas of defense and clubhouse leadership. However, since recovering from a broken elbow sustained during the 2001 season—a process that took all of 2002—the switch-hitting Varitek had emerged in his early thirties as a two-way threat, batting .273/.351/.512 with 25 home runs in 2003. Still, Varitek was separated from Posada by his relative impatience, lesser home run power, and his enforced benching every five days so that Doug Mirabelli could be abused by Tim Wakefield. Mirabelli made the most of his opportunities offensively, but the combined production didn't equal what Posada did on his own.

LEFT FIELD

Yankees: Hideki Matsui	
Projected AVG/OBP/SLG	.279/.360/.451
Projected VORP	26.8

Red Sox: Manny Ramirez	
Projected AVG/OBP/SLG	.314/.410/.582
Projected VORP	57.1

In 2003, Hideki Matsui came to the plate with 507 runners on base, third most in the game. He drove in 18 percent of them, a strong but unexceptional number. This was enough to push him across the 100 RBI mark, considered by many to be the hallmark of a strong season. In this, Matsui was an artistic success but a practical disappointment. A slugger in Japan with a career-high 50 home runs in his last Yomiuri Giants season, Matsui became a marked ground-ball hitter in the states, pounding 2.2 balls into the dirt for every one hit into the air. He hit into 25 double plays, second most in the league, and his home run total shrank to 16.

Even if Matsui rediscovered the uppercut that earned him the nickname Godzilla, it was unlikely he'd be half as productive as Manny

Ramirez. The Sox may have been eager to deal Ramirez because of his frequent mental lapses on the bases and in the field, his occasional and inexplicable self-removal from the lineup, and, most important, the sheer size of his contract, but it certainly wasn't because of his offense. A career .317/.413/.598 hitter through 2003, Ramirez's credentials were impeccable. Among active players, he was:

- Third in slugging percentage (.598), first among right-handed hitters
- Third in isolated power (.281), first among right-handed hitters[4]
- Third in marginal lineup value (.380), second among right-handed hitters[5]
- Sixth in batting average (.317), fifth among right-handed hitters
- Seventh in on-base percentage (.413), third among right-handed hitters
- Fifteenth in home runs (347), ninth among right-handed hitters
- Sixteenth VORP (Value Over Replacement Player) (684.2), tenth among right-handed hitters

A hardworking future Hall of Famer—despite the absences, he ranked third in games played among players in his age group—Ramirez was capable of driving his manager and teammates crazy (a talent shared by more than a few of the greatest players in baseball history). The Sox had to keep Ramirez—before and after the A-Rod deal no one else would take on his salary—but it was a bit like wanting diamonds and settling for platinum; in this Panglossian outcome the worst alternative had the highest of upsides.

CENTER FIELD

Yankees: Bernie Williams	
Projected AVG/OBP/SLG	.285/.374/.440
Projected VORP	25.9

Red Sox: Johnny Damon	
Projected AVG/OBP/SLG	.282/.351/.421
Projected VORP	14.7

For most of his career Johnny Damon had been as overrated as Bernie Williams was underrated. Damon's ability to run and turn slapped singles into doubles gave him a lot of curb appeal, whereas Bernie Williams's patience and hesitant, inhibited base-running concealed a stretch of eight seasons (1995–2002) few center fielders in history could match: he batted .321/.406/.531 with 194 home runs, a batting title, and four Gold Gloves. The excellence came to a sudden halt in 2003, when the thirty-four-year-old Williams, hobbled by a bad knee, missed 43 games and never found his stroke, finishing with .263/.367/.411 averages. This signified a major decline in value because, as of 2002,

BERNIE'S MAGIC EIGHT: VALUE OVER REPLACEMENT, 1995–2002				
YEAR	VORP	MLB RNK	AL RNK	CF RNK
1995	62.0	15	11	1
1996	68.2	21	14	3
1997	70.2	13	7	2
1998	78.7	12	8	2
1999	90.6	6	3	1
2000	68.2	27	11	5
2001	66.8	26	9	2
2002	75.5	11	6	2

Williams's defensive abilities had gone from mediocre to unacceptable. He remained a productive hitter for his position, but the sheer number of singles that fell in front of him had begun to nullify his offensive contributions.

For 2004, the Yankees attempted to duck the issue of Williams's decline with half-measures, none of which made very much sense. The plan seemed designed with an eye toward Kansas City center fielder Carlos Beltran, who would be a free agent after the season. The Yankees would make no long-term commitments that would prevent them from offering Beltran a job. On January 6, the Yankees signed veteran center fielder Kenny Lofton, thirty-seven, to a two-year contract. Lofton and Williams would compete in spring training for the center-field job, with the loser expected to be the everyday designated hitter.

There were several problems with this scenario. In his time of decrepitude, Lofton was no longer suited to be an everyday player. Even as a young man he had not been a great defensive center fielder, and he was no longer young. On offense, Lofton, a left-handed hitter, had long struggled against left-handed

BERNIE'S MAGIC EIGHT VS. HISTORY: BEST EIGHT-YEAR STRETCHES BY CENTER FIELDERS AS PER WINS ABOVE REPLACEMENT		
Players	Years	WARP 3
Willie Mays	1958–65	97.2
Mickey Mantle	1954–61	94.1
Ty Cobb	1910–17	86.6
Joe DiMaggio	1937–42 + 1946–47	85.2
Tris Speaker	1909–16	82.9
Ken Griffey Jr.	1991–98	81.9
Duke Snider	1949–56	74.0
Richie Ashburn	1951–58	73.3
Bernie Williams	1995–2002	71.7
Kirby Puckett	1986–93	70.8
Billy Hamilton	1891–98	69.0
Jim Edmonds	1997–2004	68.9

pitchers. He would need to be platooned. While both Williams and Lofton might have provided acceptable offense in center field, neither would be strong offensive contributors at DH, a hitter's position. In addition, if Lofton forced Williams to DH, Jason Giambi would have to play first base every day, creating another defensive problem and one that risked injury to Giambi.

Giambi's early tendonitis was a blessing in disguise, limiting his playing time at first. Shaping the roster so that Giambi was boxed into playing first was asking for trouble. As if sensing this, the Yankees signed two mediocre first basemen, Tony Clark and Travis Lee, further clouding the issue of just who would play when. As the spring wore on it became clear that Yankees manager Joe Torre's two priorities were showing loyalty to Williams and placing a strong defender at first base.

This gave the Red Sox a double chance to steal a march on the Yankees. Damon had always been a better defender than Williams. Given left fielder Manny Ramirez's frequent flights of fancy in left, and injuries to right fielder Trot Nixon, Damon's presence in center was a necessity. At the plate, Williams and Damon were converging. At age thirty-five, Williams was unlikely to return to peak form, giving Damon the offensive edge if he could get his inconsistency (alternating .300 seasons with .270 seasons, or even .250) under control.

RIGHT FIELD

Yankees: Gary Sheffield	
Projected AVG/OBP/SLG	.297/.387/.515
Projected VORP	44.2

Red Sox: Trot Nixon	
Projected AVG/OBP/SLG	.284/.372/.511
Projected VORP	28.5

The Yankees right field situation had been a soup du jour disaster in 2003, the position occupied on any given day by Raul Mondesi, Karim Garcia, Juan Rivera, and David Dellucci. That winter the team had a choice of two big-splash solutions, Gary Sheffield, thirty-five, and Vladimir Guerrero, twenty-eight. Sheffield was coming off of the best year of any right fielder in the game, while Guerrero had been limited by injuries, but the seven-year age gap made Guerrero the safer long-term investment, even though the two players were quite evenly matched as hitters:

GUERRERO VS. SHEFFIELD, 1998–2003														
	G	AB	H	2B	3B	HR	BB	K	SB	CS	AVG	OBP	SLG	FRAA	VORP
Guerrero	905	3411	1112	204	32	222	362	442	120	67	.326	.395	.600	-56	424.8
Sheffield	856	3070	961	162	9	199	549	356	77	28	.313	.419	.566	-17	420.9

Whether because of Guerrero's herniated disc, the same injury that had cost the Yankees a year of Dave Winfield's services in 1989, or because Sheffield's uncle, Dwight Gooden, was one of his inner circle advisers, Yankees owner George Steinbrenner chose the older man. Meanwhile, the Red Sox stayed the course with Trot Nixon, their 1993 first-round draft choice. Nixon had a belated peak year in 2003 as a twenty-nine-year-old, batting .306/.396/.578 with 28 home runs. It was a terrifically valuable season, but in many ways he was still the same player he always was, a platoon outfielder miscast as an everyday player. In 2003, Nixon batted just .219/.296/.375 against lefties. His lifetime record against them was even worse: .213/.298/.332. The Duquette regime had been slow to accept the necessity of Nixon's sitting against southpaws. Theo Epstein moved faster, signing the muscular right-handed outfielder Gabe Kapler four days after he was released by the chronically confused Colorado Rockies. In 2003, Kapler had batted .326/.386/.446 against left handers. Kapler was the only true outfield reserve on the roster; that is, he was not someone the team wanted to see every day. Should anything happen to Nixon, the Red Sox's fallback plan was to move Millar to right field, opening up first base to David Ortiz, Dave McCarty, or Brian Daubach. This would also free playing time for returning Red Sox outfielder Ellis Burks, a slugging right-handed hitter whose gnarled legs now limited him to designated hitter duties.

DESIGNATED HITTER

Yankees: Ruben Sierra	
Projected AVG/OBP/SLG	.255/.309/.408
Projected VORP	2.0

Red Sox: David Ortiz	
Projected AVG/OBP/SLG	.278/.361/.533
Projected VORP	28.7

Boston was well-fixed at designated hitter with the find of 2003, David Ortiz. New York's plans were much shakier, centered as they were on the Giambi/Lofton/Williams love triangle. Sierra, thirty-eight, entered the picture when an appendectomy sidelined Williams for the first few days of the season. As soon as Williams returned, Lofton hit the disabled list, allowing Sierra to hold on to the job a while longer.

In 2003 the average American League designated hitter had hit .260/.348/.439. It was possible, though unlikely, that Sierra's home run stroke might allow him to approach or surpass that .439 slugging percentage mark.

As for on-base percentage, the chronically impatient Sierra had posted an OBP of .330 or higher just three times in his career, most recently in 1991.

The Yankees were in a productivity catch-22: If Giambi were the everyday DH, then either Lofton or Williams couldn't play and the substitute first basemen would sink the offense. If Giambi played first base, the center-field/DH combo wouldn't be able to provide adequate offense. It was a no-win situation.

PITCHERS: STARTING ROTATION

Yankees	Proj. ERA	Proj. VORP
Mike Mussina, RHP	3.31	56.3
Kevin Brown, RHP	3.58	38.9
Javier Vazquez, RHP	3.22	61.7
Jose Contreras, RHP	3.56	24.4
Jon Lieber, RHP	4.44	21.1

Boston	Proj. ERA	Proj. VORP
Pedro Martinez, RHP	2.49	70.0
Curt Schilling, RHP	3.35	55.8
Derek Lowe, RHP	4.28	27.9
Tim Wakefield, RHP	4.44	26.8
Bronson Arroyo, RHP	4.35	16.7

A much noted aspect of both teams' starting rotations was the complete absence of left-handed pitching. For Boston, this was not unusual, since Fenway Park, with its claustrophobia-inducing left field wall, discouraged a reliance on lefties. Conversely, Yankee Stadium, with its short right field line, encouraged the Yankees to stock their team with lefty hitters. For the Red Sox, this meant they would be giving up the platoon advantage against their rivals as long as their starting pitcher remained in the game. To mitigate the disadvantage, they would have to count on lefty middle relievers like Alan Embree and Bobby M. Jones, the latter a pitcher whose poor control would undoubtedly carry him back to Pawtucket as soon as Byung-Hyun Kim came off the disabled list.

THE BULLPEN

Yankees	Proj. ERA	Proj. VORP
Mariano Rivera, RHP	2.97	19.8
Tom Gordon, RHP	3.22	25.3
Paul Quantrill, RHP	4.07	11.2
Felix Heredia, LHP	5.34	3.1
Gabe White, LHP	4.46	6.0
Donovan Osborne, LHP	9.42	−7.2

Boston	Proj. ERA	Proj. VORP
Keith Foulke, RHP	3.15	24.8
Mike Timlin, RHP	3.83	14.8
Alan Embree, LHP	4.05	11.7
Bobby M. Jones, LHP	5.50	0.0
Ramiro Mendoza, RHP	4.57	11.4
Scott Williamson, RHP	4.11	14.9

In fielding a rotation devoid of left-handers, the Yankees would be sacrificing the traditional benefits enjoyed by lefties in their park—a capacious left-center field where long fly balls went to die. Both teams would have preferred to start at least one southpaw, but neither team had a lefty pitching prospect ready. This forced both teams to the meat markets. There was little for sale. In the winter of 2003–2004, few lefties were available—even considering the customary dearth of lefty starters in this world.

Both Boston and New York coveted Randy Johnson, but he would not approve a trade to Boston and the Diamondbacks could not work out a trade with the Yankees. For Brian Cashman, that left only subjourneymen like Brian Anderson. Cashman accurately assessed what was left among the free agents, a group that included Anderson, Mark Redman, Ron Villone, Terry Mulholland, John Halama, Damian Moss, Kenny Rogers, Glendon Rusch, Bruce Chen, Shawn Estes, Darren Oliver, and Sterling Hitchcock as being of limited worth. Lefties who moved through trades were of the same quality: Mark Hendrickson, Joe Kennedy, Eric Milton, and Boston's Casey Fossum. The only exception was former Yankee Ted Lilly, dealt from Toronto to Oakland. In fact, the two best lefties on the market were *leaving* New York: David Wells, who had been freed when the Yankees declined his 2004 option, and Andy Pettitte, whom the Yankees, or so Pettitte claimed, had pursued halfheartedly.

The departure of three fifths of their rotation seemed to have little effect on New York's off-season priorities; the team marched into the winter intent on solving the problems of the 2003 team, which had strong starting pitching and ragged middle relief, rather than those of the coming 2004 team, which had neither. The new starting rotation, which now boasted thirty-nine-year-old Kevin Brown, thanks to the December trade of Jeff Weaver, Yhency Brazoban, Brandon Wheedon, and cash to the Dodgers, contained many question marks. It was no sure thing that Brown, a pitcher who had spent 289 days on the disabled list during his career, could withstand the ravages of age and injury; that Jon Lieber could still pitch; or that Jose Contreras, Cuba's version of the Cowardly Lion, could find his courage.[6] As the season opened, only Mussina and Vazquez seemed anything like a good bet.

As for the bullpen, Chris Hammond, a lefty who wasn't good at retiring his own brethren, was traded to the A's. Free-agent righties Tom Gordon and Paul Quantrill were signed. Donovan Osborne, a Torre Cardinals alumnus who had pitched just seventeen games in the previous four years, was invited to spring training and made the team as a swingman. He would be the third lefty, joining incumbents Felix Heredia and Gabe White. With three lefties in the pen, the Yankees hoped to keep David Ortiz and his portsider friends from taking them deep in the middle innings.

Boston's pitching options required less guesswork. In 2003, Boston's rotation had been unremarkable except for Pedro Martinez, a state of affairs greatly improved by the acquisition of Schilling and the promotion of Bronson Arroyo, twenty-seven, from Pawtucket. Arroyo had failed to establish himself in the majors in extended trials with the Pirates from 2000 to 2002, but Boston trusted what they saw with their own eyes. Such confidence in their own sensory impressions is not a quality enjoyed by the Yankees, who, strangely biased against their own evaluations, can only be impressed by what a player does outside of New York. Arroyo could never have made the Yankees. Pedro Martinez was visibly aging, but even an easily fatigued all-time great was still an asset. Schilling was terrifically durable, not having been disabled for a pitching-related injury since March 2000. Lowe and Wakefield were erratic but durable; Wakefield had made just one visit to the disabled list in his career. Lowe never had. Whatever the level of their performances, they would be there at the end.

The final report card: The two clubs looked very closely matched, but the Yankees had taken a great many risks while the Red Sox had taken comparatively few. The Red Sox still had to hit their marks, but any student of the off-season figured that the Yankees were going to have to have guessed right more often. The pennant was a matter of whose assumptions would give way first, and when.

—STEVEN GOLDMAN

5

VARIETIES OF RELIEF
APRIL 8–9, 2004

At the beginning of the regular season, the Red Sox wanted to show their opponents something they hadn't seen in a while: a fully functioning bullpen. The bullpen had been the team's only glaring weakness in 2003, and for the first few games in 2004 . . . well, it actually looked like it might be the only glaring weakness in 2004.

On April 8 and 9, the new Foulke-fronted bullpen blew two games in a row. In the first contest, against the Orioles, Tim Wakefield came out of the game after his knuckleball lost its knuckle, leaving only balls. It took him over a hundred pitches to slog through five and a third innings. The Boston bullpen came in to work. Alan Embree got three strikeouts. Mike Timlin finished the seventh by being on the mound when Brian Roberts was caught stealing, then struck out Tejeda. Scott Williamson pitched two innings, mostly uneventful, and then, in the tenth, it was time to unveil Keith Foulke, the shiny new expensive closer.

Melvin Mora doubled, went to third on a wild pitch, but Foulke escaped the crisis with a strikeout. Raffy Palmiero was intentionally walked, and Javy Lopez hit a short fly to Johnny Damon, who caught the ball and threw Mora out at home.

Then Bobby Jones allowed the winning run in the thirteenth inning.

The next night, they did it again. Bronson Arroyo left the game in the sixth, having given up four runs. Two innings later, Mike Timlin gave up three runs and turned the ball over to Alan Embree, who managed to do almost as much damage while only getting one out. Five runs, four outs.

Relief pitcher Keith Foulke

The resemblance to the 2003 bullpen was eerily depressing, at least for the fan in the stands and the man on the street. At a cursory glance, nothing seemed to have changed since the closer-by-committee failures of the year before, when the Sox blew enough late-inning leads to drive the sneering local wolves into a howling frenzy. How could the hated Yankees have a dominating stopper like Mariano Rivera in the pen to snuff out all late-inning rallies, while the Sox settled for a bunch of no-names? In the last days of the old regime, the Red Sox seemed to rent off-the-rack closers by the season. After

BOSTON SAVES LEADERS 1996–2004		
1996	Heathcliffe Slocumb	31
1997	Heathcliffe Slocumb	17
1998	Tom Gordon	46
1999	Derek Lowe/Tim Wakefield	15
2000	Derek Lowe	42
2001	Derek Lowe	24
2002	Ugueth Urbina	40
2003	Byung-Hyun Kim	16
2004	Keith Foulke	32

1997, only Derek Lowe was able to hold the closer's job for two years in a row (given the erratic nature of Lowe's performance, "hold" is a generous assessment). Heathcliffe Slocumb begat Tom Gordon whose injuries begat Tim Wakefield and Derek Lowe who begat Ugueth Urbina who begat . . . no one and everyone. In Boston, the day of the closer had ended—for a moment.

Inside Fenway's warren of offices, however, cooler heads, the heads that had reengineered the bullpen, prevailed. And so did the bullpen, in particular Keith Foulke. In the first four-game series with the Yankees on April 16–19, Foulke appeared in three, saved two of them, then added two more saves in the ensuing series with Toronto. In all, he pitched five times in six days, saving four games. He pitched five innings, allowed three hits and one run, walked none, and struck out four.

In Foulke, the Sox had a pitcher who could snuff out a rally at any time—the seventh, eighth, ninth, tenth, eleventh, you name it. The legacy of the previous season's bullpen experiment was the belief that overall talent was more important than strict bullpen roles and a flexibility regarding the use of Foulke or any other reliever. Although the team would go on to use Foulke in a conventional way, his dominance—combined with Terry Francona's willingness to stretch the closer's role to smothering eighth-inning uprisings—would play a big, critical role in Boston's pennant drive.

The idea of expanding the closer's role is not so much an innovation as a reversion to a strategy of the 1950s and '60s that had since been discarded—for no good reason, many thought—as the concept of the relief pitcher evolved into an essential, but overspecialized, weapon.

Joe McCarthy, the great Yankees manager of the 1930s, once said that it's not important to have pitchers who start; it's important to have pitchers who finish. By this he meant starting pitchers who didn't falter, who didn't look over their shoulder to the bullpen, but instead paced themselves and closed out the opposition in innings seven through nine without making the manager sweat too much. Within just a few years, that philosophy had become antique. It was gradually, grudgingly accepted that not every arm was up to throwing 150 pitches every time out and that it was advantageous to have a talented, fresh pitcher available to take over when the starter's battery went dead.

By the 1960s, the stoic starting pitcher was no longer in vogue. It was acceptable for Whitey Ford to say, "I'll have a great season if Luis Arroyo's arm holds out."[1] Indeed, Ford's relief ace Arroyo led the league in saves and Ford himself won the Cy Young award. Ford and Arroyo were part of an accelerating historical process that now deemphasized durable starters in favor of durable relievers. The best pitcher in the bullpen was expected to relieve at any time in the game and no matter what the situation—ahead, behind, tied, early, late. This sturdy specimen further evolved, or perhaps devolved, into a pitcher who could only pitch one inning at a time, and then only with a lead. This trend reached its apotheosis in Dennis Eckersley, Tony LaRussa's rehabilitation project of the late 1980s, who rode the one-inning-an-outing program to three consecutive pennants, a championship, 387 saves, and a spot in the Hall of Fame.

Before Eckersley, having a strong ace reliever in the bullpen was considered essential to a team's success, but after him, every team *had* to have its own version of the Eck. Not having one was considered a fatal weakness by everyone . . . everyone except Theo Epstein, Bill James, and the 2003 Boston Red Sox. The idea of a closer-by-committee implies that a team uses its best couple of pitchers in the situations where it would normally employ a single, conventional modern closer. What the Red Sox had tried to do was much more complex, and the rewards potentially much higher: Theo Epstein intended to build a new kind of bullpen, one where all men were equal but every man was a king.

In this, he was violating the strict division of labor of the modern bullpen, which had to include:

- A *closer*: best reliever, pitches the ninth inning when the team is ahead by one to three runs.
- A *setup man (lefty)*: best noncloser left-handed reliever, pitches the eighth inning when the team is ahead by one to three runs and there are more lefties than righties due up in the eighth.
- A s*etup man (righty)*: best noncloser right-handed reliever, pitches the eighth inning when the team is ahead by one to three runs and there are more righties than lefties due up in the eighth.
- A *left-handed specialist*: left-handed guy who can only pitch to left-handed batters, used to get one out and slow down games that are in danger of finishing in under three hours.
- A *long relief/mop-up*: someone who can pitch four to five innings if the starter is injured or gives up six home runs in the first two innings.
- *Everyone else*: pitches when the game is tied or if the team is behind.

Bill James, one of baseball's most influential thinkers, was hired by the Red Sox in November 2002. James's series of *Baseball Abstract*s were groundbreaking books in which he tested many of baseball's basic beliefs to see if they held up to objective scrutiny. Over time, he had come to think of the way managers utilized their bullpens as a waste of resources. "Essentially, using your relief ace to protect a three-run lead is like a business using a top executive to negotiate fire insurance," he wrote in his *New Historical Baseball Abstract*. "While it was necessary to limit a relief pitcher's role, many modern relievers now are working 70 to 85 innings a season—*and they're not even working the right 75 innings*."[2]

James's position was generally misunderstood. He didn't argue for a closer-by-committee approach; he argued that there was no need for a modern closer at all. As James wrote, it is "far better to use your relief ace when the score is tied, even if that is the seventh inning, than in the ninth inning with a lead of two or more runs." A great pitcher will protect nearly all of those leads, James argued. But a bad pitcher would, too. He was entirely right.

Consider Shawn Chacon, a pitcher with the Colorado Rockies in 2004. In 63 innings of work, he allowed 71 hits. The averages against him were .282/.414/.500, which is to say that he turned the average hitter into Hideki Matsui. He struck out 52 and walked 52 batters. A good strikeout-to-walk ratio runs about 2:1. Chacon's ERA in 2004 was 7.11. Based on his actual contribution to his team, he was no better than a scrub you could pick up hanging around outside a local 7-Eleven. Chacon was eight runs *worse*. So let's say you're at a game and Chacon comes in to pitch the ninth inning. In an average outing on his way to getting three outs, he'll walk a guy, strike out a guy, give up at least one hit, and probably one run.

Shawn Chacon would end the year with 35 saves, three more than Keith Foulke. Yet Foulke helped his team, while Chacon damaged his. When the play-by-play data for Foulke's appearances is examined, it shows that he contributed 4.4 wins above replacement (WXRL) to the Red Sox, whereas Chacon, at –1.7, would have done better to step aside for someone from the local beer league. This is a commonplace occurrence among relievers, who accumulate soft saves while actually pitching quite poorly. Baseball is a game in which even the very best hitters will make an out nearly 70 percent of the time, and the worst pitcher in the game is capable of getting three outs before three runs are scored the vast majority of the time. Even some relievers who have achieved as many as forty saves in a season have failed to contribute much to the winning effort:

Year	Name	IP	SV	ERA	VORP	WXRL
1992	Rick Aguilera	66.7	41	3.78	9.83	0.13
2002	Jose Jimenez	73.3	41	3.56	9.80	0.47
1992	Lee Smith	75.0	43	3.36	8.01	–0.20
1993	Mitch Williams	62.0	43	3.34	7.29	–0.19
2004	Danny Graves	68.3	41	3.95	4.29	1.80

A closer operating at the peak of his profession might add somewhere between six and ten wins above replacement. (See the WXRL entry in the leader list, Appendix III.)

The closer role has become more and more limited, an easy path to saves and lucrative contracts. If "closer" is defined as the reliever with the most saves on his team, the rate of successful saves by closers has gone from the 70 percent range—a low of 69 percent in 1974—to almost 90 percent today. A reasonable argument might be made that the bullpens of the 1970s contained fewer talented, potential starters, but that does not begin to explain the steady, constant increase in successful save percentages across baseball. It is the limited, three-out stints that have slanted the odds in favor of the closer.

In James' view, a team should have its best relief pitcher throw two innings when it's tied or up by one in the seventh inning or on. In 2000, Rany Jazayerli of Baseball Prospectus analyzed reliever usage patterns in situations where a team would most benefit from using its relief ace, as measured by impact (in parentheses, below), which is the percentage increase in the chances of winning a game.[3] For instance, if the team could be expected to win 60 percent of its games when up by one run, but would expect to win 70 percent if it used its closer, then the impact would be .100:

Home		Visitor	
1) Top 9th, lead by 1	(.170)	1) Bottom 9th, lead by 1	(.223)
2) Top 9th, tied	(.160)	2) Bottom 8th, lead by 1	(.158)
3) Top 8th, lead by 1	(.123)	3) Bottom 9th, tied	(.155)
4) Top 8th, tied	(.115)	4) Bottom 8th, tied	(.122)
5) Top 7th, lead by 1	(.096)	5) Bottom 9th, lead by 2	(.113)
6) Top 7th, tied	(.092)	6) Bottom 7th, lead by 1	(.111)
7) Top 9th, lead by 2	(.080)	7) Bottom 8th, lead by 2	(.108)

Conversely, the closer has almost no impact when used in many ninth-inning "save situations":

Home		Visitor	
Top 9th, lead by 1	(.170)	Bottom 9th, lead by 1	(.233)
Top 9th, tied	(.160)	Bottom 9th, tied	(.160)
Top 9th, lead by 2	(.080)	Bottom 9th, lead by 2	(.113)
Top 9th, lead by 3	(.038)	Bottom 9th, lead by 3	(.055)
Top 9th, lead by 4	(.019)	Bottom 9th, lead by 4	(.027)

Jazayerli's decision tree suggests that James's argument is a workable, efficient idea. The closer's importance declines even in textbook save situations, such as a lead of three runs. His impact when used by the visiting team in, say, an eighth-inning tie, is more than twice that of when he is used to protect a three-run lead in the ninth inning.

As Boston's "senior baseball operations adviser," James was in a position to conduct an experiment in applied baseball theory during the 2003 season. With Theo Epstein, he finally had someone in power willing to listen to him. The Red Sox set out to try this arrangement with a bullpen that might, if dressed up in a really fearsome costume and red contact lenses, scare a particularly gullible child. In descending order by value, the bullpen consisted of Mike Timlin, a standard-issue reliever with a reputation for succeeding when the pressure was off; Alan Embree, a left-hander of no great regard; Brandon Lyon, a vanilla pitcher whose hit, walk, strikeout, and home run numbers were about average in both the majors and the minor leagues; Chad Fox, a chronically injured pitcher who only looked good after the Sox gave up on him in August; Bob Howry, former White Sox closer/middleman who had been going in reverse since 2000; Steve Woodard, control-oriented, busted starter with a bad injury history; and Ramiro Mendoza, a versatile but inconsistent starter/reliever (formerly with the Yankees) who had problems staying healthy.

But the Red Sox had violated James's vision; his original idea was a bullpen with no closer, but with consistent overall talent that would allow the closer role to be shared among equals. Unorthodox bullpen structures had worked before. Ten years earlier, the Expos had run an all-righty bullpen (Gil Heredia, Mel Rojas, Tim Scott, Jeff Shaw, John Wetteland) that was outstanding. In 2004 the Angels would go virtually the whole year without a left-handed reliever. The Angels pen had a 3.47 ERA and struck out 494 batters while only walking 186. It wasn't theory but mediocrity that made a mess of the 2003 Red Sox experiment. Boston had the twenty-eighth-best bullpen in baseball as ranked by earned run average. The bullpen unit went 30–27, with an ERA of 4.83. With the second Gulf War on, the Sox bullpen was called "the Boston division of the Republican Guard" on ESPN's *SportsCenter*.[4]

James and the team were subject, unfairly, to great derision, both in baseball and out. "Well, anybody who thinks the seventh inning is like the ninth inning should put on a uniform and go out and experience it for him-self," said then Anaheim closer Troy Percival. Then Oakland A's pitching coach Rick Peterson sneered, "Tell Bill James to come into a clubhouse that has just blown a three-run lead in the ninth inning. It's an absolutely horrific feeling. Nothing can deteriorate the confidence of a ballclub like losing a game in the ninth."[5]

In principle, it could have worked. Prior to the season, Oakland gen-eral manager Billy Beane had endorsed Epstein's committee plan. "I think we get so locked into things that we don't always use common sense," said Beane. "Does it make any sense to have your best reliever waiting in the bullpen when the game's tied in the seventh or eighth? By the time the ninth inning comes, it might be a three-run game. A lot of guys can get those last three outs. Why waste your best pitcher there?"

Toronto GM J. P. Ricciardi had supported it as well: "I think we've cre-ated this mind-set of what we're supposed to do and everybody's follow-ing it, whether it makes sense or not. If you feel like you have a dominant closer, then go with him. But if you don't . . ."

Besides a lack of talent, and a spate of injuries, the experiment suffered from the fact that Little had never been on board with the program. He picked relievers based on whatever had happened recently, and who he thought was hot. When that didn't work he'd reshuffle. He might try to turn someone like Brandon Lyon into an unofficial closer, and then abandon the idea after a bad outing. These indecisive tactics managed to combine the worst characteristics of both the modern and the historical approach. One of the reasons Little balked at pulling Pedro Martinez from Game Seven of the 2003 ALCS was that his relief choices hadn't been sufficiently outlined for him.

The Sox shored up the bullpen through trade and internal promotion and limped through the year. They acquired Reds reliever Scott Williamson and former Diamondbacks closer Byung-Hyun Kim, used him as a starter, then, giving in to Little, moved him to the pen. Kim was gen-erally effective as the closer. At the very least, he relaxed the other reliev-ers: "The bullpen-by-committee thing, in theory, if everybody was healthy, it probably could have worked, but for whatever reason, nobody was healthy," Alan Embree said. "We lost four of those guys and had to make do with what we had. Then after that, you're being criticized for anything that goes wrong. The manager's getting hammered by people asking 'How could you have the nerve to go and do that?' and players are thinking you're horrible, you can't pitch, but once we got that group together, Kim came in and settled everything down, and we're having fun now."[6]

But it hadn't been enough, and the front office had migrated back toward the conventional end of the spectrum, with Foulke as the modified "closer." Like Mariano Rivera, Foulke was a closer who could throw more than one inning when required but, also like Rivera, infrequently came into tie games. What most people didn't know was that, while Foulke lacked Rivera's name recognition, he had been the more valuable of the two in the five years preceding the 2004 season. Here's their value using VORP, along with their rank among pitchers who made at least 50 percent relief appearances.

Year	VORP	Rank
1999 AL Keith Foulke	51.2	1
2000 AL Keith Foulke	35.6	2
2001 AL Keith Foulke	33.6	2
2002 AL Keith Foulke	25.5	10
2003 AL Keith Foulke	37.7	4

Year	VORP	Rank
1999 AL Mariano Rivera	36.8	5
2000 AL Mariano Rivera	31.2	7
2001 AL Mariano Rivera	30.4	5
2002 AL Mariano Rivera	14.5	35
2003 AL Mariano Rivera	32.9	7

Despite this, Mariano Rivera was regarded as the greatest reliever in all of baseball while Keith Foulke had been fired (by a soon-to-be-fired manager) from his closer role in Chicago after a couple of bad outings, and traded to the A's. Of course, Rivera had been dominant for much longer than Foulke. The 1999–2003 five-year comparison ignores years of Rivera's dominance when Foulke was still improving. Overall, the numbers aren't close, though both are in the top ten modern relievers:

Name	VORP
Rich Gossage	323.5
Mariano Rivera	**304.3**
Dan Quisenberry	258.4
John Franco	255.7
Rollie Fingers	255.1
Jesse Orosco	254.5
Mike Jackson	252.9
Doug Jones	252.1
Lee Smith	243.9
Keith Foulke	**243.2**
Tom Henke	233.9

To close the gap with Rivera, Foulke would have to put up two more great seasons while Rivera cheered him on from the box seats, but that doesn't diminish his place among the all-time greats at the position.

Foulke had also slipped from the spotlight for a time. One of the curses of a reliever is that because they work in such short stretches, it only takes a couple of bad appearances to make them look bad. In 2002, when White Sox manager Jerry Manuel pulled him out of the closer role, Foulke's full-season line was superb (2.90 ERA, 77 IP, 58 K, 13 BB, 7 HR). But Manuel had lost faith in Foulke's ability to get critical outs, and looked to the slightly younger Damaso Marte as the team's closer-of-the-future. Because the relatively short (six feet) Foulke did not resemble the prototypical closer or possess a fastball in the mid-90s, it was easy to dismiss him as a flash in the pan.

Trying to keep Billy Beane off an undervalued player was futile. To get Foulke he traded the much less effective Billy Koch, whom Beane had acquired and used in easy-save situations to rack up gaudy closer-type numbers. Foulke repaid Beane's faith by dominating as an A (2.05 ERA, 43 saves, 88 K, 20 BB, 10 HR in 86.6 IP), but Oakland doesn't get much media attention, and their early playoff exit (ushered out by the Red Sox) denied Foulke the opportunity to demonstrate on a national media stage that he still had it.

But now he was in Boston's bullpen, and finding a pitcher the team could slap the "closer" label on had freed the front office to tweak other parts of the delicate construction otherwise known as a baseball team.

—DEREK ZUMSTEG

CALVIN SCHIRALDI: INDUSTRIAL-STRENGTH FLUKE

No discussion of the Red Sox and their bullpen would be complete without mention of the rise and fall of Calvin Drew Schiraldi, the hero and goat of the 1986 season. Nearly twenty years later, Schiraldi remains an ambiguous lesson, one that can be claimed by both the radical "any pitcher can be a successful closer" lobby and the ultra-orthodox "it takes a special heart, soul, and liver to withstand the pressure of inning nine" reactionaries.

Schiraldi played a large role in the Red Sox drive to the World Series in 1986, but he had experienced considerable success as a pitcher previously. As a teammate of Roger Clemens on the University of Texas's 1983 NCAA championship–winning squad, Schiraldi's exploits were heralded before he signed his first contract. Calvin Schiraldi, not Clemens, was the ace of that squad, and Schiraldi was both an All-American and Most Outstanding Player of the 1983 College World Series. In that year's amateur draft, Schiraldi was selected twenty-seventh overall by the New York Mets—eight picks behind teammate Clemens.

After two middling seasons in the Mets organization, Schiraldi joined the Red Sox after the 1985 season, coming to Boston in the Bobby Ojeda trade. After starting the 1986 season in Pawtucket, Schiraldi was called up to the majors in July, just after his twenty-fourth birthday. By August, Schiraldi was spinning a streak of ten straight appearances without giving up a run. Schiraldi's workload went from garbage time in losses to protecting leads. With the Red Sox steaming toward their first postseason since Pudge Fisk's 1975 World Series squad, Schiraldi supplanted Bob Stanley as Red Sox closer and was a perfect 9-for-9 in save opportunities.

Then came the postseason. Schiraldi pitched well against the Angels in the League Championship Series, giving up a single run in four outings as the Red Sox beat the Angels 4–3 to advance to the World Series. Then, in the Series title bout, Schiraldi's story turned ugly. After notching the save in Game One, Schiraldi gave up disastrous hit after hit in Games Six and Seven. Ray Knight had a field day against him, going 2-for-3 with a home run, and Schiraldi became the first pitcher ever to be tagged with the loss in both Games Six and Seven. If Bill Buckner's failure to handle Mookie Wilson's grounder was the dominant image of the Mets–Red Sox World Series, a despairing Schiraldi with his head buried in a towel in the dugout ran a close second.

Although Schiraldi was only twenty-five years old at the start of the 1987 season, his career had peaked. As the Red Sox slid back to the pack, so did Schiraldi, whose 4.41 ERA was exactly three points higher than his banner 1986 performance. The Red Sox jumped on the chance to acquire proven closer Lee Smith from the Chicago Cubs in the off-season, and Schiraldi headed off to the National League, where the Cubs and San Diego Padres couldn't figure out what to do with him. In 1991, it took the Texas Rangers only 4.2 innings to decide to move on without Schiraldi, and he was out of the majors for good.

Calvin Schiraldi is Exhibit A in the argument that not all relievers can handle the stress of closing. Through a failure of confidence, Schiraldi's career went from ascendant to average in one fell swoop. In the pressure cooker of the closer's role on the largest stage in baseball, he let himself and his team down, and never recovered from it.

How uncommon is it for a reliever to have one great season so out of place with the rest of their career? WXRL is the best metric for evaluating the value of a relief pitcher's season. Put simply, it distills all the facets of a reliever's performance we can measure into a single number, depicting the change in expected wins given a reliever's performance and the situation he was brought into, adjusted for park, league offensive level, opposing batter quality, and (deep breath) compared to a replacement-level reliever. From the years 1972 to 2004, we took pitchers with at least four seasons of fifty innings pitched in relief and compared their best season by WXRL to their second-best season. This allowed us to isolate the pitchers with one huge relief season, like Schiraldi, while ignoring pitchers who never had a particularly good year or strung together a series of them. The fluke column is the difference in value between the two seasons.

RANK	NAME	YEAR	WXRL	YEAR 2	WXRL2	FLUKE
1	Willie Hernandez	1984	9.155	1985	2.924	6.231
2	John Hiller	1973	9.640	1978	3.883	5.756
3	Tom Murphy	1974	5.164	1977	-0.270	5.434
4	Doug Corbett	1980	7.932	1986	2.778	5.153
5	Bob James	1985	5.926	1983	1.753	4.173

RANK	NAME	YEAR	WXRL	YEAR 2	WXRL2	FLUKE
6	Donnie Moore	1985	6.040	1986	2.073	3.968
7	Aurelio Lopez	1979	7.929	1983	4.082	3.847
8	Tom Burgmeier	1980	6.593	1982	2.965	3.629
9	Jeff Lahti	1985	4.586	1982	1.073	3.513
10	Dan Spillner	1982	4.259	1981	0.922	3.337
. . .						
38	Calvin Schiraldi	1986	2.877	1989	0.696	2.181

For industrial-strength flukes, look no further than some of Schiraldi's contemporaries in the 1980s. Tigers closer Willie Hernandez easily takes the cake with his Cy Young-winning 1984 campaign, when he pitched about as well as Schiraldi's 1986 season—for almost three times the innings. There are sad stories in the top ten as well. Bob James enjoyed 32 saves and a 2.13 ERA in a career-high 110 innings as the White Sox's closer in 1985; he'd be released by the White Sox only two years later, unable to kick a substance abuse problem. Donnie Moore pitched well for the California Angels in 1986, but not as well as he had in 1985; his part in the Angels failing to turn a 3–1 ALCS lead over Boston into a World Series berth was linked to his suicide in 1989. There is also the literally heartwarming tale of John Hiller, who worked his way back to dominance after a massive heart attack in 1971.

Like Schiraldi, most of these pitchers were high-round draft picks who were expected to be successful major league starters, because, with few exceptions, that's where major league relievers come from. Like Schiraldi, they had a single season where they were able to put their skills to good use as terminators from the bullpen, and they weren't able to repeat those campaigns.

It's possible that Calvin Schiraldi just mysteriously lost it in 1986, but there's another plausible explanation: He was pitching over his head all year, wasn't as good as he performed, and never caught lightning in a bottle again. It's less dramatic, but after 2004, so are most explanations for past Red Sox championships lost.

—DAVE PEASE

6

WALKING, WOUNDED
APRIL 16–18, 2004

The Red Sox had begun the season like 31 other World Champions before them: by losing on Opening Day. (For whatever it is worth, eventual champions play somewhat better on Opening Day than they do the rest of the year. In the tiny 100-game sample, they've won 67 times with one tie—a .666 clip compared to the champs' overall .624 wininng percentage.) After Opening Day, the Sox played .500 ball until meeting up with the Yankees for the first time on April 16 at Fenway Park.

The Yankees had begun their season early with a trip to Japan, a grueling proposition but also a convenient one for those predisposed to use fatigue and jet lag as excuses for poor performance. (One Yankee, reliever Paul Quantrill, had a more legitimate case when he would later blame his struggles on an injury to his right knee sustained on the trip.) The Yankees had more gaps than most in their early schedule, though, and a rainout on April 13 against Tampa Bay allowed them to play just one game in the four days leading up to the first Red Sox series, in Yankee Stadium. The Sox, too, had lost two games to rainouts and had played just once, so it was two well-rested groups of players who squared off in Boston.

There was a time when the first meeting of the season between the Red Sox and Yankees was a bellwether of things to come. Boston dominated these games in the teens, New York in the 1920s, '40s, and '50s, much as they did the standings. The predictive power of these games had long since waned. The Red Sox had won six of the last seven first encounters with the Yankees, but had finished behind New York in the standings each and every year in that run.

The Red Sox after beating the Yankees
on April 19, 2004

Since the last time the World Champion banner was hoisted at Fenway Park in 1918, the Red Sox had managed to finish ahead of the Yankees in the standings on only eighteen occasions. During that time they won the season series just twenty-five times. The last time the Red Sox had managed to beat the Yankees in the standings *and* on the field was 1990, the final year of a three-year run of doing so. Fortunately, the drama of the rivalry was immune to statistical reality.

Owing to the quirkiness of spring weather and the ramifications of Major League Baseball's Pacific overtures, Javier Vazquez found himself making just his second start two weeks into the season. Boston's lineup was patchy with substitutes, notably Pokey Reese and Gabe Kapler, who replaced the injured Nomar Garciaparra and Trot Nixon. But the Sox got all over Vasquez in the first inning, popping two home runs and taking advantage of errors by Jason Giambi and Derek Jeter to total four runs. They won going away, 6–2, but it would have been a worse beating had the Red Sox not hit into three double plays and run their way into a fourth. By the time Vazquez left in the sixth, he had given up another home run and been touched for nine hits. Tim Wakefield, meanwhile, pitched only a single 1-2-3 inning out of seven, but went home with the victory when Boston's bullpen closed out the Yankees with no further damage.

In the second game of the series, Mike Mussina, previously a pitcher of predictable stability, got cuffed around like a Dickensian schoolboy. The Yankees had now played eleven games and he already had four decisions, three of them losses. It was a freak of the early-season scheduling; the world had not seen a pitcher with this high a percentage of his team's decisions since Wilbur Wood roamed the earth. Against the Sox on April 17, Mussina had an especially nasty second inning, walking two men and surrendering a single to load the bases before forcing in two runs with yet another walk, followed by a hit batsman. In all, he gave up four walks and left trailing 4–1 after the fifth. Mussina's opponent, Curt Schilling, also walked four—and gave up six hits and a home run, yet still managed to hold the Yankees to a single run in six and a third innings. Final score: 5–2, Red Sox.

Derek Lowe was not as lucky in the third game, allowing twelve base runners in less than three innings and leaving with the game nearly out of reach. The only positive note for Boston was the failure of the Yankees'

Jose Contreras to capitalize on the best run support the Yankees had mustered since their 12–1 win over Tampa Bay back in Japan. The Cuban Contreras, one of the most popular refugees since Albert Einstein, blew up in the third inning, much to the thrill of the Red Sox faithful, the same people who had wrung their hands when the Yankees wrested him away from the Sox prior to the 2003 season. The last laugh turned out to be on the Yankees, who had paid millions for an obviously nervous pitcher who threw hard but was effective only for moments at a time, who tipped his pitches and had the general air of a man for whom pitching was a Kafkaesque nightmare, which, to be fair, had been a description of how he was living not long before. But the Yankees took the series' third game, 7–3.

In the fourth game, Bronson Arroyo and Kevin Brown had mirror-image outings that resulted in a 4–4 tie by the time they were both gone in the seventh. The Sox won the game in the eighth when three of their lesser lights combined to get a run

LOWEST OBP (NONPITCHER, 75 PA MIN.), 1985–2004					
		Year	Team	OBA	PA
1.	Marty Castillo	1985	Tigers	.138	87
2.	Jeff Schaefer	1992	Mariners	.139	78
3.	Rich Gedman	1991	Cardinals	.140	100
4.	Enrique Cruz	2003	Brewers	.145	76
5.	Mike Laga	1988	Cardinals	.147	102
6.	Brian Hunter	1993	Braves	.153	85
7.	Ron Karkovice	1987	White Sox	.160	95
8.	Cesar Crespo	2004	Red Sox	.165	79
9.	Al Pardo	1985	Orioles	.167	78
10.	Ryan Minor	2000	Orioles	.170	88

across. Dave McCarty doubled with one out. Cesar Crespo, who did as little with seventy-nine at-bats as anyone in recent memory (see chart), contributed a groundout that advanced McCarty to third. Kapler singled him home and Keith Foulke sealed the deal.

Especially gratifying for Boston was how ineffective Alex Rodriquez had been in the series. The should-have-been/would-have-been/could-have-been-a-Red-Sox A-Rod made his first trip to Boston in pinstripes a memorable one, going hitless in the three games. Not that Rodriguez deserved any ridicule; after all, he had been more than willing to shed some of his salary to play for the Red Sox, so any schadenfreude over his poor showing in the series should have had less to do with the man himself than with the simple fact that it was the despised Yankees who had acquired him. The supernaturally inclined might have read great things into A-Rod's 0-fer; in his career, he had seldom gone any three consecutive games without a hit, and rarer still was a series as futile as this. Here are the other worst series of his storied nine-year career:

August 16–18, 1997, vs. White Sox: 1 for 17 (one walk)
September 22–24, 2000, vs. A's: 1 for 16 (two runs scored)
September 3–6, 1999, vs. Red Sox: 1 for 17 (home run, two RBI)
June 25–27, 1999, vs. Rangers: 1 for 13 (one walk, two runs scored)
June 22–24, 2001, vs. A's: 1 for 13 (one run scored)
April 1–3, 2002, vs. A's: 0 for 12 (one walk)
July 6–8, 2001, vs. Padres: 0 for 12 (one walk)

Rodriguez's futility was contagious. The Yankee starters' batting averages looked like this:

Derek Jeter	.175
Bernie Williams	.167
Alex Rodriguez	.257
Jason Giambi	.204
Gary Sheffield	.265
Jorge Posada	.281
Hideki Matsui	.262
Ruben Sierra	.194
Enrique Wilson	.167

Thanks to the innovation of listing batting averages in box scores, the Yankees looked bad—somewhat worse, in fact, than they actually were. To declare the Yankee bats dead at this point was to miss the signature quality of their attack: They were still walking. What George Steinbrenner's fabulous largesse had bought them was a lineup filled with patience. The team was leading the league in walks—five a game—just as it had in 2002 and 2003.

They had also been hit by the most pitches, giving them an extra dozen base runners. Still, ballplayers pride themselves on base hits, not body hits, and to their hypercompetitive egos a walk is *not* as good as a hit. They were leading the league not only in walks but also in cussing and abuse of inanimate objects. "I just sense that there's a lot of frustration here, the way they are throwing helmets and bats," manager Joe Torre told the New York *Daily News* on April 11. "They're not mad at anybody, just mad at themselves. It's something they're going to have to get through and be themselves. They're not letting the game come to them. They're being overly aggressive."

Torre was referring to his players' attitude toward balls *in* the strike zone, not out of it. At least they were getting the bat on the ball. Through April 25, only Tampa Bay, Minnesota, and Baltimore had struck out fewer times in the American League. That means that a more-than-average number of Yankee outs came on balls put into play, a clue that they were, in reverse of Wee Willie Keeler's famous dictum, hitting them where the fielders were. To that point in the season, the Yankees were unambiguously the worst team at turning batted balls into hits. The bottom three teams in that category looked like this:

Tampa Bay	.309
Toronto	.304
New York	.260

The team leader was the Texas Rangers at .377 and the league average was .329—compared to which the Yankees' numbers were staggering, given the quality of the lineup. The low standing was actually a harbinger of a change for the better; bad luck can only last so long before a few hits fall in. It was just a matter of time before the cosmos would compensate the Yankees.

The Yankees were averaging just four runs per game and even Derek Jeter was being booed at home. Jeter, who had gotten a free pass from Yankee loyalists on his questionable fielding for the better part of a decade, was now being scapegoated for events beyond his control. True, it's hard to explain "regression to the mean" to someone who has paid $50 for a ticket and watched a third straight home loss to the hated rivals, but if the old adage "They're due" ever meant something, it was now.

After the Yankees rebounded somewhat by taking two of three from the White Sox (while Boston was doing the same to Toronto), they were swept at home by Boston. It was the first time in sixteen years that the team had lost the first two series of the year to the Red Sox. The Red Sox were now 12–6 and had amassed half those victories at the expense of the Yankees. This left New York at 8–11. In the Yankees' very next game, the gods of fortune relented. They survived another poor outing from Mike Mussina and defeated the A's, 10–8. They got ten hits on twenty-eight balls in play. Fully half of them were of the bleed-and-bloop variety, an indication of how sincerely Fate was repaying her debt to them.

One of the biggest hits of the Oakland game came with the bases loaded and nobody out in the eighth. Gary Sheffield splorked one off the end of his bat and it rolled out to second baseman Frank Menechino. Had he been positioned differently, the A's four-run lead might have been safe, but all he could do was knock it down and a big inning was under way. "The ball I hit that went for a hit and got a run in, that was one of those things that happens when you get a break," Sheffield said later. "When you get breaks, you can win."

The team also drew six walks. The wonderful thing about walks and the players who are predisposed to draw them is that they, like the adult segment of the entertainment market in an economic downturn, are impervious to changing conditions. When the hits started coming again, it would not be at the expense of the walk total, but at the expense of the out total. It was a textbook turning of the law of averages. The Yankees followed that victory with seven more in a row, averaging over eight runs per game in the process. When the sun finally set on this particular cosmic correction on May 5, they were 16–11 and tied for first place with the Red Sox.

The good news for Boston was that they were holding their own with the B team in place at a number of positions. Pokey Reese, a player whose offensive capabilities were the inverse of his defense capabilities and would normally have been a top candidate for the title Least Likely to Play for Boston, had done little to reverse his reputation as an all-glove contributor. For the month of April he hit worse than even his career low the previous year in Pittsburgh, .220/.254/.254. The zaftig Gabe Kapler was only slightly better, failing to hit a home run or, until the last day of the month, even a double. (Kapler, who departed for Japan in the off-season, generates the least amount of power per cubic inch of mass outside, perhaps, of the Democratic Party.) In total, Reese, Kapler, and the other Red Sox lesser lights, including Ellis Burks, Crespo, and McCarty, did amazingly little damage in the month of April—either to opposing pitchers or Boston's chances. Combined, they came to the plate 213 times, hit one home run, walked only 10 times, and produced a line that reads .197/.235/.243. Anything Nixon and Garciaparra contributed on their return was going to be gravy. If the Red Sox could survive a month like this and still go 15–6, then perhaps this was their year after all.

—JIM BAKER

7

ARMS AND THE MAN
APRIL 25, 2004

On April 25, Pedro Martinez took the mound against the New York Yankees at Yankee Stadium. Although Martinez would struggle with consistency throughout the season, this start was vintage Hall of Fame–bound Pedro. He held the Yankees to four hits, striking out seven and allowing no runs. And then, even though the score was only 2–0 in Boston's favor . . . even though Derek Jeter, Alex Rodriguez, and Gary Sheffield would be up in subsequent innings . . . even though Martinez was one of the greatest pitchers of all time and the drop off from him to anyone else was bound to be dramatic . . . even though Martinez had thrown just 105 pitches . . . he was sent to the showers. Martinez was replaced by Scott Williamson, who pitched a perfect two innings for the save. The Red Sox got their win and their ace survived to pitch another day, and therein lay a lesson in applied baseball theory.

Before the twenty-first century, one would be hard-pressed to find similar examples of an ace pitcher's premature exit. It is safe to say that Walter Johnson, Lefty Grove, or even Tom Seaver never left a game under similar conditions. Even as the age of the complete game ended and the reign of the closer began, most managers and starting pitchers were extremely reluctant to change pitchers in such a situation. By pulling Martinez out of the game, the Red Sox showed that they were full-fledged members of one of the quietest revolutions ever in the history of the most reactionary of all sports.

The following chart shows the number of starts in which a pitcher threw a given number of pitches, in every presidential election year going back to 1988, as far back as we have pitch count data:

PITCH COUNT

Year	101–110	111–120	121–130	131–140	141+
1988	782	563	337	151	60
1992	754	493	282	101	29
1996	805	595	316	78	14
2000	1079	806	330	60	5
2004	1251	632	144	11	3

It was just fifteen years ago that a still effective starting pitcher would be left in a game with complete disregard for his pitch totals. Orel Hershiser, a veteran pitcher and the defending Cy Young winner, threw 170 pitches in a 1989 start and blew out his shoulder the following spring. The same year, the Yankees allowed a promising lefty named Al Leiter, then only twenty-three years old, to throw 174 pitches, and an assortment of arm injuries would limit Leiter to a total of just nine innings over the next three years.

As teams wised up to the notion that pitch count totals exceeding 140 are abusive, their frequency dropped in half every four years until they became virtually extinct. But throughout the 1990s, pitch count totals in the 130s dropped much more slowly, while those in the 120s showed no significant decline at all.

Since 2000, however, there has been a sea change in pitchers' workloads. The decline of pitch counts greater than 130 has accelerated; between 1988 and 2000, the number of major league starts exceeding 130 pitches dropped from 211 to 65, a 69 percent drop. They have dropped another 78 percent, from 65 to 14, in the last four years alone. The most profound change, though, has been in the pitch counts between 121 and 130. Between 1992 and 2000, the frequency of these starts actually rose by 1 percent, even after factoring in the four extra teams added to the majors in that span. After stubbornly holding for the entire 1990s, pitch counts in the 120s have dropped by 56 percent in four years. That premium pitch count totals have plummeted at a dizzying pace represents one of the biggest fundamental changes in the game over the past five to ten years—and yet it has received almost no attention.

What happened? A perfect storm of events, all of which have worked to bring pitch counts lower, came together in the 1990s. The first and most fundamental step was simply making the data available. Pitch count data simply does not exist prior to 1988, when it began being charted to satisfy the statistical revolution in baseball. That data slowly made its way to the public in the form of expanded box scores that began proliferating in the early to mid-1990s. Until pitch counts became available, we had no idea that, say, Bobby Witt threw 158 pitches in a single game in 1990—the year before he tore his rotator cuff.

Data is the lifeblood of analysis, and once the data was available, it could be shown that high pitch count totals did, in fact, increase injury risk. It was now possible to systematically compare outings where pitchers did a lot of work without relying on incomplete estimates like innings pitched. In research presented in *Baseball Prospectus 2001*, and available at www.baseballprospectus.com, Keith Woolner and Rany Jazayerli undertook that very study. In the first part of the research, Woolner looked at a pitcher's performance in the weeks just before, and the weeks immediately after, a high pitch count outing. The research showed that pitchers decline significantly more after a high pitch count. The trend starts around 100 pitches, and becomes even more pronounced around 120 pitches. The Pitcher Abuse Formula PAP = MAX(0,(NP-100)^3) was derived from the observed data. This was the first documented evidence that high pitch counts lead to a risk of short-term ineffectiveness.

In the second part of the research, Woolner compiled an injury database for all starting pitchers over a several year span for whom relatively complete pitch count data was available. Injured pitchers were matched up with other pitchers of similar age with a comparable lifetime total of pitches thrown. Thus, pitchers of similar age and workload could be compared to see if how that workload was distributed (more starts with lower pitch count, or fewer starts with high pitch count) was related to the risk of getting injured. In other words, did pitchers with a higher lifetime Pitcher Abuse Point per Pitch Thrown (PAP/NP) have a greater probability of getting injured? Once again, the evidence did indicate that PAP/NP was a better indicator of risk than total pitch counts, or innings pitched alone. The PAP/NP metric was dubbed Stress, and typically ranges from 0 to 100. Consistent lifetime stress levels above roughly 30 start to noticeably increase the chance of injury.

This was persuasive, but it takes a seminal event to move academic research into the real world. Just such an event occurred in spring training

1999, when twenty-one-year-old Cubs wunderkind Kerry Wood, fresh off a Rookie of the Year campaign and his legendary 20-strikeout game, blew out his elbow. Suddenly, his workload as a rookie, when he averaged over 112 pitches a game and threw as many as 137 in one start, came under the microscope.

In response, that summer the Detroit Tigers declared that they would not allow their prized rookie, Jeff Weaver, to throw more than 110 pitches in a start (he topped out at 111 that season). The following year, über-agent Scott Boras publicly berated the Cardinals for breaching an agreement to limit his young client, Rick Ankiel, to no more than 110 pitches per start. Suddenly, pitch counts were everywhere—updated every inning on radio broadcasts, talked about on ESPN's *SportsCenter*, tracked on stadium scoreboards. Once recognized, pitch count data permanently changed the landscape of baseball. And in 2004 perhaps no one benefited more from this knowledge than Pedro Martinez.

Few pitchers in baseball history can approach Martinez in terms of sheer dominance, but fewer still match his frustrating blend of ability and fragility. No episode illustrates this quite like the 1999 American League Divisional Series, when after one of the most magnificent seasons in pitching history—23-4, 2.07 ERA when no other starter in the league was under 3.44—Pedro opened the series against the Indians with four scoreless innings, then departed with a back injury that allowed the Indians to come back and win the game. The Sox were able to force a fifth game, setting the stage for his miraculous return out of the bullpen in Game Five—throwing six hitless innings after the two teams had combined for sixteen runs by the middle of the third.

That was not an isolated incident. Pedro missed half of the 2001 season with right shoulder inflammation, and on his return the following April it became clear that his fastball had permanently lost some zip. He missed a few starts in 2002 with a hip injury; he spent a month on the DL in 2000 with a strained oblique muscle; he spent a month on the DL in 2003 with a strained latissimus dorsi (a large muscle on the trunk of the body). The Sox tried various changes to his regimen to keep him from breaking down. For years, the team tried to give him five days of rest between starts whenever possible. This didn't really work, as his twenty-two missed starts between 2001 and 2003 show. What made 2004 different was that for the first time, the Red Sox not only carefully protected Martinez *between* starts, they also protected him *during* his starts. To wit, Martinez was kept on a much tighter pitch count in 2004 than in any prior season.

Martinez's workload had been slowly declining even before 2004. Between 1997 and 2000, Martinez made 12 starts of over 130 pitches. Between 1997 and 1999, he made 11 starts of over 120 pitches each year. After his shoulder injury in 2002, he never made another 130-plus pitch start. In 2004, Martinez wouldn't make a single start of even 120 pitches. It's not that the Sox babied Martinez. While he topped out at 117 pitches, Martinez exceeded 100 pitches 26 times in 2004, matching his career high, and his average pitch count of 105.8 per start was his highest total since 2000. The Sox simply made a deliberate decision to keep Martinez in a strict 100–120 pitch range than to let him throw 130 pitches one outing and 80 the next.

In some ways, the 2004 season would turn out to be his worst. His 3.90 ERA was the highest of his career, and the highest relative to the league since 1996, the year before he became *Pedro Martinez*. But Martinez was still awfully good. For the Red Sox, having Martinez pitch at the very peak of his abilities was perhaps less important than simply having him pitch at all. On that score, 2004 would be a resounding success. For the first time this century, Martinez would not miss a start all season. He would match his career high with 33 starts in the regular season—last set six years before. Most important, though, his pitch count regimen would help keep him healthy into October, when he would make 4 starts in the postseason and (not counting a relief tune-up in Game Seven of the ALCS) post a 3.46 ERA in 26 innings.

Ironically, in this one instance, baseball's awareness of pitching matters outpaced its ability to appreciate something as simple as the differences in offensive value between an oafish home run–hitting designated hitter and an agile, singles-hitting first baseman. The elements of run creation had been understood for better than twenty years, but the news hadn't penetrated to some of the game's more stubbornly backward outposts. Once again, the Red Sox would capitalize on another team's intellectual lethargy.

—RANY JAZAYERLI

8

"YOU WANT ME TO HIT LIKE A LITTLE BITCH?"
MAY 5, 2004

Anyone could have had him. David Ortiz, left-handed slugger, defensive liability, offensive and emotional center of the Red Sox, had spent six years in the Twins' system. Six frustrating years being jerked up and down the organizational ladder as baseball people questioned his attitude and tried to change his style of hitting. Six years struggling to stay healthy and stand out among the young hitters. Six years that ended when he was unceremoniously released in December 2002.

Just eighteen months later, Ortiz, not talented enough to hold a job with the Twins, was saving Boston's season, and hardly for the last time. On May 5, Boston had lost five straight games of their current road trip, three at Texas followed by the first two of their four-game set at Cleveland. The consecutive sweeps of the Yankees and Tampa Bay that preceded the trip had nearly been squandered. With a record that had fallen to 15–11, the team seemed to be making a beeline for .500.

At first, the May 5 game, a contest of incompetence between the diminutive Byung-Hyun Kim and the towering Jeff D'Amico, seemed unlikely to reverse the team's fortunes. Though Ortiz had taken a first-inning pitch from D'Amico and put it over the fence for an early 1–0 lead, Kim had given it right back and more, starting with a home run to Omar Vizquel. By the end of the second, the Red Sox were down 3–1. During the five-game losing streak, the Sox had averaged three runs a game, so offensive confidence wasn't exactly spiking. Bill Mueller led off the top of the third inning with a

David Ortiz argues a call

single and was forced at second by Pokey Reese. Johnny Damon flied out for the second out. Mark Bellhorn kept the inning alive with a single to right that moved Reese to second base. Ortiz took the very next pitch and parked it in the right field bleachers for three runs. The Sox were back on top, 4–3, and would go on to win the game, 9–5. It would be the first of four straight wins, a streak that got the team back on its 100-plus win pace.

Just a year earlier, on May 5, 2003, Ortiz, in his first year with the Sox, had been hitting only .226/.329/.387 with one homer and 10 RBIs. He'd played in only nineteen of the team's thirty-two games, failing to distinguish himself as he alternated between first base and designated hitter in a four-player game of musical chairs. Stardom was unthinkable; Ortiz couldn't even stay in manager Grady Little's starting lineup for three days in a row. Ortiz's Boston tour was shaping up to be a replica of his time in Minnesota. That *that* Ortiz—limited, cumbersome, injury-prone—was a key to the Boston renaissance and on his way to Most Valuable Player status was one of the more unlikely stories in baseball. And how it happened is a revealing lesson in player-valuation philosophies.

Seventeen-year-old David Americo Ortiz was signed by the Seattle Mariners out of the baseball hotbed of Santo Domingo, Dominican Republic, in late 1992. Taking his mother's maiden name, David Arias spent 1993 in the Dominican Summer League, hitting .264 with 7 homers in 61 games while playing mostly at third base, an oddity for a left-handed thrower. By the time he reached the United States, he was a first baseman, beginning his professional career in the rookie-level Arizona League. He struggled in his first year, so the Mariners sent him back to Arizona, where he was much more successful, hitting .332/.403/.538 and making the league's All-Star team.

Arias/Ortiz continued to flourish during his first full-season campaign, hitting .322/.389/.509 with 18 homers for the Wisconsin Timber Rattlers of the Midwest League, and at the end of the 1996 season he was on the move again. Just under the waiver-wire trading deadline, the Mariners shored up their infield by acquiring third baseman Dave Hollins from the Twins for a player to be named later. Two weeks later, Arias/Ortiz became that player; he shed the Arias and David *Ortiz* returned, this time to stay.

The six-four, 230-pound lefty sped through the Twins system in 1997, playing half a season apiece at Single-A Fort Myers and Double-A New

Britain, tasting Triple-A Salt Lake City, and arriving for a September cup of coffee with the Twins, where he hit .327/.353/.449 in 49 at-bats. All told, Ortiz hit 32 homers and drove in 130 runs over the course of his four stops. *Baseball America* anointed him the Twins' number-two prospect, and *Baseball Prospectus 1998* compared his upside to that of Dave Parker—the young, productive Parker, not the later model.

Ortiz began the 1998 season as the Twins' starting first baseman. He hit .306/.375/.531 over the first five weeks, but he broke his right wrist and missed two months. The injury sapped his power; he slugged only .400 upon his return, finishing with a .277/.371/.446 line (and 9 home runs). It was a credible season for a twenty-two-year-old rookie. However, Twins manager Tom Kelly often sat him against lefties or lifted him for a pinch hitter late in ball games, and the management's list of his liabilities grew from there. The Twins somehow decided that despite his power and potential, Ortiz's poor conditioning, attitude, awkwardness around first base, and difficulty with lefties warranted turning the first-base job over to Doug Mientkiewicz, a slick fielder with limited offensive potential. Rather than use Ortiz as the designated hitter, a job recently vacated when Paul Molitor retired, the Twins, who have one of the most leisurely player-development schedules in the game, banished Ortiz back to Salt Lake, where he languished through the entire 1999 season, mashing 30 homers while hitting .315/.412/.590. The only action he saw with the Twins was a futile 0-for-20 September call-up.

Ortiz's demotion exemplified a chronic problem the Twins appeared reluctant to confront. Kelly carried a torch for glovemen, and this leather fetish had started to damage the team. A young player with a bat had no chance of making a living in Kelly's world. As time marched on, he clashed with an increasing number of young Twins. The fallout from the desultory 1999 season exiled four players to Salt Lake City: Mientkiewicz and two other starters, second baseman Todd Walker and left fielder Chad Allen, as well as semi-regular catcher Javier Valentin. Mientkiewicz complained early in that season that, while playing for Kelly, he felt he was "walking on eggshells." Walker, traded to Colorado in July, was even more direct: "I think Kelly can go to the extreme when he talks about what a guy can or can't do. Especially what he can't do."

It was a wasted year developmentally, and the team suffered as well. The Twins declined by seven wins as Mientkiewicz hit an anemic

.229/.324/.330, pitiful for a shortstop, let alone a first baseman. DH Marty Cordova had an adequate season (.285/.365/.464), but his 14 homers were second on the team to Ron Coomer's 16. That the Twins would give 501 plate appearances to the thirty-two-year-old Coomer, a versatile mediocrity who by this point could barely keep his OBP above .300, was telling. It had been four years since a Twin had topped 21 homers, but the team would be damned if their best hope to reach that plateau did so anywhere but in the rarified air of Utah.

(Eventually, Ortiz, Walker, and Mientkiewicz would all play for Theo Epstein, who, in contrast to the Twins' limited imagination, acknowledged these players' faults and moved on, utilizing them in appropriate roles. At times—as in the case of Walker, a butcher at second base but a productive hitter for the middle infielder—the Sox overlooked his faults until they could find someone better, understanding that half a solution to a problem is better than none at all.)

Ortiz regained his locker at the Hubert H. Humphrey Metrodome in 2000, slotted as the Twins' DH and picking up where he left off. His numbers—.282/.364/.446 with just 10 home runs—suggested stagnation, perhaps self-inflicted. As Ortiz would later tell *The Boston Globe*, "Something in my swing was not right in Minnesota. I could never hit for power. Whenever I took a big swing, they'd say to me, 'Hey, hey, what are you doing?' So I said, 'You want me to hit like a little bitch, then I will.'" But Ortiz got off to a roaring start the next year, hitting .311/.386/.611 through May 4 when another broken wrist put him on the shelf, this time for two and a half months. (He broke it sliding into home plate, but still managed to homer in his next at-bat before the pain won out.) On his return in July, his power suffered, as did the rest of his batting stroke; he hit only .202/.298/.418 and finished with a .234/.324/.475 line overall. Injuries dogged his 2002 campaign as well; bone chips in his knee cost him a trip to the OR and four weeks on the shelf. His .272/.339/.500 line was an improvement, and his 20 homers set a career high.

By this time Ortiz was twenty-seven years old and with enough service time to qualify for arbitration, a process that might easily triple his $950,000 salary. This was bad news for the Twins, whose 2002 payroll of $41.8 million placed them twenty-sixth among Major League Baseball's thirty teams (on top of which, the new Collective Bargaining Agreement signed that summer would raise the minimum salary from $200,000 to $300,000). The Twins were coming off not only an AL Central title, their first taste of success since their 1991 championship, but also the death-scare of contraction. Their leap into contention had been in no small part the result of the jelling of a nucleus of young hitters who had arrived in 1998 and 1999—Cristian Guzman, Torii Hunter, Jacque Jones, Corey Koskie, Mientkiewicz, Ortiz, and A. J. Pierzynski. (Please note that the franchise that produced Jim Kaat, Harmon Killebrew, Bert Blyleven, Kirby Puckett, Kent Hrbek, Gary Gaetti, Chuck Knoblauch, Mark Funderburk, and Paul Thormodsgard had not lost its penchant for leading the league in signing ballplayers with unusual names.)

But the team's success came at a cost. Hunter, Jones, Mientkiewicz, and Ortiz all reached arbitration eligibility at the same time, the point at which salaries can, from miserly billionaire owner Carl Pohlad's point of view, start spiraling madly out of the control of a small-market team. The price of the Twins' success was about to become prohibitive. At the same time, the system that produced these players was prepping yet another batch—Michael Cuddyer, Michael Restovich, Lew Ford, Justin Morneau, Matt LeCroy, Bobby Kielty, Michael Ryan, Dustan Mohr, and Jason Kubel. All were useful ballplayers, many interchangeable with each other and with the previous cohort—except at the defensive skill positions of catcher, shortstop, and center field, where the Twins chose to settle, respectively, on Pierzynski (at least until top prospect Joe Mauer could arrive), Guzman (for no good reason), and Hunter (whom they would sign to a four-year, $32 million contract before arbitration).

Some twenty years before this, Bill James, in his *Baseball Abstract* series, had observed the workings of what he called the Defensive Spectrum, which ran from positions requiring the least defensive skill to the most: 1B-LF-RF-3B-CF-2B-SS. James noted that as players age, they tend to drift leftward on the defensive spectrum; rarely does a player shift to the right with any success. (Famous exceptions include relocation of outfielder Mickey Stanley to shortstop by the Detroit Tigers in time for the 1968 World Series; Earl Weaver moving the oversized Cal Ripken Jr. from third base to shortstop; and catchers who have sometimes moved to first base, third base, or the outfield corners.) The lower standards on the left end of the spectrum make finding, say, a slugging first baseman a much easier proposition than finding a good-hitting center fielder. And so it was with the Twins, even if they didn't subscribe to any Jamesian doctrine. With all those young, productive hitters, they had relatively little need for the pricier Ortiz; they could just as easily plug in Matt LeCroy at DH for one tenth of what they might wind up paying Ortiz, about whom they had several complaints, anyway. So, on December 16, 2002, the Twins released Ortiz, four days before they would have been obliged to offer him a contract, triggering a process that likely would have led to an arbitration hearing.

That December 20 nontender date was a cause célèbre around the majors in 2002. In the wake of that summer's labor clash, the owners had strengthened their resolve to tighten their fiscal belts, particularly when it came to avoiding the kind of arbitration cases that a player like Ortiz represented—about to get expensive but not necessarily worth the money, at least to an organization with younger, cheaper alternatives. By avoiding arbitration, not only could teams free up more salary (either to pocket or else to divert to players who truly made a difference), but they could also saturate the free-agent market with low-cost alternatives. And *this* idea, which had been around since the dawn of free agency in the mid-seventies, had shaken Marvin Miller, the powerful leader of the players' union at the time, but had also drawn his admiration. As he recounted in his autobiography, *A Whole Different Ballgame*, maverick Oakland A's owner Charlie Finley introduced the idea:

> *There was Finley, maybe the only original thinker in the group, saying, "Hey, what's the problem? Let them be free agents every year. It will flood the market with players; it'll keep salaries down." It was so logical, so obvious, that to this day I can't understand why other owners didn't think of it. All I can imagine is that they had such a fixation on power, such an abhorrence of the idea of the players winning any kind of freedom, that they refused to consider an idea that clearly was in their own economic interest.*

Much to Miller's relief, the other owners ignored Finley's epiphany. But in 2002 the lesson was not entirely lost on a group of owners who had spent a quarter century on the losing end of labor battles and had been reminded of that fact all summer long. In all, forty-six players were officially nontendered—that is, not offered a contract—at the 2002 deadline, and not surprisingly, many of them were first basemen, including Brad Fullmer of the World Champion Anaheim Angels, Travis Lee of the Philadelphia Phillies, and Brian Daubach of the Boston Red Sox. As different as the Red Sox and Twins organizations' philosophies might have been, the Daubach decision reflected similar thinking. Daubach had enjoyed a solid trio of seasons as the Sox's regular first baseman; coming off his age-thirty season, he had hit .266/.348/.464 with 20 homers, good but unexceptional numbers. He had made $2.325 million in 2002, and was certain to receive an even more expensive arbitration reward. Looking down the same barrel of the arbitration gun that the Twins had with Ortiz, the Sox front office concluded they could replace Daubach, a player who had most likely maximized his capabilities and was poised to decline, and get a better bang for their bucks.

Lacking a farm system as productive as the Twins', Epstein and company needed to gather talent more creatively. They did so with an array of moves that illustrated the many backroads a team can use for player acquisition. In mid-December, the Sox traded minor league pitcher Josh Hancock to the Philadelphia Phillies for Jeremy Giambi. The twenty-eight-year-old younger brother of Jason had been purged from Oakland in a trade that purportedly had disciplinary motives. Split between two teams, the lefty Giambi had hit a robust .259/.414/.505, but the Phillies had just signed top-notch slugger Jim Thome, making the arbitration-eligible Giambi expendable. Shortly after the trade, Epstein inked Giambi to a $2 million deal.

A month later, the Sox created a small-scale international incident by disrupting a transactional formality, netting another candidate for the first-base job. Kevin Millar of the Florida Marlins, a versatile thirty-one-year-old righty coming off a .306/.366/.509 campaign, looked to be yet another player squeezed by economic pressures. Players with limited fielding finesse and offensive profiles in the middle of the range for first basemen were being left unprotected. Looking abroad for a larger payday, Millar had signed a two-year, $6.2 million contract with the Chunichi Dragons of Japan's Central League. To free him to sign that contract, the Marlins had to put Millar on waivers for the purpose of giving him his unconditional release. The Sox violated an unspoken protocol that read, "Thou shalt not mess with other teams' waiver moves, lest yours be similarly messed with," and claimed Millar. As a veteran player, Millar had the right to reject such a claim, and he did. But the real world intruded on behalf of Boston. The looming threat of the U.S. invasion of Iraq—including a U.S. State Department caution which said that "U.S. citizens and interests [abroad] are at a heightened risk of terrorist attacks"—forced Millar to reconsider, and over the course of a month of negotiations, a deal was hammered out by which the Sox would buy him from the Marlins for about $1.5 million, with the Dragons compensated for their headaches as well. Shortly after that, Millar agreed to a two-year, $5.3 million deal.

As the Millar saga unfolded over the winter of 2002–03, the Sox were busy hedging their first-base bets. First there was Earl Snyder, a onetime Mets prospect who had languished in their system for four years before being sent to Cleveland in the Roberto Alomar trade. A quick look was all the Indians needed to lose interest in him. The Sox wasted no time and snagged him. Then came Dave Nilsson, a lefty-hitting catcher/first baseman with a career line of .284/.356/.461 who had been out of the majors since 1999. He had earned All-Star honors as a Milwaukee Brewer, but had left the majors for a noble reason: to represent his native Australia in the 2000 Olympics. The Sox invited him to camp as a nonroster player. Finally, the Sox reached an agreement with David Ortiz on a one-year, $1.25 million deal.

"David has shown the ability in the past to also hit left-handed pitching, not every year, but he's shown he can do it," Epstein said in announcing the signing. "The upside is him as an everyday player." Ortiz was something less than a priority, but certainly more than an afterthought. The flurry of moves left the Sox with more than enough left-spectrum types to go around, but the ranks were thinned when Nilsson had second thoughts and retired, and Snyder earned himself a ticket to the Red Sox triple-A team in Pawtucket. The team's opening day 2003 lineup against Tampa Bay left-hander Joe Kennedy featured Millar at first base and Giambi at DH. The next night, facing a righty, Ortiz started at first, Giambi was the DH, and Millar sat. Then Millar started at first base, Giambi played left, and Ortiz sat . . . and so it went. Each day brought a new permutation in Grady Little's lineup. Needless to say, the players just *loved* the uncertainty.

Despite the lineup juggling, the Sox rolled through the first month of the 2003 season with an 18–9 record. But the first-base/DH jumble never jelled. In May, Ortiz (.212/.311/.346) and Giambi (.136/.309/.318) wilted. Millar was good to go at .300/.356/.556, but with the other two struggling, Little had to enlist regular third baseman Shea Hillenbrand for first-base duties because another third baseman, Bill Mueller, was too hot to bench. Ortiz heated up in May, hitting .333/.393/.549, but still had only 2 homers as the month ended, earning him the nickname "Juan Pierre" (after the Marlins' bunt-happy speedster). Giambi struggled to cross the Mendoza Line, batting .197 (eventually, he was found to have a torn labrum), but the crowd at the corners thinned out when Hillenbrand was sent to Arizona for reliever Byung-Hyun Kim. June found Ortiz continuing to hit, but not for power (.324/.420/.541 with only two more homers).

It wasn't until two weeks before the All-Star Game that Ortiz finally found the stroke the Twins had tried so hard to suppress: He ripped 6 homers, including 5 over a three-day span. Four came on back-to-back nights in the Bronx, helping the Sox to 10 runs each night. The rest of the season appeared just that easy for Ortiz, as he clubbed 27 homers in July, August, and September, finishing with 31. Not only had he solved the Sox's DH problem, but suddenly he had become a mainstay in the heart of their order—an imposing trio consisting of Manny Ramirez, Nomar Garciaparra, and himself. His surprising season earned him fifth place in the AL Most Valuable Player vote, just ahead of those two teammates. Not a bad return on a $1.25 million investment.

Ortiz had a taste for Yankee pitching in 2003, hitting .327/.383/.745 with 6 homers in the regular season and homering twice in the American League Championship Series. His performance against the Yankees caught the notice of owner George Steinbrenner. Early in September, ESPN reported that "the Boss implored the GM [Brian Cashman] to sign" Ortiz in the off-season. Cashman later denied it, telling *Newsday*'s Jon Heyman, "We didn't have an organizational meeting where Ortiz's name was discussed. . . . It only came up when we saw on *SportsCenter* that he was on the verge of signing with the Red Sox. That's when the question [from Steinbrenner] came up: Why didn't I get him? I always liked that guy." Cashman later tweaked his boss by remarking that with Jason Giambi and Nick Johnson already on hand, what was he supposed to do, corner the market on first basemen?

With Jason Giambi coming off his first year in pinstripes, one in which he'd hit .314/.435/.598 with 41 homers and 122 RBI, and highly touted Nick Johnson slated to alternate first-base and DH roles, a move for Ortiz would have made little sense for the Yanks. Giambi's seven-year, $120 million contract made him untradable even in the best of times. Johnson, though his arrival had been delayed due to a mysterious wrist injury, was the jewel of an otherwise decrepit Yankee farm system, an on-base machine with developing power and a reasonable amount of defensive skill. But for all of Steinbrenner's bluster, he was on to something. According to Baseball Prospectus's PECOTA system, Ortiz was projected to slightly outperform Johnson:

Johnson	.259/.363/.455, 18 HR, 9.6 VORP
Ortiz	.274/.355/.504, 17 HR, 16.0 VORP

The projected difference in the two players' performances, 6.4 runs above replacement level, amounts to about two thirds of a win. (Studies have shown that for every ten runs above replacement a player adds, the team will add roughly one additional win.) In reality, the *actual* gap turned out to be about twice that, with Johnson's huge edge in OBP no match for Ortiz's big edge in power:

Johnson	.284/.422/.472, 14 HR, 34.8 VORP
Ortiz	.288/.369/.592, 31 HR, 48.6 VORP

A cynic might note that Ortiz's low price tag was another reason he never wound up in pinstripes; the Yankee front office isn't exactly known for bargain hunting. The reasoning goes something like this: Why sign a big, slow first baseman to a one-year, $1.25 million deal when you can lock one up for seven years at a hundred times the price? But, to be fair, despite the Yankees' legendary greed, the big slugger didn't fit their needs, and the front office acted appropriately.

For the Red Sox, Ortiz filled not only a spot in the lineup but a void in the clubhouse. On a team whose three superstars (Nomar, Manny, and Pedro) often resembled moody single-named divas in their standoffish relationships with the media, Ortiz had an easy rapport with reporters.

He made efforts to encourage fellow Dominican Ramirez to open up. "I've talked to him a lot and he understands that we need to talk to [reporters] sometimes to let people know about some things," Ortiz told the Associated Press. Teammates nicknamed him "Big Papi" and fans took to Ortiz as well, christening him "Cookie Monster" after the googly-eyed Muppet. The Sox rewarded Ortiz for his fine first season with them by signing him to a one-year deal worth just under $4.6 million, plus incentives. The move had the potential to backfire; as a player who had taken a great leap forward in just about every category, including his novel ability to stay healthy for a whole year, during his age twenty-seven season (the statistical peak age of ballplayers), Ortiz could have been expected to regress to the mean. Nearly quadrupling his salary was a calculated gamble that may well have had nonperformance-related elements thrown in—a chemistry deal from a front office not enthralled with the concept of chemistry.

It may be that Ortiz's role in maintaining harmony in the clubhouse was a factor when the Sox upped the ante in May 2004, signing Ortiz to a two-year extension worth a minimum of $12.5 million and a club option for 2007 worth $7.75 million. On a team with the key contracts of Martinez, Garciaparra, Derek Lowe, and Jason Varitek expiring at the end of the season, the move made further sense. Martinez and Garciaparra had reached somewhat acrimonious standoffs in negotiations suspended prior to Opening Day. Ortiz's was the rare deal that the club completed in season. Ironically, Ortiz himself credited Martinez with convincing him to stay, telling a TV reporter, "[Martinez] told me, 'The best move you can make is to sign with Boston, stay around here.' . . . You don't get all your happiness from money. You get your happiness from the guys around you."

Unlike the previous year's slow start, Ortiz, version 2004, wasted no time spreading happiness around. He stroked 3 home runs in the season's first week, and

BIG PAPI AMONG GIANTS: BEST SEASONS BY RED SOX DESIGNATED HITTERS						
	Year	AVG	OBP	SLG	EqA	VORP
1. Jim Rice	1977	0.320	0.376	0.593	.313	76.0
2. Manny Ramirez	2001	0.306	0.405	0.609	.335	75.4
3. David Ortiz	**2004**	**0.301**	**0.38**	**0.603**	**.321**	**71.3**
4. Mike Easler	1984	0.313	0.375	0.516	.311	61.5
5. David Ortiz	**2003**	**0.288**	**0.369**	**0.592**	**.315**	**48.5**
6. Jose Canseco	1996	0.289	0.400	0.589	.323	44.6
7. David Ortiz	**2005**	**0.302**	**0.383**	**0.567**	**.323**	**42.1***
8. Jose Canseco	1995	0.306	0.378	0.556	.314	41.6
9. Orlando Cepeda	1973	0.289	0.349	0.444	.280	36.7
10. Jack Clark	1991	0.249	0.373	0.466	.304	34.3
11. Reggie Jefferson	1997	0.319	0.357	0.470	.288	32.6

*Through July 23, 2005

101

finished April hitting .301/.383 /.602, virtually identical numbers to the ones he put up over the course of the 2003 season (.301/.380/.603). Ortiz's performance was no fluke, and at $4.6 million, he was looking like a bargain. The Red Sox had nurtured a star. Ironically, he still had the same weaknesses that the Twins had spotted. Ortiz was still vulnerable to lefty pitching, showing a considerable platoon differential over the course of his career:

	%PA	AVG	OBP	SLG	ISO	HR/PA	BB/PA	K/PA
vs. Left	25.5	.251	.317	.454	.203	3.4%	7.9%	20.6%
vs. Right	74.5	.288	.373	.540	.262	4.9%	12.2%	18.9%

In 2004, Ortiz got by far the most exposure of his career against lefties, and performed at a level in line with his career numbers against them. Given that Fenway tends to punish lefty pitchers in general, that the Sox are built for the park and likely to turn the lineup over more frequently, and that Ortiz has become such a fearsome hitter against righties during his Boston years (.320/.410/.663), it was well worth the team's while to write his name in the lineup every game and ignore the fact that he'd likely face the occasional lefty specialist in the late innings.

The Twins had taken Ortiz's problems and exacerbated them—chiefly by trying for years to shorten Ortiz's swing. Red Sox hitting coach Ron Jackson, on the other hand, encouraged Ortiz to "load up," drawing power from his bulk. "Think of what it's like to get ready to throw a punch," explained Jackson. "If you really want to hit somebody hard, you've got to draw back. That's what I mean by loading up. That's what we had David work on." The adjustments enabled Ortiz to take advantage of Fenway's dimensions, hitting balls off and over the Green Monster in left field as well as ripping them down the cozy right field line.

It's easy to criticize the Twins for failing to value Ortiz correctly and to laud the Sox for seeing his worth, but the reality is more nuanced and a matter of emphasis. Both saw him as a not particularly nimble hitter at the left end of the defensive spectrum, where talent was abundant, and therefore not particularly worth a big-dollar gamble once he reached arbitration eligibility. But the Twins focused on what Ortiz couldn't do—play defense effectively, stay healthy, hit to the opposite field, hit lefties well enough to justify playing full-time—and moved on to cheaper options when the bill came due. The Red Sox recognized what he could do—hit for power, take advantage of the unique dimensions of Fenway Park, show reasonable plate discipline, and become part of an effective rotation at DH and first base. They saw him for what he was, a budding superstar at a bargain-basement price.

—Jay Jaffe

9

THE CAVEMAN CLEANS UP
MAY 21, 2004

In mid-May, the Red Sox hit some turbulence. Derek Lowe continued to have rough outings followed by rougher outings, including a shelling by an awful Royals team. The Red Sox split a series with Toronto, a team otherwise known as the Hidden Failure of the Sabermetric World. They then dropped two of three to Cleveland, including a game that finally got Byung-Hyun Kim pulled from the rotation and sent to Pawtucket.

But mid-May witnessed a far more publicized event: Johnny Damon trimmed his beard, the facial fur that had elevated him from mere ballplayer to a beloved figure of fun who combined the essence of athlete, religious figure, and Wookie. Sadly, it had taken an act of sloth on Damon's part—if that's not too strong a term for growing a beard—to raise the public's awareness of this key cog in Boston's new baseball machine, for Damon was that rarest of things, a two-way center fielder who could contribute both offensively and defensively.

Damon's 2003–2004 off-season had been an odd mix of infirmity and hyperactivity. "I was pretty much in bed for a month, month and a half," he said. "I had migraines every day. I only started to feel better in December, after a chiropractor adjusted me." He had let his hair grow long, down to his shoulders, and stopped shaving. For exercise, he began to race cars. On foot. By running down the street in the middle of the night. "I live on a street [in Orlando, Florida] where there's a twenty-five-mile-per-hour sign and the cops get you if you go anything over. I'd wait on the side of the street at night and when cars started coming, I'd race them to my house, so I know I can go at least twenty-five [mph]. I think I

Johnny Damon celebrates scoring a run

scared the cars and they'd speed up a little more because they'd see a cave-man running after them."[1] (It's unlikely that Damon can run 25 miles an hour; when Michael Johnson ran the 200-meter dash in 1996 in the Olympics in Atlanta in 19.32 seconds, he was going about 23 miles an hour.)

Whatever his foot speed, it became clear in the spring of 2004, when *The Passion of the Christ* was raking it in at the box office, that Damon had his own cross to bear—he looked like Jesus Christ. Not as Jesus might have actually looked (Semitic), but like the bearded, white, Anglo-Saxon Jesus on the cross of a suburban church. This resemblance was hardly lost on Damon, who began jokingly blessing his teammates during spring training. However, he admitted that, as a Christian, he was a little uncomfortable with some of the fans' reactions: "There's the thing with the Damon Disciples, and fans in some ballparks have yelled 'You're no Jesus! You're no Jesus!' Well, no kidding. Those fans are smart, aren't they? Jesus is amazing to me and a lot of others. I can't fathom a comparison. In no way would I ever have long hair and a beard just to look like Jesus." Still, "What Would Jesus Do?" bracelets, keycard lanyards, shot glasses, and Teflon-coated bullets were replaced in Boston by Red Sox gray-market T-shirts reading "What Would Damon Do?"

Here's what Damon would do: On May 21, Damon shaved his beard to benefit literacy programs (the flowing locks were left untouched), and when it grew back in, he kept it trimmed. The Wookie now looked merely like a hippie, and it was enough to redirect the media's and fans' attention away from his grooming and back to his game.

Overheard B.T. (Before Trim):
"Oh my God, he totally looks like Charles Manson!"
"No way! He's totally the unfrozen caveman lawyer!"
"You two are so stupid. He's Jesus!"

Overheard A.T.:
"Dude, this guy can play him some baseball."

Indeed. Ten years before, Johnny Damon had been the future of the Kansas City Royals, part of an outfield of prospects some thought would bring glory back to a franchise that hadn't won a division title since the team won a World Series in 1985. He was probably the most gifted of the draft class of 1992, a group that included Phil Nevin, Derek Jeter, Shannon Stewart, and Jason Kendall, all of whom were selected ahead of him. At twenty, he had dominated his elders in the Carolina League, hitting .316 with 25 doubles and 13 home runs, making good contact, a tough out who would take his walks if given nothing to hit.

Damon made the majors at twenty-one, but needed three years to establish himself as a quality ballplayer. Meanwhile, the predicted Royals renaissance never materialized. The products of their farm system could not overcome mismanagement of nearly every aspect of the franchise. In Damon's five years with the team, they never won more than seventy-five games in a season, and by 2001, Damon was in Oakland. Damon and the A's should have been good for each other, but they were out of phase. The A's had traded for the Royals outfielder for all the same reasons the Red Sox would later sign him as a free agent. But Damon got off to a terrible start and needed a late-season surge to get his stats up to .256/.324/.363, his worst season since 1996, when he was twenty-two. Though the A's considered Damon "a delightful human being" and "a pleasure to be around," in the final analysis the team felt he was "an easily replaceable offensive player"—and Damon was allowed to depart as a free agent.[2]

At twenty-eight, Damon was still at the peak of his career, an offensive threat with speed at a premium defensive position. He was a good bet to age well, since a fast runner, when he slows down, will still be above average in speed, whereas players who are slow to begin with calcify and become stationary objects. He signed with Boston for $31 million over four years in a deal that solved the Red Sox center field problem, which was named Carl Everett, a fragile, volatile player who was suspect both defensively and psychologically. Damon's speed on the base paths would give the offense a dimension other than power, something critics of the Red Sox had been demanding for better than fifty years. While Damon never racked up huge season stolen base totals (at least not by the standards of the 1980s run-rabbit-run era of base stealers), he sometimes displayed crazy foot speed that decided games. Boston had not seen anything like him since the short tenure of Tommy Harper in the early 1970s.

Damon's contract was one of the few of the premarket-correction deals that doesn't look wildly extravagant today, but it didn't seem that way at first. His first season in Boston, 2002, was relatively strong (.286/.356/.443), but he crashed to earth in 2003, losing about 25 percent of his production from the previous year. Worse, the year ended badly. The Red Sox were bounced from the postseason by the Yankees, and Damon slammed into Damian Jackson during the fifth game of the American League Division Series against Oakland, suffering a concussion. Damon batted just .200 in the decisive series with the Yankees.

Damon had also clashed with Red Sox former manager Grady Little, who felt Damon's late-night hijinks interfered with his ability to play. "I found out from him that I might have been partying too much," Damon said. "I was like, 'No, I'm out eating food or I'm hanging out with my girl-friend or some teammates, but by no means was I ever unable to play.'"[4] Little had missed the point. Damon was a friendly, fun-loving guy who fit in well with the self-described "Idiots" style of Boston's clubhouse.

In many respects, Damon had always been a victim of baseball's infatuation with worn-out ideas. One of them was that a batting order is composed of nine players, generally arranged according to an irrational ancient formula:

BATTING	PLAYER
#1	A singles hitter with base-stealing speed. It would be nice if he liked to take a walk as well.
#2	Another contact singles hitter, who can execute the hit and run, and make "productive" ground outs.
#3	The team's best overall hitter or best combined batting-average-plus-power threat.
#4	The team's second-best average-plus-power threat, with a heavy emphasis on power.
#5	The team's next-best power threat, but he probably hits for less of an average than the two guys in front of him and he strikes out a lot.
#6	A player whose offensive skills don't instantly suggest a place higher in the order.
#7	Generally a lesser version of the #5 hitter; the main reason he's batting seventh is because the manager wanted to avoid having two consecutive strikeout threats.
#8	He married the owner's daughter.

#9   In the National League, a pitcher. In the American
          League, someone who slept with the owner's daughter.

For a good deal of his career, and even in his first two years with Boston, Damon presented a problem for his managers because he didn't fit neatly into any of the categories described above. He didn't get on base enough to be the lead-off batter. He'd been roughly league average in that category for all players from 2002 to 2003 with league-average power while playing in a park that greatly favored hitters. The last time he'd been a top hitter was as a Royal in 2000, when he had hit .307 with a .382 on-base percentage and a .495 slugging percentage. On the other hand, he was too fast not to bat leadoff. Average OBP, above-average speed, above-average slugging percentage. Hmmm—it was a mix that didn't correspond to any of the traditional definitions of batting-order position.

Then there was his defense. The primary attribute of a center fielder is defense, and in this regard Damon was not what he seemed. He was below average for his position, as measured by errors. His fielding percentage (total chances/total chances + errors) was .986. But fielding percentage, which measures something called errors, was a slippery metric that just so happens to penalize good fielders. Take a hypothetical center fielder with tremendous speed who gets 50 percent more fly balls than an average fielder and who, when he gets to them, makes errors at the same rate as everyone else. He turns an additional 150 hits into outs and makes five more errors. Despite having put up a season for the ages (and almost certainly putting his team into the playoffs), he would be endlessly cited by the talking heads for leading the league in errors by a center fielder. This more or less described Johnny Damon.

Fortunately, there are more sophisticated ways to assess defense, ones that account for a player's range—his quickness, speed, and therefore ability to be in a position to field more balls. The best of these methods, *Baseball Prospectus*'s take on fielding runs, was developed by Clay Davenport. Whereas zone rating is an observational method based on dividing the field into somewhat arbitrary areas of responsibility, Davenport's fielding runs are based on how many more plays a fielder made than one would expect, considering the statistics of the pitcher and the other fielders on the team. Damon shows up as about average in fielding percentage and zone rating, but, according to Davenport's defensive translations, in 2004, Damon saved *eight runs* more than an average center fielder, his best performance in his career (followed by seven in 2000, six in 2001, and five in 2002). The Red Sox perceived Damon's defensive value (so did the A's, for that matter), which was heightened in their particular case by the presence of a visitor from outer space named Manny Ramirez in left field. Ramirez's range was limited by his tendency to treat every fly ball as if it were a unique, previously unencountered situation.

Damon's hidden defensive virtues were all the more exciting when you considered his tremendous offensive value to the team. Even adjusted for the friendly confines of Fenway Park, Damon was the best-hitting center fielder in the American League. His eventual 2004 season numbers of .304/.380/.477 made him one of the twenty most valuable players in the league and its most valuable center fielder, as measured by Value Over Replacement Player (VORP)—or how many more runs a player was worth to his team than his theoretical, but realistic, replacement (see chart).

2004 AL LEADERS, VORP			
Player	Team	Pos	VORP
1. Vlad Guererro	Anaheim	RF	88.5
2. Ichiro Suzuki	Seattle	RF	80.9
3. Melvin Mora	Baltimore	3B	73.6
4. Miguel Tejada	Baltimore	SS	73.0
5. David Ortiz	Boston	DH	71.3
6. Travis Hafner	Cleveland	DH	70.9
7. Carlos Guillen	Detroit	SS	70.5
8. Manny Ramirez	Boston	LF	68.6
9. Garry Sheffield	New York	RF	63.4
10. Ivan Rodriguez	Detroit	C	63.1
11. Alex Rodriguez	New York	3B	62.3
12. Mike Young	Texas	SS	60.1
13. Derek Jeter	New York	SS	59.7
14. Hideki Matsui	New York	LF	57.5
15. Erubiel Durazo	Oakland	DH	57.2
16. Javy Lopez	Baltimore	C	56.3
17. Mark Teixeira	Texas	1B	52.6
18. Johnny Damon	**Boston**	**CF**	**51.0**
19. Aubrey Huff	Tampa Bay	3B	50.5
20. Aaron Rowand	Chicago	CF	50.0

The way to make the most of this kind of valuable commodity is to get him as many plate appearances as you can and that's exactly what the Red Sox did. "The only thing I told him," Francona said when he became Boston's manager, "is I want him to get on base. I don't care if he walks, hits, or bunts. I think he understands that if he's on base, our offense is going to be in the right direction."[5]

The teams with players at the skill positions—catcher, second base, shortstop, and center field—who can also provide offense even a touch above average have a huge advantage over the opposition. Every team can find a poor-fielding but burly hitter to play first base, so any advantage there is marginal. It's on the right side of Bill James's "defensive spectrum," where Club A has Jim Edmonds in center and Club B has Endy Chavez, that games are won and lost. Since 1996, few teams had more all-around strength in the skill positions than the Yankees, with their core of Jorge Posada, Derek Jeter, and Bernie Williams. However, the one flaw of these great Yankee teams was that they often put relatively unproductive players at the left end of the spectrum. From 1996 through 2004 the Yankees averaged 886 runs a season. This is very good, but not great. The 2004 Red Sox did not make the same mistake. (The slight discrepancy between Damon's own numbers and the numbers in this table is the result of the twelve games in which Damon did not play center field.)

The Red Sox got tremendous offensive contributions where other teams could not, and where other teams had an easier time

POSITION	2004 AL AVERAGE			2004 BOSTON		
	AVG	OBP	SLG	AVG	OBP	SLG
C	.264	.326	.410	.293	.386	.497
SS	.274	.327	.420	.273	.308	.408
2B	.259	.320	.397	.264	.360	.434
CF	.280	.339	.430	.296	.370	.460
3B	.269	.343	.449	.264	.358	.411
RF	.275	.344	.436	.306	.362	.461
LF	.281	.347	.448	.287	.379	.565
1B	.266	.346	.447	.270	.346	.467
DH	.263	.345	.439	.293	.380	.567

finding bats, the Red Sox played the biggest, baddest bats possible.

In Oakland, Damon had felt constrained by the team's dictate to wear out pitchers. "It's definitely a lot harder to hit when you pattern your game around taking pitches," he said. In Boston, though also a mecca of on-base-percentage baseball, the caveman was freer to be himself. With essentially the same lineup behind him in 2004 as in 2003, Damon scored twenty more runs. Twenty runs is huge—worth two wins in the standings.) The great irony was that, in 2004, Damon would still see as many pitches per plate appearance, 4.1, as he had in 2003.[6]

Not long after Damon's tonsorial trim, a grooming move that would soon see him named one of *People* magazine's "50 Sexiest" celebrities of 2004, the Red Sox suffered every team's dreaded, but inevitable, fate: a spate of injuries. Damon's productivity provided much needed insurance during the storm, but Theo Epstein had taken out other policies as well. In fact, he had one of baseball's most coveted hole cards.

—DEREK ZUMSTEG

10

THE HOLY GOSPEL OF ON-BASE PERCENTAGE
MAY 23, 2004

Baseball is a game of mimicry. Every year, someone wins the World Series and the twenty-nine other teams try to figure out the latest winning formula and copy it. The Cardinals of the eighties won with speed? Let's build a roster full of jackrabbits. The 2002 Angels had a dominating bullpen? Let's get a bunch of power arms for the late innings. The Red Sox, like every other team in 2004, had no such role model to follow because, although the Florida Marlins' 2003 championship was a satisfying story of a cash-poor underdog that came out of nowhere to charge through the playoffs and knock off the Yankees, there wasn't much of a lesson there. More than any other factor, the Marlins won thanks to luck. As noted in *Baseball Prospectus 2004*, Florida traded for players who, once outfitted in Marlin teal, black, and silver, suddenly performed far above the wildest optimist's dreams.

Sure, the 2004 Red Sox had some breaks go their way—no team has ever won a World Series without the benefit of a few leprechauns. However, they experienced an alarming number of injuries, especially in the season's first half, and the lesson there was that they were able to overcome the loss of several top players and hang in the race while everyone healed. It wasn't a matter of luck, but of the ballclub's design, plus an appearance from God—the Greek God of Walks, Kevin Youkilis.

Youkilis's divine intervention didn't occur until the Sox were nearly one quarter of the way through the season, battling for first place in the

Kevin Youkilis, the
Greek God of Walks

AL East. On Thursday, May 13, Terry Francona gave third baseman Bill Mueller what he called a routine day off (Mueller would get to pinch-hit, however, singling in his one time up). In Mueller's stead, the Sox shifted starting second baseman Mark Bellhorn to third and used Cesar Crespo at second. A light-hitting utility infielder who was out of baseball in 2003, Crespo would go on to post a horrendous line of .165/.165/.215 in fifty-three games of part-time duty in 2004. Boston fell, 12–6, to the Blue Jays, although Crespo contributed two hits. Still, the Red Sox were concerned about losing Mueller for any length of time. Though outshone by sluggers like David Ortiz and Manny Ramirez, the five-ten, 180-pound Mueller had established himself as one of the most valuable weapons in Boston's arsenal in 2003. Mueller hit .326, winning the American League batting title. And he wasn't some Punch-and-Judy singles hitter; his 2003 season set the example for all American League third basemen:

AMERICAN LEAGUE THIRD BASEMEN, RANKED BY VORP (2003)

	Team	PA	AVG	OBP	SLG	VORP
Bill Mueller	BOS	600	0.326	0.395	0.540	65.2
Eric Chavez	OAK	654	0.282	0.350	0.514	61.7
Hank Blalock	TEX	615	0.300	0.350	0.522	50.9
Corey Koskie	MIN	562	0.292	0.393	0.452	46.6
Joe Randa	KCA	566	0.291	0.343	0.452	32.8

Mueller led AL third basemen in batting average, on-base percentage, slugging average, and Value Over Replacement Player (VORP). Though Mueller had always been a solid on-base threat in his first seven seasons with the Cubs and Giants, he'd also lost gobs of playing time to injuries. His knees were the main culprit; he'd had them tweaked, fretted over, and surgically repaired so often that teams wondered if he'd ever be good for an entire season again, especially since he was entering his mid-thirties. In 2003, Mueller had beaten the odds, posting a career year and staying healthy throughout most of the season.

Mueller exemplified the team's belief that on-base ability was a player's single most important offensive trait. The new Red Sox approach held that every out was precious and should be fiercely protected, from the top of the batting order down to the bottom. The idea may seem obvious to some: The more runners you put on base, the better a team's chance of scoring. The fewer outs a team makes, the longer it can extend innings, wear out opposing pitchers, and put crooked numbers on the board. Fifty years earlier, Branch Rickey had espoused the virtue of getting on base in an essay for *Life* magazine entitled "Goodby [*sic*] to Some Old Baseball Ideas":

> *In my experience probably the most important single thing in batting has been the mental attitude of the hitter going to the plate. The most gripping moment in any field of sports comes when batter faces pitcher. Batter and pitcher eye each other. Psychologically one or the other is in command before a ball is thrown. But can you measure this? Could you measure the arrogance of a Rogers Hornsby as he got ready to take his cut? Walter Johnson's utter indifference to the identity of any batsman who ever faced him?*
>
> *Eyesight is another variable factor. Babe Ruth's eyes were so quick, it is said, that he could read the label of a phonograph record while it was spinning. I suppose there is a way to get an optometrist's rating on hitters' eyes, but that could not help fix a formula. But the ability to get on base, or On Base Average, is both vital and measurable.*

Yet for as long as some of the game's brighter minds have understood the concept, many teams still haven't taken the lesson to heart. Whenever a team signs Tony Womack to be its starting second baseman . . . whenever a manager orders a first-inning bunt by the number-two hitter . . . whenever a general manager trades a good, young hitter with on base ability for a mediocre pitcher . . . the ghost of Branch Rickey sighs deeply.

When Epstein signed Mueller for two years at just $4.2 million (plus a $2.5 million 2005 option) prior to the 2003 season, the price reflected Mueller's bad knees, but it also showed how many teams would still overlook a supposedly one-dimensional player if that dimension was getting on base.

Although improved statistical analysis has shown that a team's batting order is an overrated element in run production, it is not irrelevant—even a one percent improvement in run production over the course of the season can mean an additional win. It is common sense to structure the lineup so as many runners as possible are on base for the power hitters. Though used in multiple lineup spots in his 2003 season, Mueller saw the most action as Boston's number-two man. In 168 at-bats batting second, he racked up a gaudy line of .345/.399/.524, roughly on par with his equally impressive overall numbers that year. No one appreciated that more than Manny Ramirez and David Ortiz. However, heading into the 2004 season, Theo Epstein did not allow himself the luxury of assuming that Mueller would duplicate his 2003 numbers. He knew that 2003 marked just the third time in his seven seasons as a big-league starter in which Mueller had played more than 130 games.

Before their May 13 loss to Toronto, the Red Sox led the AL East by half a game over the Yankees; one Mueller-less day later they'd dropped to second. The next night, Mueller was a late scratch for the lineup, but the Sox smacked the Jays, 9–3, with Crespo collecting two more hits in Mueller's stead. Francona wanted to rest Mueller for the last two games of the Toronto series. He penciled him in for the start of the Tampa series on May 18. The starting third baseman—the one who put up monster numbers a year earlier—needed a couple of days off to heal? Fine. Crespo's hitting a little, and who knows, maybe he'll break out at age twenty-five. Why tinker with the roster? Some complacency could have been forgiven, even expected.

But Boston's front office reacted differently, sensing the perils of a little roster inertia. In battling teams like the Yankees in the AL East, plus serious wild card contenders like the Angels, A's, and others, even a single game lost through bad management might mean the difference between playing golf and postseason baseball. Just two days after Mueller first sat out, less than twenty-four hours after the Sox acknowledged an injury, they recalled the twenty-five-year-old third baseman Kevin Youkilis.

Francona immediately inserted Youkilis into the lineup, spotting him eighth against the Jays. The new third baseman responded, going 2-for-4 with a homer in a 4–0 win. The win vaulted the Sox right back into first place, underlining the importance of valuing every game, every transaction. As if to drive the point home, Crespo, batting ninth and playing shortstop, went 0-for-4, with a dropped pop-up.

That the Red Sox brought Youkilis up was to Epstein's credit; that the team had a major league–ready replacement rarin' to go in Triple-A

Pawtucket was to Dan Duquette's credit. Though frequently criticized for his aloof, taciturn dealings with the always harsh Boston media, Duquette did a credible job of building some competitive Red Sox teams, often taking fliers on players unloved by scouts, both with freely available older talent and in the amateur draft. Youkilis was Exhibit A for this strategy. Scouts had been unimpressed by the big-time hitter at the University of Cincinnati, despite a .405/.549/.714 line in his final year. Youkilis had a slightly doughy six-one, 220-pound frame and was derided by bird dogs as an unathletic player with a suspect glove and limited upside. Still, Duquette and company saw something they liked and grabbed him in the eighth round of the 2001 draft. He was the 243rd pick overall, which is to say that baseball's collective wisdom held 242 players to be more talented.

The move immediately paid dividends. Though old for his level, Youkilis still did what a good prospect should in the short-season New York–Penn League, banging out a .976 OPS (on-base percentage plus slugging percentage). Youkilis drew 70 walks in just 260 plate appearances, netting him a Bondsian OBP of .512. Skeptics still dismissed him as a college-trained hitter taking advantage of overmatched teenagers. This was demonstrably false. Not every college-trained hitter who just turned pro walks 27 percent of the time. In fact, none do.

The next year brought more of the same. Though his power continued to lag, Youkilis zoomed through three levels, finishing the season in Double-A. His OBPs that year included a .433 mark in the South Atlantic League, .422 in the high-A Florida State League, and a .462 mark at Double-A Trenton. By the time Theo Epstein took the reins as the new GM in November 2002, word of Youkilis's on-base prowess had spread. In 2002's *Moneyball*, Michael Lewis made the "Greek God of Walks" famous by writing about the Oakland A's GM Billy Beane's burning desire to have him. Other teams were catching on, as well. Obviously, Epstein was not about to let him go cheaply—and he didn't. Though Youkilis again struggled in the power department in 2003 (just 6 homers in Double-A), he still posted a massive .487 OBP, drawing 86 walks and getting hit by 15 pitches in just 417 plate appearances. Despite a rough finish to his 2003 season in Pawtucket—followed by an improved early showing there in 2004—Epstein knew he had an able replacement ready should Mueller go down with an injury.

Youkilis's rousing May 15 debut marked the start of a hot streak, both for the rookie and the team:

Date	Youkilis Results	Red Sox Result
5/15	2-for-4, HR	Won, 4–0
5/16	2-for-4, two singles	Lost, 3–1
5/18	Sat for Mueller	Won, 7–3
5/19	Sat for Mueller	Won, 4–1
5/20	1-for-4, single	Lost, 9–6
5/21	2 BBs in 4 PAs	Won, 11–5
5/22	1-for-4, single	Won, 5–2
5/23	2 BBs in 4 PAs	Won, 7–2
5/25	2B, 2 BBs in 4 PAs	Won, 12–2
5/26	Single, BB in 4 PAs	Won, 9–6
5/27	BB in 4 PAs	Lost, 15–2
5/28	2-for-4, 2 doubles	Won, 8–4

The Sox went 9–3 over this twelve-game stretch. All Youkilis did was hit .313, with a .463 on-base percentage. Though he tailed off some later in the year, the Sox were in good hands, even when Mueller hit the disabled list, missing six weeks. Kevin Youkilis, the supposedly overmatched, unathletic slob who'd be lucky to even sniff the majors, had arrived.

Mueller's injury was one of several key blows suffered by the Sox in the season's first two months. Nomar Garciaparra missed the first nine weeks of the season to severe Achilles tendonitis. A double shot of left quad problems and a herniated disk in his back shelved Trot Nixon for the season's first ten weeks. Byung-Hyun Kim sat out most of April with shoulder inflammation, posted one great start and two brutal ones, then got knocked out for most of the rest of the year. While Youkilis performed admirably in the third-base role, the other injury replacements had a rougher go of it. Pokey Reese briefly won a legion of followers with his glovework at short in place of Garciaparra, but the love affair ended quickly when Red Sox Nation discovered Reese's disastrous hitting (by season's end he'd posted a line of .221/.271/.303). Though Kevin Millar did an adequate job in right field replacing Nixon, Dave McCarty struggled in Millar's vacated first-base slot. The Sox would eventually upgrade the bench, adding players like Doug Mientkiewicz and Dave Roberts at the deadline to act as insurance and improve the team's late-inning defense.

While replacement players helped carry the Sox through their injuries, the team's core players—Schilling, Ramirez, Ortiz, and Damon—were all living up to expectations and then some. Few fans would have put Mark Bellhorn in the same category as those headliners before 2004. Bellhorn had spent most of his career as a reserve to that point. Finally granted full-time duty in 2002 with the Cubs, he put up huge .258/.374/.512 numbers. Even then, his manager, the media, and fans all criticized him for his defense and especially for his high strikeout total (144, or about one for every three at-bats). After a slow start in 2003, he landed in Colorado, then became available again that off-season. In baseball, as in life, people tend to focus on what an individual can't do, not on what he can. When most teams looked at Bellhorn, they didn't see a hitter with power and good walk rates, an infielder who could play multiple positions, or a cheap commodity still in his peak years. They saw strikeouts—without considering that strikeouts are scarcely worse than other outs when taken as a whole (see more about this in the sidebar to Chapter 11). They didn't consider that Bellhorn's offensive production more than made up for his defensive mediocrity, especially compared to the typical light-hitting second baseman. Where others saw weaknesses, the Red Sox saw opportunity. Bellhorn's high walk rate fit Epstein's high-OBP prototype, and he grabbed him for the princely sum of a player-to-be-named-later. Garciaparra's injury propelled Bellhorn into the starting job at second base, with Reese taking over at short.

Bellhorn hit just .194 in April, causing many observers to tout Reese for the everyday second-base job when Garciaparra returned. But, on closer examination, Bellhorn's numbers were deceptive: even while hitting anemically, he'd still managed a .323 on-base percentage and .404 slugging average. Reese could manage only .254 in both categories in the season's first month. Call it coincidence, but when Francona scratched Mueller from the May 13 starting lineup against the Jays, Bellhorn shifted his game to another gear. In the next sixteen games, he hit .288, with a .397 OBP and 17 RBI. The streak launched what would become the second-best season of Bellhorn's career (.264/.373/.444), despite his spending three weeks on the disabled list in August. Although he played just 138 games, he finished a close second to

Alfonso Soriano in VORP among AL second basemen. He had struck out a staggering 177 times—but nobody in Boston's front office blinked.

The best part was that Bellhorn made only $490,000. In addition to Bellhorn and the über-cheap Bill Mueller, Kevin Millar proved a deal at $2.65 million a year in 2003 and 2004, with a $3.5 million option for 2005. Indeed, Epstein's propensity for finding cheap sources of on-base percentage in his two years as general manager was unsurpassed by anyone in the game. Even Ortiz's $4.6 million salary in 2004 was a steal; his $1.25 million deal in 2003 was outright larceny. That kind of intuitive bargain hunting, which allowed the Sox to go the extra dollar elsewhere, whether to sign a top free-agent reliever like Keith Foulke or to lock up a star hitter like Ortiz, has become a hallmark of the Epstein regime.

Would a roster so deep in high OBP players help protect the Sox in 2004 against the inevitable losing streaks of any team's season? As the team readied for a makeup game against the Orioles and a five-game road trip, they were about to get a taste of their own resilience.

—JONAH KERI

EXTRA INNINGS

ON-BASE-PERCENTAGE SCRIPTURE

"All right, so Cobb and DiMaggio and a couple of others said I took too many close pitches, 'begging walks,' that I should have gone for the close pitch when we were behind and needed runs. Al Simmons used to say that I was 'helping the enemy.' My argument is, to be a good hitter you've got to get a good ball to hit . . . My argument is, if the guy behind me is a .300 hitter, and having walked me, they *have* to pitch to him . . ."—TED WILLIAMS

"They think they're bein' unlucky, but they'll be unlucky all their lives if they don't change."—CASEY STENGEL, YANKEES HALL OF FAME MANAGER, ON HITTERS WHO MAKE OUTS BY SWINGING AT BAD PITCHES

"If you don't swing at bad pitches, they have to throw you a good one." —GATES BROWN, TIGERS HITTING COACH, 1979

"A walk is not as good as a hit, but it is more nearly so than any other offensive event . . . A .400 batting average is gaudy, but unaccompanied by a high number of walks or extra base hits, it is not a great performance."—JOHN THORN AND PETE PALMER, *THE HIDDEN GAME OF BASEBALL*, 1984

"I wish there was a way to convince some players of the importance of walks . . . Don't misunderstand; I'm not saying that a player should go to the plate with a bat glued to his shoulder. Rather, I'm saying that a guy should lay off bad pitches. It sounds so simple, but it's not. A player who can do it . . . gives you another dimension."—EARL WEAVER, ORIOLES HALL OF FAME MANAGER

"What makes a good leadoff hitter? Deion Sanders had speed, but he wasn't the ideal leadoff hitter. What was his on-base percentage? The criteria shouldn't be speed, it should be getting on base."—JACK MCKEON, REDS MANAGER, 1997

"I like walking. I enjoy that part of the game. And I have a lot of trust and belief in the guys behind me."—ALEX RODRIGUEZ, 2000

"We are a team that doesn't walk. When you don't walk and you don't get runners on base, then the stats are going to catch up to you." —PHIL GARNER, TIGERS MANAGER, 2000

"Fans will look at batting average, but on-base percentage is the most important thing. That's what I gauge myself on. I always try to stay around that .400 level."—JEFF CIRILLO, ROCKIES INFIELDER, 2000

"Walks have been underappreciated. It's lost in the stats sheets. It lost its appeal somewhere. Another thing lost in the stats is on-base percentage. That's the most important thing in baseball. If nobody's on base, nobody scores."—RICKEY HENDERSON, PADRES OUTFIELDER, ON SETTING THE CAREER WALK RECORD, 2001

"Even if he [Tim Raines] doesn't make the club, the fact that he is in camp will help a lot of guys—Peter Bergeron, Orlando Cabrera, a lot of guys who, in the minors, didn't have any idea how to take a walk. . . . Raines is a master. I'd like to see that happen before I get on, see a couple of

those guys with a .400 on-base percentage."—**FELIPE ALOU,** EXPOS MAN-
AGER, ON HAVING OUTFIELDER TIM RAINES IN SPRING TRAINING FOR THE EXPOS,
2001

"Offensively, the two most important parts of your lineup are your No.
1 hitter and your No. 4 hitter. You need somebody who can have a good
on-base percentage. Sometimes it's a guy who's not a burner whose
strengths don't include stealing bases. You can't steal bases if you don't
get on."—**MIKE HARGROVE,** ORIOLES MANAGER, 2001

"I think the main thing is on-base percentage. If you still have a good on-
base percentage and drive in runs, the strikeouts don't really matter."
—**JEROMY BURNITZ,** BREWERS OUTFIELDER, 2001

"To me, on-base percentage is important, more so than walk ratio or
home runs. If you're on base, you can do something. You can manufac-
ture runs. You get on base, everything else goes up. I've always wanted
a .500 on-base percentage. I've always had one around .430 or .440. I
should be able to get on base, if I'm patient enough."—**BARRY BONDS,**
GIANTS OUTFIELDER, 2002

"The game comes down to runs and outs. You want to score more runs
than the other team before you run out of outs. The way to do that is to
get on base as much as possible, and there is a correlation between seeing a lot of pitches and having a high on-base percentage."—**CHRIS
ANTONETTI,** INDIANS ASSISTANT GENERAL MANAGER, 2002

"To me batting average is an overrated statistic. It doesn't really tell the
whole story like on-base percentage or slugging percentage. Really,
that's what offense is: on-base percentage and slugging percentage."
—**STEVE PHILLIPS,** METS GENERAL MANAGER, 2002

"On-base percentage is very important. A high on-base percentage
means you're accepting a lot of walks, so that means the pitcher is
throwing more pitches. So that means you'll get into the middle-inning
pitchers quicker. And middle relief is the weaker part of a pitching staff.
If you can face more weaker pitching, you have a better chance to win."
—**GENE MICHAEL,** YANKEES HEAD SCOUT, 2002

"It'd be nice to cut down on them. But I think as long as you get your on-base percentage up around .400, it doesn't matter. That's the way I look at it."—Mariners first baseman **Richie Sexson,** on cutting down on his strikeouts, 2005

"I'm just looking for guys to get on base and score runs, doing what they are supposed to do out there. [Drawing walks] is huge. If you swing at pitches that aren't strikes, you get yourself out."—**Ned Yost,** Brewers manager, 2005

"Every batter needs to behave like a leadoff man and adopt as his main goal getting on base."—The first tenet of **Sandy Alderson**'s batting "system" for the Oakland A's.

"It's kind of like in scripture now because everybody reads [*Moneyball*]. They only hear what that book says and they can't look past it. I heard a guy in the stands yell, 'Hey Youk, get a walk.' I'm like, 'What, you don't want me to hit a three-run homer here and win a ball-game?' I've had more people come up and go, 'Hey, do you go up there looking for a walk?' I'm like, 'Are you crazy? If you go up looking for a walk, you'll be sitting down in about four pitches.' Hopefully I can shed it some day."—Red Sox infielder **Kevin Youkilis** on his nickname, The Greek God of Walks

—Compiled by Baseball Prospectus

11

A STREAK
OF INSIGNIFICANCE
MAY 29–JUNE 8, 2004

I nevitably, every team suffers some kind of let down, sometimes relative in scope to its quality level and sometimes surpassing it. Losing five of six is the kind of lapse to which all but the most stalwart of teams is prone (the 116-win Seattle Mariners of 2001 are one such exception). Beginning on May 27, following a five-game winning streak, the Red Sox and their followers slipped quietly into a funk.

The rough patch began when the Sox dropped a 15–2 decision to the A's, then continued when the Mariners edged Boston, 5–4, at Fenway Park on May 29. Seattle gave its starter Freddy Garcia something they hadn't yet provided him in 2004: run support. The Sox and Tim Wakefield were down 5–0 to the then-current American League ERA leader by the third inning, but rallied back to within a run by the sixth. This chased Garcia, who would be shipped off to the White Sox within a month. The Mariners wasted six base runners from that point on, but it mattered not—Boston was done scoring for the day. The next day they survived a fairly pedestrian start by Curt Schilling, a blown save by Keith Foulke, and a 0-for-6 day by David Ortiz to outlast Seattle, 9–7. Spare part Dave McCarty won the game in the twelfth with a two-run homer, his second.

The game featured two hits by the single most obscure member of the 2004 World Champion Red Sox: Andy Dominique. Playing in just his third major league game, the twenty-eight-year-old catcher came to the plate with two out in the bottom of the eighth and the Sox down 7–6. They had

What losing looks like

just coughed up a 5–1 lead in the top of the inning and had rallied to score once and now had the tying run on third. Dominique, pinch-hitting for Pokey Reese, responded with a single to right that would send the game into extra innings. Dominique, who would get into only a handful of other games, had just batted safely for the last time in 2004.

A rainout makeup from early April ruined the Red Sox travel plans for Memorial Day. Instead of getting to the West Coast early, they had to stay home and host the Orioles. Derek Lowe absorbed a beating so sound that not even the Red Sox offense, who so generously supported him most of the time, could save him. It was the third consecutive disaster or near-disaster of a start, and his ERA soared to 6.84. He walked four and struck out none, a low number even for him. Fortunately, the game would prove to be the nadir of his season.

From there, the team rushed to the West Coast to meet the franchise that seemed most determined to usurp Boston's position as the league's second-best funded club, the Anaheim Angels. New owner Arturo Moreno had landed free agents like Vladimir Guerrero, Kelvim Escobar, and Bartolo Colon, and the Angels' record, 30–20, almost matched Boston's 31–20. This, their first meeting of the year, perfectly illustrated the inequities of major league scheduling in the interleague play era. The Red Sox would play two in Anaheim now, return in July for a four-game set, and Anaheim would finally show up in Fenway for three games at the end of August. This imbalance—six home games for Anaheim, three for Boston—would unfairly penalize the Sox in the case of two clubs headed for a wild card showdown.

The Angels took the first game of the set when Angels middle relievers Kevin Gregg and Francisco Rodriguez shut the Red Sox out for four innings and former über-closer Troy Percival held on for the 7–6 win. The loss, combined with a Yankee victory over Baltimore, dropped Boston a game out of first. They didn't know it at the time, but they had just spent their last moments in first place for the rest of the season.

In the second game of the set, Vladimir Guerrero inflicted rare pain on Pedro Martinez and the Boston bullpen. It's one thing to drive in nine runs with a grand slam and a couple of other multi-RBI hits; it's another to come to the plate five times, as Guerrero did, and drive somebody home on each and every one of those occasions. RBI as a counting stat has long been exposed as overrated and the very concept of clutch hitting has also been similarly downgraded, but the devastating effect of Guerrero's personal slugfest can't be denied. The great sucking sound heard that day was the sharp intake of breath of every general manager who had passed on Guerrero's free agency owing to concerns over the time he had missed to back problems the previous season.

Martinez had surrendered a 2-run homer, 2-run double, and sacrifice fly to Guerrero, but was still leading, 7–5, heading into the home sixth because Angels starter Jarrod Washburn—the best-supported pitcher on the planet up to that point of the season—was even less effective. Martinez appeared to calm down in the fifth but surrendered a hit to leadoff man David Eckstein (one of his five) and a walk to Chone Figgins to lead off the sixth before giving way to Mike Timlin. (The first three batters in the Angels' order came to the plate fifteen times and either had a hit, walk, or sacrifice fly in fourteen of their plate appearances.) Guerrero greeted Timlin with a 3-run shot to put Anaheim ahead to stay and the Sox a further game behind New York.

Two days later in Kansas City, Tim Wakefield allowed thirteen base runners in less than seven innings, threw a season-high 116 pitches in the process, and Boston now trailed New York by three and a half games.

It was June 4, and the Red Sox had just played six games against four different opponents and managed to lose to each of them at least once. The Red Sox had managed, depressingly, to lose to an unusual variety of teams in that short span, thanks to anachronistic scheduling reminiscent of baseball of the 1870s.

More disturbing was that, during the nine-game stretch that began with two victories and concluded with the loss to Kansas City, Red Sox pitching had epitomized bad. In 1988, our forefather Bill James invented the Game Score system of rating pitcher performances. All starting pitchers begin with a Game Score of 50 and proceed either to add to it, by striking men out or getting through innings without allowing anyone to score, or subtract from it, by surrendering base runners and runs. In 2004, eighty-six pitchers threw enough innings to qualify for the ERA title. The average Game Score among this group was 50.7. For its last nine games, Boston's starting pitchers had averaged a Game Score of 34, with only two above-average performances:

5/26: 36 (Lowe)
5/27: 16 (Arroyo)
5/28: 54 (Martinez)
5/29: 33 (Wakefield)
5/30: 56 (Schilling)
5/31: 19 (Lowe)
6/1:   34 (Arroyo)
6/2:   19 (Martinez)
6/4:   38 (Wakefield)

The lowest AGS in 2004 belonged to Brian Anderson of the Royals. The second lowest—42.4—was the property of Mr. Lowe. While National Leaguers have better Game Scores than those in the American League (thanks to the absence of designated hitters), a run of consecutive games in which only two pitchers score above 40 is evidence of possible disaster. It was the kind of run a team like the Royals might expect, but not a team trying to keep the Yankees within earshot. Had the Red Sox bats not risen to the occasion and scored nine runs twice in this period, they would have lost eight of those nine, instead of six.

While the Red Sox, and their fans, were in the midst of the team's losing streak, it might have been futile to point out one of baseball's odd little statistical truths: early- and midseason losing streaks are a lot less meaningful than they appear. Teams have endured worse than the Red Sox streak and have not only lived to tell about it but have thrived. Between the advent of divisional play and the 2004 season, 176 teams made the playoffs. Twelve of them, including the 1996 World Champion Yankees, suffered losing streaks *as long as their longest winning streak*. Another ten playoff-bound teams suffered losing streaks *longer than their longest winning streak*. Here are those ten, beginning with the longest losing streaks:

2001 Astros (longest losing, 8; longest winning, 5)
This is the largest reverse differential between winning and losing streaks ever for a playoff team in the multidivision era. What is more, these Astros had not one but two losing streaks longer than their longest winning streak. With nine games left to go in the season, they dropped six straight before recovering to win two of their last three. This allowed the

Cardinals to tie them for the division lead on paper, but the Astros were awarded the division on the basis of head-to-head competition. Streakwise, Houston compensated for these pratfalls with three different five-game winning runs.

1976 Phillies (longest losing, 8; longest winning, 6)

Of the ten teams that have managed this feat, the Bicentennial Phils managed the most wins—101. They actually had two six-game losing streaks, one of which began with a three-game wipeout by the Reds, the team that would later sweep them out of the playoffs. (Ironically, the Phillies were the one team against whom Cincinnati played sub-.500 ball in 1976, losing seven of the nine other contests.)

1996 Padres (longest losing, 8; longest winning, 6)

After breaking their losing streak on June 15, the Padres dropped five more consecutive games (for a total of thirteen losses in fourteen games). They added another five-game losing streak for good measure, and added two six-game winning streaks. The Cardinals swept them out of the playoffs in the first round.

1999 Mets (longest losing, 8; longest winning, 6)

The second-most successful team on this list with ninety-seven wins, the '99 Mets are better known for their seven-game losing in late September than they are for the eight-game pre-All-Star-break swoon. With two weeks to go in the season, they were just a game out of first and had a fairly comfortable four-game lead for the wild card. By the time they recovered to win four of their last five, they were forced to play the Reds in a one-game playoff for the wild card, winning that but eventually losing to the Braves in the NLCS. The two long losing streaks were offset by a second six-game win streak and two five-gamers.

1982 Angels (longest losing, 8; longest winning, 7)

This was a team that did things in bunches. Their eight-game losing stretch was ended by one of their two six-game winning streaks. They also dropped seven in a row, but two five-game win streaks helped compensate. In the '82 American League Championship Series, they jumped out to a 2–0 lead on the Brewers, only to drop three straight in a rehearsal for their even more devastating playoff loss to the Red Sox four years later.

1995 Yankees (longest losing, 8; longest winning, 7)

Shortened season or no, this was another seriously streaky team: The Yankees found themselves four games below .500 on August 28. From that point on, they went 25–6 to land themselves in the playoffs for the first time in fourteen years. In addition to the streaks mentioned above, they won six in a row three different times and five twice. They also had two five-game losing streaks interrupted by a single victory.

1984 Royals (longest losing, 7; longest winning, 6)

At the end of their seven-game slide, the Royals record stood at 9–18. Fortunately for them, these were uninspired days in the American League West, and they were able to grab the division crown in spite of also developing a six-game losing streak along the way—and amassing only eighty-four wins.

1991 Blue Jays (longest losing, 7; longest winning, 6)

The only thing standing between the Jays and a twelve-game win streak was a 1–0 loss to David West and the Twins on July 4, which preceded a five-game winning streak and was followed by a six-game one.

1996 Orioles (longest losing, 6; longest winning, 5)

The O's won eleven of their first thirteen games, which made it easier to absorb their early-season six-game losing streak. They won five straight on three separate occasions, but totaled the second-fewest victories of the teams on this list—eighty-eight.

1997 Yankees (longest losing, 6; longest winning, 5)

Four winning streaks of five games each was the compensation here.

Of the ten teams on this list, only the Jays went all the way. Since 1969, of the 176 teams to make the playoffs, 22 had losing streaks equal to or longer than their longest winning streak. Two of those (9.1 percent) won the World Series. Of the other 154 teams to make the playoffs, teams with winning streaks greater than their longest losing streak, 33 (21.4 percent) won the World Series. Teams with longer losing than winning streaks may not fare well in the postseason, but teams with especially long winning streaks don't enjoy much of an advantage either. No playoff team has ever won more in a row than the Oakland A's of 2002, yet their twenty-game run was just a memory when they were bumped off, once again, in the first round of the playoffs. If it is indeed possible to "learn how to win," wouldn't school be in special session in a winning streak of a dozen or more games? Fifteen playoff-bound teams have won at least twelve games in a row, yet only two of them—the 1991 Twins and the 1982 Cardinals—went all the way. As a group, the twelve-plus streakers have performed at a .422 clip in the playoffs. Strangely, more World Champions show up with ten- and eleven-game losing streaks (four for each of them).

How should we think about the fact that teams that won at least twelve games in a row do poorly in the postseason? Is what a team does when it's not streaking a better indication of their true strength? As an experiment, let's subtract the number of games won by these clubs during their longest streak and substitute it with the number of games they would have won had they played at the same winning percentage they did during the nonstreak portion of the season. In other words, the 2002 A's were a .585 team outside their 20-game march. A .585 winning percentage on 20 games is good for about 12 wins. At 95 wins instead of 103, would they have even qualified for the playoffs? In their case, the answer is no. Six of the other longest streakers also would not have made it, and one, the 1977 Phillies, would have tied. It is a testament to the vagaries of the postseason, though, that one of the teams eliminated in this experiment is one of the two champions these fifteen produced—the '82 Cards. Three other such clubs, including the champion Twins of '91, would have barely squeaked in by a single game.

Is this all so much statistical self-amusement—that teams with twelve-game winning streaks do *worse* than those with ten- and eleven-game winning streaks—or does it actually prove anything? Perhaps only this: While having a lengthy winning streak may predispose a team to get *into* the playoffs, it is no predictor of success once *in* the playoffs.

What, then, is a streak? Think of it as a massive correction performed sequentially.

The reason we know this is the Pythagorean record. Baseball is a complex game with a very simple objective: to score more runs than the other team. To that end, it would make sense that the best team in a given season is not only the one with the most wins, but also the one that scores the most runs in relation to the runs they allow. In his 1980 *Baseball Abstract*, Bill James demonstrated that a team's total runs scored and allowed do indeed have a predictable relationship to wins and losses. In nearly every case, this equation—

$$\frac{(\text{runs scored})^2}{(\text{runs scored})^2 + (\text{runs allowed})^2} = \text{winning percentage}$$

—produced a result that almost exactly matched a team's actual record. Because the equation's three squares are reminiscent of the Pythagorean theorem ($a^2 + b^2 = c^2$), its result has been dubbed a team's Pythagorean record.

Over time, James's followers, including BP's own Clay Davenport, discovered that this formula was not only a bridge from runs to wins, but that the resulting winning percentage was a stronger in-season predictor of future team performance than actual record. As a result, a team's Pythagorean record came to be used as a barometer of the true quality of that team. In his 1982 *Abstract*, James wrote, "In 1981 the standard error of these calculations was 3.69 [wins]; over time it has averaged 4.30 wins per team-season. This is to say that we do not really expect that the team which scored 700 runs and allowed 600 would win *exactly* 93 games, but that they would win 89 to 97 games most of the time." To Davenport, however, the predictive power of the Pythagorean record proved that such deviations were not simply random—that is, a team that outperformed its Pythagorean record had been in some way lucky or overly efficient, while a team that underperformed its Pythagorean record had been unlucky or inefficient.

At the beginning of the twenty-first century, the Pythagorean record revealed to Red Sox fans the existence of an alternate reality in which their team had just won three American League East titles that they'd been denied in actuality. In 2000, the defending World Champion New York Yankees won the American League East by two games, despite trailing Boston by one game according to their Pythagorean record. The Red Sox failed to make the playoffs that year, while the Yankees went on to win their third-straight World Championship. In 2002, the Yankees again finished the season one Pythagorean win behind the Red Sox, yet won the East by a whopping ten games, forcing Boston to once again watch the postseason on television. In 2004, the Red Sox finished the season with 98 wins, exceeding their Pythagorean record for the first time since 1999. Vexingly, the Yankees finished with a Pythagorean record of 89–73, but in actuality won 101 games and the division.

RED SOX	ACTUAL			PYTHAGOREAN			
	W	L	Pct	W	L	Pct	Diff.
2004	98	64	0.605	96	66	**0.593***	2
2003	95	67	0.586	94	68	0.580	1
2002	93	69	0.574	100	62	**0.617**	−7
2001	82	79	0.509	83	78	0.516	−1
2000	85	77	0.525	86	76	**0.531**	−1
1999	94	68	0.580	92	70	0.568	2
1998	92	70	0.568	94	68	0.580	−2
Avg.	91.3	70.6	0.564	92.1	69.7	0.569	−0.86

YANKEES	ACTUAL			PYTHAGOREAN			
	W	L	Pct	W	L	Pct	Diff.
2004	101	61	0.623	89	73	0.549	12
2003	101	61	0.623	96	66	**0.593**	5
2002	103	58	0.640	99	62	0.615	4
2001	95	65	0.594	89	71	**0.556**	6
2000	87	74	0.540	85	76	0.528	2
1999	98	64	0.605	96	66	**0.593**	2
1998	114	48	0.704	108	54	**0.667**	6
Avg.	99.9	61.6	0.619	94.6	66.9	0.586	5.29

*Boldface denotes Pythagorean division winner.

True believers in the Pythagorean record would view those three seasons as the sad but true results of a capricious game in which the best team does not always prevail. However, while the Pythagorean record is a stronger predictor of future performance during a given season, by the time the sample has grown to 162 games, actual record is as good or better an indicator of the quality of a team. In other words, in the final accounting, the Red Sox were exactly what they were meant to be, no cheating by the cosmos, no mercurial God playing dice with the universe.

With luck removed from the equation, the Yankees' ability to consistently exceed their Pythagorean record becomes a subject of great interest; their ability to transcend the limitations of runs scored and allowed is akin to defying gravity. Rather than be satisfied with the facile explanation of sustained good luck, we can now ask, "What is it the Yankees are doing to achieve this?" Knowing the answer would have been especially handy in 2004, when the Yankees became just the third team in history to beat their Pythagorean records by twelve or more games:

		ACTUAL			PYTHAGOREAN			
Year	Team	W	L	Pct.	W	L	Pct.	Diff.
1905	Tigers	79	74	0.516	65	88	0.425	14
2004	Yankees	101	61	0.623	89	73	0.549	12
1984	Mets	90	72	0.556	78	84	0.481	12
1954	Dodgers	92	62	0.597	81	73	0.526	11
1972	Mets	83	73	0.532	72	84	0.462	11
1924	Robins	92	62	0.597	81	73	0.526	11
1970	Reds	102	60	0.630	91	71	0.562	11
1943	Braves	68	85	0.444	58	95	0.379	10
1961	Reds	93	61	0.604	83	71	0.539	10
1932	Pirates	86	68	0.558	76	78	0.494	10

With the exception of the mid-fifties Brooklyn Dodgers and the mid-eighties New York Mets, every team on the list also fell short of their Pythagorean expectations in one of the following two seasons, indicating that there is something exceptional occurring when a team consistently exceeds its Pythagorean record, as the Yankees did during the seven consecutive seasons in which they and the Red Sox finished first and second, respectively, in the American League East. During that time, the Red Sox fell short of their Pythagorean expectations by an average of 0.86 games per season, while the Yankees exceeded theirs by an average of more than five and a quarter games per year.

So what were the Yankees doing? They were losing big and winning small. It was often said that the 2004 Yankees had 61 "comeback wins." Though this term was never properly explained (if a team trails 0–1 in the second inning, scores two in the third, and wins 16–2, is that a comeback win?), it suggests a great number of small-margin wins. On September 1, 2004, the Yankees also suffered the largest margin of defeat in franchise history when the Cleveland Indians pounded them, 22–0. Simply removing that one loss adds two wins to the Yankees' Pythagorean record.

Looking at the fourteen Yankee and Red Sox teams from 1998 to 2004, the 2004 Yankees were just one of two with a greater average run differential in their losses than in their wins. The 2001 Yankees, who exceeded their Pythagorean record by 6 games, won 95 games by an average margin of 3.58 runs while losing 65 by an average of 3.83. The 2004 Yankees, meanwhile, won 101 games by a similar average of 3.59 runs, but lost their 61 games by an average of 4.49 runs, the greatest average margin of defeat of the fourteen teams by more than a third of a run and almost a full run more than the average margin of defeat.

Conversely, of those fourteen teams, the 2002 Red Sox's average margin of victory exceeded their average margin of defeat by the greatest amount (more than a third of a run more than the second closest team, the 1998 Sox). The 2002 Red Sox's average margin of defeat was 3.13 runs, while their average margin of victory was 4.41, easily the largest of the fourteen teams in question. As one might expect, that team fell the farthest short of their Pythagorean record, finishing seven wins below expectations.

The question now becomes whether there is something about the makeup of those teams that leads to these patterns of losing big and winning close or vice versa. In July 1999, Rany Jazayerli and Keith Woolner performed a study for BP that suggested that teams with good bullpens (which they defined as "only those relievers used in tight games") are more likely to exceed their Pythagorean record while teams with bad bullpens are more likely to fall short. The basic logic is that a team with strong relievers can protect small leads and thus win close games, while a team with poor relievers has to win big lest its poor relief pitching turn a slim lead into a loss. The former holds true for the 2004 Yankees, who in Tom

Gordon and Mariano Rivera had an absolutely dominant pair of short relievers who combined for a 2.08 ERA in 168⅓ innings converting 57 saves and recording 36 holds. Meanwhile, the 2002 Red Sox bullpen lost 22 games, and other than left-handed specialist Alan Embree, a midseason acquisition, no Boston reliever recorded more than five holds that year.

By the same logic, teams with good bullpens that also happen to have poor starting rotations are more likely to overachieve by winning small and losing big, while the opposite is true for teams with weaker bullpens but excellent rotations. Again, this is supported by the 2004 Yankees and the 2002 Red Sox. The 2004 Yankees' starting pitchers posted a combined 4.82 ERA, almost a third of a run worse than league average. Only Orlando Hernandez finished the season with an ERA under 4.00, doing so in just 84.2 innings of work. Conversely, the 2002 Red Sox had an outstanding 3.52 starters ERA, thanks largely to dual twenty-game winners Pedro Martinez (2.26) and Derek Lowe (2.58) and the 2.39 ERA of swingman Tim Wakefield. Meanwhile, both teams finished second in the major leagues in runs per game on offense (to one another). The 2002 Red Sox pounded opposing pitching, but dominated opposing hitters, leading to a tremendous average margin of victory, but their downfall was a shaky bullpen, which resulted in numerous close losses. The 2004 Yankees routinely engaged in slugfests with the opposition, frequently outlasting them due to a strong back of the pen, but occasionally falling so far behind in the early going that manager Joe Torre forced an unfortunate starter or long reliever to take one for the team, running up the team's runs allowed in the process.

NUMBER OF GAMES

Margin of Victory/Defeat	2004 Yankees (+12)	2004 Red Sox (+2)	2002 Red Sox (−7)
+5 or more	27	36	34
1 to 4	74	64	59
−1 to −4	33	42	50
−5 or more	28	20	19

As it turns out, the true measure of a team is not its ability to score a lot of runs over the course of a season while allowing few, but its ability to outscore its opponent on any given day, be it 1–0, 10–1 or 20–19—proving once again that it's not how you play the game but whether you win or lose.

Despite the early June losing streak, the Pythagorean record, comfortably in its in-season role, suggested that the Red Sox were due to turn things around. They could console themselves on June 5 with the thought that Curt Schilling was pitching against the Royals in the second game of the series. One auspicious aspect of this matchup for Boston: Schilling was as unlikely to issue a walk as any American League starter other than Brad Radke of the Twins; the Royals, on the other hand, continuing a tradition as old as the franchise, were among the least likely teams to take one. Schilling had pitched a complete game against Kansas City the previous month, striking out eight without walking a batter. This time he was not nearly as sharp, but he was good enough to take an 8–3 lead into the seventh, when he began to fatigue. Matt Stairs worked Schilling for a rare walk in the seventh, later scoring. (Stairs would go on to be the team leader in walks with 49; as an indication of the Royals deficiencies in this regard, Stairs led the team while starting only 117 games.) The Red Sox won, 8–4, ending their short nightmare.

The next start went to Derek Lowe, who was much better this time out, yet still had to rely on his mates for some midgame comeback drama. Since becoming a starter in 2002, Lowe had been on the receiving end of the most generous run support in all of baseball. Here's the run support received by Boston starters and their rank among American League leaders:

2002
6.84: Lowe (second in the American League)
6.45: John Burkett (sixth)
6.23: Martinez (eighth)
5.57: Wakefield (sixteenth)
3.97: Frank Castillo (thirty-seventh)

2003
7.26: Lowe (first)
6.03: Martinez (eighth)
5.83: Wakefield (thirteenth)
5.25: Burkett (twenty-fifth)

2004
7.54: Schilling (first)
7.29: Lowe (second)
6.07: Wakefield (eleventh)
5.79: Arroyo (fourteenth)
5.60: Martinez (twentieth)

This support has allowed Lowe to rack up a Hall of Fame–caliber winning percentage. In reality, he has pitched more like a .500 pitcher over the course of his starting career, as these Baseball Prospectus metrics show:

Actual Win-Loss/Expected Win-Loss
2002: 21–8 / 16–8 (Luck rating: 4.7—thirty-second-highest in baseball)
2003: 17–7 / 11–13 (Luck rating: 12.2—third-highest in baseball)
2004: 14–12 / 8–16 (Luck rating: 10.1—third-highest in baseball)

Lowe finished the fifth inning trailing 3–0 after holding the Royals to a walk and three hits, one of them a 2-run homer by Mike Sweeney. In the top of the sixth, the Red Sox rallied against Royals starter Chris George. In 2003, George had enjoyed Lowe-like support and almost single-handedly proved the folly of paying more than modest attention to pitchers' win-loss records; he went 9–6 and nearly led the team in wins despite coughing up 22 homers in just 93⅔ innings and accumulating an ERA of 7.11. In the sixth, George allowed his fourth and fifth walks of the day, and that was the end of him. Jason Grimsley came in to relieve and that was the end of the Royals. After allowing another walk and a 2-run single to David Ortiz. Grimsley departed in favor of Jose Cerda, who allowed two more hits and another walk. By this time it was 5–3 and it could have been worse if Jason Varitek hadn't hit into a double play to end the inning. Mike Timlin then entered the game to hold the lead. The hold statistic is justly derided for being too forgiving of a poor performance—a middle reliever is credited with a hold when he enters a game in a save situation, records at least one out, and exits without having given up the lead whether he allows no runs or twenty—but Timlin's performance was the kind the statistic was invented to credit. He hurled three perfect innings before handing the ball to Keith Foulke to close out the game.

This was, in a way, textbook Boston Red Sox baseball: The team got a passable performance from its worst pitcher, a textbook middle relief job, an effective closeout, and an offense that worked the opposition for seven walks. Lowe got the win from the bench. Come October, he would go on to repay the Red Sox for their earlier offensive favoritism.

San Diego and David Wells were next. On June 2, Pedro Martinez's worst start since April 2003 had helped perpetuate the crisis atmosphere. Now he would be asked to sustain the recovery. Martinez went eight, walking one, hitting one, and surrendering two hits. Boston scored a run on doubles by Gabe Kapler and Johnny Damon to win the first 1–0 game at Fenway Park since the 2001 season. More remarkably, the Red Sox did not draw a walk, just one of the three times it happened all year. The first was in their 5–4 victory over the Yankees on April 19. The other occasion was the 8–2 victory over Baltimore on July 30. They were also held walkless once in the playoffs, the Game One 10–7 loss to the Yankees.

With these three wins, the starting pitcher mini-crisis came to a close. In the end, Boston would have one of the two most stable rotations in baseball. Their five designated starters started 157 of their games. (Oakland matched this number, and eventual World Series opponent St. Louis got 154 out of their five starters.) By contrast, the Yankees only got 126 starts out of their five most-active pitchers and gave starting assignments to a total of 12 different hurlers, proving that rotation stability is not a prerequisite for team success. But it helps: Of the top eight clubs in this category, five were playoff teams and only one of this group, the much-improved Tigers, finished below .500. Any manager who doesn't have to sweat the identity of a starting pitcher is a happier manager.

Not that Terry Francona was done thinking. The rotation may have been stable, but his infield was not. The organization would soon be forced to confront the diminished possibilities of one of baseball's biggest stars, Nomar Garciaparra.

—JIM BAKER AND CLIFFORD J. CORCORAN

12

NOMAR'S SPRING AND REGRESSION TO THE MEAN
JUNE 9, 2004

Pedro Martinez's 1–0 win over the Padres on June 8 set the stage for a Red Sox revival. After four straight losses, the team had reeled off three straight wins. Their 34–23 record was still second best in the league and optimism about the team's pitching ran high. But the Red Sox remained two and a half games behind the red-hot Yankees, and serious doubts about the health of Bill Mueller and Trot Nixon, as well as the irrefutability of Pokey Reese's limitations, dampened the atmosphere. The offense needed a nudge from Nomar. Now, after fifty-seven games without their star shortstop, the Red Sox were getting him back.

Along with Alex Rodriguez and Derek Jeter, Garciaparra belonged to the Holy Trinity of shortstops, the best troika at the pivotal position since Cal Ripken, Alan Trammell, and Robin Yount dominated the position in the 1970s and 1980s—maybe the best trio ever. Nomar was the 1997 AL Rookie of the Year, a seven-time .300 hitter, a six-time 20-home-run hitter, a five-time All-Star and MVP top-ten finisher, and a two-time batting champ. He had been the heart and soul of the Red Sox for the last eight seasons.

Garciaparra had burst onto the scene in 1997 with one of the best starts by any shortstop. The following stats are batting average, on-base percentage, slugging percentage, and Equivalent Average (EqA), which is an all-in-one stat that takes offensive contributions and boils it down to one number with a scale similar to batting average. Thus a .260 hitter is average, a .300 hitter is very good, and a .200 hitter is Rey Ordonez:

Nomar Garciaparra tests his
inflamed Achilles tendon

Year	Production	Age
1997	.306/.342/.534, .291 EqA	23
1998	.323/.362/.584, .315 EqA	24
1999	.357/.418/.603, .335 EqA	25
2000	.372/.434/.599, .340 EqA	26

Note the accelerating batting average, OBP, and EqA numbers. Even in the current high-offense era, Garciaparra's .340 EqA in 2000 achieved rarefied air. Just one shortstop (Alex Rodriguez) has topped a .340 EqA in the last decade. Only twenty players have done it all told, every one of them an elite player such as Bonds, McGwire, Sosa, and Pujols.

Player	Years	Ages	AVG/OBP/SLG	Composite EqA
Arky Vaughan	1932–1935	20–23	.337/.422/.502	.325
Nomar Garciaparra	**1997–2000**	**23–26**	**.337/.386/.577**	**.320**
Alex Rodriguez	1996–1999	20–23	.314/.371/.567	.314
Hans Wagner	1898–1901	24–27	.341/.394/.490	.308
Derek Jeter	1996–1999	22–25	.319/.391/.467	.303
Cal Ripken Jr.	1982–1985	21–24	.297/.362/.490	.302
Ernie Banks	1954–1957	23–26	.288/.347/.533	.296

Even removed from the traditionally limited world of shortstops, it was a career-starting run that rivaled some of the all-time greats. Here is a sample (chosen at random) of twelve fast-starters, pre– and post–World War II, with the first year, as above, defined as the first season in which the player played a minimum of a hundred games:

Player	Years	Ages	AVG/OBP/SLG	Composite EqA
Ted Williams	1939–1942	20–23	.356/.481/.642	.368
Frank Thomas	1991–1994	23–26	.326/.449/.596	.368
Johnny Mize	1936–1939	23–26	.346/.425/.605	.341
Albert Pujols	2001–2004	21–24	.333/.413/.624	.338
Lou Gehrig	1922–1925	22–25	.342/.437/.630	.337
Joe DiMaggio	1936–1939	21–24	.341/.397/.622	.325
Mickey Mantle	1952–1955	20–23	.303/.408/.542	.325
Mel Ott	1928–1931	19–22	.323/.427/.547	.321

Nomar Garciaparra	1997–2000	23–26	.337/.386/.577	.320
Jimmie Foxx	1928–1931	20–23	.327/.423/.598	.314
Vladimir Guerrero	1998–2001	22–25	.323/.384/.604	.314
Ken Griffey Jr.	1989–1992	19–22	.301/.366/.494	.311

A start of this historic caliber raises expectations sky-high. Since Garciaparra had improved in each of his first four seasons, it was only natural to expect him to continue to do so. Granted, he was a little older than Ted Williams, Joe DiMaggio, and Mickey Mantle in his first four years, but he was entering the 2001 season at just twenty-seven, an age at which many players hit their peak. There were even whispers that Nomar would take a real run at a .400 batting average, a feat not accomplished since fellow Sox Williams turned the apparently obsolete trick in 1941.

On March 5, 2001, Garciaparra appeared shirtless on the cover of *Sports Illustrated*, holding a bat and glaring. The caption read: "A Cut Above: How Boston's Nomar Garciaparra Made Himself the Toughest Out in Baseball." The article by Tom Verducci marveled at Garciaparra's ability to hit any pitcher in any situation. Nomar, Verducci explained, usually had no idea who that day's starter was, and almost never watched video, except of himself. The article noted that Garciaparra's .372 batting average in 2000 was the highest by a right-handed hitter since Joe DiMaggio hit .381 in 1939. "Sweat and science have made Garciaparra . . . perhaps the toughest out in baseball," fawned Verducci, "and, according to Ted Williams himself, the first man in 60 years who could hit .400."

All across America, Red Sox fans winced. Everything about it pointed to a jinx: the beefcake pose, the fate-tempting Williams endorsement, and of course the fact that being on the cover of *Sports Illustrated* had jinxed countless athletes in the past. But, although some say the magazine should be called *Santeria Illustrated* for its voodoo-like influenza, there is a down-to-earth reason why so many of its cover boys soon take a turn for the worse. The further any trend drifts toward one extreme or another, the greater the force that pulls that trend back toward the average. The phenomenon is known as regression to the mean, and it explains why an athlete, who is on the cover precisely because he has approached or reached the limits of his excellence, is almost certainly going to experience an imminent decline.

Fate, however, had more in mind for Nomar than mere regression. Two days after the *SI* cover story hit the newsstands, a team physician diagnosed him with "a small longitudinal split in an ECU (extensor carpi ulnaris) tendon . . . and inflammation of the tendon." There was speculation that he also might have broken some bones and suffered a "cubital tunnel" injury. Cubital tunnel syndrome refers to pressure on the ulnar nerve behind the funny bone, causing numbness and tingling in the ring and small fingers of the hand. Though the injury often occurs as a result of gradual wear, a direct hit on the tunnel can damage the ulnar nerve and surrounding area.

NOMAR BEFORE THE FALL:
TOP SINGLE-SEASON EqA BY SHORTSTOPS

	Year	Team	EqA	WARP
1. Arky Vaughan	1935	PIT-N	.372	15.3
2. Alex Rodriguez	2000	SEA-A	.346	14.3
3. Honus Wagner	1908	PIT-N	.344	14.9
4. Lou Boudreau	1948	CLE-A	.341	13.3
4. Alex Rodriguez	1996	SEA-A	.341	13.9
5. Nomar Garciaparra	**2000**	**BOS-A**	**.340**	**11.3**
6. Derek Jeter	1999	NYY-A	.337	11.0
6. Cal Ripken	1991	BAL-A	.337	14.9
7. Robin Yount	1982	MIL-A	.336	11.8
8. Nomar Garciaparra	**1999**	**BOS-A**	**.335**	**11.0**
8. Alex Rodriguez	2001	TEX-A	.335	13.5

And a direct hit is what Nomar had suffered a year and a half before, on September 25, 1999, when Baltimore reliever Al Reyes hit Garciaparra on the wrist with a pitch. Though the initial injury seemed to have little lingering effect—Garciaparra played the entire 2000 season with some pain and discomfort, but missed no games due to the injury— it would change Nomar's career forever. Given that he hit .372 that season, you'd have forgiven Brian Daubach for standing in front of the pitching machine, arm dangling over the heart of the plate, hoping that something vital got broken.

"There wasn't a time when I felt like I even needed to ice it," Garciaparra would later say, but the spring 2001 recurrence rang alarm bells. Garciaparra quickly developed extensive swelling in the wrist and couldn't grip a bat or throw a ball. The team hoped that he'd be fitted with a soft cast, wear it for a week or two, and rehab quickly. Garciaparra was adamant about avoiding surgery, but less than two weeks later, after an independent review of an MRI and X-rays, doctors raised the possibility. A week after that, Garciaparra had his cast removed, hoping the wrist had healed enough for him to avoid surgery. He started on a regimen of exercises designed to increase the mobility of his wrist and get it back into playing shape. His intention was to be ready for Opening Day—just two weeks away. Less than a week after that, though, a hand specialist persuaded Garciaparra to go under the knife, which he did finally at the start of April, just three days after the Red Sox, under the gun with an April 1 deadline, exercised Garciaparra's $11.5 million option for the 2004 season—three years away.

Garciaparra would play in only twenty-one games in 2001, and the Sox would struggle to an 82–79 record. Though he bounced back to post robust EqAs of .300 and .294 in 2003 and 2004—tremendous production compared to most shortstops in baseball history—the numbers were still way down from his remarkable 1999 and 2000 efforts. The surgery had only minimized the pain and done nothing to prevent recurrence. Though Garciaparra shielded most of the recurrences from public view, it's likely that his wrist had flared up dozens of times since 2001, triggered by everything from weather to overusage to how he slept. It took the Red Sox a while for the cold reality of the situation to sink in: They still had Nomar, one of the best in the game and a great asset to the team, but never again would they have "Nomaaaaaaaaah!"

Nonetheless, the Sox were hoping to hammer out a contract extension by Opening Day 2004 that would keep Garciaparra in Boston well into his mid-thirties. The figures were rumored to be for four or five years, at about $13–$14 million a year. Before the discussions could really warm up, though, the team developed doubts about the wisdom of offering a player with his injury history a contract lasting so many years. Talk of $70 million contracts soon faded. As if confirming the team's judgment, Garciaparra unexpectedly showed up at camp wearing a cast on his lower right leg. It was a Grade 2 sprain, meaning the Achilles tendon was partially torn. With such an injury, the foot has to be immobilized, the weight taken off it with a boot and crutches. The injury heals slowly as blood struggles to flow to the affected area (tendons are ill-served by the circulatory system, being something of a side road off the blood highway). When reports of his injury first circulated in March, the Red Sox indicated Garciaparra would miss just a few games with what they thought was a bruised right heel. After just two games off, Garciaparra returned to the lineup for a March 10 contest against the Reds. All seemed well.

An MRI taken March 18 "revealed mild tendonitis but showed no structural deficits." He remained out. Ten days later, the Sox placed Garciaparra on the disabled list. While Garciaparra sat, questions began cropping up. How had he hurt himself? Some hinted at an undisclosed, soccer-related injury. When would he be back? No one seemed to know. Would he be 100 percent when he returned?

When Garciaparra jumped back into the lineup on June 9, 2004, the joy was tainted by mistrust. Red Sox fans had staked their hopes on Garciaparra in the past, only to see him sidelined at key moments. Would this Achilles tendon injury that cost him the season's first nine-plus weeks wreck his season the way his wrist injury wrecked his 2001 season and limited him for the next two years? Even if he returned to full health, here was a player four years removed from his best season, and a month shy of his thirty-first birthday.

Batting fifth between Manny Ramirez and Jason Varitek on his first day back, Nomar managed a single in two at-bats, a respectable first effort of the season. But the team's bats mostly fell silent, as Brian Lawrence and the Padres rolled to an 8–1 win. Back in the fifth spot the next day, the shortstop slammed a two-run double to lead a five-run fifth inning that propelled the team to a 9–3 rout of San Diego. The Sox got a scare when Garciaparra was hit by a pitch just above the left knee in the seventh inning. Manager Terry Francona joked after the game, "He said the good news was when he got hit by the pitch the other areas didn't hurt." The gallows humor continued the next day. About stumbling over second base while fielding a ball up the middle in the ninth, Nomar quipped, "Somebody just moved the bag. . . . I'll have to get with the grounds crew on that."

After taking two of three from the Padres, Boston's offense struggled with the Dodgers in town, putting up only eleven runs in three games at Fenway. Nomar sat out the first game of the Dodgers series, then took an 0-for-5 collar in the series' last two games. Though he drew two walks and even stole a base in the series, he had failed to stroke an extra-base hit since his return, and he certainly didn't look like the line-drive machine of old. The Sox packed their bags and headed to a struggling batter's favorite spa, Coors Field, but Garciaparra managed just a single in four trips in a 6–3 loss. He rapped a pair of singles in game two, but the Sox lost again, 7–6. Suddenly Boston found itself five and a half games behind the Yankees, and 6–7 for the month of June.

Game three brought better tidings. Derek Lowe, the owner of a 6.84 ERA entering June, logged an amazing seventeen ground-ball outs to just one flyout against the Rockies, pitching seven shutout innings in a start that could have served as a primer on how to pitch well at Coors Field. David Ortiz banged out three hits, Johnny Damon, Reese, and the recently activated Trot Nixon two each. The Sox stormed to an 11–0 win, picking up a game on the Yankees. The best news of all was Garciaparra's 3-for-5 performance. The highlight came in the seventh, one out after an Ortiz homer, when Nomar lashed a line drive into the gap in left-center and legged out a triple, suggesting that maybe, just maybe, his Achilles had healed.

As the team pulled into San Francisco, the Red Sox offense was in for a sterner test since the spacious dimensions of SBC Park tends to smother well-hit balls. (In 2004, it was about 10 percent harder to hit a home run in San Francisco than in the average National League park; the uniquely talented—possibly uniquely fueled—Barry Bonds hit 18 percent of all home runs hit in the park.) Boston's bats picked up where they had left off in Colorado, pounding out fourteen hits and five homers en route to a 14–9 win. Garciaparra managed just one hit in five at-bats, but for the second straight game the one hit was a triple. After a scheduled day off to rest his recuperating leg—a 6–4 Red Sox loss—he returned to the lineup for the rubber match on June 20. A win would lift the Sox back over .500 for the month; a loss would drop them to 8–9. Against a dominating Jason Schmidt, the Giants' ace, the Sox managed a paltry one hit and lost, 4–0. Batting in the cleanup spot, Garciaparra went hitless.

By the time the Sox returned home to host the Twins and an inter-league series with the Phillies, the natives were restless. A couple of Yankee losses kept the AL East margin at four and a half games. Boston's lead in the wild card race—a topic under increasing discussion—had shrunk to one game. With a three-game set in the Bronx just a week away, Boston needed to hold serve at home.

Once again, an offensive outburst gave the Sox hope for a turnaround. The team collected thirteen hits against Kyle Lohse and the Minnesota bullpen, romping 9–2. Though Garciaparra went just 1-for-5, his one hit seemed a harbinger of his complete recovery. Up 3–1 in the bottom of the seventh, the Sox started stringing together hits. After a two-run double by David Ortiz made it 5–1, the Twins decided to walk the always potent Manny Ramirez with runners on second and third and pitch to Garciaparra. Pitcher Joe Roa may have thought he was facing the diminished hitter Garciaparra had been the last two weeks, but at last he became Metronomar, the erstwhile hitting machine, and smashed a Roa pitch over the wall in center field, a grand slam. The Fenway faithful cheered lustily. Sure, this was the supremely hittable Joe Roa, not some late-inning flame-thrower, but with two triples and a homer in the last four games, and hits in five of his last six, it looked like Garciaparra had finally turned a corner. When he followed with three more hits over the next two games, the heart of the Red Sox appeared to be beating again.

But the Sox dropped the last two games of the Twins series. The series' rubber match was decided in the tenth inning, when a Garciaparra error led to the Twins' winning run. When the Sox followed by erupting for twenty-six runs and two wins out of three against the Phillies, Nomar suddenly went cold again, going 1-for-12.

When the sun rose June 29, the damage to the good ship Red Sox was extensive. The team had fallen to five and a half games out of first, had gone 11–12 in June, and Garciaparra's return, it had to be said, had been a bust. In fifteen games, the shortstop had managed a brutal line of .233/.277/.400. Nomar was not the defensive asset he once was, either, and the Sox could have been forgiven—this was a frightening thought—for wondering whether Pokey Reese wasn't such a bad option after all.

The stage was set for a showdown with the Yankees. But while Derek Jeter would make highlight reel history with an ill-advised swan dive into the third-base side seats, Nomar Garciaparra took a nosedive on the field, going 2-for-8 with two harmless singles in the series' first two games, then taking a day off in the third matchup. His absence from the thrilling, thirteen-inning series finale symbolized his increasing irrelevance. He was fading away, becoming a ghost, a memory, right before fans' and teammates' eyes.

—JONAH KERI

13

BETTER WINNING
THROUGH CHEMISTRY
JULY 1–3, 2004

In a world where much is still made of the primitive notion of team chemistry, the July 1–3 series in Yankee Stadium would have to be considered the big chemistry test for the 2004 Red Sox team. The circumstances this time were not as innocent as those of April's trip. The Yankees had now been in charge of first place for the past month. Over the past eight games, the Red Sox had gone 3–5 and surrendered a further two games to the Yankees, hitting the field in the Bronx on June 29, five and a half games out of first. If the gap wasn't closed in this series, it would be time to start thinking constructively about the wild card.

It was around this time that Johnny Damon introduced the concept that the Red Sox were "just a bunch of idiots." Desperately needing a label or catchphrase, the media (having beaten 2003's "Cowboy Up" to a bloody pulp), jumped on it indiscriminately. As inexplicable as "Cowboy Up" is going to be decades from now when those too young to remember it try to decipher its meaning, the "Idiots" tag will be an even greater linguistic nut to crack in that it did nothing to describe the team. Honed by some of the finest minds in the game, the brand of baseball played by the Red Sox was anything but idiotic. Even Kevin Millar, the player most closely associated with the phrase, is someone who makes the most out of his modest skills by intelligently playing the type of game that best utilizes those skills. The history of baseball is littered with the prematurely extinguished careers of men who never latched on to this simple concept.

151

Ramirez and Mueller, embracing the
concept of team chemistry

The media, though, used to decades of sullen Red Sox teams lacking in both esprit de corps and joie de vivre, were quick to exploit this angle. The 2004 Sox, it was said, had something their forebears did not: team chemistry—whatever that is. One thing it surely *wasn't* was a prerequisite for a winning team. Consider the 1986 Red Sox, remembered for their "25 players, 25 taxicabs" approach to team bonding. They came within one out of winning it all. If chemistry is such an important component in a team's makeup, then it should have been impossible for this House of Negativity team to roar back from a three games to one deficit to defeat the Angels in the American League Championship Series, or to rally from a 5–2 deficit down to their last two outs in Game Five. By contrast, the 2003 "Cowboy Up" Red Sox, with custom-made T-shirts and all manner of love for their fellow man, were driven off before reaching the World Series.

Derek Lowe faced Javier Vazquez in the opener of three. Lowe had spent the month of June in an ERA-reduction program. This entailed shutting out the Dodgers for seven innings on June 11 and then doing the same to the Rockies, in Coors Field no less, on his next rotation turn. His subsequent outing was a little more problematic—four runs in seven innings against Minnesota—but there was now reason to believe his mates might not have to brace him with their usual offensive pyrotechnics in order to ensure a victory. As it turned out, even his typical allotment of seven runs wouldn't have been enough. Lowe surrendered a career-high nine runs in five innings, the coup de grâce coming when Tony Clark relocated a batted ball to the very distant center field bleachers. Earlier, Derek Jeter and Alex Rodriguez had engineered a double steal that set up a two-run single by Lowe nemesis Hideki Matsui. Final: Yankees 11, Red Sox 3.

It was still possible for Boston to leave New York with a better résumé than the one they brought to town, and when the first three Red Sox batters singled in the top of the first off Jon Leiber to take a 1–0 lead of the second game, it appeared they might do just that. But the promising rally was doused when Manny Ramirez hit into a double play and Nomar Garciaparra fouled out. The lead held, though, and the Sox doubled it in the sixth when David Ortiz, who had also driven in the first run, homered over the right field fence. The Red Sox loaded the bases with nobody out in the seventh and the Yankees summoned Felix Heredia to keep things close. With his ERA at 7.45, he had not been asked to do much heavy lifting; an inspection of the final scores in his previous four outings illustrate the relaxed climate in which Heredia had been working: 2–13, 3–9, 11–6, and 11–3. Yet heavy lift he did, setting down first-inning ralliers Johnny Damon and Mark Bellhorn to bring up Ortiz. Heredia got him looking. It was not to be Ortiz's worst moment of the inning. In the home half, Tim Wakefield, who had been cruising with a three-hitter, began to tire. He hit Gary Sheffield with a pitch and then with one out walked Matsui. Scott Williamson relieved and got a second out, but then walked the bases loaded before departing himself (to the dismay of his teammates) with arm trouble. Mike Timlin came in and appeared to have preserved the shutout when he induced Clark to hit a hard grounder to Ortiz at first that squirted through his glove into right field. (One has to wonder if it was in the moments just after this play that the Red Sox began contemplating a move to get Doug Mientkiewicz from the Twins, which they did a month later. If the Red Sox were going to go down in flames again, they'd be damned if it was because they had the wrong man playing first base.)

The error, or equipment failure, as Ortiz later explained, tied the score. In the next inning, an inaccurate throw by Garciaparra put Kenny Lofton on second base. Jeter then sacrificed him to third as part of a continuing campaign to make the Yankee shortstop the most inappropriate sacrifice bunter in the major leagues. Jeter laid down 16 sacrifices in 2004, a stunning total given the Yankees' firepower and Jeter's talent as a hitter. Looking at the top ten sacrificers for 2004, National League pitchers fill most of the bottom half of the list (Livan Hernandez and Kris Benson being the most accomplished there) with shortstops filling the top half. Royce Clayton of Colorado (24, 13 in Coors Field), Adam Everett of Houston (22), and Omar Vizquel of Cleveland (20) were the only players who had more sac bunts than Jeter. They are all men of sub-.400 slugging means, while Jeter's slugging percentage was .471 on the season. Bunting when you hit 44 doubles and 23 home runs a year is an act of unjustifiable modesty. Jeter had been sacrificing about three times a year for the seasons leading up to 2004, so perhaps this was compensation for his perception that he was not contributing earlier in the year when his batting average was depressed. No matter what the reason, it was wasteful—and, as it turned out, moot. Sheffield doubled and Lofton could have skipped home from second. An insurance run was added and Mariano Rivera was at his maddening best, striking out the side in the ninth.

A blowout loss and a blown late lead set the Red Sox stage for the third game, one that players raised in a media-intensive world understood to be a classic well before it was over. It was a marvelous game. Had these same events transpired between two lower-tier clubs in a stadium occupied by nine thousand people, it wouldn't have been any less of a masterpiece. On the grand stage of Yankee Stadium in the midst of the most heated rivalry in the sport, though, it was as magnificent a spectacle as an unrehearsed form of entertainment can muster. Consider the game's plot points:

- Pedro Martinez hitting Gary Sheffield in the first inning, sending the Yankee faithful into a retribution-obsessed frenzy. Memories of the previous year's playoff melee with departed coach Don Zimmer were instantly revived.
- A fresh-faced rookie pitcher (Brad Halsey) holding his own in his third big-league start.
- Jason Giambi, ostensibly sans parasite, appearing for the first time in five games.
- The Red Sox rallying from a 3–0 deficit.
- Pokey Reese performing an injury-defying act to snare a pop fly.
- Both teams loading the bases in extra innings and failing to score.
- Alex Rodriguez returning to shortstop, the position Jeter should have volunteered to vacate when A-Rod came on board the previous winter for the defensive betterment of the team. As it turned out, A-Rod would make just one other appearance there all year.
- Red Sox defensive shenanigans in the twelfth inning, in which five men were in the infield with the participants swapping gloves for maximum efficiency.
- The Yankees overcoming a 4–3 deficit in the bottom of the thirteenth.

Rodriguez's appearance at short was necessitated by Derek Jeter's all-out dive into the stands down the left field line to snare a pop-up to end the twelfth inning. Never mind the $60 million gap in their team payrolls, the prevailing attitude at the time was that this effort, more than any other, illustrated why it must always be so that the Yankees win out over the Red Sox. In fact, it was the opening sentiment of the AP wire story on the game: "Bloodied and bruised, Derek Jeter showed just why the New York Yankees always seem to come out ahead of Boston."

If Yankee fans were genuinely stunned and concerned as they watched their team captain, a victim of forward momentum, hurl himself Kurt Cobain–style into the crowd, there was ample reason: In addition to jeopardizing his season, Jeter's play was, on a percentage basis, not an especially smart one. Baseball has had its share of players who met unfortunate ends when tampering with immovable objects like railings, dugout steps, and walls. Red Sox third baseman Bill Mueller was playing for the Cubs in 2001 when his knee collided with the structural integrity of Wrigley Field brick, ending a very nice season. The most extreme cautionary tale relating to barrier avoidance is that of Pete Reiser, a player who made a big noise in his first full year in the majors (1941) and then slowly unraveled after frequent collisions with the unpadded fences of the day. Entire book chapters have been dedicated to what Reiser's career could have been had he just played with a little more caution. As it was, according to unofficial counts, he was hauled off the field horizontally at least ten times, leaving as his legacy an unnecessarily and unfortunately sketchy career. Another reckless charger of stationary objects was Earle Combs, the Hall of Fame center fielder of the Yankees, who lost several years of his career to unpadded barriers and whose retirement was hastened by a wall-induced, nearly fatal skull fracture.

In his 1982 *Baseball Abstract*, Bill James wrote eloquently on this very topic, using as his focus former Red Sox third baseman Butch Hobson, a former Crimson Tide quarterback who was, by that time, playing for the Angels. James contrasted Hobson's style of balls-out, hell-bent-for-leather play with that of Royals center fielder Amos Otis. He wrote: "Two years ago I saw a game in Kansas City in which the fans unmercifully booed Amos Otis, who had only given them about one good decade, because in one inning he pulled away from two balls he might have caught. First, he shied away from the wall on a drive that hit about seven feet high. Then he pulled up and played a ball on a hop when he might have caught it had he dived for it. *Might*, I say. The Kansas City fans will never forgive Amos for being a percentage player, but the Yankees scored only one run in that inning and Otis would drive in two before the game was over and the Royals had won."

As James points out, playing baseball like it's a football game is not in anyone's best interest, thanks to baseball scheduling. A game played once a week over the course of about four months invites a certain devil-may-care attitude from its participants. A game played virtually every day for six months, however, requires day-to-day durability, and that in turn requires a certain degree of self-preservation. In the course of a season, a team must inflict about 4,375 outs on its opponents, give or take, and to treat any one of them (except in the most extreme circumstances) as a matter of life and death is to lose sight of the big picture. This isn't to say that a player should never hustle except in critical situations, but that reckless endangerment of self—especially for players who operate significantly above replacement level, as Jeter did—is extremely ill-advised. Yet somebody like Jeter—indeed, almost any athlete who reaches the pros—simply does not know how to play any other way, and his momentum on the play probably made diving into the stands preferable to any other action. You cannot ask a player of this type to simply turn off the adrenaline. On a rational basis, though, with millions and millions of dollars at stake, another eighty-six games to run in the schedule, and the Yankees nearly certain of a return to the postseason, a little discretion can buy a lot of later valor.

Nomar Garciaparra, who was taking advantage of a scheduled off-day to rest his Achilles tendon, watched the play, as he had watched the entire game, huddled in the shadows of the dugout. His behavior, which could only be interpreted as either a sulk or a lack of interest in one of the more fiercely contested games of the teams' storied rivalry, conveyed the impression that he was not really a member of the team. Throughout the entire extra-inning contest, Garciaparra was nailed to the bench, a combustible chemical no sane team would want in its mix of personalities. Though Terry Francona tried to take the blame for not using his great shortstop, Garciaparra's impassivity, his apparent lack of interest in getting into the game, damaged, if not destroyed, his reputation in Boston.

Swept by the Yankees and left for dead, the entire team could have been excused for just slowly fading away, chemistry or no chemistry. Boston left town eight and a half games behind New York in the American League East. Red Sox fans could have been forgiven for wondering whether they had in fact been rooting for a downwardly mobile major league baseball team disguised as a powerhouse.

—JIM BAKER

THE FANNING FALLACY

The strikeout might be somewhat embarrassing on an individual basis, but it is clearly no hindrance to a productive offense.

During their three-game sweep by the Yankees, the Red Sox added twenty-eight more strikeouts to their rising season total; they would go on to lead the league in strikeouts and "achieve" the second-highest count in American League history. (The National League team record is much higher; with pitchers batting, there is an almost guaranteed extra strikeout per game above and beyond what a designated hitter chips in. In 2004, as a result of interleague play, Boston's pitchers would contribute only twelve Ks to the cause.) Here are the five easiest teams in American League history to strike out, along with their league rank in runs scored per game:

1996 TIGERS: 1,268 STRIKEOUTS
League rank in scoring: 11
Counter king: Melvin Nieves, 158
Most proficient: Nieves, 37%
Not with the program: Alan Trammell, 14%

There were a lot of things holding back the '96 Tigers and how often they were striking out was not one of them. They surrendered 241 home runs—the most ever served up by a pitching staff. The batters had the worst OBP in the league. They were just 17 walks shy of having the fewest in the league. An honorable mention has to go to Phil Nevin who did what he could in the few at-bats allotted him. He struck out 11 times in 21 trips to the plate.

2004 RED SOX: 1,189 STRIKEOUTS
League rank in scoring: 1
Counter king: Mark Bellhorn, 177 (16th all-time)
Most proficient: Bellhorn, 34%
Not with the program: Orlando Cabrera, 10%

Garciaparra was right there with Cabrera. Also not especially with the program was Johnny Damon at 11 percent.

1997 ATHLETICS: 1,181 STRIKEOUTS
League rank in scoring: 11
Counter king: Jose Canseco, 122
Most proficient: Ernie Young, 33%
Not with the program: Rafael Bournigal, 9%

The last of the really bad A's teams, they began their five-year improvement run the very next year. The building blocks were in place, though, as they were first in the league in walks and attempted the fewest stolen bases. Their problems were on the other side of the ball as the most wins they got out of a starting pitcher were six from Ariel Prieto. The highest VORP among anyone who started a game was 12.2 and belonged to Jimmy Haynes.

2002 YANKEES: 1,171 STRIKEOUTS
League rank in scoring: 1
Counter king: Alfonso Soriano, 157
Most proficient: Jorge Posada, 28%
Not with the program: Juan Rivera, 12%

The Yankees had five men in triple figures in strikeouts (and two more in the high 90s) and boy, did it ever cost them (just kidding). They led the league in walks and were second in home runs. Someday a club will come along that will have every one of its regulars striking out 100 times. By then, let's hope it is understood how little it matters.

2000 ATHLETICS: 1,159 STRIKEOUTS
League rank in scoring: 2
Counter king: Ben Grieve, 130
Most proficient: John Jaha, 39%
Not with the program: Terrence Long, 13%

A younger Mark Bellhorn was on hand, putting up 6 Ks in just thirteen at-bats. That places Bellhorn on three of these five teams, as he also spent his rookie year with the '97 A's, contributing 70 Ks to the cause. These A's led the league in homers, had the second-most walks and tried the fewest steals.

The 2004 Red Sox, spurred on greatly by the addition of Bellhorn, increased their team total by 250 strikeouts over 2003. This affected the offense so little that a case cannot even be made that there was an impact. Scoring dropped by 12 runs, a 1 percent difference. The team's league-leading on-base percentage held at .360.

For contrast, let's look at the Yankees. As we can see from the above, New York was whackin', watchin', and whiffin' with the best of them two years ago. Although Tony Clark, one of the men who drove the '96 Tigers to fanning immortality, was now on hand (with a 36 percent strikeout rate), the Yankees of 2004 still managed to clip 189 strikeouts off their team total from 2002. Not much changed. Their team OBP was about the same—.354 to .353—and they scored the exact same number of runs.

Here, then, we have two teams playing in the same period of time in the same division against the same opponents—in other words, the perfect teams to compare. One trimmed their total and the other ladled them on and neither saw any discernible difference in its offensive output.

What else, besides bats with a tendency to elude balls, do four of the above five teams have in common? That's right, they are drawn from the ranks of clubs run by progressive general managers. Sandy Alderson, Billy Beane, Brian Cashman, and Theo Epstein are men who understand that the stigma of the offensive strikeout is an undeserved one and don't let it stand in the way of assembling a good ballclub.

—JIM BAKER

14

BROTHERS OF
THE MIND GAME
JULY 6–8, 2004

After playing the Clanton Brothers to New York's Wyatt Earp in the Not-OK Corral of Yankee Stadium, Boston faced the possibility of reprising their disappointing 2002 season, when they had missed out on a playoff appearance by failing to keep up with the American League West's dueling duo, the A's and the Angels.

After going south to lose two out of three to the perennially contending Braves in Atlanta, the Sox came home to face the A's, whom they now trailed by a distressing three games in the wild card race. Statheads will point out that any game is equally valuable in the standings, but as the season goes on the prospect of actual playoff elimination inevitably lends the proceedings a new intensity. Losing three to the A's would hamper the front office with the trading deadline coming up at the end of the month. Winning the series would put them in a much stronger negotiating position since potential trading partners would not be able to use Boston's desperation as leverage.

The series was all the more dangerous because this would be Boston's first home stand against the A's since the two teams met in the playoffs the previous fall. The Athletics would be playing with the bitter memory of the fifth and final game of that series. It had been an ugly affair, marked by a fracas between Jason Varitek and Eric Byrnes at the plate, Manny Ramirez's leisurely admiration of the home run that gave Boston the lead, and Derek Lowe's obscene antics on the mound as the Sox

Oakland A's general manager,
Billy Beane

clinched. Boston had given the A's plenty of motivation to play hard against them now, at a time when what the Red Sox really needed were weak opponents.

The rivalry between the Red Sox and the Athletics represented something greater than a grudge match. This was a struggle between like-minded rivals. Oakland general manager Billy Beane and Theo Epstein shared philosophical viewpoints. Both had become dedicated to the school of offense centered on high on-base percentages and power while disdaining the batting average, the sacrifice bunt, and the stolen base. Both believed in the power of informed decision-making, seeking input from both scouts and statisticians, the search for undervalued sources of on-base percentage, and the targeted spending of money rather than mere profligacy.[1] But there was an important difference: Beane had to cope with the financial limitations of Oakland's relative trickle of a revenue stream, while Epstein's version of "moneyball" had a flood of money behind it.

Beane and Epstein both prized the same things in players, but where Beane would often have to work out deals to get them to Oakland—trading salaries away in order to take on salaries—Boston could afford to acquire players like Keith Foulke or Johnny Damon through free agency—former A's, in fact, who had become too expensive for the team. The Red Sox roster was a great compliment to Beane and the A's. It was as if Boston were a major studio producing a knockoff of a critically acclaimed indie film.

Recognizing that base runners equal runs equal wins isn't rocket science. Long before Pete Palmer, Bill James, or Baseball Prospectus, John McGraw, Joe McCarthy, and Earl Weaver were running offenses focused on getting men on base. This is the most important thing a lineup can do. Beane once boasted he wanted to field an offense that would post a .400 OBP. That wasn't the ranting of an ideologue, but a practical objective; to win, a team needs an offense that creates as many opportunities to score runs as possible. Every spring some manager will chirp that he thinks the answer to his team's problems will be more speed on the base paths, cutting down on strikeouts, or playing "fundamental" baseball. Indeed, there is something "fundamental" about all this: the fundamentally flawed assumption that you'll score more runs if you start giving away outs with the running game, the hit and run, or having nonpitchers bunt. Not that these tactical weapons don't have their place and time in a team's repertoire, but over the six-month march through the baseball season, the benefits of spending outs to get runs are surprisingly modest. In every game, a team's offense has twenty-seven outs to live. Giving away outs hastens mortality. It's chain-smoking for the jockstrap set.

Beane's pragmatism embraced minor league performance data. He understood that, translated correctly, this information could identify productive players who had been dismissed by the baseball establishment. Even better, having been dismissed, these players would come cheaply. Oakland became a place where hitters like Geronimo Berroa and Matt Stairs, and pitchers like Cory Lidle and Jason Isringhausen, could launch successful careers. He aggressively used every means available—not just free agency, but waivers, minor league free agency, and the minor league Rule 5 draft (in which players not protected on the forty-man roster may be purchased by other teams) held every December at baseball's winter meetings. Beane reinvented the three-way deal, treating every team's roster as a potential source of whatever chits he needed to acquire the object of his desire.

Epstein could afford to splurge on undervalued offensive threats since he was underwritten by Fenway Park's sold-out schedule and revenue from the New England Sports Network, which the team owned. Beane knew the value of David Ortiz and Curt Schilling, but even had he succeeded in bringing them to Oakland he wouldn't have been able to keep them there for long. Nor could he contemplate, as Epstein had, taking on a contract the size of Alex Rodriguez's in the act of unloading a contract the size of Manny Ramirez's.

In some ways, Epstein exceeded Beane's devotion to the big inning philosophy. His team basically retired the sacrifice bunt. In 2004, the Red Sox would attempt just seventeen of them (two executed by pitchers during interleague play) while the A's called for thirty. And while Beane was satisfied with okay-hit, good-glove Scott Hatteberg at first, Epstein happily turned the base over to the iron-gloved but thumping duo of David Ortiz and Kevin Millar. He treated his defensive first basemen, Dave McCarty and Doug Mientkiewicz, strictly as late-inning substitutes.

But the real value of the "Oakland way" was the strategic advantage of a lineup loaded with patience. When batters take pitches, they run up pitch counts. If the opposing starter is worn out by the fifth, sixth, or seventh innings, your lineup is going to spend an inning or two hitting against the bottom of the bullpen. If the other team counters by using its better relievers earlier, you still gain an advantage *within* a series by wearing out the opponent's bullpen.

Case in point: On Monday, August 9, 1999, in the first game of a series against the Yankees, the A's were getting shellacked early. For Oakland, every game was critical; although six and a half games back of the Rangers for the AL West coming into the series, they were only a game out in the wild card chase. After Jimmy Haynes and then Mike Oquist had been hammered for eight runs in the second, the odds of the A's coming back and winning the game were remote. But Beane knew that if the lineup forced Yankees starter Hideki Irabu to labor, perhaps Oakland would get into the Yankees' pen and affect who was available to Joe Torre in the second and third games of the series. He sent a reminder down to the dugout to make Irabu work for every strike; as a result, Torre pulled the Japanese hurler after four innings and six runs, and had to use three relievers, including key setup men Mike Stanton and Ramiro Mendoza, to close out a 12–8 win. Stanton, who had already pitched the previous day, now wouldn't be available for Tuesday's game. When Roger Clemens faltered in the sixth inning of that game, Torre left him in, despite allowing four runs in six innings, sending him out again in the seventh to give up a fifth run. It was a nice example of using one game to limit the opponents' tactical options in a subsequent game. Stretched out over a season, that can mean a lot of runs off of pitchers who aren't among the league's best.

Although they were three games up on the Red Sox in the race for the wild card, Oakland was limping along at this point of the season. Superstar third baseman Eric Chavez was on the DL with a broken hand, and his replacement, utility man Mark McLemore, lacked Chavez's quickness and arm. The top dog among Oakland's trio of ace starters, Tim Hudson, had just broken down two weeks before, landing on the DL with a strained abdominal muscle. Although morally battered after dropping two of the three in Atlanta, Boston was coming home at physical full strength.

In the first game, former Cy Young winner Barry Zito faced Tim Wakefield. Both clubs had the prior Monday off, so both pens were relatively rested. The flutterball had been working for Wakefield in his previous pair of starts against the Twins and Yankees, but he'd been crushed in the pair of games before those, walking 7 and allowing 15 runs in 8.1 IP. He'd also had his troubles against the A's in the past, allowing 13 runs in 21 IP the previous pair of seasons. Just like his signature pitch, Wakefield was all over the place.

As it turned out, this was a game where almost nothing went wrong for the Red Sox. Wakefield cruised through the first four innings, facing only one batter over the minimum and working through the A's lineup economically enough, using only 11, 12, 12, and 14 pitches in those frames. Through seven frames, he'd given up four base runners and no runs. Meanwhile, the Sox lineup made Zito work, getting two men on in the first on 23 pitches before coming up empty. They scored three runs in the second on Bill Mueller's first hit in Fenway since early May, a 3-run home run, while making Zito throw another 24 pitches. Zito's defense hadn't helped. McLemore had bobbled an easy double-play grounder, settling for a force at second. When the reliable Scott Hatteberg Bucknered an equally easy grounder on the next play, instead of the inning being over, the Sox had men on second and third with one out and Mueller up. One hundred pitches is a commonly accepted limit for starting pitchers; Zito wasn't going to make it through the fifth inning at this rate. He didn't. In the fourth, he gave up a pair of hits, walked in a pair of runs, and gave up two more on lefty-killer Kevin Millar's two-out double.

Up 7–0 after four is a point where some lineups might let up; Boston's didn't. When rookie Justin Lehr came in to start the fifth, the Sox chased him with four quick runs, forcing A's manager Ken Macha to turn to his better relievers with more than three innings yet to go. The Sox made Oakland use their best middle reliever, Justin Duchscherer, and their top setup men, Jim Mecir and Ricky Rincon, just to finish out an 11–0 loss. The victory highlighted the immense benefits of having a healthy lineup without a weak spot; David Ortiz went 0–6 and stranded a dozen base runners, but the team could shrug it off because 8-9-1 hitters Doug Mirabelli, Mueller, and Damon reached base fifteen times.

Getting into the A's pen in the first game gave the Sox a strategic advantage in the second game of the set, when Mark Redman faced Pedro Martinez. Redman gave up solo home runs to two of the first five hitters he faced. In the second, after letting Nomar lead off with a home run, he endured an ugly series of at-bats: Millar walked, Varitek pasted an RBI double, and Bill Mueller singled through Hatteberg's wickets, moving Varitek over to third. Redman finally got his first out on his twenty-fourth pitch in the inning, inducing spot starter Gabe Kapler to pop out, but Johnny Damon followed with an RBI single to make it 4–0. McLemore then made another bad situation worse. Rather than eating a hard smash by Mark Bellhorn, he rushed a desperate throw across the diamond that bounced away down the right field line, allowing both Mueller and Damon to score and make it a 6–0 game only one out into the second inning.

Meanwhile, without his best fastball, Martinez worked in and out of trouble, but spotted to a six-run lead, he could afford to take a few chances. Desperate for innings, Macha sent Redman out in the third, but with another run across and two men on base, he brought in Duchscherer. Duchscherer took the game through the sixth, essentially removing him from Macha's tactical menu for the third game of the series. Even then, both Chad Bradford and Lehr had to toss an inning apiece to close out an 11–3 laugher.

The Sox were now only a game back of Oakland, with Curt Schilling taking the mound against rookie Rich Harden in the second of the set. McLemore wasn't in Oakland's lineup. Once again, the Sox mauled the A's starter, but without Duchscherer to turn to, Macha had to leave Harden on the mound through a forty-two-pitch fifth inning that added three more runs to Boston's 4–0 lead. Like Pedro the day before, Schilling didn't have his best stuff, leaving in the sixth inning after allowing eleven hits, but Alan Embree stranded Schilling's last pair of base runners, preserving Boston's 7–3 after six.

But here Francona's overmanaging of the bullpen hurt the Sox. He had used his best relievers to close out the second game, a game he'd won. He used his top lefty-righty setup duo, Alan Embree and Mike Timlin, to pitch the eighth between them, and Foulke to finish in the ninth. Using three pitchers to tackle the last pair of innings with an eight-run lead proved to be a profligate use of a finite resource. In the third game, he pulled Embree in the seventh, sending Timlin out instead. Timlin gave up a run, a couple of hits, and tossed twenty-one pitches; he clearly wasn't on. Rather than continuing to cycle through his pen, Francona chose to let Timlin pitch a second inning he wasn't up to, allowing a quick pair of hits to lead off the eighth and make the game 7–5. Foulke came in with a man in scoring position, who scored on an opposite field single by Hatteberg, who then came home on a booming triple by Jermaine Dye.

The Red Sox offense's battering of the Oakland pen would eventually provide a final gift. With the game tied in the bottom of the eighth, Macha did the best thing he could, bringing in closer Octavio Dotel. It was Dotel's first appearance in the series, and he shut the Sox down for two frames. That carried the game into extra innings, on a travel date. Using Dotel for another inning or two would probably handicap his availability at the beginning of the A's next series, and Macha had already used Rincon and Mecir in the sixth and seventh innings, and Duchscherer had done a long stint in the series' second game. Macha was down to submariner Chad Bradford, or Lehr in his third straight game. Bradford's throwing motion makes him tough on right-handed hitters, but he struggles with left-handers, which the Sox would put up against him en masse in the tenth inning: Varitek, Bellhorn pinch-hitting for Pokey Reese, Damon, Mueller, and Ortiz.

Forced to choose between two dubious options, Macha used Lehr in his third straight game. It even looked like it might work for a frame, when Lehr got Varitek and Bellhorn out, but then Damon singled and Mueller doubled him home, and the Sox had a sweep and a tie for the wild card with three games left before the All-Star break.

The Red Sox had had more than their share of luck in the series. They didn't have to face either Hudson or Mulder, and the one member of Oakland's vaunted three-ace rotation they did face, Zito, was the least fearsome of the trio. After the rout of the first game, Boston's two aces faced the bottom of Oakland's rotation. The absence of Eric Chavez had made a significant difference, not simply in terms of what he might have done at the plate, but because of what McLemore had failed to do in the field as his replacement.

Still, the Red Sox had managed to win without either Pedro or Schilling at their best, and Wakefield had rattled off his third consecutive quality start. The offense was clicking, chewing up Oakland starters and forcing Macha to use people just to finish ball games he'd already lost.

It was, both philosophically and on the field, the best possible baseball to be playing.

—CHRIS KAHRL

15

BASEBRAWL
JULY 24, 2004

O n July 24, Red Sox catcher Jason Varitek shoved Yankees third baseman Alex Rodriguez. As a result, the momentum of Boston's season changed and a Red Sox World Series victory was preordained—or so the theory goes. This belief, in which cause and effect struggle vainly to achieve a plausible relationship, became popular both with fans and the Red Sox themselves, and it should surprise no one, since violence is a spectacle that lends itself to symbolism, while diplomacy is a prolonged and boring stretch of reality that puts all observers—and not a few of the participants—to sleep. Actions not only speak louder than words, but they can really shut up your opponent.

Future Hall of Famer Rogers Hornsby had perhaps the first and last word on this on June 16, 1925, when, as manager of the Cardinals, he got into a three-way beef at home plate with the umpire and Phillies' manager Art Fletcher. After jawing for a few moments, Hornsby suddenly socked Fletcher in the face. Later, when asked why, Hornsby reasoned: "Well, I wasn't making any progress talking to him."[1] Similarly, on September 23, 1974, Ted Simmons of the Cardinals, a masked catcher, ignited an all-out fight by socking the batter at the plate, Bill Madlock. Asked why he had thrown the first punch, Simmons said, "I didn't like the way he was looking at me."[2]

As far back as the nineteenth century, teams have looked at a good fight as a preemptive strike against failure. "We were a cocky, swashbuckling crew and we wanted everybody to know it," John McGraw said of those brawling 1890s Orioles, "and as a result we won a lot of our games before the first ball was ever pitched."

Jason Varitek gives A-Rod a facial

So if people believed that Jason Varitek propelled them to the championship when he socked Alex Rodriguez in the mouth with his catcher's mitt, they were only subscribing to a very old bit of baseball wisdom, which, as it turns out, has absolutely no basis in reality.

In the third inning of the Yankees–Red Sox contest at Boston on July 24, Alex Rodriguez stood in against Bronson Arroyo. The Yankees were leading 3–0. Rodriguez had knocked in the winning run the night before. Arroyo's first pitch hit Rodriguez on the elbow. Rodriguez, figuring he was being paid back for his Friday-night heroics, swore at Arroyo. One of the catcher's many jobs is to intercept enraged batsmen on their way to the mound whenever such an occasion might arise. Jason Varitek jumped in front of Rodriguez, who then turned his rage on the catcher. Varitek cut the conversation short by attempting to force his catcher's mitt into A-Rod's mouth. The inevitable brawl followed, after which four players were ejected: Rodriguez and Varitek, Kenny Lofton of the Yankees, and Gabe Kapler of the Red Sox. Yankees starting pitcher Tanyon Sturtze, bleeding from his ear, bore the only obvious wounds, but stayed in the game.

In the bottom of the third, the righteously motivated (as far as they were concerned) Red Sox scored two runs on a single, double, and two groundouts. In the bottom of the fourth, Nomar Garciaparra singled with runners on second and third to give the Red Sox a 4–3 lead. This situation lasted until the top of the sixth, when the Yankees seemed to put the game away with a six-run inning. The Red Sox opened the bottom of the sixth with a hit and a walk off of Juan Padilla, who had relieved Sturtze in the fourth. Now Joe Torre went to his third pitcher of the game, Paul Quantrill. Quantrill, already well into a slump that dated from the team's ill-advised season opener on turf in Japan, gave up a single to Kevin Millar, loading the bases. Bill Mueller hit a sacrifice fly— 9–5. Mark Bellhorn doubled, scoring Trot Nixon to make it 9–6. Johnny Damon singled—9–7. Reserve catcher Doug Mirabelli, in the game for the banished Varitek, struck out, bringing David Ortiz to bat. Torre, desperate to prevent Ortiz from getting another big hit against the Yankees, went to the sole left-hander in his bullpen, the unsustainably wild Felix Heredia.

Heredia walked Ortiz, loading the bases. Incredibly, Torre left Heredia in to face Manny Ramirez, one of the game's marquee sluggers and a right-hander. Heredia walked him, too—9-8. Torre finally went to his fourth pitcher of the inning, rookie Scott Proctor, who struck out Garciaparra to end the frame. Leading off the top of the seventh, Ruben Sierra homered off Mark Malaska, giving the Yankees a two-run cushion at 10-8. The score held going into the ninth inning.

In the bottom of the ninth, the Yankees did what they had done every year since 1996, calling in Mariano Rivera to protect a late-inning lead. A future Hall of Famer by acclamation, Rivera almost never blew a save in a big game ... except those rare times when he did. He was so consistently effective that those rare losses—the last game of the 1997 American League Divisional Series, Game Seven of the 2001 World Series—were chalked up to the caprice of the cosmos. Perhaps the Yankees should have phoned Mount Palomar before bringing in Rivera on this day. In one of his last hurrahs as a member of the Red Sox, Garciaparra led off the inning with a double. He moved to third base on Trot Nixon's fly out to right field, and Millar drove him in with a single—10-9. Terry Francona inserted Dave McCarty as a pinch runner. The move turned out to be irrelevant, because the next batter, Bill Mueller, worked the count to 3-1 then blasted the next pitch out of the ballpark. Final score: Red Sox 11, New York 10. Rivera's invulnerability had once again been exposed as a myth.

Mueller had hardly touched home plate before the game was being cast as a rite of passage. "Following the rhubarb, the donnybrook, and the ejections, the Sox finally woke from their stupor," Sox fan Stephen King wrote two days later in his diary of the season. "If this is the place where the season turns around—and stranger things have happened—then you can give Jason Varitek the MVP for getting in Alex Rodriguez's face."[3] The Red Sox, too, had already decided on the game's meaning. "You're never out of it if you continue to fight," Terry Francona said after the game. "I hope we can look back at this day a while from now and say that this brought us together." "I think that's the best thing that ever happened to us," said David Ortiz. "It's the start of something good."[4]

Even after the World Series, the club still held to this conviction. "The turning point of our season [was] either the July 24 comeback win against the Yankees, or the trade of Nomar Garciaparra six days later," Bill James told Baseball Prospectus. "One of those two is cited by most everybody as the point at which the season turned."[5]

In fact, the aftermath of the July 24 game was not nearly so dramatic. Going into the July 23–25 series against the Yankees at Fenway Park, the Red Sox had gone 4–6 in their last ten games. In the ten games following the brawl, including the final game in the Yankees series, they went 5–5. It wasn't until eleven days later, on August 7, that the Red Sox kicked off a sustained winning streak, going 19–4 over the remainder of the month. While it is possible that residual feelings of machismo lingered after the brawl, the Red Sox certainly took their time about displaying their new-found confidence.

Perhaps because brawls have never been fully cataloged, studies of the impact of a good fight on won-lost record have never been conducted. However, studies similar in intent have been attempted. In 1993, Stats, Inc. studied the effect of "emotional wins" on won-lost record, looking for the winning afterglow that was presumed to follow such uplifting moments. They defined an emotional win in four ways:

- Team is trailing by three or more runs in the ninth inning, but comes back to win.
- Team is trailing by five or more runs at some point during the game, but comes back to win it.
- Home team only—opponent scores in extra innings to take the lead, but the home club comes back to win.
- A no-hitter.

Using data from 1992 only, they found that teams received no detectable lift in games following an emotional win.[6] Baseball Prospectus repeated the study using all games from 1972 to 2004. In that period there were 1,957 "emotional wins." The typical emotional-win team had a winning percentage of .506 (.503 in all "nonemotional" games). The cumulative season record was 155,373 wins and 153,587 losses, or an average of 80.393 wins and 78.481 losses per team (the strike seasons pulled the average season down from 162 games).

Repeating the same process, using only games happening in the thirty days following an emotional win (regular season games only, and if the season ended before thirty days were up, only the rest of the regular season was counted). In the month following an emotional win, teams went 24,245–24,264 for a winning percentage of .500, a drop of 0.0031 points of winning percentage. That amounts to an expected 12.38886 wins and 12.3986 losses in the month following an emotional win. In short, there was no consistent effect in the month following an emotional win.

The same uncertainty of effect applies to every other physical confrontation in the history of the game. Baseball Prospectus examined a representative sample of major brawls (actual fights, not just posturing), some fifty in all (for a complete list, see Appendix II), and we could find no clear examples of teams that were propelled into the post-season by physically abusing an opponent, or being themselves abused. The good teams stayed good and the bad teams stayed bad.

On May 7, 1923, the first-place New York Giants, defending World Series champions, were playing the last-place Phillies in Philadelphia. The Giants were leading 9–1 in the fourth, having knocked the Phillies' starter out before he could record an out. Phillies pitcher Phil Weinert threw one high and tight to Stengel. Deciding he had been thrown at, Stengel snapped. (His manager later accused him of having come to the park "stinking of cheap gin," but Stengel claimed he was merely wearing fresh aftershave lotion after a pregame trip to the barber.) He heaved his bat at the pitchers mound, then charged. A violent scrap ensued. It took two policemen and Phillies manager Art Fletcher (there he is again, the Zelig of baseball brawls) to separate the combatants, and an additional policeman was needed to drag Stengel, now out of control, back to the bench. The game rolled on. The Phillies scored a few more runs, but so did the Giants. Final score: Giants, 13; Phillies, 8. At the time of the fight, the Giants had won six of their previous ten games. The Phillies had lost seven of their previous ten. After, the Giants went 7–3 on their way to their third consecutive pennant, while the Phillies' destiny was unchanged as well. They finished at the bottom of the second division for the sixth consecutive season.[7]

That's the typical example. More ambiguous is the result of the fight between the Yankees and the Washington Senators in the first game of a July 4, 1932, doubleheader at Washington. Both were good teams with a tradition of bad blood between them. Trailing the Yankees, 3–2, in the bottom of the seventh inning, Senators outfielder Carl Reynolds collided with

Yankees catcher Bill Dickey when scoring the tying run. Dickey, who had been knocked unconscious on a similar play the day before, jumped to his feet and smashed his fist into Reynolds's jaw, breaking it in two places. Reynolds, thinking he had made a clean play, was dusting himself off and never even saw Dickey coming. The usual bench-clearing mess occurred, with players, coaches, fans, and policemen scuffling on the field before play was resumed.

The fight was a blow to both teams. Dickey was suspended "indefinitely" by the American League, by which it was meant that he would sit roughly as long as it took for Reynolds to recover—a period expected to last six weeks or more (ultimately the punishment was defined as a one-month suspension without pay and a $1,000 fine—in all, Dickey lost about $4,000 of his $14,000 salary). The Yankees lost one of their biggest tactical advantages, a catcher who was hitting .332 with power (although they still had Babe Ruth and Lou Gehrig, poor lambs). He was replaced by Art Jorgens, a .220 hitter with no power. The Senators had to do without their starting right fielder, a career .320 hitter—nearly for life, as it turned out. Two weeks after the incident, Reynolds choked on his own vomit when he threw up with his mouth wired shut. Saved by a pair of scissors, he returned to the field on August 14.[8]

In the ten games that preceded the brawl, the Yankees had won seven games and lost three. In the next ten they went 6–4. During Dickey's absence they went 18–10, only a one-game decline from their record before July 4. In first place on Independence Day, they stayed there and went on to win the World Series. The Senators, the team with the nearly dead player, were invigorated. The Senators had lost seven of their previous ten games going into July 4 and rested in fourth place with a lazy 40–34 record after the events of the day. They lost four straight to the Indians after the Yankees left town, then, like the Red Sox, were belatedly energized. They won nine straight games and stayed hot for the rest of the season, going 53–27 (.663). Yet they failed to challenge the Yankees, won just two of their five remaining meetings, and finished in third place.

The many notorious Red Sox–Yankees brawls are no more conclusive:

May 30, 1938, at Yankee Stadium: Yankees outfielder Jake Powell and Red Sox shortstop/manager Joe Cronin fought in front of the pitcher's mound while a Stadium-record crowd of 83,533 looked on. Red Sox pitcher Archie McKain hit Powell in the stomach with a pitch. Powell, who had violent inclinations to begin with, charged the mound. Cronin got there first and the two lit into each other. "Both Cronin and Powell were ordered off the field, but that by no means ended the fighting," wrote John Drebinger of *The New York Times*. "For as Cronin passed through the Yankee dugout, his only means of exit, several Yanks followed him. This induced the three umpires . . . to do the same, and presently the other players also dashed from view, leaving the record crowd to view in bewilderment nothing but the grass."[9] The Yankees had gone 3-6-1 in the ten games prior to the fight and went 5–5 after. The Red Sox had gone 5–5 in their previous ten games, 6–4 in their next ten. The Yankees won their third consecutive pennant and World Series that year, the Red Sox finished second, nine and a half games out. They went 6-8-1 against the Yankees the rest of the way.

May 24, 1952, at Fenway Park: Sharing the field for pregame warm-ups, infielder Billy Martin of the Yankees and outfielder Jimmy Piersall of the Red Sox, two of baseball's more volatile personalities, were somehow allowed to get within taunting range of each other. Violent words quickly escalated to actual violence under the stands. The fight was interrupted by coaches from the two teams. The Yankees, three-time defending world champions, had gone 8–2 in their last ten games. The Red Sox had gone 4–6. After, both teams went 6–4 in their next ten games. Boston lost eleven of sixteen remaining games with the Yankees.

June 21, 1967, at Yankee Stadium: The Red Sox, 32–31 and in fourth place, took on the Yankees, 28–34 and in ninth place. In the top of the second inning, Yankees starting pitcher Thad Tillotson hit Red Sox third baseman Joe Foy in the helmet. In the bottom of the frame, Red Sox starting pitcher Jim Lonborg hit Tillotson in the shoulder. Tillotson, in what was destined to be the one memorable moment of his big-league career, jawed at Lonborg on the way to first base. Suddenly a revenge-minded Foy went tearing across the infield to get at Tillotson. Both dugouts emptied. Yankees outfielder Joe Pepitone was injured. It took twelve policemen to restore order. Later in the game,

Lonborg hit pitch hitter Dick Howser on the helmet; Howser collapsed while standing on first base (he missed five games). The Sox, 6–4 in their previous ten matches, went 7–3 in their next ten and went on to win the American League pennant on the last day of the season. The Yankees, destined to stay in ninth place, went 6–4. They still lost ninety games. The Red Sox went 6–2 against the Yankees the rest of the way.

August 1, 1973, at Fenway Park: Red Sox catcher Carlton Fisk and Yankees catcher Thurman Munson had been rivals for the title of best catcher in the American League and there was no love lost between the two. In the top of the ninth inning the game was tied, 2–2, and Munson was on third base with one out. With light-hitting Yankees shortstop Gene Michael at the plate, the suicide squeeze was called. Munson came running down the line, Michael stuck his bat out—and missed. Munson's only chance was to knock the ball out of Fisk's glove. The two collided with tremendous force. Fisk held on to the ball, then pushed Munson away from him. Munson punched him. Michael jumped in and the dugouts and the bullpens emptied. Both catchers were ejected from the game, which the Red Sox won 3–2 in the bottom of the ninth. "There's no question I threw the first punch, but he started it," said Munson, displaying the cavalier disregard for causal relationships that characterizes the whole concept of fighting-inspires-winning.[10] Tied for first place at the time of the fight with a weak .550 record, the Yankees went 9–18 in August and rapidly dropped out of the race, though they went 4–6 in the days after the scuffle. Concurrently, the Red Sox went 5–5, but finished August with a strong 18–13 record and rose from fourth place (though just two and a half games out) to second place, eight games behind the Orioles. They went 4–1 in their remaining games against the Yankees.

May 20, 1976, at Yankee Stadium: With the Red Sox trailing 1–0 in the sixth inning and the Yankees at bat, Lou Piniella was on second when Otto Velez singled to right off Bill Lee. Piniella tried to score, but Evans' throw had him beat. There was a collision and Fisk and Piniella came up fighting. Suddenly both teams were on the field. In the wild melee that ensued, Lee's pitching shoulder was wrecked after Graig

Nettles threw him to the ground. The next day Lee called Billy Martin a Nazi and the Yankees "Steinbrenner's Brown Shirts."[11] The Red Sox came back to win the game, hitting three home runs and a triple for eight runs in the final three innings. "Until the fight, we were too complacent," Carl Yastrzemski said. "That seemed to shake us up, and just in time, too."[12] Shaken, stirred, or none of the above, the defending American League champion Red Sox went just 5–5 in their theoretically emotional next ten games, as compared to 7–3 before. They went 6–11 against the Yankees during the balance of the schedule.

Red Sox adviser Bill James has said, "It is one thing to build an analytical paradigm that leaves out leadership, hustle, focus, intensity, courage and self-confidence; it is a very, very different thing to say that leadership, hustle, courage and self-confidence do not exist or do not play a role on real-world baseball teams."[13] This is undoubtedly true, but precisely what roles these qualities play is open to interpretation and can't be quantified. It's impossible to weigh the effect of these qualities compared to talent, health, the schedule, and all of the other variables that change a team's possibilities on a daily basis. This is especially true in the case of the 2004 Red Sox. All we can say about them is that whatever newfound confidence the glove in the face actually inspired, it failed to manifest until Game Four of the American League Championship Series, when the collapse of the Yankees could be traced to that team's exploitable flaws, without any reference to fisticuffs.

The tenacity of the belief that a baseball team can succeed with violence when talent fails is an expression of humanity's need to tell simple stories to explain mystifying events, such as the complex process by which a team flips its switch from "loser" to "winner." For some, electricity strikes from the sky because of static charges in clouds and the ionization of the air. For others, it's because Zeus hurls thunderbolts. Either way you get lightning. For some, the Red Sox won a World Series because, on the whole, they were a little smarter—and perhaps a little luckier—than the competition. For others, they won a World Series because a few guys lost their tempers. Either way, though, as July came to an end, you had a team that suddenly had to answer a rather high-class question: Is it possible for a baseball club to have too much offense?

—STEVEN GOLDMAN

DRAFT-WISE BUT CAREER-FOOLISH

Jason Varitek signed a monster contract during the 2004–2005 off-season to stay with Boston for four years at $10 million a year. If, at the end of this new contract, he never plays another game of professional baseball, he'll have made just shy of $60 million during his career. It's a lot of money, but it's not nearly as much as he would have made had he not played hard to get as a youthful draftee acting under the informal guidance of agent Scott Boras.

A highly prized catching prospect, Varitek was selected in the first of his three drafts in 1990 when the Houston Astros picked the Lake Brantley High School (Longwood, Florida) graduate in the twenty-third round (608th overall). Varitek decided to forsake the ham sandwich the team offered him to sign and went to Georgia Tech. He became a collegiate star, playing for Team USA at the 1992 Olympics in Barcelona and being named *Baseball America*'s College Player of the Year for 1993.

YEAR	AGE	SALARY
1998	26	$170,000[1]
1999	27	$237,500
2000	28	$375,000
2001	29	$1,800,000
2002	30	$3,500,000
2003	31	$4,700,000
2004	32	$6,900,000

Varitek became eligible for the draft again in 1993. In the months before June, it was rumored that Darren Dreifort and Alex Rodriguez would be picked for the first two spots by the Seattle Mariners and Los Angeles Dodgers, with the Mariners possibly passing on Dreifort because of concerns over his salary demands. While Boston was rumored to be interested in Varitek, they drafted Trot Nixon with the seventh pick. Varitek was the twenty-first pick, by the Twins.

According to the NCAA, amateur players aren't supposed to have agents, so instead players are "advised" by agents who counsel them out of the goodness of their hearts and their insatiable thirst for doing good deeds. You can almost hear it:

"Hey there, kid, I'm Scott Boras. I understand you might be drafted soon."

"Gosh, there have been an awful lot of scouts at my games, and hanging around my house, too. I had wondered why that was."

"Good thing I happened to be passing by. I represent all the biggest baseball stars in their contract negotiations and, in my copious spare time, I travel the country righting baseball wrongs. I'd be more than happy to answer any questions you might have about the draft, and even help you come up with a negotiating strategy and deal with the press for you."

"Would you really, Mr. Boras? That would be great! Except, you know, I don't have any money to pay you."

"Forget it, kid! I can't officially be your agent until you go pro, anyway. I can only give you some free advice. Later, when you're a pro, maybe you'll consider using me as your agent. But, hey, if you choose someone else, that's fine, too."

"Why do you keep blinking one eye like that, Mr. Boras? Is there something wrong?"

Varitek had a year of college left. With Boras's stamp of approval, he reportedly demanded a $630,000 signing bonus. The Twins were $200,000 short. After a protracted negotiation, he returned to Georgia Tech.

Varitek had another great year in school and was named the NCAA Player of the Year. Even though he had no leverage—since he was a senior, it wasn't as if he could go back to college again—just having Boras as his adviser caused his draft position to drop. In the 1994 draft, the Mariners picked him at number fourteen. Varitek was stuck.

The Mariners offered him less than the Twins did the year before: $355,000. As Mariners assistant general manager Roger Jongewaard said, "His only options are the Independent Northern League or playing in Italy."

Varitek countered by asking for more than $800,000. That fall, despite no longer being eligible to play collegiate baseball, Varitek returned to Georgia Tech to try and finish up a degree. By January, the Mariners had abandoned any hope that Varitek would sign in time to make plans for him to join the team. Varitek signed a contract with the St. Paul Saints of the Northern League. His deal allowed him to talk to and sign with any major league team and leave the Saints immediately if he wished. The Mariners bumped their offer to $450,000. Boras, by now officially his agent, claimed that, because Varitek had used up his college eligibility, he was a free agent and not subject to the draft. Major League Baseball disagreed, ruling that Seattle had exclusive bargaining rights. Boras said he would challenge that ruling. The Mariners raised to $500,000. "They know what it's going to take for me to sign, and that's market value," Varitek replied, referring to what players drafted around him received.

As late as February, the Mariners stuck to their position, saying, "We went above-budget on this offer, invited him to spring training camp, placement on our Double-A roster. If that isn't satisfactory to him, we'll go in another direction."

Had Seattle been unable to sign Varitek before the next draft, their rights would have expired and he'd have become an unrestricted free agent, though the issue likely would have gone to arbitration. In fact, the court challenges may well have shattered the draft system entirely. No Curt Flood, Varitek didn't let things get that far, finally signing on April 20, 1995. It had been the longest holdout of any amateur draft player who ended up signing.

Varitek signed in time to play 104 Double-A games, so the season wasn't a complete loss, but after his long layoff his professional career started slowly. Playing at Port City of the Southern League, he hit .224 with 14 doubles and 10 home runs. He struck out 126 times (bad) and walked 61 times (good). Repeating the level in 1995, he was a different player, making far better contact, striking out a lot less, and driving the ball for more doubles, though not home runs.

In the middle of the 1997 season, Varitek was traded with Derek Lowe to Boston in a historically poor deal that brought the Seattle Mariners Heathcliffe Slocumb, a former middle reliever who had been miscast as a closer by the Red Sox. The trade rescued Slocumb, as Boston fans had bound and gagged him and were about to throw him into the Charles River when they heard the news.

Varitek's hold-out year cost him a lot of money. It's impossible to know precisely how much, but even a conservative guess lands somewhere to the left of "quite a bit." Simply getting Varitek's career under way one year earlier would have made him a free agent after 2003. While he wouldn't have competed in 2003 numbers with Javy Lopez, Varitek would have been a year younger with better career production numbers. Lopez got a three-year, $22.5 million deal to go to Baltimore. On the negative side, Varitek wouldn't yet have his championship ring and the leadership mystique that comes with it, the reason why the Red Sox were willing to pay a premium to retain him.

As a younger free agent, Varitek would have had at least one more $10 million year in his early thirties. Possibly, it would also have meant that Varitek's next contract would come earlier, which would make him still more money. The simplistic view is that Varitek holding out for a year over a $300,000 difference easily cost him thirty times that much over the course of his career.

Or he might have done even better. Had Varitek signed almost immediately, he would have been thrown into a league to finish out that year, possibly played winter ball, and then gone into 1995 for a full-season of AA where he'd have done well. That early experience might have helped him make an easier transition from college to professional baseball if he'd started immediately and had the support of better coaching. It's possible he wouldn't have struggled so much initially and would have started better and taken less time to advance to a level where he could contribute as a major leaguer. In that case, he might well have taken over as the Mariners backup catcher at some point in 1996, and would have been a star catcher at twenty-nine or thirty, when he became a free agent in 2001 or 2002—and drawn the kind of money-mad contracts players of all kinds were getting then.

It's instructive to look at the career of his 1993 draft-mate, Alex Rodriguez. Rodriguez was also advised by Scott Boras to hold out against the Mariners in order to get a larger signing bonus, but Alex decided instead to take the money and start playing baseball immediately. It worked out pretty well for him.

—DEREK ZUMSTEG

16

NOMARGATE
JULY 31, 2004

On the issue of scoring runs versus preventing runs, Hall of Fame manager Casey Stengel once said, "I don't like them fellas who drive in two runs and let in three." Stengel's argument has a nearly symmetrical twin. He just as easily could have said, "I don't like them fellas who save two runs and strand three."

One of the unrecognized burdens of team management is keeping offense and defense in harmony. The guiding principle here is that good offence is more valuable to a team than good defense. This is most obvious in the case of the pure slugger, whose run production more than compensates for his occasional lapses at first base or in right field. However, at the skill positions, like shortstop, even an Ozzie Smith can't save his team more than 20 or so runs a season over the average shortstop; there aren't enough balls hit to the position that the average shortstop can't get, but the exemplary shortstop can. Teams get in trouble on defense when they carry too many players with weak gloves. They get in trouble on offense when they carry too many glovemen. That is why the rare two-way players, those who can contribute with both the bat and the glove, are the most valuable players in the game. Once obtained, they are not lightly dispensed with.

Nomar Garciaparra was one of these players—or had been. As the Red Sox drew nearer to the trading deadline, they were forced to confront the possibility that Garciaparra, sullenly playing out (and just as often sitting out) the last year of his contract, had changed from indispensible star into an albatross who just might prevent them from reaching the postseason. It

Nomar after making an error

was the kind of situation that one would normally like to take one's time digesting, say a good six months or so, and in someplace quiet. The Red Sox had only days to come to grips with it.

The offense was humming along in high gear, cranking out 6.3 runs per game in July after averaging 5.4 (still a very good figure) over the previous three months. Garciaparra, Bill Mueller, and Trot Nixon were all back from the disabled list. Yet the team still hadn't taken off. Besides, their offensive pace wouldn't be easy to maintain, given Nixon's persistently strained quadriceps, which was about to force him back onto the disabled list; and Garciaparra's chronic, aching Achilles, which made him questionable from day to day. Instead of picking up ground, the Sox bounced between seven and nine games back of the Yankees during July's last week. June's 11–14 record had been disappointing, and July's only modest improvement, to 14–12, was doubly so as the sands of the season began to run out. Not only had the Sox failed to keep up with the Yankees, but the team couldn't even count on winning the wild card.

It was a point in the season when every additional loss carried an ever-increasing risk of turning a holding action into a full-scale collapse. To make matters suddenly worse, Garciaparra's understudy, Pokey Reese, broke down on July 19. After playing through a torn ligament in his left (non-throwing) thumb, he was disabled by a strained rib cage. Initially, it was feared that he'd torn his oblique muscle and might be lost for a considerable stretch, if not the entire season. Reese's bat had always been weak, but in 2004 it was downright dead; his final percentages were .221/.265/.303 (the average major league player hit .270/.338/.433 that year). Reese had contributed on defense, but his offense left a massive deficit on the ledger. Theo Epstein and his collaborators were now faced with a truly horrific situation: What if Garciaparra's day-to-day status changed to out-and-out? That would mean replacing him with someone worse than Reese, and Reese was hardly worthy of being called replacement level.

On the day after Reese went on the DL, Epstein pulled off a quick deal to acquire veteran shortstop Ricky Gutierrez from the Cubs (for a player to be named later or cash). Gutierrez was far from a sure thing, though, having lost most of the 2002 and 2003 seasons to neck surgery that still seemed to hinder him—and even then, he didn't have the best reputation as a defensive shortstop. Now Epstein didn't have to close his eyes to get a picture of what "worse than Reese" looked like.

Gutierrez was not a long-term solution because he represented little more than a human in a baseball uniform whom the team could put at short if all other options failed. (If Garciaparra had been the star, and Reese his replacement-level substitute, Gutierrez was somewhere below that, worse than replacement level, better than hotel doorman level or kangaroo level or whatever lies a step beyond desperation.)

What the Red Sox needed was a superior glove at the position. A single statistic made that clear: the number of *unearned runs* the team had allowed. In July, Derek Lowe had surrendered a team-high thirty runs, of which eight were unearned. As a groundball-generating pitcher, Lowe was the most defense-dependent member of Boston's rotation. The unearned runs, not to mention the forty-five hits allowed in thirty-five innings pitched, weren't entirely his fault, the front office knew all too well, but a symptom of a larger problem. As of July 31, the Red Sox were already the least effective team among the contenders at converting balls in play into outs. (Generally speaking, every ball in play, with the obvious exception of home runs, is a potential out; looking at the different rates at which teams actually succeed in catching the grounders and fly balls that come their way is a good way to compare defenses.)

DEFENSIVE EFFICIENCY FOR AL CONTENDERS AS OF 7/31/04

Anaheim	.7095
Oakland	.7074
NY Yankees	.7034
Texas	.7033
Boston	.7029

Just the small difference in defensive efficiency between the Red Sox and the Angels already had been worth, since the beginning of the season, approximately thirty runs.

As a group, pitchers can generally expect up to 10 percent of their runs allowed to be unearned runs.[1] For the Red Sox, that figure was almost 15 percent, close to a select group of which they did not want to be a member:

185

TOP TEN UNEARNED RUNS ALLOWED TEAMS, 1969–2004

Team	Year	R	ER	UER	UER %
Dodgers	1972	527	434	93	17.6
Twins	1972	535	444	91	17.0
Dodgers	1983	609	506	103	16.9
Padres	1975	683	570	113	16.5
Giants	1976	686	573	113	16.5
A's	1978	690	577	113	16.4
Giants	1971	644	539	105	16.3
Cardinals	1975	689	578	111	16.1
Giants	1969	636	534	102	16.0
Giants	1974	723	608	115	15.9

Though only one team on the list, the '78 A's, was truly execrable, this was not a group of teams that went on to great things; the '83 Dodgers and '71 Giants both won the NL West, if barely, and were quickly routed in the Championship Series. Some of Boston's problems were a function of errors; the team was on its way to a total of 121 miscues, fifth-most in the majors. The team was not only failing to reach balls, but when they did manage to reach them, they, too, often fumbled.

The defensive problems were even deeper than they appeared, because while Garciaparra hadn't been a dramatically overrated defensive player like Derek Jeter, he had his own problems. In 2003, he'd been a below-average fielder, allowing, over the season, nine runs more than the average shortstop.[2] That had been when he was relatively healthy and able to play a full season. Now he was in disrepair. He was pressing in the field, trying to make plays he couldn't physically handle. Conceding that defensive metrics are the crudest tool in a baseball statistician's toolbox, objective measures confirmed that Garciaparra had been no defensive asset. In the following table, Garciaparra is compared using three fielding metrics: range factor, a simple measure of plays made per inning in the field; zone rating, in which the field is divided into areas of responsibility for each fielder; and Clay Davenport's fielding runs above replacement, which shows how many runs the player saved versus a replacement-level player at the same position.

GARCIAPARRA'S GLOVE

Stat	Garciaparra	AL Rank
Range	3.87	13/14
Zone rating	.694	14/14
Fielding runs	−4	12/14

To a certain degree, the overall softness of the defense was just the price of assembling an offensive powerhouse. Neither David Ortiz nor Kevin Millar was considered the second coming of Keith Hernandez. Mark Bellhorn's play at second had always encouraged his managers to look at him cross-eyed. Since tearing up his knee in May, third baseman Bill Mueller seemed to be moving gingerly. However, they all could hit. Garciaparra could, too, but, as a result of his defensive decline, it now looked as if Epstein had really overshot the mark. The Red Sox had become what Stengel had warned against—a team that drove in two runs while letting in three. To paraphrase Socrates, "The most knowledgeable man is he who knows he knows nothing. The second-most knowledgeable man is he who at least knows he has nothing at shortstop." By this standard, the Red Sox were just bursting with knowledge, but that didn't bring them any closer to an attractive solution. Terry Francona and the front office understood that Garciaparra would need rest down the stretch, perhaps as many as twenty of the remaining sixty games. That meant forty games from a player at less than his best at a key defensive position, and twenty more that would have to be started by the likes of Pokey Reese or—gulp—Ricky Gutierrez.

Epstein's options were limited. The farm system lacked a blue-chip shortstop, and even if it had one, bringing him up would have meant adding a player without subtracting one, crowding the infield without necessarily making it better. Nomar Garciaparra was both the main problem and the only solution, the only chit valuable enough to be redeemed for the solution to himself. In a most convenient coincidence, baseball did have one patsy franchise that was always willing to make a deal, and they had a star shortstop. The cynicism with which the Montreal Expos (now Washington Nationals) had been run—and run down—by Major League Baseball is a topic that transcends the scope of this book, but the one thing a team with a need could count on was that Expo general manager Omar Minaya was happy to talk about filling it. Operating a franchise co-owned by the other twenty-nine teams, Minaya had few responsibilities beyond fielding a simulacrum of a big league ballclub, and if he enjoyed himself by dealing for other people's turkey contracts or fading prospects, his twenty-nine employers appreciated and respected him all the more for it. Minaya had agreeably let superstar slugger Vladimir Guerrero walk as a free agent without a pro forma offer of arbitration. He'd dealt away his best players (notably starting pitchers Javier Vazquez and Carl Pavano) and his top prospects (Grady Sizemore). Fans would have complained about the way the team was being operated, but there weren't any because the previous stewardship of carpetbagger/owner Jeffrey Loria had run off most of the remaining diehards.

The shortstop that the Expos had on their hands was Orlando Cabrera. He was having a bad year for a bad team, but, at twenty-nine, he had established a track record of durability:

CABRERA AS AN EXPO, 2001–2004

Year	Age	Games	PA	AVG/OBP/SLG	EqA	FRAR	WARP1[3]
2001	26	162	684	.276/.324/.428	.256	54	33.9
2002	27	153	626	.263/.321/.380	.248	33	22.7
2003	28	162	691	.297/.347/.460	.275	23	49.8
2004	29	103	425	.246/.298/.336	.223	12	5.3

This was a player who didn't miss work often, and if his defense had slipped from his Gold Glove season in 2001, it was still strong. He also had a reputation for infectious enthusiasm, in stark contrast to Garciaparra's perceived hauteur and penchant for brooding, and the Red Sox could not afford to overlook it. While sabermetric orthodoxy basically ignores team chemistry, that's because there's no way to measure chemistry, not because chemistry doesn't exist. Chemistry may not have a stable relationship to success, as witnessed by famous examples of dissension-fraught winners like the Big Green Machine in Oakland in the early '70s, or the fractious Yankees of the late '70s, but it couldn't hurt.

If Cabrera bounced back offensively, chemistry or no chemistry, what would his performance mean to the Red Sox? Here are Cabrera's performances in 2003 and 2004 versus those of Garciaparra:

Player	Year	Age	Games	PA	AVG/OBP/SLG	EqA	FRAR	WARP	VORP
Cabrera	2003	28	162	691	.297/.347/.460	.275	23	6.2	49.8
Cabrera	2004	29	103	425	.246/.298/.336	.223	12	1.0	5.3
Garciaparra	2003	29	156	719	.301/.345/.524	.286	14	6.4	67.4
Garciaparra	2004	30	38	169	.321/.367/.500	.284	0	1.0	15.6

Despite Garciaparra's superior offensive value, when defensive considerations are added to the mix, Garciaparra's clear advantages begin to diminish.

The most optimistic projection had Garciaparra playing forty games out of the season's remaining sixty. How would forty Garciaparra games plus twenty Reese games compare to sixty Cabrera games? Comparing what they were doing in 2004 to what Garciaparra and Cabrera had done in 2003 in terms of offensive value, the Sox had a hard choice:

Player	G	VORP
Nomar '04	40	16.4
Reese '04	20	–2.4
Cabrera '04	**60**	**3.1**
Nomar '03	40	16.8
Cabrera '03	60	18.2

Garciaparra was performing at roughly his 2003 level in 2004; his per-game VORP rate was .420 in 2003, and .411 with Boston in 2004. If Cabrera bounced back to his 2003 level after joining the Sox, his per-game VORP rate would be .303.[4] But if they all continued their 2004 performance, the Sox would have traded 14.0 VORP from Garciaparra and Reese together for 3.1 with Cabrera. With everyone returning to 2003 form (and assuming that Reese's pokey 2004 performance would remain virtually the same), the Sox would have traded 14.4 VORP for 18.2 VORP. And if they got a Cabrera vintage 2003 for swapping out Nomar plus Pokey 2004, that would mean a bump from 14.0 VORP to 18.2, a net gain on offense.

In a sense, the real albatross was not Garciaparra, but Reese; twenty games of guaranteed offensive ineptitude wasn't something to be taken lightly when every game could mean the difference between an early vacation or October glory. If the only way to prevent Reese from taking the field was to replace Garciaparra, then it began to look like a no-brainer. Cabrera was younger, faster, healthier, and a significantly better defensive player. Even if his bat didn't recover its 2003 potency, he'd be hitting at the bottom of the game's most potent run-scoring lineup; if he hit—and he *had* to hit better than Reese—it would be gravy.

So Epstein made the deal with the Cubs and, with a tip of the cap to the trading genius of Oakland's Billy Beane, enlisted two additional partners to make it a four-way deal. Not only would the Sox get Cabrera from the Expos by sending Garciaparra to the Cubs, but they would add slick-fielding first baseman Doug Mientkiewicz from the Twins by throwing the Cubs a solid minor league hitter, outfielder Matt Murton. Mientkiewicz would give the Sox an alternative at first base that would allow Papi Ortiz to stick to DHing while making Millar a more regular option in right field, replacing the injured Trot Nixon. Mientkiewicz had not been hitting well with the Twins (.241 Equivalent Average), but his Equivalent Averages from 2001 to 2003 (.284, .265, and .290) hinted that he could do better if healthy.

Epstein was acquiring insurance so he wouldn't have to rely on a cipher from Pawtucket for the stretch drive; if everyone was healthy by October, Terry Francona would have a postseason roster stacked with quality reserves. Simultaneously, Epstein pulled the trigger on another deal, landing speedy center fielder Dave Roberts from the Dodgers for a spare Pawtucket player. Roberts's mandate wasn't to be an improvement on the starting outfielders, but simply to provide the Sox with insurance in case something happened to Johnny Damon. If nothing happened to Johnny Damon, the Sox would have a nifty pinch runner and lefty bat on the bench.

The deal done, the howling began. Red Sox Nation wailed and sat shivah. The analysis community bled through their pores. Though Epstein offered defensive considerations as his prime motivation, analysts conditioned to revere offense over defense weren't buying it. As Baseball Prospectus's own Joe Sheehan stated, "I don't think that the Sox are a better team today than they were Friday (before the deal). . . . I think they made the trade not because it makes them better, but because they didn't have it in them to stand up to Garciaparra. . . . This trade happened because Garciaparra wasn't going to come out of his full pout until he was dealt or filed for free agency."[5] Sheehan went on to observe, "The Sox are a poor defensive team, and it's hurt them so much that they're sixth in the league in runs allowed. How many fewer runs *should* the Red Sox give up?" Another Baseball Prospectus commentator chimed in with the ungenerous observation that the deal was "a craven trade-down to give the ballclub the appearance of owning some leather . . . whatever the off-field drama involved, it's [Epstein's] responsibility to smooth that out, not let it become tabloid fodder."[6] Raised on two decades' worth of analysis that said that offense was the currency with which you could buy victory, statheads simply wouldn't concede that maybe Epstein had done something that needed doing.

Epstein had taken a calculated risk, flouting the conventions of the very analysis that had sustained him in the past. In effect, the trade argued that the mind game might need to yield now and then to instinct. Still, he knew that the outcome could be as damning for him as the Larry Andersen-for-Jeff Bagwell trade had been for Lou Gorman, or the inflated expectations of Rudy Pemberton had been for Dan Duquette. Epstein wouldn't have to wait long to find out. The wisdom of the move might be debated forever, but the only proof that really mattered would be what happened on the field in the next two months.

—CHRIS KAHRL

HAIL AND FAREWELL
TO THE HOLY TRINITY

Between them, the Red Sox and Yankees had on their rosters three of the four men—Nomar Garciaparra, Derek Jeter, and Alex Rodriguez—who embodied a revolution in shortstop play that suddenly didn't look like it would survive their retirement.

From the end of the hard-hitting Honus Wagner's career (.327/.391/.466 lifetime) in 1917 until Cal Ripken's emergence in 1982, shortstop was largely the domain of defense-first players. Pee Wee Reese and Phil Rizzuto didn't strike fear into the hearts of pitchers. Lou Boudreau and Johnny Pesky were decent hitters, but with only 85 home runs between them, power wasn't their forte. The position even suffered the indignity of owning baseball's most notorious measure of offensive ineptitude—the Mendoza Line—named for 1970s shortstop Mario Mendoza and his career .215 batting average. Note the list below: from Wagner to Ripken, just a handful of shortstops were able to hit with the outfielders and first basemen.

When the five-eleven, 150-pound Ozzie Smith came on the scene in 1978, he fit nicely into the modern shortstop concept, and then some. His acrobatic defense earned him the nickname "The Wizard," but his bat was more wet noodle than magic wand. Smith didn't manage a batting average over .260 until 1985, and ended his nineteen-year career with a grand total of 28 home runs in 19 seasons. Still, Smith was proclaimed by many to be the best shortstop in the game purely by virtue of his defense. This was true at the time, but Smith was not *all* a shortstop could be.

CHILDREN OF WAGNER, FATHERS OF RIPKEN: SHORTSTOPS WHO HIT, 1918–81			
Player	Years	EQA	HR
Arky Vaughan	1932–43, 1947–48	.316	96
Ernie Banks	1953–61	.304	298
Lou Boudreau	1938–52	.291	68
Joe Cronin	1926–45	.287	170
Johnny Pesky	1942, 1946–54	.287	17
Luke Appling	1930–50	.286	45
Cecil Travis	1933–41, 1945–47	.284	27
Vern Stephens	1941–55	.283	247
Denis Menke	1962–74	.281	101
Jim Fregosi	1961–73	.279	151
Joe Sewell	1920–28	.279	49
Woodie Held	1954, 1957–69	.276	179
Eddie Joost	1936–37, 1939–43, 1945, 1947–55	.276	134
Pee-Wee Reese	1940–42, 1946–58	.276	126
Rico Petrocelli	1965–70	.274	129

Enter Cal Ripken Jr. In the spring of 1982, rookie Ripken wasn't anybody's idea of a shortstop. At six-four, 225, he was too big, it was said, to field the position. Only his manager, Earl Weaver, was able to see beyond the biases of the time, the biases of practically *all* time, which insisted that a shortstop had to be lithe, light, and little to effectively play the position. (There have been five players in major league history nicknamed "Rabbit," and each of them played shortstop for all or part of their careers.) Even if this stricture effectively ruled out putting superior hitters at the position, men who were simply *large* were reflexively reassigned. After years of carrying the good-field/no-hit (not even a little) Mark Belanger at shortstop, the visionary Weaver looked at Ripken, who had hit 25 and 23 home runs in his previous two minor league seasons, and saw not a "natural" third baseman but a shortstop who was a slugger. In a world of Ozzie Smiths, this would be a decisive tactical advantage; during 1980 and 1981, just one shortstop in all of the majors, Robin Yount of the Milwaukee Brewers, had been close to a consistent offensive asset.

Ripken quickly learned how to use his strength to compensate for a smaller man's quickness. With a strong arm, he could set up deeper than most shortstops, increase his groundball range, and use his strong arm to throw out runners from deep in the hole. Suddenly the Orioles were getting Gold Glove defense *and* 25 home runs a year from a position where most teams would be happy to get 10. The debate began: Was Ripken just a happy fluke, or were the days of the good-field/no-hit shortstops dead?

Thirteen years later, the shortstop position was still having an identity crisis. In 1995, Cal Ripken was in the twilight of his career and would soon move to third base. Ozzie Smith was a year away from retirement after nearly two decades of making impossible things look easy. Alan Trammell (.285/.352/.415, 185 career home runs) was still on the roster in Detroit but hadn't played more than sixty-three games at short in a season since 1991. The one vital star at short was Barry Larkin who, at thirty-one, was in the middle of what should prove to be a Hall of Fame career. He was a more impressive hitter than most shortstops, but wasn't putting up Ripken's power numbers. Though Ripken had proved that a big man could play shortstop, he hadn't inspired any other teams to emulate Weaver's thinking. Perhaps in the years 1982–1995, Ripken was a unique specimen; perhaps the other teams were being timid. It's impossible to say. Teams continued to rely on the Smith model, of which Cleveland's Omar Vizquel was the primary exemplar.

It took until 1996, Ripken's last year at shortstop, for his heirs to materialize. Having made Alex Rodriguez (six-two, 190) the first overall pick in the 1993 amateur draft, the Seattle Mariners did not hesitate to rush him to the big leagues. After auditions in 1994 and 1995, Rodriguez came to the majors to stay in 1996. The Yankees had had former first-round draft choice Derek Jeter (six-three, 185) up to New York for a cup of coffee in 1995. The next spring, when Tony Fernandez (six-two, 165), was injured, Jeter lucked into a job despite the organization's prejudice against its own young players. Nomar Garciaparra got his own call-up on August 31, 1996, and became Boston's full-time shortstop in 1997.

In 1997, Major League Baseball arrested its retreat to the Ozzie Smith model. Rodriguez followed his monster 1996 (.358/.414/.631) with another solid year (.300/.350/.496). Garciaparra's numbers were impressive (.306/.342/.534 and 30 home runs), while Jeter chipped in with .291/.370/.405. The Holy Trinity of Shortstops was anointed. Suddenly it was no longer acceptable to scrape by with a .250 average and a glove. The barrage continued the next year when Jeter smacked 19 home runs; Garciaparra, 35; and Rodriguez, 42. In one season, the trinity hit more home runs than Rizzuto, Smith, and Pesky had in their entire careers combined.

Between 1998 and 2000, Rodriguez, Jeter, and Garciaparra led all major league shortstops in Value Over Replacement Player (VORP) by a wide margin. Rodriguez set a new high in VORP for shortstops in 1996 (101.8), edging out a three-way tie at 100.1 among Ernie Banks's 1958, Honus Wagner's 1908, and Robin Yount's 1982. Jeter trumped him with a spectacular 1999 in which he hit .349/.438/.552 and totaled 105.1 VORP. Not to be outdone, A-Rod edged him in 2001 with 105.2 VORP and a .318/.399/.622 with 52 home runs.

By 2004, the trinity had begun to show some wear and tear. In fact, it had become more of a onesome. Traded to the Yankees, Rodriguez agreed to play third while Jeter remained at short. Garciaparra spent the year struggling with his Achilles injury and a growing negative public perception, and was traded to the Cubs. Having missed significant time in 2003 after dislocating his shoulder, Jeter struggled mightily for the first two months of 2004, eventually placing fourth among major league shortstops in VORP behind Baltimore's Miguel Tejada, Detroit's Carlos Guillen, and Texas's Mike Young.

Despite Tejada's 2002 MVP award while with the Oakland A's, this latter-day trinity was a pale copy of the original. The tide was turning again:

AL SS MARGINAL LINEUP VALUE, 1972–2005

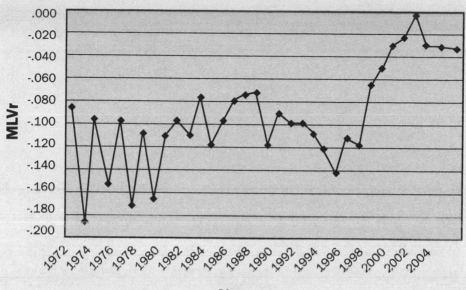

Even the Red Sox, in acquiring Orlando Cabrera, had elected to move forward without exceptional offense at short.

The National League had never even gotten the good news about shortstops. While Jeter pushed the Yankees to six pennants, Garciaparra won his batting titles and Rodriguez dominated the league in everything else. National League teams stuck with Royce Clayton, Neifi Perez, and Rey Ordonez, and cultivated new versions of the old model like Adam Everett, Jose Reyes, and Cesar Izturis.

Is shortstop so challenging a position that it's rare to find players who both field the position and hit? Was the simultaneous arrival of the trinity a fluke rather than a paradigm change, or was it the defense-über-alles mind-set of managers such as Ozzie Guillen that aborted the revolution?

Whatever the case, the age of the super shortstop seemed to be coming to an end, just as it had when Honus Wagner hung up his spikes almost ninety years ago.

—JAMES CLICK

17

INVULNERABLE
AUGUST 16–SEPTEMBER 11, 2004

ow can we explain, and what should we make of, the fact that between August 16 and September 11 the Red Sox won twenty-two of the twenty-five games they played? As we already know, an eight-game losing streak tells us little about a team's eventual fortunes, but a 22–3 stretch must surely say something about a team's destiny, right?

On the morning of August 16, 2004, it had been over two weeks since The Trade and almost nothing had changed in Beantown. The Red Sox were 64–52, a depressing ten and a half games behind the Yankees (75–42). The Rangers (64–52) and the Angels (65–53) were each a half-game behind the Athletics in the west and in a virtual tie for the wild card spot with the Sox. There was, however, good news. Boston had just finished thirteen games against Tampa Bay, Detroit, and Chicago—three of the American League's weaker sisters—and managed a healthy 8–5 record, winning the first three series before dropping two of three against the other Sox in three one-run games. The Red Sox's run differential was the best in the AL, as it had been nearly all year long. Through August 16, they had outscored their opponents 658–558, 16 runs better than the Yanks' 650–566 margin, and significantly better than Oakland (585–531), Anaheim (592–547), and Texas (613–567). And this information was more telling than you might think.

Over twenty years ago, Bill James, author of the famous *Bill James Baseball Abstracts* and now an official analyst for the Sox, discovered that a team's winning percentage could be pretty accurately deduced from its runs scored (R) and runs allowed (RA) totals, using the formula $R^2 / (R^2 + RA^2)$. By multiplying this formula's result by the number of games the team played, James could accurately estimate the team's win-loss record. Further research by BP's Clay Davenport both improved the formula's accuracy and showed that a team's winning percentage for the rest of the season would be closer to the estimated winning percentage based on R and RA than on the actual winning percentage up until that point in the season.

But this wasn't just any season. Based on the Red Sox's runs scored and runs allowed as of August 16, their record *should* have been 67–49, three games ahead of where they actually were. More important, the Yankees should have been 66–51, nine games *behind* their current pace. Based on their R and RA, the Red Sox actually should have been 1.5 games up on New York, not 10.5 games down. However, Boston's winning percentage for the rest of the season, based on their R and RA, was most likely to be .576, well ahead of the projected winning percentage of the Angels (.537) and Rangers (.536). If the rest of the season was consistent with those winning percentages, the Sox would finish at 91–71, nine games behind the Yankees (100–62) but two games ahead of the Angels and Rangers and safely in the wild card spot.

Mathematics showing that the Red Sox should have been leading, and winning, the division would have been small comfort in these dog days were it not for what happened next, a course correction during which the Sox went 22–3, climbed from 10.5 games to a mere 2.5 behind New York, and made Bill James and Clay Davenport look better and better. Beginning with sweeps of Toronto and Chicago, the Sox took six of seven from the Blue Jays and Tigers before swinging through the West Coast, where they swept the Angels and Athletics and took two of three from the Rangers in between. The Idiots finally began to slow down in Seattle, where they dropped the first and final games of a four-game weekend series. Overall, the Sox outscored their opponents 167–89 and compiled individual winning streaks of six and ten games each, wrapped around a 3–0 loss in Toronto where Ted Lilly outdueled Pedro Martinez. It was a stretch of some of the most dominant baseball of the past thirty years, propelling the Sox to the front of the wild card chase and only a couple of steps behind the division leader.

Over the past thirty years, only eleven teams have managed to win twenty-two out of twenty-five games (see table). With the exception of the 1978 Pirates and the 1990 Mets, it's a list of some of the greatest teams of the last thirty years. The 1975 Reds—the Big Red Machine—have their own place in the hearts of New England fans, having defeated the Red Sox in an intense seven-game World Series, despite the best efforts of Carlton Fisk. With the 2004 Red Sox, the list includes five World Series champion-ships (the '75 Reds, '77 Yanks, '91 Twins, and '98 Yanks), eight teams that won a hundred games, and ten teams that made post-season appearances.

TEAMS THAT WON AT LEAST 22 OF 25 GAMES IN A SEASON			
Year	Team	W	L
1975	Cincinnati Reds	108	54
1977	Kansas City Royals	102	60
1977	New York Yankees	100	62
1978	Pittsburgh Pirates	88	73
1979	Baltimore Orioles	102	57
1990	New York Mets	91	71
1991	Minnesota Twins	95	67
1998	New York Yankees	114	48
2001	Oakland Athletics	102	60
2001	Seattle Mariners	116	46
2002	Oakland Athletics	103	59
2004	Boston Red Sox	98	64

As the '90 Mets and '78 Pirates proved, however, it doesn't take a great team to get hot and win 22 out of 25. Given their winning percent-ages, the likelihoods of the Pirates or the Mets doing it were only 0.04 percent and 0.07 percent, respectively.[1] On the other end of the spec-trum, the '98 Yanks and '01 Mariners—two of the three most victorious teams in history—had a 3.62 percent and 4.76 percent chance. While those odds may sound rather low, they are only the odds of the team win-ning 22 of a *particular set* of 25 games. With 162 games in the season, however, each team effectively has 137 25-game sets (162–25) in which they could win 22 games. Looking at the problem that way, the odds of the Mariners and Yankees *not* winning at least 22 of 25 games at some point in the season was 0.13 percent and 0.64 percent, respectively—that is, for teams as dominant as the '98 Yankees and '01 Mariners, winning 22 of 25 games at some stretch in the season is almost inevitable. The Yankees did it from April 5 to May 6, 1998; the Mariners went 24–3 from May 8 to June 8, 2001.

Given the 2004 Red Sox's winning percentage (.605), the chances of them ripping off a 22–3 winning streak was 31.4 percent. They had almost a one-in-three chance to do it, and they did. The Red Sox won against weak teams and they won against strong teams. In the streak's first 13 games, they faced Toronto six times, Chicago three times, and Detroit four. In 2004, those teams had winning percentages, respectively, of .416, .512, and .444. The next 12 games, three against each team in the traditionally strong AL West, proved no sterner a test. They were a blistering 10–2.

The streak, then, was not the artificial result of a weak period in the unbalanced schedule. In theory, baseball's unbalanced schedule, readopted in 2001 after twenty-two years of balanced play, made a 22–3 stretch more likely by giving the Red Sox extra series against the weaker sisters of the AL East. But Boston's hot stretch wasn't entirely the result of a few well-timed games against Tampa Bay, Toronto, and Baltimore. The Sox may have started their streak against weaker competition, but they maintained it—when the odds of losing were growing greater—against the elite of the AL West.

In general, as the table at right shows, the Red Sox did not face a significantly easier schedule than their wild card rivals in the season's final two months. Each

OPPONENT'S WEIGHTED WINNING PERCENTAGE BY MONTH, 2004				
Month	Anaheim	Boston	Oakland	Texas
April	.498	.503	.510	.489
May	.505	.458	.483	.475
June	.527	.521	.523	.505
July	.502	.546	.506	.532
August	.476	.459	.485	.494
September	.490	.511	.494	.528
October	.562	.481	.568	.389

of the four teams faced a very easy August followed by a more difficult September, but while Boston's August was easier than either Oakland's or Anaheim's, its September was significantly more difficult. Six games against the Yankees combined with eight against Oakland, Anaheim, and Texas made September a relatively fair month for the Sox, not the cakewalk of August, but far from the brutal month of July.

If Boston's overall winning percentage hardly made the streak inevitable and the quality of their opponents wasn't the cause, perhaps it was players added in the trade of Nomar Garciaparra that provided the spark. New shortstop Orlando Cabrera hit better during the streak than he had in any year in his career, putting together a batting line of .333/.358/.556 (AVG/OBP/SLG) in 110 PAs. While those numbers seem impressive compared to his season total of .264/.305/.383, Garciaparra batted .300/.367/.500 while with the Sox, so even Cabrera's unseasonably hot bat only made a minimal difference. Doug Mientkiewicz, the other player acquired in the trade, managed only .194/.270/.300 during the streak, hardly streak-worthy numbers.

Cabrera and Mientkiewicz were brought in as much for their defense as their offense, so the pitching staff's performance could be more revealing. For the season, the Red Sox defenders allowed opposing batters to reach base 30.6 percent of the time the ball was put in play. During the winning streak, opposing batsmen managed to reach 27.9 percent of the time. This difference is significant—similar to turning their opponents' lineups from a collection of .306 hitters to .279—but the streak's relatively small sample makes it difficult to say with any confidence that the defensive improvement was more than a random fluctuation. Anyway, the defensive improvement wasn't maintained in the season's last two weeks (during which the Sox allowed runners to reach 30.2 percent of the time afterward), so it continues to be difficult to attribute the streak to the presence of Cabrera and Mientkiewicz, especially considering Mientkiewicz's limited playing time. While opposing batters were somewhat stifled, the Boston infield's double play percentage was actually lower during the streak (10.1 percent of double play opportunities) than during the rest of the season (11.4 percent). In the end, the combination of small sample size problems, Mientkiewicz's limited playing time, and the decreased double play percentage leave the causality of the improved defense highly in doubt.

Another theory: Garciaparra's departure allowed the players to stop worrying about him and his injuries and instead concentrate on baseball. It's true that during the two months following the transactions, the rest of the Red Sox lineup improved from .280/.358/.469 averages to .288/.373/.490, but most of that improvement was nullified by Cabrera and Mientkiewicz's

LEATHER NOT-SO-GOODS

The Red Sox have rarely been blessed with great interior defense. Fenway Park's invitingly close left-field wall, the Green Monster, has always placed a premium on power hitters, not acrobatic infielders. Gold Glove voters may not always be the most discriminating observers when it comes to understanding the nuances of fielding excellence (see the discussion in Chapter 9 of the flaws in conventional measurements), but it is by no means insignificant that Boston shares with Anaheim/Los Angeles the fewest Gold Gloves among American League Infielders. No Boston Red Sox infielder has won a Gold Glove in over a quarter of a century. Among American League teams, the Baltimore Orioles have accumulated the most Gold Gloves, a total of 39. Here are Boston's paltry four:

POS	Player	Year(s)
1B	George Scott	1967–68, 1971
2B	Doug Griffin	1972
3B	Frank Malzone	1957–1959
SS	Rick Burleson	1979

combined line of .269/.309/.418. In other words, the overall batting remained roughly the same with the new players added.

Then where do we look to explain the team's run? Actually, plain old statistical probability in the ebb and flow of a baseball season is as good an answer as any. Hits are not evenly distributed through the season, nor are home runs or strikeouts. Likewise, wins and losses come in bunches in general proportion to a team's overall strength. Winning streaks come and go, the result of factors too numerous to identify. Flipping a coin 162 times inevitably produces sequences of four or five or six or even eight heads in a row; it's just the natural variance in the results of a binomial system. By allowing arbitrary endpoints to be assigned to a subset of games within a season, almost any team can be made to appear either invincible or inept. From May 31 to July 2, the Red Sox struggled to an 11–17 record, but that stretch of games didn't make them any worse than the 22–3 stretch made them better.

What it did do was this: It enabled them to wake up on the morning of September 12, a mere two and a half games behind the Yankees with twenty-one games remaining, the wild card race having been exchanged for something far more precious.

—JAMES CLICK

E X T R A   I N N I N G S

BICOASTAL BLUES?

"You commence getting tired two days later from staying up all night which it wasn't 'cause you're going West and you can't even get a sandwich in the whole town."
—CASEY STENGEL ON ARRIVING IN LOS ANGELES FOR A ROAD TRIP

At the tail end of their August–September hot streak, the Red Sox left to play four series against American League West teams:

August 31–September 2: three games at home against Anaheim
September 3–5: three games at home against Texas
September 6–8: three games in Oakland
September 9–12: four games in Seattle

At the time, the Red Sox were four and a half games behind the Yankees. With just thirty games left it would be extremely hard to make up those games and take the division title. If New York went 18–12, the Red Sox would have had to go 23–8. A poor showing could cost the team any chance at the playoffs. Boston's competition for the wild card playoff berth was going to come from whichever team in the AL West didn't take the pennant. (There was no other team in wild card contention; the second-place team in the AL Central, the Indians, were 66–66.) Anaheim, first opponent on the West Coast swing, was only two and half behind Boston for the wild card.

AL WEST STANDINGS AFTER GAMES OF AUGUST 30:

Oakland A's	77–53	.592	
Anaheim Angels	75–55	.577	–2
Texas Rangers	73–56	.566	–3.5
Seattle Mariners	50–80	.385	–27

The Red Sox could not have been happy.

To the usual and customary handicaps of playing on the road—the absence of your own fans and the presence of hostile ones, a playing field tailored to the home team's advantage, the strategic disadvantage of not getting last licks in the bottom of the ninth—western trips add jet lag. By their normal clocks, East Coast players on the West Coast start their night games between ten and eleven P.M.

But statistically, how much worse do East Coast teams do on the West Coast than non–East Coast teams? Consider the table below, which contains the results of eastern time zone teams' road trips to the West Coast from 1972 through 2004. The last column, WODIFF, shows the difference between the winning percentages of East Coast and non–East Coast teams when visiting West Coast teams:

TEAM	EAST HOME WIN % VS. WEST	EAST AWAY WIN % VS. WEST	DIFF	OTHERS HOME WIN % VS. WEST	OTHERS AWAY WIN % VS. WEST	DIFF	WODIFF
ATL	.5496	.4875	.0621	.5398	.4901	.0498	–.0123
BAL	.5619	.5146	.0473	.5282	.4912	.0370	–.0104
BOS	.6229	.5214	.1015	.5661	.4952	.0710	–.0305
FLO	.5265	.3652	.1613	.5318	.4225	.1093	–.0521
MON	.5348	.4462	.0886	.5264	.4572	.0692	–.0194
NYA	.5795	.4991	.0805	.6089	.5196	.0894	.0089

(continued)

TEAM	EAST HOME WIN % VS. WEST	EAST AWAY WIN % VS. WEST	DIFF	OTHERS HOME WIN % VS. WEST	OTHERS AWAY WIN % VS. WEST	DIFF	WODIFF
NYN	.5276	.4457	.0819	.5262	.4638	.0624	−.0195
PHI	.5592	.4423	.1169	.5398	.4502	.0896	−.0273
TBA	.3684	.3509	.0175	.4523	.3650	.0873	.0697
TOR	.5064	.4829	.0235	.5276	.4594	.0682	.0447
	0.5494	0.4706	0.0788	0.5430	0.4734	0.0696	−0.0092

Most East Coast teams had a greater than normal drop in winning percentage when playing West Coast teams. Only the Yankees and Blue Jays (and the Devil Rays, who have only a few years of data to examine) had smaller drops against West Coast teams than other opponents. Aggregating across all East Coast teams, the difference comes to a little over 9 points of winning percentage. Over a full 162-game season, this would amount to about a game and a half in the standings. Of course, games played against West Coast teams amouns to a small fraction of a season, not 162 games. As such, the expected negative impact on the win-loss record of East Coast teams, due to travel, amounts to less than half of one win.

Another common belief is that road trips, particularly cross-country ones, wear more on teams later in the season. Dividing all road trips into late (after August 1) or early (before August 1) reveals that the effect is mildly, moderately real:

TEAM	LATE	EARLY	DIFF
ATL	.4754	.4967	−.0214
BAL	.5029	.5200	−.0171
BOS	.5419	.5112	.0307
FLO	.3370	.3841	−.0471
MON	.4318	.4541	−.0223
NYA	.4892	.5042	−.0150
NYN	.4842	.4242	.0599
PHI	.4175	.4537	−.0362
TBA	.2895	.3816	−.0921
TOR	.4649	.4887	−.0238
	.4637	.4743	−.0107

There's a mild effect, a loss of about 11 points of winning percentage, associated with these teams playing on the road later in the season. Given the number of games in a season played under these circumstances, it's still a small effect on the team's overall record, particularly since the team's divisional opponents are also equally vulnerable when they fly west.

The perils of West Coast swings, then, have always been somewhat exaggerated. Essentially, the Red Sox were not likely to be destroyed by this late swing, but they couldn't expect to prosper either, and since mediocrity was tantamount to conceding the eastern division race to the Yankees, the trip would very likely finish the Red Sox.

Or not. In 2004, the Red Sox went 8–1 against the three toughest teams outside their own division:

GAME	OPP	@	RS	RA	RESULT	GM#	BOSTON STARTER	OPPONENT STARTER
Aug. 31	ANA	BOS	10	7	W	130	Schilling	Lackey
Sept. 1	ANA	BOS	12	7	W	131	B. Arroyo	Sele
Sept. 2	ANA	BOS	4	3	W	132	Lowe	B. Colon
Sept. 3	TEX	BOS	2	0	W	133	P. Martinez	Wasdin
Sept. 4	TEX	BOS	6	8	L	134	Wakefield	C. Young
Sept. 5	TEX	BOS	6	5	W	135	Schilling	Drese
Sept. 6	OAK	OAK	8	3	W	136	B. Arroyo	Zito
Sept. 7	OAK	OAK	7	1	W	137	Lowe	Redman
Sept. 8	OAK	OAK	8	3	W	138	P. Martinez	Hudson
Sept. 9	SEA	SEA	1	7	L	139	Wakefield	Madritsch
Sept. 10	SEA	SEA	13	2	W	140	Schilling	Franklin
Sept. 11	SEA	SEA	9	0	W	141	B. Arroyo	Moyer
Sept. 12	SEA	SEA	0	2	L	142	Lowe	Meche

The Red Sox scored 86 runs (6.62 per game) and allowed 48 (3.69 per game), leading to ten wins and three losses. It could have been even better: Two of those losses were to the lowly Mariners.

Manny Ramirez fueled the offense. The American League's best and most consistent hitter over the past ten seasons, Ramirez smacked 7 home runs in 13 games, scoring 12 runs and driving in 13. Johnny Damon hit .405. David Ortiz hit 4 homers and drove in 11 runs. Mark Bellhorn also drove in 11. The whole team was hot, even bench contributors Gabe Kapler and the newly acquired Dave Roberts excelled while filling in for the injured Trot Nixon.

NAME	G	PA	H	2B	3B	HR	R	RBI	SB	CS	BB	SO	AVG	OBP	SLG
Manny Ramirez	13	58	15	3	0	7	12	13	0	0	7	10	.300	.379	.780
Orlando Cabrera	13	57	16	6	1	1	10	7	1	0	4	6	.314	.351	.529
Mark Bellhorn	12	57	14	5	0	2	6	11	1	0	6	13	.280	.368	.500

(continued)

NAME	G	PA	H	2B	3B	HR	R	RBI	SB	CS	BB	SO	AVG	OBP	SLG
Jason Varitek	11	49	13	3	0	0	7	2	1	0	6	7	.310	.408	.381
Bill Mueller	12	48	10	2	0	2	7	8	0	1	6	6	.250	.354	.450
David Ortiz	11	47	9	2	0	4	8	11	0	0	7	14	.231	.340	.590
Kevin Millar	11	44	10	4	0	2	9	8	0	0	6	7	.270	.364	.541
Johnny Damon	9	41	15	3	1	1	9	8	1	0	4	2	.405	.463	.622
Dave Roberts	11	40	10	5	0	1	8	7	0	1	3	5	.286	.350	.514
Doug Mientkiewicz	10	25	4	1	0	0	2	1	0	0	4	3	.200	.320	.250
Gabe Kapler	7	23	6	1	0	1	3	6	0	0	2	1	.286	.348	.476
Doug Mirabelli	6	12	2	0	0	0	1	1	0	0	3	5	.222	.417	.222
Trot Nixon	5	7	2	1	0	0	0	0	0	0	0	2	.286	.286	.429
Dave McCarty	2	4	1	0	0	0	1	0	0	0	0	1	.250	.250	.250
Pokey Reese	2	3	0	0	0	0	1	0	0	0	1	0	.000	.333	.000
Kevin Youkilis	2	5	0	0	0	0	1	0	0	0	1	1	.000	.200	.000
Adam Hyzdu	1	1	1	1	0	0	0	1	0	0	0	0	1.000	1.000	2.000
Sandy Martinez	1	1	0	0	0	0	0	0	0	0	0	1	.000	.000	.000
Ricky Gutierrez	1	1	0	0	0	0	0	0	0	0	0	0	.000	.000	.000

There were as many contributors on the pitching side of the ledger. Curt Schilling, Pedro Martinez, Derek Lowe, and Bronson Arroyo all pitched very strongly. Martinez threw 13 shutout innings across two starts. Only Tim Wakefield, who surrendered 15 runs in 10.2 innings, failed to record a win during this stretch among starting pitchers, and taking two of the three losses. The bullpen was outstanding as well, allowing only one inherited runner to score, and posting a 3.15 ERA during that stretch:

NAME	G	GS	IP	H	R	ER	BB	SO	ERA	W	L	SV
Curt Schilling	3	3	23.0	18	8	8	0	19	3.13	3	0	0
Derek Lowe	3	3	20.7	17	6	6	6	13	2.61	2	1	0
Bronson Arroyo	3	3	16.3	17	8	7	4	10	3.86	2	0	0
Pedro Martinez	2	2	13.0	6	0	0	4	15	0.00	2	0	0
Tim Wakefield	2	2	10.7	15	15	10	5	6	8.44	0	2	0
Terry Adams	4	0	5.7	6	1	1	2	1	1.59	1	0	0
Keith Foulke	6	0	5.3	7	2	2	0	4	3.38	0	0	4
Mike Timlin	5	0	4.7	5	2	2	1	2	3.86	0	0	0
Mike Myers	6	0	3.7	5	4	4	1	0	9.82	0	0	0
Ramiro Mendoza	3	0	3.3	1	0	0	0	0	0.00	0	0	0
Curt Leskanic	4	0	3.3	3	0	0	2	2	0.00	0	0	0
Alan Embree	5	0	2.7	1	0	0	0	2	0.00	0	0	0
Pedro Astacio	1	0	1.7	2	2	2	3	1	10.80	0	0	0
Scott Williamson	1	0	1.0	0	0	0	1	1	0.00	0	0	0

This was a team that had hit its stride, with solid contributions from the starting lineup, rotation, bullpen, and bench. The Red Sox not only held their ground against the Yankees, but picked up a game in the standings, closing the gap to three and a half games. In the wild card race, Anaheim fell from two and a half games behind Boston to five games behind, Texas from three games to eight games. The Red Sox could not have picked a better time to become truly bicoastal.

—DEREK ZUMSTEG AND KEITH WOOLNER

18

CRACKING THE RIVERA CODE
SEPTEMBER 17–19, 2004

With only twenty games remaining and Anaheim facing a difficult stretch through its own division, the Red Sox set their watches back to eastern standard time for the duration of the season. Except for two key series with the Yankees, the remainder of the slate was filled with games against Tampa Bay and Baltimore. The battle for Connecticut would be settled in a home-and-home series, six games in all.

The first game against the Yankees was a rain-soaked pitching duel in Yankee Stadium between Orlando Hernandez and Bronson Arroyo, whose new dreadlocks prompted manager Terry Francona to say, "It's the first time I ever looked in the mirror and was glad I was bald." The Yankees nursed a 2–1 lead through rain delays and into the top of the ninth. It was at this point that the familiar chords of Metallica's "Enter Sandman" rang through the damp air, the bullpen gate in deep left-center opened, and closer Mariano Rivera strolled to the mound to end the game, as he had done routinely in over four hundred other games since 1997.

Rivera was having one of his better seasons, with a 1.73 ERA and a league-leading 49 saves. Long one of the best control pitchers in the league, he was not quite at Curt Schilling's level of stinginess with walks, but Rivera kept his walk rate down, his strikeout rate respectable, and his home run rate miniscule. The difference between Rivera and the league-average pitcher was significantly larger when looking at on-base percentage allowed or slugging percentage allowed, than batting average allowed. While he gave up annoying bloop singles, he didn't issue free passes and didn't give up the long ball.

Uniquely, he did all of it with one pitch, a low- to mid-nineties cut fast-ball that showed an amazing propensity to elude bats or else shatter them. Depending on their role, most pitchers require a repertoire of two to four pitchers to succeed, but for Rivera, that one pitch has been enough for him to compile an almost certain Hall of Fame career.

To not only have a chance in this game, but in any conceivable post-season, the team would need to go through Rivera. Fortunately, from 2003 to 2004, the team had been far more successful than the rest of the league against him. In 2004, not including the postseason, the Sox batted .250/.375/.375 (average/on-base percentage/slugging percentage) and handed Rivera a 4.22 ERA while the rest of the league could only muster .221/.271/.265, a 1.59 ERA. The year before that the Sox hit .356/.396/.467 (a 2.70 ERA); everyone else hit .209/.246/.265 (1.48 ERA). In 2004 the Yankees had lost only one game all year in which Rivera entered with the lead or tied: on July 24 in Boston, on Bill Mueller's two-run home run in the bottom of the ninth.

The Red Sox would take this game, too. Thanks to a solo home run from John Olerud and five scoreless innings of relief by Tanyon Sturtze and Flash Gordon, the Yankees carried a 2–1 lead into the top of the ninth inning. As he had countless times before, Joe Torre called for Rivera. Trot Nixon, the first batter to face Rivera, walked on a six-pitch at-bat, and Francona sent Dave Roberts out to pinch-run. Rivera threw three straight strikes to Jason Varitek, but as the catcher went down swinging, Roberts stole second base. Rivera fell behind, 2–1, to Kevin Millar, then hit him with a pitch. Francona pinch-ran for Millar with Gabe Kapler. Rivera then fell behind again on Cabrera, who singled to right on a 2–1 pitch, scoring Roberts and moving Kapler to second. Tie game. Rivera then got his second swinging strikeout of the inning, retiring Kevin Youkilis on four pitches, but Johnny Damon, rapidly establishing himself as Rivera's personal Antichrist, singled to center on a 1–1 pitch, scoring Kapler and giving the Red Sox their first lead of the day. One pitch later, Mark Bellhorn grounded out to end the inning. In the bottom of the frame, Keith Foulke did what Rivera could not, retiring the Yankees in order to end the game.

Boston's rally against Rivera moved the Red Sox to two and a half games behind the Yankees. Had they not beaten Rivera in this game and the July 24 contest, they would have been six and a half games behind, with no chance at the division title. (Boston's success against Rivera would continue into the postseason and then into 2005, when Rivera would pitch the ninth inning in the last two games of the 2005 season's opening series against the Sox at Yankee Stadium. Rivera entered the second game of the season with a 2–1 lead in the ninth and allowed a home run to Jason Varitek, but was rescued by Derek Jeter's home run in the bottom of the ninth, which gave the Yankees the victory. The following night, Rivera again entered the game in the ninth to protect a one-run lead. This time, the Red Sox made sure the bottom of the ninth wouldn't spoil their night, scoring five runs against Rivera. While Alex Rodriguez's ill-timed error meant that only one of the runs was earned, Rivera still walked three men and allowed three more hits on his own.)

Why didn't Rivera's magic work against Boston in the first two years of the Theo Epstein administration? For one thing, Rivera was simply overworked; Yankees manager Joe Torre had Rivera throw more innings in 2004 (78.2) than any other year that he's been their closer except 2001.

Rivera had thrown 10.2 innings against the Sox all year. Of course, it helps to remember that the 2004 Red Sox were not only one of the most potent lineups of the last decade, but also one of the most patient. Since 1990, only three teams have averaged at least four pitches per plate appearance: the 1994 Tigers, the 2000 Mariners, and the 2004 Red Sox. The Fenway hitters weren't simply fouling pitches off or looking at strikes, either; only the Yankees, Giants, and Indians saw a higher percentage of balls in 2004. (Removing intentional balls and, effectively, Barry Bonds moves the Sox up to number three.)

Upon taking over as general manager of the Red Sox in the winter of 2002, Theo Epstein and farm director Ben Cherington made Ted Williams's *The Science of Hitting* required reading throughout the minor league system. They sought out hitters at the major league level who subscribed to the Splendid Splinter's recommended discipline: Watch a couple of strikes go by while waiting for that perfect meatball to drive in the gaps or out of the park. While there's still some debate that this strategy does in fact yield higher power numbers, the hitting philosophy based on Williams's ideas guided the Epstein administration's free-agent signings and led them to league-leading totals in on-base percentage, slugging percentage, runs scored—and strikeouts.

The major flaw in Ted Williams's waiting game is this: *If* the opposing pitcher isn't the kind to fall behind in the count, *if* he throws strikes and walks few batters, the Red Sox philosophy might fold in on itself as hitters continually fall behind in the count. Patience and power should work only against league-average pitchers or worse, or hurlers who are just a little bit too wild for their own good.

On the surface of things, this does seem to have been the case in 2004. Extreme control pitchers—those who walk fewer than two and strike out fewer than six batters per game—faired better than usual against the Sox in the 65.2 innings they threw in 2004.[1] Boston batters hit .287/.323/.472 against them, scoring only 5.35 runs per game. But then again, extreme control pitchers who keep their walk totals down do well against nearly everyone. Relax the definition of control pitchers to include pitchers who managed three or fewer walks per game—still well short of the league average—and suddenly the Sox did extremely well: 6.23 runs per game, hitting .308/.362/.500. With just that small increase of one walk a game by the opposing pitcher, the entire Boston lineup went from hitting like Craig Biggio to hitting like Javy Lopez (circa 2004, not 2002).

How'd they do against power pitchers, who as a group tend to have high totals of strikeouts, walks, and home runs? Power pitchers like to take care of their own business with little help from the defense, challenging hitters to make contact with their overpowering pitches. The truly great power pitchers, such as Schilling or Randy Johnson, are adept at keeping their walk rate down while keeping the strikeout rate up, but on the whole they tend to be a little wild. Against flamethrowers, the Sox didn't fare quite as well as they did against the control pitchers group, hitting .250/.357/.443 on the season.

Or did they? Dig a little deeper and an interesting fact emerges. The Sox maintained their power and on-base numbers against the power-pitching group at almost exactly the same levels as they did against the control pitchers. Against the control-pitching group, the Red Sox slugged .500, but managed only .443 against the power boys, a significant drop—at least on the surface. In fact, that difference is very misleading; the Sox actually showed *more* power against the power-pitching group.

The reason for this is that slugging percentage can be skewed by players with high batting averages. A better measure of a team's power is isolated power (ISO), or slugging average minus batting average. ISO provides a measure of total bases *after first base* per at-bat. Two hypothetical players—one who hits a single every time up and one who hits a home run every fourth time up—would have identical slugging percentages, but the latter player would certainly have more power than the former. The perfect real-world example is the Mariner's slap-hitting artist Ichiro Suzuki. The 2001 Most Valuable Player automatically has nearly a .100 point advantage over the rest of the league in slugging because of his .372 batting average. But while Ichiro's .455 slugging percentage was well above league average, he was clearly not among the upper half of sluggers in the league. His ISO of only .083 denotes his actual power, not his unending string of singles.

Against the control pitchers group, the Sox had an ISO of .192 (.500 minus .308) while against the power-pitching group they had an almost identical ISO of .193 (.443 − .250). Likewise, their on-base percentage was nearly identical (.362, .357). Essentially, *the only difference between Boston's results against power and control pitching is that the walks they drew against power pitchers became singles when they faced control artists*. The lineup hit for the same amount of power while simply adapting to the pitcher's tendencies to either walk or challenge the hitters. It's as if the style of pitching didn't matter to Boston batters.

The reason for this consistency was not that each individual Red Sox hitter did well against both kinds of pitching, but rather because team management had assembled a lineup that was nearly equally divided into two groups of players: one that did well against the control artists, and one that did well against the power pitchers. Mark Bellhorn (.270/.407/.522), Millar (.302/.436/.585), Damon (.273/.392/.503), and Nixon (.286/.407/.524) all performed better against the power pitchers in the league than they did against the control group. Bill Mueller (.387/.446/.698), Gabe Kapler (.306/.351/.403), David Ortiz (.386/.442/.719), and Kevin Youkilis (.338/.408/.515) all favored the control group. The only two players who performed equally well against both pitching approaches were Manny Ramirez and Jason Varitek.

The lineup balance left opposing pitchers no way out. Oakland's Mark Redman, one of the game's softer throwers, has found most of his success not in striking batters out, but in keeping them off the bases. Discounting his games against Boston, in 2004, Redman struck out a mere 4.78 batters per game while walking 3.1—not impressive totals, but better than league average. Against the Red Sox his game plan fell apart. While Redman achieved a 4.22 ERA against the rest of the league, the Sox touched him up for a healthy 10.93, hitting .371/.429/.700 against him including 5 home runs in just 14 innings. It wasn't the walks that did Redman in, though; it was the Sox waiting for their pitch and creaming it when they got it, thus maintaining their power against one of the league's more extreme control pitchers. Their patience—not biting at a control pitcher's marginal offerings—earned them fatter pitches later in the count.

Another Oakland hurler, Barry Zito, used the exact opposite approach, almost that of the classic power pitcher, though he lacks the velocity usually associated with top strikeout men. He didn't have much success against the Sox either, allowing them a .319/.396/.574 line. Other pitchers similar to Redman or Zito, such as Baltimore's Rodrigo Lopez, had great success against the Boston lineup. But it would be a mistake to infer too much. There were almost no common features among pitchers who fared well against the Sox and those who did not. The difference in the Red Sox's performance against certain pitchers lies more in the inherent statistical noise of baseball than in any key factor. Boston employed a group of hitters who were adaptable and potent, equally impressive against whatever the rest of the league could throw at them.

While that kind of adaptability comes in handy over the long haul, it still doesn't explain the Sox's undue success against a pitcher like Rivera, who belongs to a third class of pitchers: the elite. By virtue of his high-strikeout, low-walk style of pitching, Rivera doesn't fall into the traditional power or control pitcher groups. And you can't group all pitchers who share Rivera's style and analyze how the Red Sox did against them for the simple reason that Rivera is one of a kind. There are no truly similar pitchers in terms of approach or results.

If Rivera's style of pitching does not explain why Boston was so successful against him, perhaps the key factor is familiarity. And there the numbers have something to say. Due to the unbalanced schedule, the Sox see Rivera quite often. Rivera pitched against seventeen different teams in 2004, but he faced only four teams six times or more, the four comprising the American League East. Against the thirteen teams he faced fewer than six times, he allowed an ERA of 0.45 in 40 innings; against the other three: 3.59 in 38.2. Every team in the AL East scored on Rivera. The rest of baseball mustered two runs on a Bengie Molina home run in Anaheim. Pitching is as much about deception as it is about talent. The trend held true in 2003 as well. The two teams that saw Rivera the most, Boston and Baltimore, handed him a 2.28 ERA while the rest of the league mustered but 1.41. For hitters, familiarity breeds contentment.

Interestingly, and contrary to the league norm, Rivera's success diminished the more often he saw a team. Most pitchers' ERAs improved the more familiar they were with a team and its lineup. Pitchers who only faced a particular team once had an ERA of 4.89 while pitchers who faced teams ten, eleven, twelve, and thirteen times had ERAs of 2.82, 3.09, 2.78, and 2.20, respectively. Rivera's ERA decline is likely related to his reliance on a single pitch. Batters improve against Rivera when they've had some experience recognizing Rivera's cut fastball. Pitchers with a real repertoire, on the other hand, use their increasing knowledge of batters' tendencies to fool them with pitch selection as well as location.

With Rivera's number in their back pocket and their first division title since 1995 in their sights, the Sox came to Yankee Stadium on Saturday looking to close the gap to one and a half games. It took them less than half an hour to lose the game when Derek Lowe allowed five runs in the bottom of the first on his usual collection of walks and bleeders. By the end of the fifth, they were down 12–0 to Jon Lieber. On Sunday, Martinez strolled to the mound to face Mussina, hoping to get the Sox back within two and a half, but two runs in the first didn't help. When Martinez's day was done, he'd allowed eight runs in five innings, failing to get a single out in the five-run sixth inning. Mike Mussina held the Sox to one run in seven innings, and the Yankees had all but wrapped up the division.

"They put us in the rearview mirror a little bit," Francona said euphemistically after the game, since it was closer to the truth to say that, for all postseason intents and baseball purposes, the Yankees could no longer even see the Red Sox behind them. At least the Angels had dropped two of three to the surprising Rangers over the weekend, so Boston had held its ground in the wild card hunt.

—JAMES CLICK

19

DECONSTRUCTING PEDRO
SEPTEMBER 24–26, 2004

When Pedro Martinez took the Fenway Park mound to face the Yankees on Friday, September 24, the game itself had no postseason implications. Trailing by four and a half games in the American League East standings with ten to play, the Red Sox had faint hope of catching the Yankees, and with a six-game lead for the wild card, they had little need to try. Nonetheless, the right-hander with the Jheri curls was the object of much anxiety and scrutiny. It had been a rough year for Martinez. During his first six seasons in Boston, he'd been nearly indomitable, winning two Cy Young Awards, leading the league in strikeouts four times, and posting an ERA of 2.26, less than half of the park-adjusted league average. But his right shoulder now showed the wear and tear of nearly 2,300 major league innings, he'd lost about five miles per hour on his famous fastball, and his seven-year, $90 million contract with the Red Sox was due to expire at season's end. Though the Sox had picked up his $17.5 million option for 2004 the previous spring, Martinez was not cutting the team any slack in negotiating a new agreement. As April closed, a mix of machismo and frustration over stalled negotiations drove him to declare himself a free agent at season's end.

Now, with the exact sum of his next multimillion-dollar contract riding on every game, Martinez had cause to worry; despite his 16–7 record, he had looked very beatable lately. His ERA stood at an unsightly 3.69, good for nearly anyone else, but almost a run and a half higher than his average over his entire Red Sox career. As free agency and his thirty-third birthday approached, his durability was in question. He could ill afford a bad performance and still hope to walk away with a guaranteed contract that befit a legend. The wintertime acquisition of Curt Schilling hadn't helped his bargaining position. Schilling's even keel, robust health, media-savvy manner, and pedigree as a Yankee-killer threw Martinez's moodiness and fragility into relief. The arrival of Schilling, a new alpha male to sit atop the pitchers' pecking order, proved that there would be life after Martinez for the Sox.

The thought of deferring to Schilling rankled Martinez. It was the rare case of a younger lion being displaced by an older one. "I don't know how people are going to have the guts to tell me they're going to push me back [in the rotation] . . . but if they did it, I wouldn't argue. I'm only an employee here that does his job."

A CASE STUDY

PEDRO, WITHOUT QUALIFICATION

During his tenure with the Red Sox, Pedro Martinez was often called the best pitcher in baseball. This is an insult. In fact, he's the best pitcher ever.

One of the best ways to gauge a pitcher's effectiveness is to compare how many runs he allowed (earned and unearned) per nine innings to how many a league-average pitcher would allow in the same ballpark. Baseball Prospectus uses a couple of different metrics to do this. The first, Runs Allowed Plus (RA+), is calculated by taking the league-average runs allowed, multiplying it by a park factor—which expresses the percentage by which a player's home ballpark inflates or deflates run scoring—then dividing that by the pitcher's runs allowed, and multiplying by 100. An RA+ of 100 is league average, an RA+ of 120 is 20 percent better than league average, and an RA+ of 200 is twice as good as the league average.

While some measures of pitcher success focus on earned run average, there are three reasons to consider unearned runs in the process: the arbitrary nature of official scoring and error attribution, the problems with theoretically reconstructing an inning to determine unearned runs, and the argument that pitchers are culpable for *all* the runs they allow. The pitchers that are good at preventing earned runs are also good at preventing unearned runs.[1]

Among pitchers with a minimum of 150 innings pitched in a single season, Pedro Martinez recorded the highest single-season RA+ of all time (post-1890) as a member of the Red Sox in 1999. Martinez also recorded the ninth best RA+ mark in 1999. Here are the top twenty RA+ figures for 1890–2004:

#	NAME	YEAR	TEAM	RA+	#	NAME	YEAR	TEAM	RA+
1.	Pedro Martinez	2000	BOS	293	11.	Dean Chance	1964	LAA	225
2.	Greg Maddux	1995	ATL	278	12.	Joe Wood	1915	BOS	218
3.	Walter Johnson	1913	WAS	273	13.	Ron Guidry	1978	NYA	212
4.	Dutch Leonard	1914	BOS	271	14.	Walter Johnson	1912	WAS	208
5.	Mark Eichhorn	1986	TOR	254	15.	Greg Maddux	1997	ATL	207
6.	Dwight Gooden	1985	NYN	245	16.	Billy Pierce	1955	CHA	205
7.	Greg Maddux	1994	ATL	237	17.	Sandy Koufax	1964	LAN	204
8.	Bob Gibson	1968	SLN	236	18.	Tom Seaver	1971	NYN	204
9.	Pedro Martinez	1999	BOS	225	19.	Cy Young	1901	BOS	204
10.	Roger Clemens	1997	TOR	225	20.	Kevin Brown	1996	FLO	203

He was just as dominant over a period of years. The top twenty composite RA+ figures for all pitchers since 1890 with over 1,500 innings:

#	NAME	IP	RA+	#	NAME	IP	RA+
1.	Pedro Martinez	2296.0	163	11.	Christy Mathewson	4780.7	134
2.	Ed Walsh	2964.3	146	12.	Mordecai Brown	3172.3	134
3.	Walter Johnson	5914.7	145	13.	Carl Hubbell	3590.3	134
4.	Lefty Grove	3940.7	142	14.	Lefty Gomez	2503.0	133
5.	Whitey Ford	3170.3	138	15.	Cy Young	7354.7	133
6.	Hoyt Wilhelm	2254.3	138	16.	Pete Alexander	5190.0	133
7.	Roger Clemens	4493.0	137	17.	Harry Brecheen	1907.7	133
8.	Addie Joss	2327.0	137	18.	Greg Maddux	4181.3	133
9.	Randy Johnson	3368.0	137	19.	Curt Schilling	2812.7	132
10.	Sandy Koufax	2324.3	135	20.	Jim Palmer	3948.0	132

A second way to measure a pitcher's effectiveness is to calculate how many more runs a pitcher prevented than a league-average pitcher would have in the same ballpark. Baseball Prospectus uses a statistic called Runs Prevented (RP) to do so. RP is calculated by subtracting the pitcher's runs allowed from the park-adjusted league runs allowed, multiplying by innings pitched, and dividing by nine. Martinez is one of only four post–World War II pitchers to have a season ranked among the top twenty in this category:

#	NAME	YEAR	TEAM	RP	#	NAME	YEAR	TEAM	RP
1.	Cy Young	1901	BOS	116.1	11.	Cy Young	1902	BOS	77.8
2.	Walter Johnson	1913	WAS	96.6	12.	Bob Feller	1940	CLE	77.7
3.	Walter Johnson	1912	WAS	95.9	13.	Lefty Gomez	1937	NYA	77.2
4.	Pedro Martinez	2000	BOS	84.7	14.	Lefty Gomez	1934	NYA	76.9
5.	Dolf Luque	1923	CIN	84.3	15.	Lefty Grove	1930	PHA	76.6
6.	Lefty Grove	1931	PHA	82.3	16.	Claude Hendrix	1914	CHF	76.4
7.	Red Faber	1921	CHA	81.8	17.	Joe McGinnity	1903	NYN	74.2
8.	Roger Clemens	1997	TOR	81.1	18.	Dwight Gooden	1985	NYN	74.1
9.	Joe McGinnity	1904	NYN	79.2	19.	Sandy Koufax	1966	LAN	73.0
10.	Carl Hubbell	1936	NYN	79.1	20.	Lefty Grove	1936	BOS	72.4

Here are the top twenty career RPs among pitchers post–1890:

#	NAME	IP	RP	#	NAME	IP	RP
1.	Cy Young	7354.7	1053.2	11.	Tom Seaver	4782.7	516.6
2.	Walter Johnson	5914.7	860.6	12.	Pedro Martinez	2296.0	484.6
3.	Kid Nichols	5056.3	753.6	13.	Randy Johnson	3368.0	477.2
4.	Lefty Grove	3940.7	673.2	14.	Carl Hubbell	3590.3	472.5
5.	Roger Clemens	4493.0	651.5	15.	Bob Feller	3827.0	462.0
6.	Pete Alexander	5190.0	615.7	16.	Jim Palmer	3948.0	439.5
7.	Warren Spahn	5243.7	558.5	17.	Eddie Plank	4495.7	438.4
8.	Christy Mathewson	4780.7	544.8	18.	Whitey Ford	3170.3	420.9
9.	Amos Rusie	3544.7	524.8	19.	Ed Walsh	2964.3	400.0
10.	Greg Maddux	4181.3	520.5	20.	Mike Mussina	2833.3	372.9

The top twenty cumulative RP figures for pitchers during Martinez's time with the Red Sox (1998–2004):

#	NAME	IP	RP	#	NAME	IP	RP
1.	Pedro Martinez	1383.7	352.3	11.	Mariano Rivera	482.0	145.4
2.	Randy Johnson	1634.0	294.6	12.	Al Leiter	1360.0	145.1
3.	Curt Schilling	1570.0	246.8	13.	Bartolo Colon	1503.0	144.3
4.	Kevin Brown	1261.7	215.9	14.	Jamie Moyer	1473.7	133.6
5.	Greg Maddux	1583.0	200.0	15.	Barry Zito	981.0	126.0
6.	Tim Hudson	1240.7	184.7	16.	John Smoltz	639.3	120.4
7.	Mike Mussina	1471.0	182.2	17.	Freddy Garcia	1199.3	113.6
8.	Roger Clemens	1453.0	170.4	18.	Armando Benitez	508.7	113.2
9.	Tom Glavine	1544.0	168.6	19.	Brad Radke	1435.3	112.4
10.	Keith Foulke	587.0	150.9	20.	Jason Schmidt	1258.7	108.0

By any measure, the Red Sox had enjoyed the best years by the most dominant pitcher of all time.

—JAY JAFFE

He had been feisty even in defeat the weekend before, after being blown out in the Bronx. After the game, Martinez complained to the press about umpire Bruce Froemming's strike zone, the blustery conditions, even the commentators. On learning that the Yankee broadcasters were attributing his poor showing partly to back trouble, he told reporters, with his customary flair for hyperbole, "YES Network wants me to die." Regarding the team's back-to-back blowouts at the hands of the Yankees so late in the season, he boasted hollowly, "If we get to the playoffs, believe me, we're not going to be the ones who are scared."

Now, on Friday, September 24, the Red Sox faithful watched as Martinez labored to redeem himself after the previous Sunday's debacle. He worked out of trouble in the first, striking out Bernie Williams to end the inning. After a 1-2-3 second, he gave up two runs to the Yanks in the third on nothing more impressive than a gap single by Alex Rodriguez. Manny Ramirez knotted the game with a two-run blast over the Green Monster in the bottom of the inning, and then Trot Nixon put the Sox ahead in the fourth with a solo shot. The Yanks pulled even in the sixth thanks to a leadoff walk, a double, and a sacrifice fly, but a Johnny Damon homer in the seventh gave the Sox a 4–3 lead.

At that point, Martinez had thrown 101 pitches. With the terminal fate of the last Red Sox manager staring Francona in the face, no one in his or her right mind thought he'd leave Martinez in the game, but Francona stunned fans of both sides by sending Martinez back out for the eighth inning. When previous manager Grady Little had seen the handwriting on the wall regarding his future in Boston, he had claimed his place in the Sox tortured legacy: "I'll be another ghost, fully capable of haunting." Inconceivably, Francona seemed determined to join him.

The move backfired almost instantly. Hideki Matsui golfed Martinez's second pitch of the eighth into the Red Sox bullpen in right-center-field. Francona stayed on the bench. "If I run out there after two pitches," he said later, compounding his irrationality by leaving Martinez out there, "it makes it look like I wasn't making a good decision before the inning." Francona appeared possessed by the spirits of his predecessors, who spent decades putting pathologies ahead of winning. Martinez stayed in, Bernie Williams doubled, Jorge Posada struck out, and Ruben Sierra slapped an RBI single to give the Yanks a 5–4 lead. By the time Francona came out of his trance and went to his bullpen, the damage was done.

Martinez was a reporter's dream after the game. After a moment of contrition ("How many times had my team given me the lead? I wanted to bury myself on that mound . . ."), he proceeded to deliver several immortal lines of tabloid catnip, so dense with ambiguity and cunning that it suggested Martinez had hidden verbal talents that rivaled his physical ones. "What can I say—I just tip my hat and call the Yankees my daddy. . . . I can't find a way to beat them at this point. . . . I wish they would [expletive] disappear and never come back."

In just a few sentences, Martinez had accomplished a great deal: he had dropped his defiant air to pay grudging tribute to the resourceful opposition, cast himself as the underdog in the minds of both teams' fans, and underscored his own impending free agency with a subtle threat to defect to the enemy. Martinez became the wild card's wild card.

Amusing fodder though it made, Martinez's "daddy" quote had been no idle comment. Over the course of his Red Sox career up to that point, he had made thirty starts against the Yankees, including three in the postseason. The Yanks had prevailed in nineteen of those games, including nine of eleven since July 19, 2002. Even though the Yankees had been dominant—winning three World Series and five pennants during Martinez's seven years in Boston—the Yankees' mastery of so dominating a pitcher defied expectations and eluded easy explanation—unless you haven't read the first half of this book and still believe in The Curse.

In the twenty-seven regular season starts against the Yankees—a small sample size, equivalent to just under one season's worth of data—Martinez's win-loss record was just 9–10, a .474 winning percentage. In his 176 other games pitched for the Sox (including two relief appearances in 1999), he owned a record of 108–27, an astronomical .800 winning percentage. However, a pitcher's individual record of wins and losses (and, some would argue, every aspect of his performance except strikeouts, walks, and home runs allowed) can be misleading since it is greatly dependent upon the pitcher's supporting cast. The offense must score runs for him, the defense must make plays behind him, the bullpen must take over when he tires, and the manager must make correct decisions. Did Martinez receive a disproportionate lack of support while pitching against New York?

The answer is no. In the 27 games, the Yankees held a 17–10 edge but only outscored Boston by just 10 runs, 101–91. Based on that run distribution, a simple Pythagorean calculation predicts that the Yanks should have won 55.2 percent of the time, roughly a 15–12 edge. A more rigorous calculation using the Pythagenport method, which accounts for the per-game run environment, predicts that the Yanks should have won 54.8 percent of the time, or 14.7 times out of 27. The Sox thus underperformed in this sample by 2.3 games.

If Red Sox run production doesn't provide the answer, we'll have to look closely at Martinez's numbers—against Yankees versus against everybody else (EE):

	IP/GS	ERA	K/9	BB/9	K/BB	HR/9	HP/9	WP/9	BABIP
vs. NY	6.67	3.30	11.50	2.65	4.34	0.80	0.80	0.45	.298
vs. EE	6.92	2.40	10.86	1.91	5.68	0.65	0.46	0.16	.281

The most glaring stat in those two lines is the difference in ERAs. Against the Yanks, Martinez allowed nearly one more earned run per nine innings than against everybody else. He pitched fewer innings per start, and though he struck out 6 percent more hitters, he yielded 38 percent more walks and 23 percent more homers. In addition, he plunked 74 percent more hitters and was about three times as likely to throw a wild pitch. While Martinez's numbers against the Yankees aren't as good as the rest of his stellar line, they are still excellent, particularly in regard to his strikeout rate (which actually increased) and his control. His increased walk rate, however, carries repercussions that will be examined in more detail below.

Perhaps the Yankee pitchers just overachieved against the Red Sox. As we know, management has tailored a sabermetrically ideal offense of high on-base and slugging percentages, partly to take advantage of Fenway's batter-friendly left field and right field fences. While the latter-day Dan Duquette teams were not offensive juggernauts, over the course of Martinez's tenure with the Sox, the team's offense has averaged 5.34 runs per game in a league averaging 5.00 runs per game. The Sox ranked in the American League's top three in runs scored four times out of those seven years, leading the league in the past two and finishing second the year before. Nevertheless, Boston scored only 3.37 runs per game in Pedro Martinez's starts against the Yankees, just under two runs less per game. Take away his first start (May 31, 1998) in which they scored 13 runs, and that average falls to exactly 3 runs per game. Credit for much of this goes to the Yankee pitching, which ranked sixth or better in ERA among American League teams every season in this span; four times, they were in the top three. Joe Torre did an excellent job of aligning his rotations so that one of his team's top pitchers squared off against Martinez. More often than not, his pitchers lived up to their reputations.

	GS	QS	IP	ER	ERA
Mussina	7	7	54.0	10	1.67
Pettitte	6	4	33.7	22	5.88
Clemens	3	2	16.0	4	2.25
Hernandez	3	3	24.0	3	1.13
Cone	2	2	13.0	4	2.77
Wells	2	0	13.0	6	4.15
Vazquez	1	1	6.0	2	3.00
Halsey	1	0	5.3	2	3.38
Lilly	1	0	5.0	3	5.40
Mendoza	1	0	4.7	4	7.71
TOTAL	27	19	174.7	60	3.09

With the exception of a couple of disastrous eight-run starts by Andy Pettitte, the Yankee starters never allowed more than four runs in any of the twenty-seven games, they recorded quality starts (pitching six innings or more, allowing three earned runs or less) over two thirds of the time, and they allowed more than one run per game less than the team's aggregate ERA of 4.18 over that seven-season span.

Mike Mussina, in particular, deserves the title of Martinez's archnemesis—or "daddy," if you will—with the Yankees winning five of their seven head-to-head starts. The stats of Ramiro Mendoza and Roger Clemens are distorted by one start in which Clemens departed after one inning with a pulled groin muscle; Mendoza allowed one run in 5.7 innings of excellent relief and the Yanks prevailed.

While pitchers' win totals can be misleading, it's worth noting that the Yanks were able to offer up pitchers who won at least 150 games in the big leagues in 20 of those games, venerable and acclaimed hurlers if not uniformly of Hall of Fame caliber. Fourteen of those starts were by pitchers who have won more games than Pedro's 182 major league victories.

Another piece of the puzzle: While the Yankees starters excelled, the Boston bullpen underperformed. From 1998 to 2004, the Sox bullpen posted a 4.10 ERA, just a few ticks lower than the starters' 4.16 ERA. Yet in support of Martinez in those Yankee games, Sox relievers came on to pitch 60.3 innings and allowed 33 runs—a 4.92 ERA. That's about 5.5 runs more than expected. In the eight games in which Martinez didn't get the decision, the bullpen went 1–7. Twice they blew leads Martinez handed them. Four times they lost after he departed with a tied score. Once, the offense came from behind after he left to take a lead, only to have the bullpen give it back. Just once, on April 13, 2002, did the Sox come from behind and have the bullpen back it up to turn a potential Martinez loss into a win.

What about the Yankee offense? Did the sight of a Boston uniform energize their bats? As mentioned before, the Yanks drew considerably more walks off Martinez per nine innings than his other opponents. And they did have higher batting averages and slugging percentages against him than other teams did—but only slightly.

	PA	AVG	OBP	SLG
Yankees Against Pedro	748	.215	.286	.334
Others Against Pedro	4750	.205	.256	.314

In the context of the current era's offensive explosion, these numbers are still staggeringly low. Essentially, the Yankees went 17–10 against Martinez with a lineup that was no more productive than nine Tony Womacks.

In that low-scoring offensive environment, every little edge has value. Those extra hits, extra walks, and extra hit-by-pitches all add up to one thing: more pitches for Martinez. Not by a huge amount; Martinez threw an average of 4.7 more pitches per game against the Yanks than against other teams. They also averaged 0.11 pitches more per plate appearance, or 2.9 percent more, than other hitters did against Martinez. Those are small numbers, and they may not mean much, but in a pitcher with a limited number of bullets such as Martinez, every pitch matters. The Yankees' strategy against Martinez was summed up by *The New York Times* beat writer Buster Olney in September 2000: "The pattern in the games has generally been the same— they force Martinez to work hard early in the game, driving up his pitch count and tiring him, and if they can't muster runs against him, then they get him out of the game in the middle innings and attack the Red Sox bullpen."

In his 1998–2000 heyday, Martinez averaged well over seven innings per start and routinely went above 110 pitches. In the year of his shoulder injury and the two years following, he averaged closer to 6.5 innings and 100 pitches per start:

	#p/GS	IP/GS	BFP/GS	OBP	ERA
1998	114.1	7.08	28.8	.277	2.89
1999	112.1	7.18	28.8	.247	2.07
2000	109.1	7.48	28.2	.213	1.74
2001	99.4	6.48	25.3	.252	2.39
2002	103.3	6.64	26.2	.253	2.26
2003	97.9	6.44	25.8	.271	2.22
2004	105.8	6.58	27.4	.299	3.90
TOTAL	106.8	6.86	27.4	.260	2.52
vs. NY	110.4	6.67	27.7	.286	3.30
vs. EE	105.7	6.92	27.3	.256	2.40

In 2004, his pitch count per start climbed by about eight from the year before, but those extra pitches weren't converted into extra outs; he lasted only 0.14 innings longer per start, or 1.6 batters per start, depending on which way it's measured.

Note that even in his heyday, Martinez generally hasn't gone much beyond twenty-seven hitters faced, or three times through the order. When he's stuck around long enough to see the lineup a fourth time, the results have been ugly:

								MARTINEZ VS. NYY (1998–2004)				ALL P VS. NYY		
PA#	PA	H	2B	3B	HR	BB	SO	AVG	OBP	SLG	AVG	OBP	SLG
1	250	42	7	1	5	12	92	.183	.245	.287	.270	.349	.448
2	241	54	13	1	5	10	70	.240	.285	.373	.282	.353	.478
3	203	37	7	1	4	23	53	.210	.308	.330	.298	.373	.478
4	54	12	3	0	2	8	15	.286	.434	.500	.306	.387	.464

In their first appearance, Yankee hitters struck out more than twice as often as they got hits, but the ratio improved with each trip to the plate.

On the fourth trip to the plate—small sample size alert—Martinez was raked over the coals like a minor leaguer.

The deterioration of Martinez's performance can be seen in runs allowed by inning. For comparison, the runs allowed (RA) by all starters in 2004 are on the line below Martinez's.

#	1	2	3	4	5	6	7	8	9
IP	27	27	27	26	25	23	17	6	2
RA	2.67	2.33	2.00	2.77	1.44	6.26	6.35	10.50	0.00
04	5.17	4.42	4.95	5.24	4.89	5.36	4.72	3.21	3.17

Against the Yankees, bad things tended to happen to Martinez after five innings. Martinez's RA in innings one through five was 2.25—positively vintage Pedro Martinez, the guy in the catalog. From inning six and onward, it was 6.56, nearly triple the rate of the previous innings. By comparison, the general population of pitchers in 2004 posted an RA of 4.93 in innings one through five, and of 4.88 in innings six and onward. In a word, Martinez had an earlier-than-average tipping point. The 2003 ALCS Game Seven and the September 24, 2004 start are but two examples of a larger trend that saw 33 of the 68 runs scored off Martinez by Yankees coming in his final inning or fragment of an inning pitched.

Why did Pedro Martinez's performance against the Yankees fall short more often than not? The blame for the pitcher's own failures must be shared with ineffective relievers, unproductive hitters, ineffectual managers, and a Yankee team that rose to the occasion to beat the best in the business. Not until the Red Sox assembled a capable supporting cast, and a manager capable of taking the baton from Pedro when necessary, would the daddy talk stop and the chance to end more than eight decades of disappointment begin.

—JAY JAFFE

"WHY DON'T WE JUST WAKE UP THE BAMBINO AND I'LL DRILL HIM."

In his seven years in Boston, no part of the Red Sox-Yankees rivalry symbolized both the intensity and the futility of the Sox's plight better than the Dominican's battles with the Bronx Bombers. Reeling off a starting nine of memorable highlights:

- *September 10, 1999:* As a heavily Dominican crowd cheered him on, Martinez twirled a one-hit, seventeen strikeout masterpiece in Yankee Stadium, marred only by a Chili Davis homer.

- *October 16, 1999:* In an American League Championship Series showdown at Fenway Park, Martinez squared off against former Sox ace Roger Clemens. Much to the delight of the Boston crowd, Clemens was chased in the third, while Martinez pitched seven shutout innings and the Sox prevailed 13–1. This was Boston's only win of the series and the only postseason loss suffered by the Yankees in their march to a second straight world championship.

- *May 28, 2000:* In an ESPN Sunday-night broadcast for the ages, Martinez met Clemens in their first regular season duel. The game lived up to the names on the marquee, as Martinez tossed a four-hit shutout and won, 2–0.

- *May 30, 2001:* Facing the Yankees for the second time in as many starts, Martinez avenged a 2–1, complete-game loss by striking out thirteen over eight shutout innings and winning 3–0 at Fenway Park. Afterward, a fed-up Martinez told reporters he was tired of answering questions about his pinstriped foes: "Look, I don't believe in damn curses. Why don't we just wake up the Bambino, and I'll have him face me and maybe I'll drill him in the ass."

- *June 4, 2001:* The Bambino bit back. Though he struck out ten, Martinez departed after six less-than-dominant innings, having allowed a 4–1 lead narrow to 4–3. He could only watch as the Sox bullpen yielded three runs in the seventh. Boston tied the game in the top of the ninth, but supersub Luis Sojo drove in the winning run in the bottom of the inning.

- *September 7, 2001:* Still searching for his first win since the Bambino quote and having missed two months with a frayed rotator cuff, Martinez was removed after yielding three runs in three innings. As the dysfunctional team's season unraveled in spectacular fashion—capped by the firings of manager Jimy Williams and acting pitching coach John Cumberland as well as frequent clashes between players, including Martinez, and presumptively lame-duck GM Dan Duquette—Martinez was shut down for the year.

- *October 11, 2003:* An ALCS rematch with Clemens devolved into an ugly theater of the absurd, with Martinez in the lead role. The drama featured a purpose pitch behind Yankee Karim Garcia's head, both benches clearing, taunting laced with enough obscenities to give a prudish lip-reader a heart attack, the surreal scene of Martinez throwing down seventy-two-year-old Yankee coach (and former Sox skipper, circa Bucky F. Dent) Don Zimmer, and two Yankee players brawling with a Sox groundskeeper in the bullpen. When the dust settled on the bizarre battle royale, the Sox lost 4–3, giving the Yanks a 2–1 edge in the best-of-seven series.

- *October 16, 2003:* With the American League pennant on the line, the ultimate rematch between Martinez and Clemens looked as though it was going decidedly in the Sox favor when Clemens was pulled in the fourth after yielding three runs. Martinez carried a 5–2 lead into the bottom of the eighth inning, but as his pitch count crossed the century threshold, Sox manager Grady Little resisted, calling upon his bullpen.

The Yankees strung together four straight hits to tie the game before Martinez departed, and won in the eleventh on a walk-off homer by Aaron Boone. Little subsequently lost his job.

- *July 1, 2004:* Trying to prevent a sweep in Yankee Stadium, Martinez fell behind 3–0 early, but survived for seven gritty innings, departing after the Sox tied the score. But he was just a bit player in a larger drama, as the game went well into extra innings. Derek Jeter took the stage and created the highlight film of the year with a headlong leap into the stands to catch a foul ball that ended the twelfth inning. The Yanks won it in the thirteenth, while an injured and visibly dismayed Nomar Garciaparra could only look on.

—JAY JAFFE

20

REFRAMING HISTORY
OCTOBER 5–8, 2004

If curses truly existed, they would have to include some fine-print language that defined their scope and limitations. Babe Ruth had more power than any player of his day, but not enough to authorize biblical plagues and the shattering of nations. With no blanket policy, his curse would have to be finite in its applications. With hindsight, it's now possible to say exactly what the curse on the Red Sox would have covered:

> The team shall lose its last game of consequence in any given season; or shall have its primary opponent be victorious in its last game in any given season.

The second part of the clause would cover seasons in which the Red Sox were eliminated from contention when the league/division/wild card winner clinched its own victory on the season's last day. (The wrathful Ruth surely would have anticipated expansion and divisional play.) The Red Sox curse would *have* to read like this because, on many occasions, they did anything but choke in big games.

Heading into the American League Divisional Series against the Anaheim Angels, the Red Sox were favored, proving once and for all that believing in curses and karma might be all well and good, but when money is on the line, there is no greater skeptical realist than a Las Vegas oddsmaker. Curse or no Curse, the Red Sox have had a fair share of happy outcomes in such showdowns—more than a lot of teams, more than a myth of perpetually cosmic injustice could comfortably explain. For our purposes let's say a happy outcome is a pennant, division title, or wild card berth. In the postseason, it's a series won. Unhappy outcomes are postseason series lost. In the regular season, let's define it as years in which the Red Sox were within hailing distance—say, five or fewer games—of first place (or the wild card) with about a month to go in the season. Here, then, are the numerous happy outcomes for the Red Sox since 1946:

1946 Regular Season: Teams have blown double-figure leads in baseball history, but it's extremely rare. After taking over first place earlier in the season, the '46 Red Sox upped their lead to eleven games on July 14 with a doubleheader sweep of the Indians and maintained that as a steady cushion the rest of the way.

1967 Regular Season: You wouldn't think going 4–4 at the end of an intense, four-team race would be enough to carry the day, but it was for Boston in 1967. Of the four clubs, only the Tigers played better (5–4) while the Twins (3–5) and White Sox (2–6) both essentially tanked. It's a strange curse that would cause the other teams to choke worse than you do.

1975 Regular Season: It's hard to argue that a season in which the first-place team played 160 games and the runner-up just 159 involved a close pennant race, but the Baltimore Orioles were just off the Red Sox stern for most of September.

1975 Postseason: The Red Sox brushed aside the three-time defending World Champion Oakland A's with relative ease. The A's enjoyed just one lead in the entire Series, that coming in Game Two. It was gone by the bottom of the fourth inning. During the regular season, the A's had had a better record while playing in a better division, but, having lost franchise player Catfish Hunter to self-inflicted contractual shenanigans (and, ultimately, the Yankees), the team had a short rotation—two dependable starters backed by improvisation and guesswork. This led A's manager Alvin Dark to some curiously self-destructive decisions. In game one of the best-of-five series he chose to pass over Vida Blue, his best starter, in favor of his second-best, Ken Holtzman. Both were left-handers, presumed to be at a disadvantage at Fenway

Park, but Dark didn't trust his best right-handed starter, Dick Bosman. The Sox won that game, principally because the A's fell apart defensively. Blue started the second game, but Dark panicked and yanked him when the Sox opened the fourth inning with four consecutive hits. The A's went on to lose the game. After a day off, the series resumed in Oakland with the A's facing elimination. Dark, or perhaps owner Charles Finley, determined that the best chance of winning was to start Holtzman on two-day's rest. (The manager and the owner were not on the same page at that moment, to say the least; two days before the start of the eries, Dark was quoted as saying, "Unless he changes his ways, Finley's going to hell.") Holtzman seemed like a good idea for exactly three innings before the veteran and three-time defending World Champions were doomed to defeat, proving that it's not only the Red Sox who have been distracted and made monumentally poor decisions in key postseason situations.

1986 Regular Season: The Yankees hung in there for most of the summer before fading in September. At one point, the Red Sox got their lead up to ten games. In a spurt of late-season ennui, the Sox lost five of their last six to make the final standings look a lot closer than they actually were.

1986 Postseason: Much has been written about the infamous/famous Game Five of the American League Championship Series of 1986, but, had the Angels won that one instead of Boston, attention would have been focused instead on Game Four. In that contest, Roger Clemens was cruising along with a five-hit shutout heading into the ninth before giving up three straight hits and giving way to ineffective relief from Calvin Schiraldi. The Red Sox eventually lost in the eleventh, setting up the elimination that never came. The World Series, of course, would end up on the "unhappy" side of the ledger.

1988 Regular Season: Looking at the standings for '88, it would appear there was some excitement afoot here as five teams finished within three and a half games of first place. The truth is, the Red Sox lost six of their last seven, giving posterity a false impression of the race's tightness. The

Sox had a five-game lead with nine games to go—a slightly better cushion than the '64 Phillies—but held on to win the division.

1990 Regular Season: Here's a classic case of the Sox coming up big when they had to. On September 28, the Blue Jays came to town tied with Boston with identical 84–72 records. Boston won the first two games of the series and dropped the third. Both teams split their next two games (against Chicago and Baltimore, respectively), making a tie still possible. The Sox put it away with a 3–1 victory while the Jays lost to the Orioles. One can argue that this represented more of a Toronto collapse than a Boston triumph since the Jays went 2–6 in their last eight games. Boston was 6–2 in the same period, though, so they must get their due for behaving properly when their main foe was stumbling.

1995 Regular Season: There should be a slang term for this type of pennant race—one in which the main pursuer in the first half fades big time in the second half while the main pursuer of the second half struggles in the early going. Whatever you want to call it, it's the perfect scenario for the front-runner. Such was the Red Sox's happy fate in 1995. They had a fifteen-and-a-half-game cushion as late as September 6 when the Yankees swept them and drove to the wild card title as part of a 22–6 run. Boston still finished with a comfortable seven-game cushion.

1998 Regular Season: On August 30, Boston had an eight-game lead on Texas in the wild card hunt. Toronto was ten games behind. Two weeks later, the Jays had crept to within three games as Boston went 4–10. The Rangers were not much farther behind, either. At that point, Boston righted the ship and went 9–5 the rest of the way, keeping pace with Texas's 9–4 record and besting Toronto's 7–5.

1999 Regular Season: In mid-August, Boston had a slight edge on the A's in the wild card. A head-to-head meeting resulted in a split of four games. From that point on, however, the Red Sox posted the best record in the league and fairly well cruised to the wild card spot.

1999 Postseason: One could argue that this was the finest hour of the "Curse era" Red Sox prior to 2004. Down two games to none to Cleveland, the Red Sox did not so much rise up as blow the world out from under the Indians' feet, winning the final three games of the American League Divisional Series by a combined score of 44–18. The finest moments came last, when, trailing 8–7 after three innings of the deciding game, Pedro Martinez emerged from the bullpen to throw six no-hit innings in the greatest relief appearance in postseason history.

2003 Regular Season: The Red Sox entered the final month of the season two games behind wild card front-runner Seattle on the strength of a four-game sweep of the Mariners the week before. A 17–9 September flourish put them into the postseason hunt for the first time in four years.

2003 Postseason: How close did Boston come to an early death after falling behind Oakland two games to none? Consider the events in the top of the sixth, in which Boston surrendered its 1–0 lead. If not for all manner of tomfoolery on the base paths, the A's would have scored at least one and perhaps two more runs. In the seventh, the A's had the bases loaded with one out and failed to score. In Game Four, the Red Sox rallied from a two-run deficit in the bottom of the eighth to win 5–4. In the decider, the A's had the tying and go-ahead runs on in the ninth but failed to score.

In fourteen seasons, when the team had a shot at going all the way as late as August, the outcome was a happy one. On the unhappy side, the Red Sox lost nine playoff series and World Series as well as a number of pennant races they could have won but did not: 1948, 1949, 1950, 1972, 1974, 1978, 1991, and 2000. Two more seasons—1977 and 1996 (for the wild card)—are borderline collapses. Of these, 1991 probably gets the least ink but was the most serious fade. With two weeks to go in the season, the Red Sox were just a half-game out of first. A 3–11 record sent them plummeting out of the race. The 1948 season, with its lost playoff game, has gone down in history as another of Boston's tragic losses, but in rivalry terms it was a smashing success, with the Red Sox eliminating the Yankees from a three-way race with the Indians on the penultimate day of the season, then pummeling them again on the last day to force a playoff with Cleveland. Similarly, one could also make a case that 1978 should count in both the happy and unhappy categories because of Boston's remarkable recovery from their failures of early September. Closing the season with an eight-game winning string to force a playoff, when a single loss would have meant the end, should probably count for something in the grand scheme of things.

Leaving 1948 and 1978 on the negative ledger gives the Red Sox a total of eighteen unhappy outcomes to fourteen happy ones since 1946. During the same period, the curse-free Yankees were 60–19 in such situations. Prior to 1995, the Indians were 3–7. Since then, they've gone 11–6, albeit without winning it all. Since World War II, the Tigers have been 7–7, winning it all three times. The White Sox, over the same time period (1946 to present), have gone 4–11.

In the ALDS, the Red Sox held many practical advantages over the Angels, especially in the batter's box. For the second year in a row, Boston had led the league in on-base percentage, posting a mark of .360 in both seasons. While the Red Sox did not draw as many walks as the 1949 version of their team (the Ted Williams–led group that holds the all-time team record with 835 passes) or even the 2004 Yankees, they got on base better than any other team in the majors. In 2004, there were 115 players who totaled at least 100 at-bats and managed an OBP of at least .360. Nearly one in ten of these men played for the Red Sox for at least some portion of the season: Manny Ramirez, Jason Varitek, Kevin Millar, Johnny Damon, David Oritz, Trot Nixon, Mark Bellhorn, Doug Mirabelli, Kevin Youkilis, Bill Mueller, and, before he was traded, Nomar Garciaparra. Only the Braves, with seven such players, came close to Boston in this regard. The Yankees, Orioles, and Phillies had six each, but a more typical number was four and two teams—Pittsburgh and Seattle—had just one each.

On the other side of the diamond, the Angels had shown, much like in their championship year of 2002, that it was possible to reject the walk as an important offensive weapon and still win enough games to make the post-season. Only three Angels cleared the .360 OBP mark: Vladimir Guerrero, and, in part-time play, Jeff DaVanon, and Robb Quinlan. As a team, Anaheim finished dead last in the league in walks while Boston finished second. This was about as close as it gets to a battle of polar opposites.

But what about our Las Vegas oddsmaker? What would he make of walk discrepancy heading into the 2004 American League Divisional Series? Keep in mind, of course, that the Angels pitching staff was slightly stingier than average in the walks department (3.1 per game to a league average of 3.3), theoretically canceling a bit of the Red Sox advantage.

Well, the Red Sox continued where they left off in the regular season and came very close to setting the record for most walks drawn per game in a best-of-five series.

More than anything, it was patience that won the series for the Red Sox. The Red Sox dominated the Angels, sweeping the series in three games by a combined score of 25–12. Nine of the Red Sox's twenty-five runs were either scored by a player who had walked, aided by a walk, or, in one case, driven in by a walk. It was this, along with the Boston's usual bashing, that allowed Curt Schilling and Pedro Martinez a little breathing room. Only the third and final game caused the Red Sox any real difficulty. Boston carried a 6–1 lead into the top of the seventh inning, but a bases-loaded walk to Darrin Erstad was followed by a Vladimir Guerrero grand slam to tie the game. The game remained tied until the bottom of the tenth, when David Ortiz staked an early claim to Legendry Postseason Hero status when he knocked the first pitch he saw from Jarrod Washburn out of the park for a game-winning, series-winning homer. Contrary to the ossified thinking espoused by baseball philistines who insist that a postseason series can only be won by teams whose tactics hark back to the small-ball, bunt-and-run game of the dead-ball era, the Red Sox won by sticking to their plodding but effective walks and power philosophy.

When it was over, they had compiled the second-best walks-per-game mark yet recorded in a best-of-five series:

7.5: Los Angeles Dodgers vs. Pittsburgh Pirates, 30 in four games (1974)

6.7: Boston Red Sox vs. Anaheim Angels, 20 in three games (2004)

6.4: New York Yankees vs. Seattle Mariners, 32 in five games (1995)

6.3: Florida Marlins vs. San Francisco Giants, 19 in three games (1997)

6.2: Houston Astros vs. Philadelphia Phillies, 31 in five games (1980)

(Two of those teams—the '95 Yankees and '80 Astros—lost their series; the Yankees, in part, because their pitchers allowed the Mariners twenty-five walks of their own. The '74 Dodgers were already on their way to making this list after three games, but solidified their position at the top by drawing eleven walks in the final, a 12–1 victory. Jimmy Wynn had a Bondsian nine walks in nineteen plate appearances.)

The Red Sox clinched a postseason berth earlier than the Angels, which gave them another advantage: They were able to set their rotation. The Angels, who only put the A's away for good on the day before the season ended, could not throw their best pitcher, Kelvim Escobar, at Boston in the first game. In terms of VORP, the matchups looked like this:

Game One: Curt Schilling (72.9) vs. Jarrod Washburn (22.4)
Game Two: Pedro Martinez (51.2) vs. Bartolo Colon (22.2)
Game Three: Bronson Arroyo (24.7) vs. Kelvim Escobar (53.2)

Neither Schilling nor Martinez was especially sharp in their starts, but with runs pouring in for their side like water through a busted dike, they didn't have to be. They were both good enough, although the most important moment for either of them and the team came not on the mound but away from it, when Schilling sent Red Sox Nation into collective cardiac arrest by showing obvious signs of physical discomfort once Game One was already in hand. The one matchup advantage the Angels enjoyed was neutralized by Arroyo, who actually turned in the best game of the three Red Sox starters. However, he was long gone by the time a decision was reached in the tenth inning, courtesy of David Ortiz.

The Angels did not go quietly except in Game One, in which they were pretty much done by the fourth inning. They were still just a run down heading into the ninth inning of Game Two, and ran Game Three into an extra frame before succumbing. As often happens in extremely short series, a few players never get untracked. In this case, Garret Anderson and Chone Figgins did little to aid the cause. Better players than they have been burned by such small exposures, though, so finding offensive goats in a three-game sweep is often an exercise in gratuitous cruelty. Besides, with Jerrod Washburn (Games One and Three) and Kelvim Escobar (Game Three) getting cuffed around but good, not to mention the bullpen contributing a 7.20 ERA, Angel offense was perhaps academic.

The Red Sox sweep of the Angels was not the most convincing victory of the seventy best-of-five series in baseball history to date, but it was fairly extreme. (The title of Most Convincing belongs to the Yankees and their back-to-back three-games-to-none victories over the Rangers in 1998 and 1999. While they outscored Texas 9–1 the first year and 14–1 the second, a case could be made that the 9–1 sweep was the more telling, because in '99 the Rangers at least leveraged their sole run into a brief lead—something they failed to do in '98. Of the twenty-seven such series that resulted in sweeps, the 2004 Sox scored the fourth-highest number of runs. The 1969 Mets and 1970 Orioles set the record with twenty-seven and the 2000 Cardinals came close with twenty-six. Conversely, though, Boston allowed the second-most runs ever in a sweep. Only those Mets, playing in the first National League Championship Series ever, allowed more, letting fifteen Braves score in what still remains, thirty-five years later, the sweep with the highest total score.

The sweep of the Angels was not even the Red Sox's most convincing series win ever. Their 1975 dismantling of the A's takes that prize. The important thing was that the Sox advanced and did so without the great drama that has so often attended their late-season and postseason endeavors. They were leaving that for later.

—JIM BAKER

21

INSULT AND INJURY
OCTOBER 16, 2004

Although it may remain—especially to those who aren't reading this book—a bone of contention as to whether a dead Babe Ruth haunted the Red Sox from 1918 until October 2004, one thing is inarguable: The team's reversal of fortune can be attributed in some significant part to a real cadaver. Whenever the story of the 2004 Red Sox is told by knowledgeable people, Schilling's ankle, and the impromptu cadaverous research done to help stabilize it, will be the centerpiece. The decisive moment of the season did not take place on the field but on an operating table, when Curt Schilling consented to undergo an experimental procedure, and team physician Dr. Bill Morgan attempted to sew up the Red Sox championship prospects with a needle and thread.

In reality, the Red Sox spent most of the season dealing with one injury after another. The medical staff dealt with many more injuries than average, finishing twenty-fifth out of thirty teams in days lost by players to the disabled list. Red Sox history is littered with promising ballclubs that could have won if not for injuries. Ted Williams's 1946 World Series contribution was muted by an injury suffered during an ill-considered pre-series exhibition. Jim Rice had to sit out the 1975 World Series with a broken hand. Dwight Evans wandered through the team's historic 1978 collapse in a concussive daze. The 2004 Red Sox could easily have joined this dubious roster. It was only the sound construction of the team and a superb performance by the support staff that enabled it to keep good solid players on the field while the starters received treatment sufficient for them to hobble back out to their positions.

Curt Schilling and team doctor Bill Morgan before game 4 of the ALCS

The athletic training staff of Jim Rowe and his assistants, Chris Correnti and Chang-Ho Lee, along with the team's cadre of consultants, led by team physician Bill Morgan, had their work cut out for them from nearly day one of spring training. Nomar Garciaparra showed up for camp with an Achilles tendon injury. The cause isn't clear to this day, attributed variously to a spring training foul ball off the area, an intramural soccer match, and the Bambino himself, whose curse had apparently taken up residence in Garciaparra's ankle. Trot Nixon was also shelved with a herniated disk that defied diagnosis. Morgan himself eventually gave up speaking to the press about Nixon's return, telling *The Boston Globe*, "My prediction skills haven't been so good lately."

Nixon injured his quadriceps during the rehabilitation of his spinal injury, pushing his 2004 debut to mid-June. The leg injury lingered, putting him back on the DL from late July into mid-September and leading many to question the rehabilitation plan. The pair of injuries cost the Sox an approximate 170 man-games with more to come. Ramiro Mendoza's damaged right shoulder was unable to hold up. Scott Williamson tried to pitch through a ruptured elbow ligament only to end up on a surgeon's table where his elbow was described as looking "like a car bomb went off inside." Bill Mueller missed time with leg problems, Pokey Reese was felled by an oblique strain, and Mark Bellhorn broke his thumb. All told, the 2004 Red Sox, a team with a well-respected medical staff, lost nearly a thousand days to the disabled list. In comparison, the Yankees lost around six hundred days and the Cardinals, their eventual World Series opponent, was one of the league's healthiest teams, losing only about five hundred. Only Arizona had more DL time, and the Diamondbacks weren't in contention after the ceremonial first pitch on Opening Day.

Given the team's dire medical straits, the story of Curt Schilling's retinaculum tear is almost implausible. The player who was most severely damaged turned out to be the player who managed to stay active all season. Of course, Schilling was the obvious candidate for the Iron Man role, since he has long had a reputation as a workhorse with a gritty determination that bordered on the self-destructive.

Schilling's injury was often described in the media as an ankle sprain or a torn tendon. Neither was medically correct. He had a different problem, a retinaculum tear that inhibited rotation. There are important differences between the two injuries, befitting the complexity of the foot and ankle. They make up one of the most complex structures in the body, also one of the most commonly injured and slowest healing. The foot and ankle contain twenty-six bones (one quarter of the bones in the human body); thirty-three joints; more than a hundred muscles, tendons (connecting muscles to bones), and ligaments (connecting bones to other bones); and a network of blood vessels, nerves, skin, and fascia. These components work together to provide the body with support, balance, and mobility. There are seven fasciae (connective tissues, the "packing material" of the body) in the ankle, called the retinacula, which hold tendons in place inside a shallow groove. A structural flaw or malfunction in any one part can result in a cascading breakdown across the rest of the lower body and even the lower back.

In pitching, the ankle has two main functions. Dorsiflexion is the movement of the foot up, toward the shin. This is the action that occurs during the windup stage of the pitching motion prior to the push off. Inversion/eversion is the inward and outward motion of the ankle. An ankle sprain (the tearing of the ligaments of the ankle) affects these functions by causing pain during normal usage. A torn tendon prevents the muscle from making its normal action on the bone. A completely torn tendon prevents normal function; the contraction of the muscle has no effect on its bone. It's like trying to move a rowboat with the oars pointed out of the water.

Schilling's retinaculum tear first manifested itself on May 13 during a start at Toronto. Video of the game is inconclusive, but Schilling seems to have injured himself on a fielding play. The injury did not appear to affect Schilling's pitching motion significantly and where it did, the medical care he received from the Red Sox medical staff was effective. During the season, Schilling showed little or no indication of injury effects. His performances were remarkably consistent both before and after the injury.

The Red Sox initially tried to conceal the injury. This is typical for most baseball teams, who fear that the opposition will exploit a weakness. (They never do, as evidenced by the Yankees' "sportsmanlike" refusal to bunt on Schilling in Game Six of the ALCS.) As late as June, when the Red Sox were still insisting that Schilling had nothing more than a bone bruise, Schilling was already receiving injections of marcaine, an anesthetic agent, both before and during games. In addition, due to the shaky condition of

243

the ankle, an osteochrondral defect (a place where the bone is ground down, leaving chunks of bone floating in the joint space) was created in the talus, one of the major bones of the ankle structure. There is some evidence that it took well into July to get a definitive diagnosis.

The Red Sox medical staff was taking a calculated risk that they could keep Schilling at a functional level without exacerbating the injury. With the ankle deadened, Schilling could not tell if he was doing further damage. Each pitch carried with it the risk of a season-ending rupture. It was a gamble that few others—player or physician—would have taken.

The importance of Curt Schilling would be hard to exaggerate. It had escaped no one's notice, least of all Theo Epstein's, that recent series winners have been able to win using only two dominant power pitchers and a short bullpen. Schilling was brought to the Red Sox expressly to pair with Pedro Martinez and win the World Series. The modern-era prototype for this was Schilling's own 2001 Diamondbacks team, which paired him with Randy Johnson, though the strategy has worked throughout the game's history, going back to 1905, when Christy Mathewson and Iron Man Joe McGinnity pitched all but one inning of the five-game World Series. Working with the World Series schedule, a manager can structure his pitching rotation so that the top two pitchers on the staff can pitch roughly half the total innings of the series.

At six-five, 235, Schilling has the classic power pitcher's body. He is thick, not fat. He is tall, but not rangy. He also has the classic power pitcher's repertoire, including a 92–93 mph fastball that tails slightly. He can run the pitch up to 96 on occasion when needed, but it isn't a strikeout pitch. It tends to get popped up, perhaps due to the flatter trajectory of the faster pitch. Schilling also uses a split-fingered fastball, which looks like a fastball but drops drastically as it nears the strike zone. He also has a curveball that shows up about twice a game. It's an average pitch and he doesn't control it well.

Like Roger Clemens, Schilling's power starts in his legs and thick midsection. According to studies done by the American Sports Medicine Institute, reductions in the force generated by the hips translates into a reduction in pitch velocity. Since Schilling has had shoulder surgery twice—a tendon repair in 1995 and a radio-frequency thermal capsule shrinkage in 1999—his career has been even more dependent on a healthy lower body. Unlike pitchers of the past who were injured, lost velocity, and had to either learn to pitch on guile or sell insurance in their hometown, Schilling remained a power pitcher.

Schilling's injury came at almost exactly the one-quarter mark of the season. His strikeout numbers dropped slightly, from seven strikeouts per start before the injury to six, while his walks ticked up slightly, from one per start to 1.1. Schilling was able to pitch enough to rank third in innings, second in ERA, third in strikeouts, fourth in batting average against, and first in wins. Hurt, he was better than almost every other healthy pitcher in the American League. Normal medical care and treatment kept Schilling at or close to full function during the regular season. This ended in the playoffs.

Schilling started Game One of the American League Division Series against the Anaheim Angels. In the first inning, Schilling came off the mound to cover first, then hit the brakes when he realized he would not be needed to complete the play. Video shows that he was running forward, from the mound to the dugout, his head turned to his left to watch the play when he stepped on the edge of the grass at the first-base line. His ankle buckled under him and Schilling hobbled back to the dugout. His weakened retinaculum had ruptured.

Now, in addition to pain, Schilling had to deal with an inability to rotate his ankle. "The tear prohibited inversion/eversion," he told Baseball Prospectus. "The serious issue [was] driving and rotating off the mound." With the retinaculum torn, the tendon it formerly held in place was now popping in and out of its normal location, causing great pain and making the ankle unstable. The push-off is a key piece of the pitching motion. One look at Schilling, or any power pitcher like Roger Clemens or Mark Prior, shows one common physical trait: legs like tree trunks that can thrust their bodies forward, hurtling a ball with devastating speed and motion. With his legs effectively removed from the equation, Schilling's fastball suffered a critical decline in velocity.

Schilling came to the mound for Game One of the ALCS against the Yankees just as he had since May. He hobbled, but was feeling no pain after his injection. He had discarded a brace—"too tight," he said later. From the first pitch he struggled. He was pulling his foot from the rubber rather than pushing off. His fastball slowed to 86 mph, verging on a huge

10 percent reduction from his normal 91 to 93, and the results were not pretty. He lasted barely more than an inning before leaving the game. By the time he limped off the field, the team was on the wrong end of a 6–0 score, and it seemed unlikely that he would return even if the series lasted more than four games.

Which it looked less and less like it would. Games Two and Three were all-Yankees affairs. Jon Lieber pitched seven innings of 3-hit, one run baseball, and though the Sox threatened against a fatigued Tom Gordon in the eighth, Mariano Rivera came in to end the threat, then put down the side in the ninth. The decisive blow for the Yankees was struck by John Olerud in the sixth inning—a two-run homer that came on Pedro Martinez's 106th pitch of the game. Game Three began competitively, with the two teams tied 6–6 after three, but New York's bats exploded at that point, tallying 13 runs to Boston's 2. The 19–8 fiasco was the most discouraging loss of the year for the Red Sox.

As the Red Sox contemplated the climb back from a 3–0 deficit, the medical staff went to work. The brace discarded, Reebok was asked to design a supportive shoe. (Although it would be shown repeatedly on national television in glorious close-up, the shoe was never a factor; some suggest that it was always a high-topped red herring, designed not for support, but to cover up Schilling's blood.) Meanwhile, team physician Dr. Bill Morgan was trying to figure out if a tendon could be held in place without a healthy retinaculum to restrain it. Experimenting with a cadaver, Morgan tried to hold the tendon in one place, actually dislocated from its normal seat, by means of a few sutures through the skin. It seemed to work, but there was no way to test the stress pitching would place on it.

In the first procedure before Schilling's start in Game Six, three sutures were put in. Now there was significant swelling, bruising, and evidence of bleeding beneath the skin. Inside, there was tissue damage, bone-on-bone grinding, and more that would only be discovered after the season. Television cameras focused on the ankle as blood seeped through Schilling's sock, but the real story was that the secret sutures beneath his sock were *just* able to hold. When Schilling left the game, his ankle throbbing, only one suture was left intact. Four sutures were used in Schilling's single World Series start in Game Two, but it all opened up during the six innings he pitched. The Red Sox acknowledge that Schilling likely could not have undergone another procedure, meaning he would not have been available for another start.

It took four surgical procedures to repair the damage Schilling had done to his ankle during the season, injuries that were then exacerbated by the extraordinary measures that kept him available for the playoffs. Just a few weeks after the season—enough time to ride in the parade and inject himself into the presidential election—Schilling would have his ankle repaired. First, the osteochrondral defect was repaired. Using drills and a plug of bone and cartilage, the talus was rebuilt. The doctors then repaired the retinaculum, cleaned up some torn cartilage, and, startlingly, found a four-inch tear in the tendon itself. "It tore sometime during Game Six," Schilling said. "That's one reason it didn't dislocate much in [the World Series]. It split down the middle and wedged over my ankle bone."

Schilling would owe his second World Series ring to creative, competent medical care. His red sock, through which he literally bled for the team, would become one of the sport's great symbols of sacrifice. Schilling hobbled away with another World Series ring and another line on his Hall of Fame résumé. The doctor he owes that ring to, Dr. Bill Morgan, would also get a ring, as would many team employees. But Morgan would also get a pink slip in December, dismissed in favor of what some have termed "doctor by committee." The Red Sox plan would be to have a team of physicians from a hospital to be determined by bidding, instead of one team physician. Schilling, whose ankle problems carried into 2005, continued to consult with Morgan.[1]

As for the cadaver, in just a few years it will be eligible for the Hall of Fame in Cooperstown.

—WILL CARROLL

22

THE 510-SQUARE-INCH
WAR ZONE
OCTOBER 17–18, 2004

O ver. Really over. Finito. Last-one-out-of-the-park-please-turn-out-the-lights over. Coming back from being down three games to nono had never been done. Well, twice, but not in baseball, but in some weird sport not even played with a ball, but a puck, in a league that would go out of business the 2005–05 season.

The Red Sox were not just down three games to nothing, they were down in a most ugly fashion. Saturday night's 19–8 thrashing had been the largest margin of defeat in Sox postseason history, the most runs they'd ever allowed in a postseason game. A week after cruising into the ALCS on the strength of David Ortiz's heroics, the Sox now faced the grim prospect of being bounced out of the baseball season by the Yankees for the second straight year.

The exit didn't promise to be as painful or dramatic as 2003's stomach punch, with no Grady Little to excoriate, no Aaron Boone to hate, no defining moment burned into the brain, but it was going to hurt all the same and in an entirely different way. This Sox team suddenly had the look of something at the end of its era, with Nomar gone and Pedro possibly on his way out, with Jason Varitek about to become a free agent, with no young stars ready to rejuvenate the roster. As they headed through the mist to Fenway Park on October 17, the Sox were missing their best starting pitcher. In his first season in Boston, Schilling had become a fan and media favorite not only for his work on the mound but for his man-of-the-people

Tony Clark strikes out to end game 6
of the ALCS

mien. His accessibility was a bit self-aware—Schilling is one of the smartest people in the game, and knows the value of popular perception—but it worked in a town that looks for reasons to love its baseball players. Friday's rainstorm, which had postponed Game Three and set the series back a day, would have given him time to rest and start Game Four with his normal four days of rest. His ankle, however, would not allow it. Even if the Sox could extend the Series, he would be unable to pitch.

This was a problem, since any hope for extending the Series rested on reclaiming control of the 17- x 30-inch vertical space that is the most important piece of real estate in baseball. As Sox consultant Bill James put it in his 1988 *Baseball Abstract,* "The strike zone is the very heart of a baseball game. An inch in the strike zone means far more than ten yards in the outfield." This point, which seems so basic, is at the core of the performance analysis revolution and its reverence for on-base percentage. OPB is a far better gauge than batting average of a hitter's performance because it takes literally the old saw that a walk is as good as a hit. Properly, statistically, OBP rewards the batter who knows the strike zone. Conversely, analysts evaluate pitchers not so much by their runs allowed or ERA, which are significantly affected by defense and luck, but by their strikeout rate and their strikeout-to-walk ratios, which show how well a pitcher commands the strike zone.

The value of hitters' counts and pitchers' counts has been understood in baseball for a century, but it's only in the last twenty years that we've had actual evidence of its overwhelming importance in the form of pitch-by-pitch data. This data reveals the staggering difference between batters who fall behind in the count (in 2004 they hit .214/.223/.319 in any situation when the pitcher was ahead) and those who get ahead (.341/.478/.581). So throwing a strike on a 1–1 count can mean the difference between facing a bad utility infielder and facing Wade Boggs.

Teams that show patience at the plate draw walks and get into hitters' counts, using up the opposition's better pitchers, and eventually finding themselves hitting against the weaker pitchers hiding at the back of the bullpen. This leads to more walks and more hitters' counts. Pitchers who can counter this approach by throwing strikes give up fewer base runners, work more frequently ahead in the count, and get more innings from fewer pitches, making them more valuable to their team and decreasing the wear and tear on their arm.

All of this happens in a space 17 x 30 inches, and no group of batters has owned that space like the dynastic Yankees of the late twentieth and early twenty-first century. Since the strike-shortened 1994 season, in which they had the best record in the American League, the Yankees had led MLB with 6,978 bases on balls drawn. In the same span, their pitchers had allowed the third-fewest walks in the game, just 5,387. (Greg Maddux's Braves and Brad Radke's Twins were the only two teams to walk fewer men in that span.) The Yankees averaged 144 more walks drawn than allowed a season, an edge that played a big role in six pennants and four championships in an eight-year span.

Under Theo Epstein, the Red Sox finally embraced the concept, especially on the pitching side of the equation. To a staff that already featured one of the game's paragons of command-plus-power in Pedro Martinez, Epstein added Schilling, Mike Timlin, and Keith Foulke, all of whom had an extended track record of throwing strikes. Despite giving 188 innings to a knuckleballer, Tim Wakefield, Sox pitchers would finish second in the AL in strikeout-to-walk ratio in 2004. Meanwhile, Epstein's signings on the hitting side, like Bill Mueller and Mark Bellhorn, specialized in drawing walks, while others like Kevin Millar and David Ortiz had also shown above-average selectivity before being signed by the Red Sox. The Sox increased their walk total in each of Epstein's first two years at the helm, and moved from a .345 OBP that ranked third in the AL in 2002 to a league-leading .360 mark in both 2003 and 2004.

In the first three games of the ALCS, however, it was the Yankees who had won the battle for those 510 square inches. They'd drawn 14 walks at the plate while their pitchers had allowed a mere five. Their pitchers had struck out 24 Red Sox, while Sox hurlers had cut down just 16 Bombers. Sox starters threw just eleven innings in the first three games, seeing the fourth inning just once. The Yankees were ahead three games to nothing in large part because they'd controlled the strike zone.

In Game Four, the Sox showed some life in the battle for home plate. They worked Yankee starter Orlando Hernandez for five walks and three runs in five innings. Meanwhile, the much-maligned Derek Lowe walked no one and struck out three in his five and a third innings of work, his second effective postseason outing. One of his strikes, however, was blasted over the Green Monster by Alex Rodriguez for two runs, and his last pitch was lined by Hideki Matsui past a diving Johnny Damon in center field for a triple. He left the game with his Sox clinging to a 3–2 lead. Mike Timlin relieved Lowe and somehow managed to give up two runs without allowing a ball to leave the infield—three infield singles wrapped around a walk to Jorge Posada. It might have been worse: Bernie Williams ran into an out while trying to score on a wild pitch. Without that out, the Yankees might have scored four or more runs. Down 4–3, the Red Sox provided little excuse for excitement. In the bottom of the sixth and seventh, they went down meekly to Tanyon Sturtze, waiver bait as recently as April, then couldn't capitalize on a leadoff single by Manny Ramirez off Mariano Rivera in the eighth. The Red Sox totaled two strikeouts and no walks for those three innings despite the fact that Sturtze started five of six batters out with a 1–0 count.

In the bottom of the ninth, Fenway Park grew loud again—the way a dying man can experience a burst of energy just before passing away. Kevin Millar, one of the famed Idiots, stood in against Rivera, only the greatest relief pitcher in postseason history. Five pitches later, four of them balls, Millar was on his way to first base.

In retrospect, it's easy to say when something changed for good. That walk to Millar, with the bottom of the Sox order coming up, with the nearly infallible Rivera on the mound, looked innocent enough, a slight postponement of the Yankees' coronation. At the time, no one noticed that it was the first walk Rivera had allowed in the postseason since the 2001 World Series.

Terry Francona sent Dave Roberts in to run for Millar. The speedy Roberts had been gifted to the Red Sox at the trade deadline, when the Dodgers acquired Steve Finley to play center field and were looking to get something, anything, for their incumbent. Roberts, whose light bat limited his usefulness as an everyday player, was a great fit for a Sox team with immobile corner outfielders and a pronounced lack of speed. He didn't play much down the stretch, getting just eighty-six at-bats for the Sox, but his skill set made him a natural for the postseason roster. The line between good and great base stealers, it is sometimes said, is that great base stealers can beat you even when you know they're going to go. Some people may not have known Roberts was going—people in deep comas and perhaps the guys in Washington who planned the invasion and occupation of Iraq. Certainly the Yankees knew. It didn't matter. After two throwovers from Rivera, Roberts went on the first pitch and just beat the throw. Like a good pitcher, a good base stealer traffics in inches. The din in Fenway grew.

The Yankees, with Jorge Posada as their primary catcher, had not made controlling the running game a defensive priority, and rightly so; Posada's offensive ability more than compensates for the small number of stolen bases he allows over the average thrower (Posada caught 26 percent of opposing base runners in 2004, compared to a league average of 32 percent; in 2003, he caught 27 percent against a league average of 30 percent). It hasn't mattered much, anyway, because it has been years since an American League team used stolen bases as a primary weapon—appropriate for a league with a designated hitter in an offensive era. The stolen base has become a very specific situational play. This was the situation. In acquiring Roberts, it was as if the Red Sox had foreseen the moment.

With Bill Mueller at the plate, no one out, and a runner on second base, the possibility of a sacrifice bunt loomed. Giving up an out to advance a runner one base is rarely a sound strategy; it's another one of those sabermetric tenets that collides with received baseball wisdom. In this case, however, with the tying run on second in the bottom of the ninth, with the great Mariano Rivera on the mound and his cut fastball against an average left-handed batter on the mound, it would have been justified. Still, Francona wasn't buying it. He had Mueller swing away. After taking a strike, the 2003 AL batting champion stroked a sharp single right up the middle. Roberts's great speed and Bernie Williams's terrible arm ensured there would be no play at the plate. The Red Sox, who had yielded control of the strike zone for the better part of four games, had taken it back just in time. If the impossible was out of Boston's reach, pulling off the improbable—getting to Mariano Rivera just one time to delay their fate—was a consolation prize, a reason for fans to believe that next year would almost certainly be the year.

Of course, extra innings would provide more reasons. Having exhausted Keith Foulke with two and two third innings of work, the Sox turned to left-hander Alan Embree to start the tenth inning, although Embree had been so unreliable during the season that the Sox had acquired Mike Myers in August to serve as their lefty specialist. But Embree breezed through the tenth, then allowed a leadoff single to Miguel Cairo in the eleventh. Acting on his own initiative, Derek Jeter, owner of a career .331 batting average against lefties, laid down a sacrifice bunt.

After Alex Rodriguez lined out to Cabrera, Francona called for an intentional walk to Sheffield, then finally brought in Myers to face Matsui. Not twenty-four hours prior, Matsui had hit a long home run off Myers in his longest outing in years. He walked him on four pitches, loading the bases.

Switch-hitting Bernie Williams was up and Francona was down to his last reliever, Curt Leskanic, who'd posted a poor 5.19 ERA on the season. Leskanic had been discarded in June by the Royals, the worst team in the American League. He had walked thirty men in forty-three and a third innings, and if he wasn't the last person Sox fans wanted to see coming into the game—Mike Torrez was still alive—he was on the short list. Leskanic threw two pitches, both strikes, and then, when Williams's lazy pop fly on the second offering settled harmlessly into Johnny Damon's glove in center field, the crowd welcomed Leskanic into Red Sox Nation with a cheer that was heard all the way back in Kansas City. To show his appreciation, he came out again for the twelfth and promptly gave a seminar in strike zone management, retiring the Yankees on eleven pitches, seven of them strikes.

While the Red Sox had discovered a pitching hero in the eleventh, the Yankees by that point had run out of their best pitchers. Having used up Rivera and Tom Gordon (two innings apiece), Joe Torre brought in Paul Quantrill for the twelfth. Quantrill had been worked very hard by Torre in the season's first half and was essentially useless down the stretch, posting a 7.09 ERA in the second half. AL hitters batted .360 against him. Torre could only hope that he would revert, miraculously, to early-season form.

Ramirez promptly lined a single to left, bringing up David Ortiz. Eight days prior, Ortiz's soaring home run had swept the Angels out of the Division Series. Now, in a mismatch with a struggling pitcher, he bided his time, taking the first two pitches he saw. With the count even at 1–1, Quantrill missed—just missed—with the third pitch and the valences of the pitcher/batter relationship took over. With a 2–1 count, Ortiz had the statistically proven upper hand, and he used it to drive the ball deep into the right field bullpen, eliciting one more outburst from the damp, cold, believing masses huddled in the Fens, yearning to be free of history's weight.

For one more day, they could hope. And perhaps more than that, because they had slain the dragon Rivera, and survived the game in which they had to use their least-effective starting pitcher, and been backed into a corner with nothing but the bottom of their bullpen, a swizzle stick, and two bottles of Elmer's Glue. In a must-win game, Francona had made a series of good decisions to keep the patient alive. From his aggressiveness with his two good relievers—using Timlin in the sixth, Foulke in the seventh—to his calling off the sacrifice bunt with Mueller up in the ninth, to his management of what little relief pitching he had available to him in extra innings, Francona was a big reason why the Sox won.

On Sunday, though, the Sox would need more than some managerial genius to win. They would need Pedro Martinez, in perhaps his final Red Sox start, to provide the one thing he no longer could: innings. Sox relievers had tossed 12⅔ innings and made 289 pitches in the previous two games. Foulke, the Sox's best reliever, had stepped up with 50 pitches on Saturday night. The Yankees, a patient team in a normal week, were seeing 4.12 pitches per plate appearance in Boston, a pace that would have led the majors during the season. Moreover, they had a long history of making Martinez work, forcing him to deep counts, high-pitch innings, and, often, the clubhouse before the seventh inning was finished.

The Yankees started the fifth game with all the confidence that a tried-and-true stratagem of ten years can confer. They took nine of Martinez's twelve deliveries in the first inning. Though this earned them only a walk and two strikeouts, they were once again practicing the anti-Martinez waiting game. Mike Mussina, who'd been perfect through six and a third innings in Game One, was deeply flawed in Game Five, yielding three straight singles in the first for one run, then walking Varitek to force in a second. Martinez took the mound in the second with a 2–0 lead, determined to return to the dugout as quickly as possible: he threw ten pitches, eight of them strikes. However, Bernie Williams hammered one of them for a solo homer. At the end of two: 2–1 Boston.

In the third, the Yankees went to work. Jeter struck out on five pitches, Rodriguez flied out on six, Sheffield drew a five-pitch walk. No runs crossed the plate in the twenty-six-pitch frame, but Martinez was sowing the seeds of an early departure every time he sent another fastball toward the plate. In recent years, Martinez had become more and more like Cinderella—at the sound of his one hundredth crossing home plate he turned into just another major league pitcher. In 2003, batters hit .207 against him on pitches one to ninety-nine, and .302 after that. Martinez showed no comparably dramatic split in 2002 or 2004, but then he was rarely allowed past a hundred pitches in 2004. With the Sox bullpen in disarray and Martinez unlikely to go nine innings—or seven, for that matter—the game was reduced to a battle between the Yankees' batters' patience and Martinez's right arm. How quickly could they tire him out and force Francona into the same decision that got Grady Little all but lynched a year ago?

Eighteen pitches in the fourth. Sixteen in the fifth. Martinez had made eighty-two tosses through five frames, clinging to that 2–1 lead. He might make it into the seventh, at which time Timlin could come in, and if he could provide two innings, maybe Keith Foulke could be called upon for one. In the time it took a Sox fan to mustard up his Fenway Frank, Martinez's needle hit "E" in the sixth. Back-to-back singles by Posada and Ruben Sierra gave the Yankees two runners on with one out before Tony Clark, who had looked overmatched for most of the series, pushed Pedro to seven pitches before striking out. Martinez had now thrown over ninety pitches. On number ninety-seven, Martinez hit Miguel Cairo on the arm with a fastball, loading the bases. Derek Jeter took pitch number ninety-eight for a ball. Jeter swung and missed pitch number ninety-nine. Somewhere, a clock struck midnight.

Pitch one hundred was, in fact, a pretty good pitch, a breaking ball off the outside corner, but just as the ghost of FOX's graphic displaying Martinez's pre-post-hundred splits faded from America's television screens, Jeter reached out and poked it toward right field, where it fell between Ortiz and the foul line. Three runs came in on the double, giving the Yankees a 4–2 lead. Martinez got out of the inning, if barely, walking Gary Sheffield and getting Hideki Matsui to pop to short center field, but, as if on cosmic cue, Martinez had become a pumpkin and would now give way to lesser beings.

The Yankees were back to doing a better job managing the strike zone. Martinez had walked five and struck out six in his six innings, but Mike Mussina, after tossing nineteen pitches in a 1-2-3 sixth, had allowed just two walks and struck out seven before being lifted in the seventh. Mark Bellhorn's double leading off the inning had brought Joe Torre out and Sturtze in, but after a terrific nine-pitch walk by Orlando Cabrera—perhaps the most unlikely candidate on the Sox for such a feat—Manny Ramirez grounded into an around-the-horn double play to end the threat. The Yankees had a lead, with the almost-unbeatable Rivera almost ready to go, and in almost any other year in baseball history, the story would have ended there.

Mike Timlin, who had been such a dominant pitcher for the Sox in the 2003 ALCS, came up big in the top of the eighth. Cairo opened the inning with a double, bringing up Jeter. As he had in the eleventh inning of Game Four, Jeter, almost inexplicably, laid down a sacrifice bunt. It was an even worse decision than Saturday's; a contact hitter who frequently goes to right field, Jeter was likely to produce the same result swinging away, but with a much greater offensive upside. By failing to even try to get the run home, Jeter set up Rodriguez to be the goat, and Rodriguez, who had had a strong postseason, obliged by striking out. Timlin walked Sheffield, and then Foulke, coming off the fifty-pitch outing, came in to retire Matsui.

The Yankees had a two-run lead, a runner on second base with no one out, and the top of their lineup coming up. And they couldn't score. It would be the last moment when they were even close to reversing the series' new momentum. They never again batted with a lead, were outscored 16–5 from this point forward, and fell completely apart at the plate.

Surprisingly, Tom Gordon opened the eighth inning against David Ortiz. Torre has a long history of using Rivera for two innings in important games, but one thing he's rarely done is use Rivera for multiple innings in back-to-back games. Gordon, who along with Rivera and Minnesota's Joe Nathan, was one of the three most valuable "firemen" in the American League, seemed like a safe second choice. Certainly he was a safer choice than New York's sole lefty Felix Heredia, a famous arsonist. As if following a script in which he was the inevitable hero of the picture, Ortiz blasted a 1–0 pitch into the right field bleachers to cut the lead in half. Gordon then jumped ahead of Millar with two quick strikes before delivering four pitches out of the zone to put the tying run on base. (The Red Sox's approach after falling behind was much better than in previous games, in which they had gone to desultory hacking.) Gordon fell behind Trot Nixon, another lefty hitter, 3–1 before surrendering a single to center field that chased pinch-runner Roberts to third. Gordon went out, Rivera came in. The box score would show that Rivera blew the save. Actually, Gordon was the culprit. Rivera came in, threw eleven pitches and got three outs. Unfortunately for him, one of them was a fly to center field that allowed Roberts to scamper home to tie the game.

The Red Sox deserved all the credit in the world for the work they'd done to get to this point. Winning a postseason series, however, requires not merely avoiding the big mistakes, but catching the right breaks as well. In the ninth inning, with the score tied, the Sox caught one of the latter and watched Joe Torre make one of the former. With two outs, Foulke walked Ruben Sierra on five pitches, bringing up Tony Clark. He got ahead of Clark 1–2, then left a pitch over the plate that Clark yanked down the right field line. If the ball had gone a bit farther, the Yankees would have led 6–4. Had it bounced a little lower, the Yankees would have led 5–4. But what it did was bounce into the stands for a ground-rule double that held Clark up at third base. Cairo then popped harmlessly to Doug Mientkiewicz, ending the threat. Inches.

Had Joe Torre pinch-run for Sierra with Kenny Lofton, against a pitcher with a history of not holding runners well at first base, the stage would have been set for Lofton to steal second and score easily on the ground-rule double. This was just one example, and not even the most egregious, of the damage done by Torre's unwillingness to make tactical substitutions. In the thirteenth inning Torre made another mistake. The battery of Tim Wakefield and Jason Varitek was having all kinds of problems. Wakefield doesn't hold runners well, and Varitek never catches the knuckleball. Three balls got by him in the inning, one of which allowed Sheffield to reach after a strikeout. Using a fast runner like Lofton or Bubba Crosby in place of Sheffield or Matsui (who reached on a fielder's choice) might have allowed the Yankees to take an extra base and score on one of Varitek's misplays. Torre's management stood in stark contrast to Francona's use of Roberts, who scored the tying run in both Game Four and Game Five after pinch-hitting, once after stealing his way into scoring position. Joe Torre was outmanaged as badly by Terry Francona as anyone in LCS play since the Royals' Dick Howser beat down the Blue Jays' Bobby Cox and all his platoons in 1985. Torre neglected opportunities to create one run in so many contexts, and yet had Jeter bunt with a runner on second and no one out in the eighth inning. It was a mind-boggling performance.

For the second straight night, the Yankees played their worst baseball after the Sox had tied the game. Plate discipline deteriorated in extra innings, with almost every player going up hacking:

	PA	Pitches	P/PA	Strikeouts	Walks
Regulation	45	153	3.4	7	7
Extra Innings	19	63	3.3	9	1

The situation was actually worse than the raw numbers indicate. The three Sox pitchers (Martinez, Timlin, and Foulke) who worked in the first nine innings walked 2.3 men a game in 2004. The four who worked in extra innings walked 2.8 men a game. The Yankees, at a point in the game when their normal approach should have yielded considerable benefits, fell apart. The second P/PA figure is actually inflated because the Yankees swung and missed a lot more after the ninth than they did beforehand. Basically, they turned into the Angels, but without all those pesky hard-hit balls in play. The Red Sox had taken back the strike zone, and in doing so, they were taking the pennant right out of the Yankees' hands.

As with so many things in October, it came back once again to Papi. David Ortiz came to the plate again in the fourteenth inning. In the eleventh, the Yankees had turned to Esteban Loaiza, a midseason rotation replacement who by September had been exiled to the pen. Loaiza, inflated by a career year in 2003, had shrunk back to his normal size in 2004, unable to miss bats or throw strikes the way he had the year before. His problems were apparent in this outing. In three innings, Loaiza was able to get swinging strikes just five times, two of those from the hack-aholic Orlando Cabrera. In the fourteenth inning, he was called upon to retire Ramirez and Ortiz, two of the best hitters in the AL, in the biggest game of his life. He got Ramirez to 2–2, but couldn't get strike three and walked him. He got ahead of Ortiz 1–2, then kept working up and in, trying to prevent Ortiz from extending his arms, but he simply couldn't put a ball past him. On Loiaza's tenth pitch of the at-bat, Papi fisted a ball into short center field, a ball that the twenty-six-year-old Bernie Williams would easily have snagged. Unfortunately, it was not 1995, but 2004, and the thirty-five-year-old Williams had no chance.

Johnny Damon, his mane flapping like a victory flag, motored in from second base, and Fenway Park was once again the happiest place on earth.

—JOE SHEEHAN

23

BEAT THE DEVIL
OCTOBER 19–20, 2004

A prideful, even arrogant man whose name is usually bandied about in discussions of the game's smartest players, Curt Schilling had helped engineer his trade to Boston over the winter. He embraced Red Sox Nation like no player before him, participating in online discussions with fans, contributing candid, detailed, and sophisticated reports on issues like power versus control pitching and how a rarely used bench player can provide the critical ingredient in a team's chemistry. He even came equipped with a distaste for the New York Yankees; it was Schilling, while with the Diamondbacks, who had helped to end the Yankee dynasty in 2001. In that year's World Series he made three starts, allowing just four earned runs and winning co-MVP honors with Randy Johnson.

In acquiring Schilling for three forgettable prospects, Theo Epstein had picked up one of the great command pitchers in the game's history. Through 2003, Schilling's career marks of 2,542 strikeouts and 603 walks made him one of just three pitchers in baseball history to throw 1,500 innings with a strikeout-to-walk ratio of at least 4.0 (teammate Pedro Martinez and nineteenth-century star Tommy Bond are the others). In his three full seasons with the Diamondbacks, Schilling had whiffed nearly seven men for each one walked. He gave the Sox more of the same during the season: 203 strikeouts and just 35 walks.

The Red Sox had climbed back into the ALCS by commanding a 510-square-inch space, but their chance to push the series to a seventh game depended on a much smaller area of Schilling's right ankle, which had, in the week since his short-lived Game One appearance, given Janet

Jackson's nipple a run for Most Famous Body Part of 2004. In that game, he took the mound only thanks to heavy painkillers, despite which he was able to feel the tendon sheath in the ankle "popping." His fastball had topped out at 89 mph, and he had no bite on his breaking stuff. For a major leaguer whose best pitch is his fastball, the difference between 94 and 89 mph is the difference between success and failure.

Thanks to heavy medical creativity that would temporarily stabilize the ankle, Schilling would see if he could retrieve that critical 4 or 5 mph.

America's introduction to the innovative surgery that made it possible for Schilling to pitch at all came in the early innings of Game Six, when one of the sutures broke, and blood began seeping from the wound. FOX cameras quickly found it ("If it bleeds, it leads," as the old television news adage goes). By the time the blood appeared, however, the surgery had already proved a success. He was in the low 90s in the early innings against the Yankees, and had taken up virtually permanent residence in the strike zone. He threw 11 pitches in the first inning, 9 of them strikes. He needed just 38 tosses, 25 of them strikes, to get through the first three frames, and he allowed just one base runner, Miguel Cairo on a double, in that time. Those same three innings had taken him 58 pitches in Game One. This wasn't that Schilling. This was the one the Yankees couldn't beat in 2001.

Schilling got all the help he needed from his teammates in the fourth inning, when the Sox scored four runs after two were out. Mark Bellhorn, whose head Sox fans had been calling for just two days earlier, hit an opposite-field three-run homer that proved to be the difference. The home run was initially ruled a double by left field umpire Jim Joyce, who changed his call after consulting with his five colleagues. Bellhorn hit his homer on a 1–2 pitch from Jon Lieber, who had a devastating four-batter stretch in an otherwise effective start. In addition to the 1–2 count home run, he also got ahead of Jason Varitek 0–2 before eventually giving up a single that kept the rally going.

Questionable location and pitch selection on 0–2 and 1–2 counts plagued the Yankees all series long, but the bigger disease was pitchers who couldn't get strike three. In performance analysis, great emphasis is placed on a pitcher's strikeout rate in projecting his longevity and success. Strikeouts are a proxy for a pitcher's ability to miss bats. When a pitcher can make batters swing and miss, he can turn 0–2 and 1–2 counts into outs without risking a ball in play. Strikeout rate is the most important piece of information a pitcher can provide about himself, and long at-bats like the ones by Ortiz, Varitek, and Bellhorn were informative indeed.

Schilling gave the Red Sox seven sorely needed innings. Though he labored after the first three, he ended his night having allowed just one run on four hits, walking no one, striking out four, and tossing 67 strikes in 99 pitches. When you consider the importance of the game, the measures it took to get him to the mound, and, of course, the special nature of the Yankees–Red Sox rivalry, it's not an exaggeration to say that it was one of the greatest performances in baseball history.

After he left, the umpires would once again overturn a call in the Red Sox's favor. In the eighth inning, when the Yankees cut the lead to 4–2 and threatened to make it closer, Alex Rodriguez hit a weak ground ball down the first-base line that Bronson Arroyo gloved. When Arroyo went to tag Rodriguez, the Yankee slapped at Arroyo's glove, dislodging the ball and sending it down the right field line. Derek Jeter scored from first and Rodriguez went to second on the play. Once again, the umpires huddled, and once again, they got the call correct. Runners are forbidden from using their hands or arms to induce a dropped ball, per the umpires' manual. Rodriguez was declared out on interference, and Jeter was returned to first base. The Yankee crowd, frustrated, cold, and tired, went past the bounds of acceptable behavior in reacting to the decision, throwing debris on the field and causing a ten-minute delay that featured riot police ringing the field.

Of the people who came together to help the Sox win a championship, at least an honorable mention, and possibly a most valuable nonplayer award, goes to Richie Phillips. It was in 1999 that Phillips, then head of the umpires' union, orchestrated a misguided walkout that violated the umpires' labor agreement and allowed Major League Baseball to redefine the relationship between the umpires and the league. From baseball's earliest days, umpires had always cultivated the myth of their own infallibility. The first call was always the correct call, the only possible call. In an act of unprecedented self-immolation, Phillips persuaded the umpires to resign en masse in an effort to leverage baseball for a new contract. The move backfired; baseball accepted their resignations. Their replacements were a new, more responsive group of umpires who showed a greater interest in getting a call right than in defending a bad call, a new willingness to consult their colleagues. Were it not for that change, the Sox might well have scored two runs and allowed three in Game Six and Bronson Arroyo would be Bill Buckner, just with much stranger hair.

Despite having thrown four innings and seventy-two pitches in the previous forty-eight hours, Keith Foulke came out of the bullpen to pitch the bottom of the ninth. The workload showed, as he missed corners and lacked too much velocity on his fastball to make his change-up effective. Despite issuing a leadoff walk to Hideki Matsui and a two-out free pass to Ruben Sierra, Foulke escaped the ninth inning, striking out Tony Clark to end the game and even the series at three.

That Sierra and Clark batted in the ninth was a point of some frustration for many Yankees fans. Torre, whose style had never been to make a lot of moves with his bench, had been passive even by his own standards against the Red Sox. With Kenny Lofton and John Olerud available to pinch-hit, both more likely to hit a game-tying single than Clark, Torre stayed with the tall switch-hitter, just as he had in Game Five, and got the same result.

Torre did not have a good bench at his disposal; effectively, the Yankees had a sixteen-man roster, in contrast to the twenty-two or twenty-three useful players available to Terry Francona, but the one player on the bench who had value was Lofton. Yet Torre could find no use for Lofton in all of the situations in which Sierra batted against a right-hander, or all of the ones in which Clark batted against a right-hander; nor did he use Lofton to pinch-run all of the times the tying run was represented by a player who ran like he was carrying a piano on his back. It was another of the small edges the Yankees ceded to the Sox in the series.

All the small edges added up to one thing: a Game Seven. After the near-death experiences in Boston and the heroic comeback by Schilling in the sixth game, it would take something on the order of a plague of toads or locusts for Game Seven to avoid being anticlimactic. It was the Yankees now, not the Red Sox, whose pitching staff was bruised and beaten. The weight of history had dramatically shifted onto the Yankees; no baseball team down 3–0 had ever even forced a seventh game, much less won the series.

As the hands of fate were too blistered for anything more, this one ended early. The Yankees, who had used their three reliable starting pitchers over the past three days, were left with a choice between Kevin Brown and Javier Vazquez. Brown had alienated the team and its fans by losing a one-round fight with a dugout wall in September, breaking his left (nonpitching) hand. Vazquez had restricted his losing bouts to the mound— he had a 6.92 ERA in the second half. Brown had pitched well against the Twins in the Division Series, but lasted just two and a third innings in Game Three against the Sox. Vazquez had relieved in that game, though not very well, and tossed a poor five innings against the Twins.

Had Torre been able to find a way to activate David Cone for this one, he likely would have done so. Lacking that option, he settled on Brown, who had nothing. Four batters into the game, he'd surrendered three hits and two runs, and was rescued from a third only by some overly aggressive base-running by Johnny Damon, who got himself thrown out at the plate just ahead of David Ortiz's two-run homer.

Derek Lowe, who'd gutted out five innings in Game Four, once again came out attacking. He retired the Yankees 1-2-3 in the bottom of the inning on thirteen pitches, eight of them strikes. They were the last pressured tosses he'd have to make in the game, since Brown started nibbling at the plate in the bottom of the first, loading the bases on walks to Bill Mueller and Orlando Cabrera (who drew about one walk a week against right-handed pitchers during the season). In the second inning, Torre wasted no time calling for Vazquez.

If the Red Sox comeback began when Kevin Millar drew ball four off Mariano Rivera in the ninth inning of Game Four, it concluded when Vazquez dealt his first pitch to Johnny Damon, a fastball on the inner half of the plate. Damon, seeing an opportunity to improve his poor performance so far in the series, turned it on and sent a fly ball soaring down the right field line. When it landed, the Red Sox had a 6–0 lead, and baseball had a story for the ages.

After the game, Torre was questioned about his decision to use Vazquez rather than going early to one of the Yankees' ace relievers, Rivera or Gordon. But this was a secondary issue, dwarfed by the reality that the Yankees' $183 million roster was thin, with only three quality starters and two consistent relievers. The Red Sox players beat the

Yankee players. Terry Francona beat Joe Torre. And Theo Epstein beat the tar out of Brian Cashman. The Sox had a championship-caliber team; the Yankees had a super-sized payroll and nine guys who should have been Devil Rays.

The Sox would go on to knock out Vazquez in the fourth, going through $23 million worth of starting pitchers in three and a third innings. Meanwhile, on short rest, Lowe would throw 69 pitches in six innings, 44 of them strikes, and leave the game with the good feeling of having jacked up his market value approximately $25 million in one week's time. A free agent after the season, Lowe signed a four-year contract for $36 million, a far sight from what he looked to be worth coming off of his 5.42 ERA in the regular season. He made that money in October by throwing strikes against the Yankees.

In the seventh inning of the game, Francona did something that caused millions of Red Sox supporters to gasp—he allowed Pedro Martinez to throw an inning of relief in an 8–1 game. Few things could have riled up the subdued Yankee crowd like a chance to taunt their favorite whipping boy. Martinez's entrance raised the volume level, and the three hits he allowed to the first four batters he faced, cutting the lead to 8–3, threatened to conjure up all the ghosts Damon's homer had exorcised. As had been the case so often in the series, though, the bottom of the Yankee order proved unable to sustain the momentum. John Olerud struck out on seven pitches, Miguel Cairo flied to right field, and the ghosts—Bucky Dent and Aaron Boon, most notably—moved back to the set of *Charmed*.

The only relief for Yankee fans would be the D train, carrying them away from the scene of another team dancing on their field. For the first time ever, the Red Sox had knocked the Yankees out of the postseason, and in doing so, written a comeback story to rival the 1978 pennant race in the game's lore. Mike Torrez, meet Kevin Brown.

The fact was that the Yankees made many mistakes in this series, mistakes that could not so easily be dismissed as the product of inexperience or youth or lack of character, since it was the sacred Yankees making them. That Torre didn't use his bench, or that he decided he'd rather have Tanyon Sturtze pitching than Mike Mussina with nine outs separating him from the World Series, or that he fell in love with Ruben Sierra at the wrong time—all those contributed to the defeat. That Derek Jeter, Naked Emperor of the Infield, played bad baseball for a week, was a huge factor. That Mariano Rivera lost the strike zone at the worst possible time—with a one-run lead against a good team—had helped the Sox get off the mat.

After the series, Jeter argued that expectations had been too high, that the 2004 Yankees were not the 1996–2000 Yankees. Paul O'Neill and Tino Martinez were gone. Yet it was the most experienced Yankees, including Jeter himself, who had made the most egregious errors of judgment. It was a particularly weak attempt at self-exculpation, unworthy of a player who is supposed to be the team leader.

The Red Sox, on the other hand, didn't fold the tent when down two sets and two break points. They fixed the big problem—their abdication of the strike zone—that had put them down 3–0. They found ways to use their biggest advantage, the depth of their roster, to win games by giving the back end of it chances to succeed. The manager, even the training staff, made tangible contributions to the comeback. It was a victory not of individuals, or even of a team, but of an organization.

What happened over the course of four nights in October was a once-in-a-lifetime event occurring at the intersection of performance and luck. Luck, as the great general manager Branch Rickey said, is the residue of design. Of course, the exact alchemy didn't matter in Boston on the night of October 24. All that mattered was 10–3 and 4–3, and the joy of conquering the "evil empire" and being four games away from the end of a long, long wait.

—JOE SHEEHAN

24

THE SUBSTANCE OF STYLE
OCTOBER 23–27, 2004

One of the game's defining traits is that at times a team can look genuinely incompetent even though it isn't. Baseball's long season gives great teams many opportunities to look bad and bad teams to look great. Similarly, the season gives individual players several opportunities for games of anomalous excellence or misleading ineptitude. In any given game, the strong may stumble horribly and the isolated strengths of the weak may mysteriously align themselves. It's only natural in a sport where specific games are so disproportionately influenced by a great pitching performance or a streaky hitter.

If, say, the 1927 Yankees played the 2003 Tigers over a 162-game schedule, the Tigers would likely manage to win 25 or 30 times. A handful of those wins might even be by lopsided margins—those upside-down afternoons when Ruth, Gehrig, and Lazerri just couldn't catch up with Mike Maroth's fastball, and Dmitri Young went yard twice against a hung-over Waite Hoyt. If we put together a highlight package of those games, it would be difficult, if not impossible, to tell that the Yankees were the better team. In other team sports, those more dependent upon moment-to-moment cooperation among the players, it's different. Watching a superior basketball team outplay its opponent in all phases of the game only to miss one too many jumpers in the waning minutes, we would recognize that the better team lost. The same goes for a football team that dominates the game, but fumbles away the ball, and the victory, in the fourth quarter. But the .190 hitting shortstop who smacks two homers and a double on a day when the wind's blowing out at Wrigley? He's the new Sultan of Swat—if only for a day.

At last

St. Louis was a tremendously strong team. Their 105–57 regular season record was the best in the National League since 1998. The Cardinals outscored their opponents by 196 runs during the regular season, bigger than the Red Sox's 181-run margin. They had a deep batting order, an experienced manager, a pitching staff with no obvious soft spots, and one of the league's best defenses. While the Cardinals could not match the Red Sox's historic ALCS comeback for drama, they had plenty of momentum of their own, having won the last two games of their series against the Houston Astros in thrilling fashion.

Meanwhile, the Red Sox's rotation was ill-prepared for the World Series. The Sox might have had Pedro Martinez as their Game One starter, but Terry Francona's bizarre revenge fantasy, in which he used Martinez in relief while the Red Sox held an 8–1 lead over the Yankees in Game Seven, pushed Pedro back to Game Three. Schilling, heroic ankle and all, certainly wasn't about to start Game One on three days' rest. Bronson Arroyo would have been the next most attractive alternative, but he had been used out of the bullpen in Games Five and Six of the New York series. The rubber-armed Tim Wakefield, who had a 4.88 regular season ERA and had not pitched well in the playoffs, would get the start instead.

Taking into account the teams' performances during the regular season, and the likely pitching matchups, Baseball Prospectus analyst Clay Davenport figured that the Cardinals were 3-to-2 favorites to take the World Series. Vegas oddsmakers had it a little bit closer.

Shortstop Edgar Renteria made the first out of the World Series, striking out swinging against a Tim Wakefield butterfly on a crisp, windy Saturday evening at Fenway Park. Four days later, in St. Louis, Renteria made the last out of the series, a scrawny chopper back to Keith Foulke who flicked it to Doug Mientkiewicz for the win. In between, the Red Sox outscored the Cardinals 24–12, and out hit them .283 to .190. The Red Sox scored in the first inning of each of the four games; the Cardinals never held a lead. As championships go, it was less reminiscent of the spectacular series that have spoiled baseball fans during the past several years than of a Cowboys–Bills Super Bowl. The Sox's comeback over the Yankees had been a big-budget thriller; by comparison, the World Series was a suspense-free Merchant Ivory picture.

To some, it might even have looked like the birds were in the tank. But a deeper analysis reveals a few critical chinks in the Cardinals' armor that help explain the outcome of the series. The Cardinals' best hitters were bearing the burden of having played 173 games since Opening Day. Scott Rolen's hyperextended knee wasn't at full strength. Albert Pujols's heel, waiting for off-season treatment, was apt to bother him on any given evening. Jim Edmonds, a player whose take-no-prisoners style had long made him vulnerable to September swoons, had managed just three hits in his last 35 regular season at-bats, none of them for extra bases. St. Louis was not at full strength, with their most valuable players bearing the brunt of the trauma.

Pitching matchups also portended trouble for the Cardinals. The Cardinal pitching staff of 2004 was defined by two overriding factors that actually played into Boston's strengths:

- The Cardinal pitchers were overwhelmingly right-handed.
- The Cardinal pitchers were overwhelmingly "finesse" pitchers, rather than "power" pitchers.

The idea that left-handed hitters tend to perform better against right-handed pitchers, and vice versa, has been around since before Bill James discovered America. During the regular season, 91 percent of the Cardinals' innings pitched, and all but one of their 162 starts, were made by right-handed pitchers. Things would be no different in the World Series—in fact, the team's best left-handed pitcher, relief specialist Steve Kline, had been left off the roster with a balky finger in his pitching hand. The Red Sox were especially adept at dealing with right-handed pitchers. During the regular season, the Red Sox hit for a .280 batting average, .350 on-base percentage, and a .466 slugging average against left-handed pitchers. Those are strong numbers, and Manny Ramirez in particular gave lefties fits. But the Red Sox were more successful still against righties, producing a .283 batting average, a .364 on-base percentage, and a .475 slugging average. David Ortiz tagged righties for a .326/.411/.671 batting line during the regular season. Trot Nixon, who performed so badly against lefties that he was routinely benched against them, had a .336/.397/.552 line against righties. (Not surprisingly, Ortiz and Nixon combined for a .333 batting average and a .592 slugging average during the World Series.)

Regarding the Cardinal "finesse" pitching staff: The very best pitchers in the league—like Schilling, Mark Prior, or Johan Santana—possessed both tremendous stuff and imperial command. Everyone else fell into one of two categories, finesse pitchers or power pitchers:

- *The finesse approach:* throw strikes, locate well, keep the ball down, be willing to give up hits, and let the defense do its work. Examples: Greg Maddux, Tim Hudson, Bret Saberhagen.
- *The power approach:* overwhelm hitters with pitches that they can't catch up to. Give up walks rather than giving in. Don't leave it up to your defense when a strikeout does the job all by itself. Examples: Kerry Wood, Randy Johnson (early career), Nolan Ryan.

Power pitchers are characterized by high strikeout rates and high walk rates, finesse pitchers by low strikeout and walk rates. The Cardinal pitchers, almost to a man, were finesse pitchers. Of the primary St. Louis starting pitchers, all five had a walk rate lower than the league average during the regular season. Simultaneously, all of the starters but Chris Carpenter, who was pitching out of the bullpen during the playoffs, had strikeout rates lower than the league average. This approach had worked very well for the Cardinals. The pitchers threw lots of quick, efficient games, letting the team's excellent defense work its magic. The starters kept their pitch counts down and avoided a disabled list stint all season. The Cardinals' 3.75 team ERA was the second best in the league. The essence of the finesse approach is to let the hitter make the mistakes, and that works very well against ordinary, mistake-prone hitters.

Unfortunately for the Cardinals, that didn't describe the Red Sox. They had scored 1,910 runs over the past two seasons, more than all but three post–World War II ballclubs, and they had done it with the opposite approach. The Cardinal pitchers threw strikes and attempted to resolve at-bats quickly. The Red Sox took their time and waited for their pitch, even if it meant taking a strikeout. The Cardinal pitchers thrived by avoiding walks; the Red Sox thrived by taking them. The general rule in hitter-versus-pitcher matchups is that where there's a conflict in approach/style between a pitcher and a hitter, it favors the hitter. Left-handed batters do well against right-handed pitchers, and right-handed batters do well against left-handed pitchers. Research has also shown that batters who swing down on the ball and hit a lot of ground balls do well against pitchers who throw up in the zone and induce a lot of fly balls, while fly ball hitters do well against ground ball pitchers.

When power hitters face off against finesse pitchers, the matchup is just as favorable to the hitter. Here is a quick and dirty junk statistic: By using a pitcher's walk rate and strikeout rate per nine innings pitched, we can define each pitcher's Finesse Factor—calculated as equal to strikeout rate (strikeouts per nine innings pitched) plus two times walk rate (walks per nine innings pitched), divided by innings pitched:

$$\text{Finesse Factor} = \frac{(BB*2) + K}{IP}$$

In modern baseball, there are about twice as many strikeouts as there are walks, so by doubling the walk rate, the formula gives equal importance to the two categories. Pitchers with a finesse factor lower than 12.5 are defined as finesse pitchers. Pitchers with a finesse factor of 12.5 or greater are power pitchers. Here are the finesse factors for the St. Louis starting pitchers:

ST. LOUIS CARDINALS STARTING PITCHERS—2004 FINESSE FACTORS

	BB/9	K/9	Finesse Factor
Woody Williams	2.8	6.2	11.8
Matt Morris	2.5	5.8	10.8
Jeff Suppan	3.1	5.3	11.5
Jason Marquis	3.1	6.2	12.4
Chris Carpenter	1.9	7.5	11.3

Roughly half the pitchers in the league fell into the category in 2004, including all five of the Cardinal starters.

As it happened, the Red Sox faced more than their fair share of finesse starters during the regular season. Most of the Yankees pitchers fell into this category. The following table lists the runs, strikeouts, and walks allowed by finesse pitchers in their starts against the Red Sox, and in their appearances against the other teams in the league:

RED SOX RESULTS VERSUS FINESSE AND POWER PITCHERS

Type	vs. Red Sox				vs. Rest of League			
	IP	R/9	BB/9	K/9	IP	R	BB	K
Finesse	550	6.6	3.8	6.4	15507	4.8	2.5	5.3
Power	322	6.3	4.6	7.6	7444	4.9	4.0	7.2

Power pitchers allowed an average of 4.9 runs per nine innings pitched when facing the other teams in the league, but 6.3 runs per nine innings pitched when facing the Red Sox. That's an increase of 28 percent, which is substantial. The Red Sox had such hitting talent that they did very well against just about any pitcher that the opposition dared send to the mound. But Boston did even better against finesse pitchers. Finesse pitchers allowed 4.8 runs per nine innings against regular hitters, but 6.6 runs per nine innings against the Red Sox—an increase of *37 percent*.

Power hitters like hitting against finesse pitchers. Opposites attract. This was evident from the Red Sox's very first at-bat of the series. Johnny Damon faced off against Woody Williams, an efficient veteran pitcher who oftentimes doesn't throw ten pitches in an entire inning. Damon occupied three and a half minutes of Williams's time. He took the first two pitches, a fastball up and away, and another fastball over the outside corner for a strike. Williams went back to the outside corner with his third pitch, and Damon fouled it off. The fourth pitch, a low, late-breaking curve, might have fooled a lesser hitter. The fifth pitch was a difficult curve over the inside corner, but Damon got the handle of the bat on it and fouled it off. Williams missed with his next pitch to fill the count, then worked inside-outside-inside with his next three offerings, tough pitches all, all fouled away by Damon. Finally, on the tenth pitch of the at-bat, as Fenway's fans applauded Damon's tenacity, Williams threw a flat stomach-high fastball on the outside part of the plate. It was the most hittable pitch of the sequence, and Damon didn't miss it. He poked it into the left field corner for a double. He'd come around to score a few moments later on David Ortiz's homer, and the Red Sox would never look back.

That single at-bat exemplified the entire Series. Williams likes to get ahead in the count; Damon took the first pitch and wouldn't let him. He likes going to his curveball with two strikes; Damon was prepared and didn't bite. Williams likes to work the corners; Damon responded by fouling five pitches away. What Woody Williams doesn't have—what few of the Cardinal pitchers had—is a nasty pitch that he can blow by people. Sooner or later, he's going to throw a pitch that the hitter can handle; Damon waited ten pitches for it.

The Red Sox tortured finesse pitchers in this fashion all season long. The finesse pitchers that the Red Sox faced gave up walks at a rate of 2.5 per nine innings pitched against other clubs—but 3.8 per nine innings pitched against the Red Sox, a 51 percent increase. Waiting for the hitter to make a mistake doesn't work when the hitter doesn't make very many mistakes. Instead, the Red Sox turn the game-within-the-game around by waiting for the pitcher to make a mistake in the form of a walk, or a juicy, hittable pitch. If the pitcher has superb natural stuff, as the Giants' 98 mph Jason Schmidt did in a one-hit shutout on June 20, the Red Sox can be stymied. Most everyone else had a flaw and the Sox were going to find it. The Cards required an average of 170 pitches for the four games. They surrendered twenty-four walks during the World Series—nearly twice their usual rate—while hitting four batters. Eight of those men would come around to score, including six in Game One alone.

Meanwhile, save for a difficult series of innings by Wakefield and Arroyo in Game One that allowed the Cardinals to pull into their only tie of the series, the Red Sox pitchers made it look easy. The Red Sox starters in the final three games of the series—Schilling, Martinez, and Derek Lowe—between them threw twenty innings, and gave up no earned runs. Though Pujols hit well, the exhausted Edmonds and Rolen combined for just one hit in thirty at-bats. A factor that otherwise might have been fatal—the Red Sox defense had an off series, making four errors in each of the first two games—didn't even matter.

The party on Lansdowne Street, and in taverns and homes throughout New England and the far-flung locales that constituted Red Sox Nation, was about to begin.

—NATE SILVER

25

BEAT THE YANKEES,
BE THE YANKEES
OCTOBER 28, 2004

So the Red Sox overcame the forces of history and claimed their first World Series title since Spanish flu roamed the land. The ensuing revelry made a Led Zeppelin hotel party look like a Victorian séance. This is what fans had been waiting for, all they ever wanted—at least for the time being.

Fan bases are, by nature, a restive bunch. Give them what they want, and they're bound to bay for more of the same. The 2004 season was the realization of the most desperate hopes of generations of Sox fans, but it was also the dawn of higher standards. Just as there are the famous four stages of grief, so, in the throes of the championship season just completed, Red Sox Nation experienced the four stages of World Series bliss:

Stage 1: Orgiastic pleasure at finally attaining something so foreign, and once so out of reach.

Stage 2: Recent history is the only history that matters—we are the greatest.

Stage 3: This has been really super nice, and we'd like to do it again.

Stage 4: Don't screw this up, Epstein.

To put it in standardized-test terms—winning a championship is to Red Sox fans as OxyContin is to Rush Limbaugh. They wanted more, and they wanted it without delay. Which means the question for the team's high

Kevin Millar, Manny Ramirez, Doug Mientkiewicz, and the trophy

command was this: Now what? Which might have reminded the Red Sox front office of a famous theatrical story about the Broadway debut of the seminal Rogers and Hammerstein musical *Oklahoma*. At an after-show party, composer Richard Rogers was wondering what he should do as a follow-up. "If I were you," said the movie producer Sam Goldwyn, "I'd kill myself."

Members of the club's front office had barely begun cooking their hangover omelets when they got to work on what was certain to be an especially challenging off-season. The Red Sox entered the winter of 2004 with seventeen pending free agents, the most of any team in baseball. Among those free agents were vital (or, in some instances, nominally vital) contributors like Pedro Martinez, Jason Varitek, Derek Lowe, Bill Mueller, Orlando Cabrera, Doug Mirabelli, and Gabe Kapler. Less than a month after helping Boston win the World Series, Kapler, the team's fourth outfielder for most of the season, signed a one-year contract to play with the Yomiuri Giants of Japan. A week later, the Sox re-signed reserve catcher Mirabelli to a two-year, $3 million contract. That would be their last significant transaction before the December 7 arbitration deadline.

If a team fails to sign one of its free agents early on, but still wishes to negotiate with him, he must be offered salary arbitration by the deadline. Doing so prolongs the window for negotiation with the parent team. In addition, in the cases of top free agents (players rated as "A" or "B" free agents by the Elias Sports Bureau), should the player sign elsewhere, offering arbitration entitles the team to compensation in the form of draft picks. There is a risk, however. If the player accepts salary arbitration, the team will be on the hook for a budget-busting one-year contract.

Theo Epstein surprised many observers in the winter of 2004 by offering salary arbitration to eight free agents. In some cases—like Varitek and Martinez—it was to allow further contract negotiations. In other cases—like Lowe and Cabrera—it was to net draft picks when they inevitably signed multiyear contracts with other organizations. The Red Sox went on to receive picks for Martinez, Lowe, and Cabrera, which is significant for a franchise endeavoring to rebuild its minor league system. When it comes to arbitration decisions, reading the free agency tea leaves is an essential skill. Epstein and company correctly surmised that Lowe, a durable starter, and Cabrera, considered to be one of the few double-threats at shortstop (there was hardly any white-knuckled drama in Martinez's case), would receive arbitration-besting contract offers on the market at large. Boston got rid of players they had no intention of keeping anyway, and they get a handful of high-round draft selections for their troubles. It's a neglected way for clubs to leverage an advantage over the competition, and Boston seized it.

By mid-December, Martinez stunned Sox partisans by signing a four-year, $52 million pact with the Mets. If reports of Boston's final offer to Martinez are to be believed (something in the neighborhood of three years, $30 million), their efforts to re-sign him were ceremonial at best. In part, the decision to cut bait on Martinez was likely linked to concerns about his age and durability. The decision also betrayed a nuanced understanding of an important principle for a select group of teams: Desiring to maintain the status quo is an acceptable goal so long as decision-makers correctly understand what the status quo actually is.

In 2004 the Red Sox tallied ninety-eight wins in the regular season and won the World Series. They wouldn't mind a repeat performance. Martinez, however, had a decidedly uncharacteristic season. He had excellent peripheral statistics, but gave up 4.11 runs per nine innings. In terms of runs allowed (which is the point), it was the worst season of his career. In order to compensate for what they'd lose by parting ways with Martinez, the Red Sox would need to replace not Pedro Martinez, future Hall of Famer, but Pedro Martinez, the pitcher who surrendered more than four runs per game during the season in which they won the World Series.

Enter Matt Clement, whom they signed to a three-year, $25.5 million contract on December 17. In 2004, Clement gave up 3.93 runs per nine innings, better than Martinez and in keeping with Clement's recent history. He also cost half as much, demanded a shorter contract, and was almost three years younger. This isn't the same thing as saying Clement is better than Martinez. There is a good chance Martinez will outpitch Clement over the next few seasons. However, there is also a good chance that Martinez's 2004 season and increased fragility are indicative of a pitcher on a slope slipperier than most people think. Not only could Clement rather easily replace what Martinez meant to the Red Sox in 2004, at least in the statistical sense, but he might provide greater reliability.

Two days before they signed Clement, the Red Sox paid a premium to maintain parity at shortstop, signing Cardinals shortstop Edgar Renteria to a four-year contract worth $40 million. Boston shortstops in 2004 (Nomar Garciaparra, Pokey Reese, Orlando Cabrera, and small helpings of Cesar Crespo, Ricky Gutierrez, and Mark Bellhorn) combined to hit .273/.308/.408. Renteria, meanwhile, hit .287/.327/.401. That's a modest edge in production for Renteria. There is reason to believe that Renteria somewhat underperformed in 2004 and should boost his performance in the near future. In addition, Fenway is friendly to right-handed batters, of which Renteria is one. Baseball Prospectus's PECOTA weighted mean projection for the shortstop is .302/.356/.440. His defense is also notably better than what the Sox, on balance, got from the position in 2004.

A week-and-a-half later, Epstein knowingly overpaid to re-up Varitek for four years and $40 million. By the time the deal expires, Varitek will be thirty-seven years of age. You can count on Mordecai Brown's right hand the number of catchers who have been worth top dollar at such an advanced age. Still, Varitek was, at the time of the deal, quite productive by catcher standards, the team's acknowledged clubhouse leader, and one of the city's most popular players. "We had to get him back or the city would have rioted and the players probably would have, too," reliever Keith Foulke said.[1] In February 2005, Varitek was named team captain, the first player to receive the ceremonial title since Carl Yastrzemski. "He's like having another coach on the field," said manager Terry Francona.[2]

At the press conference announcing the Varitek contract, Epstein said, "It's not every day that you're lucky enough to find a player who embodies everything you want your franchise to be. And when you're lucky enough to have that player, you don't let him get away. And you lock him up for as long as you can and you make him the rock of your franchise." He added:

What he does for them, what kind of a stabilizer he is, not only to the pitchers, but to the whole clubhouse. A lot of things in Boston make it difficult to go through the course of 162 games—the size of the clubhouse, the intensity of the fans, the volume of media that we have . . . Jason really counterbalances that. He's the ultimate stabilizer and makes everyone around him better.[3]

Observed in a vacuum, the contract given to Varitek would be, to be frank, reckless. However, if you're going to overpay, it might as well be for talent at premium, up-the-middle positions—the ones that are so hard to fill. And the Red Sox could afford to absorb the cost if Varitek disappointed them. And in this there is an important lesson for all concerned: As much as Red Sox Nation would like to recast the ALCS win over the Yankees as a moment of blessed improbability, as much as Red Sox CEO Larry Lucchino is fond of bloviating about the "evil empire" in the Bronx, Boston now had more in common than not with that cretinous Moloch down I-95, including vast coffers, a feverish and hands-on fan base, and a "sporting gentleman" owner who very much wants to win. In other words, by using the Yankees' story as both a guide and a cautionary tale, the Red Sox can better understand the path ahead. For all the animus between the clubs and their spear carriers, the differences are more bourgeoisie hair-splitting than anything in the David versus Goliath mold. The Red Sox have more to learn from the Yankees than they do from the frugality of the A's or the yo-yo dieting of the Rockies.

The most recent collective bargaining agreement was putatively forged to level baseball's financial field. In execution, however (and probably, secretly, by design), what it has done is rein in everyone save for the especially well-heeled—notably among them, the Red Sox. With a lavishly wealthy ownership group, the highest average ticket price in baseball, and a media empire under the franchise umbrella, the Red Sox have little trouble raking in revenues and spending money at will. Principal owner John Henry thus far has been inclined to reinvest those monies in the team. The 2004 model had the highest payroll of any team ever to win the World Series.

The happy upshot of a team having so much cash lying around is that it can wittingly sign players to contracts that extend beyond their usefulness as players and overcompensate them for their present skill sets. If it's filling (or keeping filled) a hole that's not so easily filled, it can justify the excesses and treat the players as sunk costs once they become problems. It's an advantage enjoyed to such a degree by only a handful of teams. It's not particularly fair, but structural inequities in the industry at large are hardly the concern of teams high on the food chain. The off-season signings of Renteria and Varitek exemplified this principle: fill the holes, sort out the costs later. Why not do the same with Martinez? Because, once again, his innings in 2004 were replaceable by cheaper means. That wasn't the case with Varitek or, in the opinion of Boston decision-makers, Renteria.

Where Henry differs from Yankees autocrat George Steinbrenner is that he lets his baseball people make the baseball decisions. This is probably as important a difference as any, and it certainly needs to be maintained. Boston, unlike the Yankees most of the time, isn't mulishly devoted to conspicuous consumption. Prior to the 2003 season, Epstein famously raided the off-season scrap heap for David Ortiz and Bill Mueller, two players who would provide MVP-caliber seasons that year. With the signing of nontendered right-hander Wade Miller to a surprisingly low-end contract (one year, $1.5 million), it appeared he'd done it again. Just because the team has deep pockets doesn't mean Epstein's not bargain shopping. Signing, say, Raul Mondesi may grab more headlines than signing Ortiz, but look who's laughing now. Epstein also buttressed the rotation by signing veteran starter David Wells to a two-year, $8 million deal. One can question the wisdom of signing a lefty with fly ball tendencies to pitch half his games in Fenway (particularly with the prop comic defense of Manny Ramirez in left), but otherwise Wells was a sensible addition. At the time of the signing, Wells was coming off back-to-back seasons in which he'd posted stellar strikeout-to-walk ratios of better than 5.0. For all his sundry back maladies, cases of gout and fondness for domestic tall boys and brawling in diners, he had averaged more than two hundred innings per season over the previous three years. Wells was a very strong bet to be a substantial upgrade, all but aesthetically, over the outgoing and magnificently overrated Lowe.

So despite entering the off-season with newly ramped-up expectations and the prospect of massive roster upheaval, the Red Sox managed to hold serve where they needed and make modest upgrades where needed, albeit with the aid of a pair of above-market contracts. In the aggregate, the decisions of Epstein and company revealed a grasp of the concept of optimal status quo and their quasi-unique financial situation.

On John Henry's watch, the Red Sox assembled a many-tentacled front office well equipped to serve the prevailing vision. Epstein was weaned on statistical analysis, and he had a boss, Lucchino, who also bought into the principle of dispassionate analysis. In addition, Epstein had like-minded assistants and consultants in Josh Byrnes, Bill James, and Voros McCracken. At the same time, Epstein had at his disposal a coterie of seasoned advisers like Mike Port, Bill Lajoie, and Craig Shipley. The upshot is that the Red Sox, when making personnel decisions, wound up with a veritable clearinghouse of ideas and perspectives. It was Epstein's job to process the various inputs and arrive at a sound decision. And he did. Again and again.

As for amateur scouting and the more specific task of rebuilding a farm system that was left largely in tatters, the Red Sox seemed to be taking the correct tack there, as well. In their most recent Rule 4 drafts (often, and incorrectly, referred to as the "amateur draft"), their overarching approach had been to focus on college talents, which is prudent in the case of pitchers, but they weren't averse to selecting the occasional high-ceiling prep player. So they weren't needlessly circumscribing their draft approach as, for instance, the Blue Jays did. Plus, the Red Sox had the scouting budget to maintain strong presences in the Caribbean and Pacific Rim. Over all, the Sox had both the scouting resources and enough devotion to quantitative matters to fish intelligently in the talent pools in question. And they had the financial wherewithal to survive those signings that turned out to be the transactional equivalent of lighting a cigar with a one-hundred-dollar bill.

In order to retain their top prospects and still make needed trades, Boston's willingness and ability to take on salary was once again critical. The only "blockbuster" trade executed since Epstein took over is the one on November 28, 2003, that brought Curt Schilling to Boston from Arizona for Casey Fossum, Brandon Lyon, Jorge De LaRosa, and Michael Goss. Boston's willingness to absorb what Arizona considered an onerous contract lowered Schilling's price. The four players going to Arizona stood little chance of equaling the value of the single player coming back.

When a statistically inclined general manager rises to power, it's useful to keep in mind John Swift's admonition: "When a true genius appears in the world, you may know him by this sign, that the dunces are all in a confederacy against him." In the early days, Epstein, no doubt buzzed on the idea of having his own $100 million erector set, chose not to re-sign Ugueth Urbina, who logged forty saves for the Sox in 2002, telling the media that the club wouldn't be using a traditional closer. Wringing of hands ensued. While he was completely correct in seeking to put right the gross inefficiencies of modern bullpen usage, he was wrong in making even the mildest show of it. In most media circles, they harrumphed and mischaracterized the approach by calling it "bullpen by committee," which it plainly wasn't. ("Properly leveraged bullpen" would've been closer to the point, but never mind.) Then they dragged from the vaults the usual timeless cracks about spreadsheets and computers running a baseball team. That swayed the ever-credulous public against the experiment (which, in actuality, was merely a return to the way bullpens were used pre–Dennis Eckersley). The idea that the approach may have been shanghaied by flawed relievers and not by its fundamental wrongness never seemed to have occurred to anyone. The lesson: When attempting to innovate (or reinnovate) in the presence of the Boston sports media, it's best to go about it quietly and let them catch on to what you're doing six months later.

If there was a mission statement for the Red Sox of the future, it was this: be the Yankees, but smarter. Leverage the financial advantages you have to absorb sunk costs. Fill holes at above-market prices when necessary. Take on the contracts of legitimate, high-level contributors that other teams fine burdensome. Restock the farm system by a prudent, balanced approach in the Rule 4 draft and by maintaining a well-executed presence in the international talent markets. Stockpile draft picks by playing the arbitration game with aplomb. Don't neglect the sources of "freely available talent." Don't chase the big name merely for effect. When the status quo is desirable, aim for the status quo. Organizational trial balloons are best floated behind the media's back. Maintain the balance between quantitative and traditional methods of player evaluation, but always remember that one is more subjective than the other.

In the months following the 2004 World Series, the Red Sox handled themselves as a high-payroll team should. If they kept it up, winning championships would become a lot less of a novelty.

—DAYN PERRY

EPILOGUE
AUGUST 8, 2005

In the classic 1957 Warner Brothers cartoon, "Show Biz Bugs," Daffy Duck, trying to outdo the more successful Bugs Bunny and capture the love of a fickle Vaudeville audience, downs a cocktail of gasoline, nitroglycerine, gunpowder, and uranium 238 before swallowing a match and blowing himself to kingdom come. The audience loves it and clamors for an encore, but as a now-celestial Daffy explains, "I can only do it *once*."

By the time you read this, you will probably already know whether the Red Sox, at the moment holding a three-to-four game lead on the Yankees in early August, beat the odds to repeat or turned out to be one-trick ducks themselves.

In over 100 years of World Series, on only 20 occasions have the teams that won the previous year repeated:

- 1907–1908 Chicago Cubs
- 1910–1911 Philadelphia Athletics
- 1915–1916 Boston Red Sox
- 1921–1922 New York Giants
- 1927–1928 New York Yankees
- 1929–1930 Philadelphia Athletics
- 1936–1939 New York Yankees (four straight)

(First racial integration, 1947)

- 1949–1953 New York Yankees (five straight)

(First geographical realignment, 1953)

- 1961–1962 New York Yankees

- 1972–1974 Oakland A's (three straight)
- 1975–1976 Cincinnati Reds

(Free agency, 1976)

- 1977–1978 New York Yankees
- 1992–1993 Toronto Blue Jays
- 1998–2000 New York Yankees (three straight)

The chronology above is divided by three key events. In the first 50 years of World Series history (1903–1953), it was much easier for teams to repeat. Eight of the 14 repeaters, including the sole four- and five-time repeaters, played in that era. During the period, in most seasons an eight team league was really a six team league, with two clubs dependably in the business of selling hot dogs, not winning ball games. The road to winning a pennant, and therefore the World Series, was considerably foreshortened.

This changed in 1953 when the Boston Braves moved to Milwaukee, and attendance jumped from 281,278 people in 1952, last in the majors, to 1,826,397, first in the majors. The next season the Braves became the first team to break the two million attendance mark. Suddenly the owners realized that new markets meant new profits. The St. Louis Browns moved to Baltimore and drew over a million for the first time in team history. The Philadelphia Athletics drew 304,666 in 1954; the following year they drew 1.3 million in Kansas City. Prosperity bred competitiveness, as did integration, which allowed the early-adopters (non-racists) to acquire talent on the cheap, raising the overall quality of the league and further leveled its playing field.

Enter free agency in 1976, which allowed a player at the end of his contract to voluntarily leave one team and sign with another. No longer could a team retain its players indefinitely under the terms of the reserve clause, which allowed better teams to keep their teams intact longer before succumbing to entropy, the enemy of all baseball clubs.

As of this writing, the 2005 Red Sox have already had to deal with several facets of entropy, including injuries to Curt Schilling, David Wells, Keith Foulke, and Trot Nixon; another outbreak of ambivalence by Manny Ramirez, who demanded a trade that didn't happen, then said Boston was where he wanted to be; and declines in offense from Kevin Millar and Mark Bellhorn.

Unfortunately, the post-free agency repeat winners have little to offer the Red Sox in the way of advice on repeating. The 1998–2000 Yankees achieved their dominance through the unplanned convergence of strong young players up the middle—catcher Jorge Posada, second baseman Chuck Knoblauch, shortstop Derek Jeter, and center fielder Bernie Williams. With incredible offense at these normally "soft" positions, the Yankees could endure relatively weak production from the corners (first base, third base, and the outfield wings) and still have a dominating offense. With their farm system in a perpetually dry state since the arrival of Jeter and Posada, the Yankees were increasingly required to make trades for veterans whose contracts had become onerous to their teams as well as conduct annual raids of the free agent market to fill out their roster, plus splurge heavily on unknown Cuban and Japanese free agents.

The system was expensive and inefficient. Free agency cut both ways—its existence made it more difficult for a winning team to retain its core over a period of years, but it also allowed a team to bolster or replace that core on the open market. Yankees wealth assured the former, but they pursued the latter clumsily, never more so than in the 2004–2005 off-season, when they rebuilt their starting rotation (itself decimated by departing free agents after 2003) by trading for an aging Randy Johnson and signing the free agent right-handers Carl Pavano and Jaret Wright, hurlers whose record of success was as short as their injury history was long.

In truth, the best role models for the Red Sox can be found among the pre-free agency repeaters, particularly the Yankees dynasties of 1936–1939 and 1949–1953. If they had anything to teach aspiring dynasties of the modern era it is that, to paraphrase the great baseball enthusiast Thomas Jefferson, the tree of competitiveness must be refreshed from time to time with the blood of old players. Complacency and the refusal to evaluate true strengths and weaknesses can kill dynastic ambition faster than invading Russia in winter.

Joe McCarthy, manager of the first Yankees dynasty, once remarked, "You have to improve your club if it means letting your own brother go." His Yankees hewed to this dictum during those four years, for example swapping out aging second baseman and future Hall of Famer Tony Lazzeri for the younger, better fielding Joe Gordon. When, in May 1937, platoon outfielder Roy Johnson seemed to have been sated by winning the championship in 1936, McCarthy cut him on the spot and brought in rookie Tommy Henrich. Faced again with the need to prune his roster in order to win his fifth straight title in 1940, McCarthy balked at the demands of his own philosophy. Throughout the championship run, the shortstop and leadoff man was 28-year-old Frank "Cro" Crosetti, a smart, scrappy infielder who was only decent in the field and indecent at the plate. That off-season, McCarthy considered his options. He had a 22-year-old short-stop who had just batted .316/.362/.412 (approximate) with 33 stolen bases for the team's Kansas City Club in the competitive American Association. Phil Rizzuto also fielded as well as any shortstop in baseball. But McCarthy couldn't bear to bench one of his favorites and decided to give Rizzuto one more year of minor league seasoning. McCarthy left him in the leadoff spot all year, and the Yankees finished third, just two games out of first place, while, in Kansas City, Rizzuto hit .347/.397/.482. The Yankees won the 1941 championship with Rizzuto in the lineup.

Ruthless McCarthyite anti-sentimentality reached its apotheosis with manager Casey Stengel and general manager George Weiss of the second Yankees dynasty. Looking back at his first six years with the Yankees, in April 1955 Stengel said, "That's a lot of bunk about them five-year build-ing plans. Look at us. We build and win at the same time." The way that Stengel did this was to embrace depth as an asset to be mined continu-ously rather than held in reserve for some rainy day that might never arrive. Rather than accept a player who might be only good enough, he replaced him the moment someone better came long. "I made up my mind to have three Yankees for every position," he said, "and on this club I can do it." The approach had the effect of vaccinating the club against the debilitating effects of age and self-satisfaction. Even the best squad even-tually loses effectiveness as it moves into its 30s. The Yankees squad never got to this point because each year Stengel and Weiss would take at least one position away from a veteran and give it to a younger player.

In those years the Yankees repeatedly demonstrated a truth since for-gotten: a winning team doesn't have to be old or experienced, just good. In late July, 2005, Yankees manager Joe Torre said, "As an organization, young kids don't usually get an opportunity to stay around because the future is right now." This benefits neither the present nor the future; if you believe the future is now, you're not preparing for that *other* future, the one down the road. It commits the organization to a program of playing men for their experience—and, often enough, their battle-tested mediocrity. Stengel and Weiss, long dead, offered no comment.

Of course, Stengel and Weiss could not protect themselves from aging; both were retired by the Yankees after the 1960 season. Under manager (and later general manager) Ralph Houk the turnover of players was abandoned. The team ceased to invest in depth, starving its minor league system. Then the draft was enacted, further cutting into the Yankees' talent pool. After four more pennants with the team that Stengel and Weiss built, the Yankees sank like a stone.

In the aftermath of the 2004 post-season, what resonated most with the Yankees seemed to be Dave Roberts' stolen base in Game Four of the ALCS. But the Yankees, it would become clear, had missed the point of Theo Epstein's acquisition of Roberts. It wasn't about having speed at the top of the order on a daily basis, or equating speed with other talents, like hitting for power, that actually correlate to run-scoring. It was about having speed available for the select moment when it might change the course of a ball game. The Yankees mistook a canny bit of contingency planning and charged off in imitation of something that didn't actually exist. They signed Tony Womack and his feeble bat to be their second baseman and leadoff hitter. A player with no patience, no power, no ability to hit for batting average, and limited defensive skills, Womack had persisted in the major leagues because his one above-mediocre skill, speed, was beguiling to general managers (and/or their impulsive owners) who confused flash and dash with substance.

On the other hand, on December 20, 2004, the Red Sox acquired outfielder Jay Payton, infielder Ramon Vazquez, righty pitcher David Pauley, and $2.65 million from the San Diego Padres for the contingency himself. Similarly, reserve outfielder Gabe Kapler was allowed to decamp for Japan (he would be repatriated in July after Payton became disgruntled playing Kapler's old reserve role). Glove-first (and often glove-only) first baseman Doug Mientkiewicz was dealt to the Mets in exchange for a prospect. The team refused to sentimentalize players who had been useful tools in the pursuit of the 2004 championship. The divestiture of these players, along with the problematic Martinez and the erratic Derek Lowe, signaled an important understanding (intuitive or learned) of the Stengel-Weiss model: Don't let the past weigh you down.

Nonetheless, at the end of April, the Red Sox were looking up at a surprising Baltimore Orioles team. The O's were a dominating 17-7, the Red Sox a middling 13-11. A month later the Orioles had cooled somewhat but so had the Red Sox, and the four game gap between the two remained. It was only on June 24 that the Red Sox, now winning more frequently, unseated the Orioles and went into first place. Then they slumped again, losing three of four to the Orioles going into the All-Star break and then three of four to the Yankees right after. For a moment the Yankees were in first place, *again*, the Sox back in second where they had been every year since 1998.

Theo Epstein improvised. The team had to get back into first place since the competitive AL West probably meant either the Angels or the ascendent A's would be the wild card entry into the playoffs. When Bellhorn's sprained left thumb brought his season-long slump to a momentary halt, Epstein consummated a little-noticed deal. During the off-season, Boston had signed the former outfield prospect Chip Ambres to a minor league deal, and he had put up a strong season for triple-A Pawtucket. Voices around baseball began to wonder if he was the proverbial "late bloomer." On July 19, Ambres was sent to the Kansas City Royals in exchange for steady infielder Tony Graffanino. Installed at second base, Graffanino went 13-for-39 (.333) in his first 14 games. It was mostly singles, but it was more than Bellhorn had done all year. Helped by that slight extra edge, the Sox went 11-3 in those games. It was enough to blow past an aged, ill-conceived Yankees club and take a 4.5 game lead in the division race.

The title defense wasn't over, but as August began, things looked better than they had all year. With just under a third of the season to go, even a .500 record the rest of the way would require the Yankees to play at a 95-win pace to pass the Red Sox, and the Yankees hadn't done that all year. The detritus of the championship run had been left behind, with Epstein adroitly taking advantage of another contingency—Ambres—to plug one of the club's biggest holes.

The mind game continued.

—Steven Goldman

Appendix I

YAWKEY AND POST-YAWKEY RED SOX GENERAL MANAGERS

STEVEN GOLDMAN

GM	YEARS	BEST DEAL	WORST DEAL	WS
Eddie Collins	1933–1947	Cash deal: Acquired LHP Lefty Grove, LHP Rube Walberg, and 2B Max Bishop from the Philadelphia A's for RHP Bob Kline, SS Rabbit Warstler, and $125,000 (12/12/1933). Baseball trade: Acquired RHP Wes Ferrell and OF Dick Porter from the Cleveland Indians for LHP Bob Weiland, OF Bob Seeds, and $25,000 (5/25/1934).	Acquired 3B Pinky Higgins from the Philadelphia A's for 3B Bill Werber (12/9/1936).	1
Joe Cronin	1947–1959	Cash deal: Acquired SS Vern Stephens and RHP Jack Kramer from the St. Louis Browns for C Roy Partee, RHP Jim Wilson, RHP Al Widmar, OF Ellie Pellagrini, LHP Joe Ostrowski, and $350,000 (11/17/1947). Baseball trade: Acquired OF Jackie Jensen from the Washington Senators for LHP Mickey McDermott and OF Tommy Umphlett (12/9/1953).	Acquired 3B Grady Hatton and $100,000 from Chicago White Sox for 3B George Kell (5/23/1954).	0
Bucky Harris	1959–9/1960	None of note.	Acquired C Russ Nixon from the Cleveland Indians for C Sammy White and 1B Jim Marshall (trade canceled when White retired rather than report, 3/16/60).	0

GM	YEARS	BEST DEAL	WORST DEAL	WS
Pinky Higgins (Unofficial until 1963)	1960–1965	Acquired 3B Felix Mantilla from the New York Mets for RHP Tracy Stallard, INF Pumpsie Green, and SS Al Moran (12/11/62).	Acquired OF Roman Mejias from the Houston Astros for 1B Pete Runnels (11/26/62).	0
Dick O'Connell	1965–1977	Personality Trade: Acquired RHP Rick Wise and OF Bernie Carbo from St. Louis for OF Reggie Smith and RHP Ken Tatum (10/26/73). Baseball Trade: Acquired RHP Ferguson Jenkins from the Texas Rangers for OF Juan Beniquez, LHP Craig Skok, and LHP Steve Barr (11/17/75). Free agent signing: RHP Luis Tiant (5/17/71).	Acquired 1B Danny Cater from the New York Yankees in exchange for LHP Sparky Lyle (3/22/72).	1
Heywood Sullivan	1977–1983	Acquired 3B Carney Lansford, OF Rick Miller, and RHP Mark Clear from the California Angels for SS Rick Burleson and 3B Butch Hobson (12/10/80).	Sent OF Fred Lynn and RHP Steve Renko to the California Angels for LHP Frank Tanana, RHP Jim Dorsey, and OF Joe Rudi (1/23/81). Administrative: Accidentally nontendered C Carlton Fisk and OF Fred Lynn (12/20/80).	0
Lou Gorman	1984–1993	Acquired RHP Lee Smith from the Chicago Cubs for RHPs Calvin Schiraldi and Al Nipper (12/8/87).	Dealt 1B Jeff Bagwell to the Houston Astros for RHP Larry Andersen (8/30/90).	1
Dan Duquette	1993–2002	Acquired RHP Pedro Martinez from the Montreal Expos in exchange for RHPs Carl Pavano and Tony Armas Jr. (11/18/97).	Sent LHP Jamie Moyer to the Seattle Mariners in exchange for OF Darren Bragg (7/30/96).	0

Appendix II

THE COMPLETE LIST OF BASEBALL BRAWLS FROM STENGEL AND WEINART TO A-ROD AND VARITEK

COMPILED BY JASON KAREGEANNES, DOUG PAPPAS, AND STEVEN GOLDMAN

In an effort to understand the impact of emotion on winning and losing, the dark continent of performance analysis, we present eighty-one years of baseball fights and their effect, or lack thereof, on the standings. This list was completed with the aid of ejection data compiled by the late Doug Pappas.

DATE	TEAMS	PARTICIPANTS	RECORD AT TIME OF BRAWL	PREVIOUS 10	NEXT 10	MONTH	SEASON FINISH
5/7/1923	Giants–Phillies	Casey Stengel, Phil Weinart	NYG: 15–8 (1st) PHI: 6–11 (last)	NYG: 6–4 PHI: 3–7	NYG: 7–3 PHI: 2–8	NYG: 20–7 PHI: 7–23	NYG: 95–58 WS (lose) PHI: 50–104 (last)
6/12/1924	Yankees–Tigers	Babe Ruth, Ty Cobb	NYY: 26–19 (2nd) DET: 28–23 (3rd)	NYY: 4–6 DET: 5–5	NYY: 4–5–1 DET: 6–4	NYY: 12–15 DET: 14–15	NYY: 89–63 (2nd) DET: 86–68 (3rd)
5/30/1932	White Sox–Indians	Umpire George Moriarty vs. White Sox	CHW: 14–27 (7th)	CHW: 5–5	CHW: 4–6	June: 8–16	CHW: 49–102 (7th)
7/4/1932	Yankees–Senators	Bill Dickey, Carl Reynolds	NYY: 50–22 (1st) WAS: 39–34 (4th)	NYY: 7–3 WAS: 3–7	NYY: 6–4 WAS: 6–4	NYY: 20–14 WAS: 19–14	NYY: 107–47 (Win WS) WAS: 93–61 (3rd)

DATE	TEAMS	PARTICIPANTS	RECORD AT TIME OF BRAWL	PREVIOUS 10	NEXT 10	MONTH	SEASON FINISH
4/5/1933	Yankees–Senators	Ben Chapman, Buddy Myers	NYY: 8–2 (1st) WAS: 6–6 (4th)	NYY: 7–2 WAS: 5–5	NYY: 5–5 WAS: 8–2	May: NYY: 14–9 WAS: 14–12	NYY: 91–59 (2nd) WAS: 99–53 WS (lose)
08/01 & 02/1933	Pirates–Cardinals	Steve Swetonic, George Watkins; Arky Vaughan, Bill Walker	STL: 53–46 (4th) PIT: 57–44 (2nd)	STL: 7–3 PIT: 8–2	STL: 4–6 PIT: 5–5	STL: 13–11 PIT: 17–11	STL : 82–71 (5th) PIT: 87–67 (2nd)
4/29/1935	Cubs–Pirates	Roy Joiner, Bully Jurges, Guy Bush, Cookie Lavegetto	CHI: 7–5 (3rd) PIT: 6–7 (T5)	Both: 5–5	CHI: 7–3 PIT: 4–6	May: CHI: 10–9 PIT: 17–11	CHI: 100–54 WS (lose) PIT: 86–67 (4th)
8/10/1936	Cardinals–Cubs	Dizzy Dean, Tex Carlton	STL: 65–42 (1st) CHN: 63–42 (2nd)	STL: 6–4 CHN: 5–5	STL: 7–3 CHN: 3–7	STL: 13–15 CHN: 13–14	STL & CHN: 86–67 (T2)
5/30/1938	Yankees–Red Sox	Jake Powell, Joe Cronin	NYY: 19–12 (2nd) BOS: 19–16 (4th)	NYY: 3–6–1 BOS: 5–5	NYY: 5–5 BOS: 6–4	June: NYY: 17–11 BOS: 16–10	NYY: 99–53 (Win WS) BOS: 88–61 (2nd)
6/19/1940	Cardinals–Dodgers	Leo Durocher, Mickey Owen	STL: 21–30 (5th) BRO: 33–17 (2nd)	STL: 6–4 BRO: 5–5	STL: 5–5 BRO: 4–6	STL: 11–14 BRO: 17–11	STL: 84–69 (3rd) BRO: 88–65 (2nd)
5/24/1952	Yankees–Red Sox	Jim Piersall, Billy Martin	NYY: 16–14 (4th) BOS: 19–14 (2nd)	NYY: 8–2 BOS: 4–6	Both: 6–4	June: NYY: 21–9 BOS: 16–14	NYY: 95–59 (Win WS) BOS: 76–78 (6th)
4/19/1953	A's–Red Sox	Allie Clark, Sammy White	PHI: 1–2 (6th) BOS: 3–3 (3rd)	PHI: 2–2 BOS: 1–1	Both: 6–4	PHI: 6–6 BOS: 7–6	PHI: 59–95 (7th) BOS: 84–69 (4th)
7/12/1952	Yankees–Browns	Billy Martin, Cliff Courtney	NYY: 47–30 (1st) STL: 33–47 (7th)	NYY: 6–4 STL: 2–8	NYY: 7–3 STL: 2–8	NYY: 20–15 STL: 9–23	NYY: 95–59 (Win WS) STL: 64–90 (7th)
7/5/1955	Reds–Cardinals	Birdie Tebbets, Harry Walker	CIN: 36–32 (4th) STL: 34–41 (6th)	CIN: 7–3 STL: 6–4	CIN: 3–7 STL: 7–3	CIN: 14–21 STL: 15–17	CIN: 75–79 (5th) STL: 68–86 (7th)
6/13/1957	Yankees–White Sox	Larry Doby, Art Ditmar	NYY: 29–21 (2nd) CHW: 33–16 (1st)	NYY: 6–4 CHW: 5–5	NYY: 10–0 CHW: 4–6	NYY: 21–9 CHW: 17–15	NYY: 98–56 WS (lose) CHW: 90–64 (2nd)
6/25/1961	Indians–Tigers	Bob Hale, Jim Piersall	CLE: 41–30 (3rd) DET: 45–24 (1st)	CLE: 2–8 DET: 8–2	CLE: 4–6 DET: 5–5	July: CLE: 12–16 DET: 16–12	CLE: 78–83 (5th) DET: 101–61 (2nd)
8/22/1965	Giants–Dodgers	Juan Marichal, John Roseboro	SF: 69–51 (T2) LA: 72–53 (1st)	SF: 5–5 LA: 6–4	SF: 3–7 LA: 4–6	September: SF: 21–9 LA: 20–7	SF: 95–67 (2nd) LA: 97–65 (Win WS)
6/4/1967	Yankees–Tigers	Bill Robinson, Ray Oyler	NYY: 20–24 (8th) DET: 28–18 (1st)	NYY: 5–5 DET: 6–4	NYY: 4–6 DET: 5–5	NYY: 15–16 DET: 12–18	NYY: 72–90 (9th) DET: 91–71 (2nd)
7/7/1974	Expos–Dodger	Rick Auerbach, Tim Foli	LA: 58–27 (1st) MON: 39–40 (3rd)	LA: 8–2 MON: 5–5	Both: 5–5	LA: 16–13 MON: 14–19	LA: 102–60 WS (lose) MON: 79–82 (4th)
7/14/1974	Reds–Pirates	Bruce Kinson, Jack Billingham	CIN: 53–38 (2nd) PIT: 38–49 (5th)	CIN: 7–3 PIT: 3–7	CIN: 7–3 PIT: 9–1	CIN: 19–12 PIT: 18–14	CIN: 98–64 (2nd) PIT: 88–74 (1st)
9/23/1974	Cardinals–Cubs	Ted Simmons, Bill Madlock	STL: 82–71 (1st) CHC: 64–88 (6th)	STL: 8–2 CHC: 7–2	STL: 4–4 CHC: 2–8	STL: 18–9 CHC: 12–19	STL: 86–65 (2nd) CHC: 66–96 (6th)

DATE	TEAMS	PARTICIPANTS	RECORD AT TIME OF BRAWL	PREVIOUS 10	NEXT 10	MONTH	SEASON FINISH
4/20/1976	Cardinals–Mets	Lynn McGlothen, Jon Matlack	STL: 3–6 (6th) NYM: 6–5 (2nd)	STL: 3–6 NYM: 5–5	STL: 5–5 NYM: 7–3	STL: 8–10 NYM: 13–7	STL: 72–90 (5th) NYM: 86–76 (3rd)
4/26/1976	Giants Cardinals	Jose Cardenal, Bill Madlock	STL: 6–8 (4th) SF: 7–7 (5th)	STL: 4–6 SF: 5–5	STL: 5–5 SF: 1–9	May: STL: 12–15 SF: 11–20	STL: 72–90 (5th) SF: 74–88 (4th)
5/1/1976	Giants–Cubs	Charlie Williams, Vic Harris	CHC: 9–11 (4th) SF: 8–10 (5th)	CHC: 5–5 SF: 4–6	CHC: 4–6 SF: 1–9	CHC: 11–14 SF: 11–20	CHC: 75–87 (4th) SF: 74–88 (4th)
5/20/1976	Yankees–Red Sox	Bill Lee, Graig Nettles, Carlton Fisk, Lou Piniella	NYY: 19–11 (1st) BOS: 14–16 (3rd)	NYY: 5–5 BOS: 7–3	NYY: 6–4 BOS: 5–5	May: NYY: 16–12 BOS: 13–15	NYY: 97–62 WS (lose) BOS: 83–79 (3rd)
6/4/1976	Orioles–Twins	Reggie Jackson, Craig Kusick	BAL: 23–22 (2nd) MIN: 22–23 (4th)	BAL: 5–5 MIN: 3–7	BAL: 1–9 MIN: 4–6	BAL: 17–12 MIN: 12–18	BAL: 88–74 (2nd) MIN: 85–77 (3rd)
4/10/1977	Braves Astros	Cliff Johnson, Dick Ruthven	ATL: 1–2 (T5) HOU: 2–1 (T1)	ATL: 0–2 HOU: 2–0	ATL: 7–3 HOU: 3–7	ATL: 8–12 HOU: 9–11	ATL: 61–101 (6th) HOU: 81–81 (3rd)
5/7/1977	Royals–Rangers	Darrell Porter, Bump Wills, Willie Horton, Claudell Washington	KC: 15–11 (3rd) TEX: 12–10	KC: 4–6 TEX: 12–10	Both: 3–7	KC: 10–15 TEX: 11–13	KC: 102–60 (1st) TEX: 94–68 (2nd)
6/11/1977	Dodgers–Cardinals	Reggie Smith, John Denny, Elias Sosa	LA: 38–20 (1st) STL: 32–24 (2nd)	LA: 4–6 STL: 5–5	LA: 7–3 STL: 3–7	LA: 17–11 STL: 13–15	LA: 98–64 WS (lose) STL: 83–79 (3rd)
6/19/1977	Dodgers–Cubs	Reggie Smith, Rick Reuschel, George Mitterwald	LA: 43–22 (1st) CHN: 39–22 (1st)	LA: 6–4 CHN: 7–3	LA: 7–3 CHN: 8–2	July: LA: 16–12 CHN: 14–17	LA: 98–64 WS (lose) CHN: 81–81 (4th)
9/25/1977	Angels–Royals	Ken Brett, NA	KC: 99–55 (1st) CAL: 72–84 (5th)	KC: 9–1 CAL: 3–7	KC: 3–4 CAL: 2–4	KC: 25–5 CAL: 12–19	)KC: 102–60 (1st) CAL: 74–88 (5th)
5/31/1978	Expos–Cubs	Ellis Valentine, Dave Rader	CHI: 24–20 (1st) MON: 25–22 (2nd)	CHI: 8–2 MON: 6–4	CHI: 8–2 MON: 6–4	June: CHI: 14–15 MON: 12–16	CHI: 79–83 (3rd) MON: 76–86 (4th)
6/11/1978	Yankees–Angels	Mike Heath, Carney Lansford	CAL: 30–27 (2nd) NYY: 32–24 (2nd)	CAL: 4–6 NYY: 3–7	Both: 6–4	CAL: 15–15 NYY: 14–15	CAL: 87–75 (2nd) NYY: 100–63 (Won WS)
4/17/1979	Mets–Expos	Gary Carter, John Stearns	NYM: 3–4 (5th) MON: 7–2 (1st)	NYM: 3–4 MON: 6–2	NYM: 5–5 MON: 7–3	NYM: 8–10 MON: 14–5	NYM: 63–99 (6th) MON: 95–65 (2nd)
6/15/1979	Mets–Braves	Craig Swan, Phil Niekro, Bobby Cox	NYM: 24–33 (6th) ATL: 22–40 (6th)	NYM: 6–4 ATL: 3–7	NYM: 4–6 ATL: 6–4	NYM: 15–11 ATL: 13–16	NYM: 63–99 (6th) ATL: 66–94 (6th)
7/27/1979	Yankees–Brewers	Reggie Jackson, Mike Caldwell	NYY: 55–46 (4th) MIL: 61–41 (3rd)	NYY: 6–4 MIL: 8–2	NYY: 5–5 MIL: 3–7	August: NYY: 15–11 MIL: 18–12	NYY: 89–71 (4th) MIL: 95–66 (2nd)
7/28/1979	Astros–Dodgers	Ken Brett, Enos Cabell	HOU: 59–46 (2nd) LA: 44–59 (5th)	HOU: 4–6 LA: 8–2	HOU: 8–2 LA: 5–5	August: HOU: 15–11 LA: 17–11	HOU: 89–73 (2nd) LA: 79–83 (3rd)

DATE	TEAMS	PARTICIPANTS	RECORD AT TIME OF BRAWL	PREVIOUS 10	NEXT 10	MONTH	SEASON FINISH
7/29/1979	Yankees–Brewers	Lou Piniella, Jim Gantner	NYY: 55–48 (4th) MIL: 63–41 (3rd)	NYY: 6–4 MIL: 7–3	NYY: 6–4 MIL: 3–7	August: NYY: 15–11 MIL: 18–12	NYY: 89–71 (4th) MIL: 95–66 (2nd)
4/20/1980	Orioles–White Sox	Doug DeCinces, Mike Proly	BAL: 5–5 (2nd) CHW: 7–3 (2nd)	BAL: 5–4 CHW: 6–3	BAL: 3–7 CHW: 5–5	May: BAL: 15–13 CHW: 12–17	BAL: 100–62 (2nd) CHW: 70–90 (5th)
9/3/1981	Yankees–Indians	Reggie Jackson, John Denny	NYY: 56–42 (1st) CLE: 46–47 (6th)	NYY: 3–7 CLE: 3–7	NYY: 3–6 CLE: 6–4	NYY: 13–14 CLE: 15–12	NYY: 59–48 (Won 1st Half/ Lose WS) CLE: 52–51 (6th overall)
6/27/1983	Cardinals–Pirates	John Candelaria, Joaquin Andujar, Jim Bibby	STL: 34–36 (2nd) PIT: 32–36 (4th)	STL: 8–2 PIT: 2–8	STL: 4–6 PIT: 5–5	July: STL: 22–10 PIT: 16–13	STL: 79–83 (4th) PIT: 84–78 (2nd)
7/2/1983	Royals–Angels	Tim Foli, Larry Gura	KC: 36–35 (4th) CAL: 41–35 (2nd)	KC: 4–6 CAL: 5–5	KC: 4–6 CAL: 3–7	KC: 13–15 CAL: 9–20	KC: 79–83 (2nd) CAL: 70–92 (5th)
8/12/1984	Braves–Padres	Pasqual Perez, Ed Whitson	SD: 69–48 (1st) ATL: 60–58 (2nd)	SD: 5–5 ATL: 3–7	SD: 5–5 ATL: 4–6	SD: 15–14 ATL: 11–17	SD: 92–70 WS (lose) ATL: 80–82 (2nd)
5/27/1986	Dodgers–Mets	Tim Niedenfeur, Ray Knight	LA: 22–23 (5th) NYM: 28–11 (1st)	LA: 3–7 NYM: 6–4	LA: 4–6 NYM: 6–4	June: LA: 11–16 NYM: 15–9	LA: 73–89 (4th) NYM: 108–54 (Win WS)
7/1/1986	A's–Indians	Pat Corrales, Dave Stewart	OAK: 30–49 (7th) CLE: 39–35 (4th)	OAK: 2–8 CLE: 6–4	OAK: 3–7 CLE: 7–3	OAK: 14–12 CLE: 15–12	OAK: 76–86 (4th) CLE: 84–78 (5th)
7/22/1986	Mets–Reds	Ray Knight, Eric Davis	CIN: 44–47 (4th) NYM: 62–28	CIN: 6–4 NYM: 7–3	CIN: 6–4 NYM: 7–3	CIN: 16–11 NYM: 15–11	CIN: 86–76 (2nd) NYM: 108–54 (Win WS)
4/21/1987	Dodgers–Giants	Scott Garrelts, Mike Marshall, Chris Brown	LA: 8–8 (4th) SF: 11–4 (1st)	Both: 7–3	Both: 5–5	May: LA & SF: 5–5	LA: 73–89 (4th) SF: 90–72 (1st)
6/17/1987	Brewers–Twins	Jim Ganter, Dan Gladden, Tony Oliva	MIN: 37–28 (1st) MIL: 33–28 (4th)	MIN: 9–1 MIL: 4–6	MIN: 5–5 MIL: 4–6	MIN: 17–11 MIL: 13–15	MIN: 85–77 (Win WS) MIL: 91–71 (3rd)
07/07 & 08/1987	Indians–Royals	Willie Wilson, Ken Schrom; Brett Butler, Danny Jackson	CLE: 30–53 (last) KC: 45–38 (2nd)	CLE: 2–8 KC: 8–2	CLE: 3–7 KC: 2–8	CLE: 10–17 KC: 10–18	CLE: 61–101 (last) KC: 83–79 (2nd)
4/30/1988	Reds–Mets	Tom Browning, Tim Teufel	CIN: 11–11 (3rd) NYM: 15–6 (2nd)	CIN: 4–6 NYM: 7–3	CIN: 5–5 NYM: 8–2	May: CIN: 12–16 NYM: 19–9	CIN: 87–74 (2nd) NYM: 100–60 (1st)
7/24/1988	Giants–Cardinals	Will Clark, Jose Oquendo	SF: 50–36 (3rd) STL: 43–54 (5th)	SF: 3–7 STL: 5–5	SF: 7–3 STL: 4–6	September: SF: 12–15 STL: 14–13	SF: 83–79 (4th) STL: 76–86 (5th)
5/10/1989	Astros–Expos	Danny Darwin, Ed Ott, Randy Johnson, Spike Owen, Tim Raines	HOU: 14–19 (last) MON: 18–16 (3rd)	Both: 5–5	HOU: 7–3 MON: 3–7	May: HOU: 16–10 MON: 14–14	HOU: 86–76 (3rd) MON: 81–81 (4th)

296

DATE	TEAMS	PARTICIPANTS	RECORD AT TIME OF BRAWL	PREVIOUS 10	NEXT 10	MONTH	SEASON FINISH
5/31/1989	Dodgers–Expos	Pasqual Perez, Mike Scioscia	LA: 24–24 (5th) MON: 27–25 (2nd)	LA: 5–5 MON: 7–3	LA: 3–7 MON: 7–3	June: LA: 12–17 MON: 17–10	LA: 77–83 (4th) MON: 81–81 (4th)
6/3/1990	Red Sox–Indians	Roger Clemens, Stanley Jefferson	BOS: 25–23 (T2) CLE: 23–25 (4th)	Both: 4–6	BOS: 7–3 CLE: 3–7	BOS: 20–9 CLE: 14–14	BOS: 88–74 (1st) CLE: 77–85 (4th)
6/30/1990	Brewers–Mariners	Bob Sebra, B.J. Surhoff, Tracy Jones, Jeff Schaefer	MIL: 33–40 (6th) SEA: 39–38 (3rd)	MIL: 3–7 SEA: 6–4	Both: 5–5	July: MIL: 12–15 SEA: 15–12	MIL: 74–88 (6th) SEA: 77–85 (5th)
8/9/1990	Mets–Pirates	Dwight Gooden, Darryl Strawberry, Tim Teufel, Dennis Cook, Darren Daulton, Mike Ryan	NYM: 63–45 (2nd) PIT: 64–45 (1st)	NYM: 5–5 PIT: 7–3	NYM: 5–5 PIT: 6–4	NYM: 16–14 PIT: 17–14	NYM: 91–71 (2nd) PIT: 95–67 (1st)
8/20/1990	Dodgers–Phillies	Rick Dempsey, Lenny Dykstra	LA: 63–58 (2nd) PHI: 57–62 (5th)	Both: 5–5	LA: 7–3 PHI: 3–7	LA: 18–12 PHI: 11–19	LA: 86–76 (2nd) PHI: 77–85 (5th)
5/19/1991	White Sox–Blue Jays	Jack McDowell, Mark Whiten	CHA: 17–16 (6th) TOR: 22–16 (1st)	CHA: 4–6 TOR: 5–5	CHA: 3–7 TOR: 6–4	CHA: 10–17 TOR: 15–12	CHA: 87–75 (2nd) TOR: 91–71 (1st)
8/21/1991	Mets–Cardinals	Rick Cerone, Willie Fraser	NYM: 58–61 (4th) STL: 61–61 (2nd)	NYM: 0–10 STL: 6–4	NYM: 5–5 STL: 4–6	September: NYM: 12–15 STL: 13–16	NYM: 77–84 (5th) STL: 84–78 (2nd)
5/4/1992	Indians–Royals	Albert Belle, Neal Heaton	CLE: 9–18 (last) KC: 5–19 (last)	Both: 3–7	CLE: 4–6 KC: 5–5	CLE: 11–16 KC: 14–14	CLE: 76–86 (4th) KC: 72–90 (6th)
6/18/1992	Giants–Padres	Bruce Kim, Jose Melendez, Dusty Baker, Fred McGriff	SD: 35–31 (3rd) SF: 31–33 (4th)	SD: 5–5 SF: 3–7	SD: 5–5 SF: 4–6	SD: 13–14 SF: 7–19	SD: 82–80 (3rd) SF: 72–90 (5th)
6/24/1992	Reds–Astros	Glen Braggs, Rob Dibble, Pete Harnish, Ed Ott	CIN: 41–28 (1st) HOU: 32–39 (5th)	CIN: 6–4 HOU: 7–3	CIN: 7–3 HOU: 6–4	July: CIN: 16–12 HOU: 11–14	CIN: 90–72 (2nd) HOU: 81–81 (4th)
7/21/1992	Brewers–Rangers	Scott Fletcher, Dickie Thon	MIL: 49–43 (3rd) TEX: 50–40 (3rd)	MIL: 7–3 TEX: 4–6	MIL: 6–4 TEX: 4–6	August: MIL: 15–14 TEX: 11–18	MIL: 92–70 (2nd) TEX: 77–85 (4th)
6/2/1993	Angels–Blue Jays	Chad Curtis, Stan Javier, Damion Easley, Darnell Coles, Mark Eichorn, Ed Sprague	CAL: 27–23 (1st) TOR: 31–22 (2nd)	CAL: 6–4 TOR: 7–3	CAL: 4–6 TOR: 5–5	CAL: 10–17 TOR: 19–9	CAL: 71–91 (5th) TOR: 95–67 (Win WS)
6/6/1993	Orioles–Mariners	Bill Haselman, Rick Sutcliffe, Chris Bosio, Norm Charlton	BAL: 25–30 (5th) SEA: 36–30 (5th)	BAL: 5–5 SEA: 4–6	BAL: 8–2 SEA: 4–6	BAL: 20–7 SEA: 13–14	BAL: 85–77 (3rd) SEA: 82–80 (4th)
6/15/1993	Dodgers–Rockies	Keith Shepard, Jim Gott, Corey Snyder	LA: 34–28 (3rd) COL: 20–43 (7th)	LA: 6–4 COL: 5–5	LA: 3–7 COL: 6–4	LA: 14–13 COL: 11–14	LA: 81–81 (4th) COL: 67–95 (6th)

DATE	TEAMS	PARTICIPANTS	RECORD AT TIME OF BRAWL	PREVIOUS 10	NEXT 10	MONTH	SEASON FINISH
8/4/1993	Rangers–White Sox	Nolan Ryan, Robin Ventura	CHA: 59–47 (1st) TEX: 54–53 (3rd)	CHA: 8–2 TEX: 4–6	CHA: 5–5 TEX: 6–4	Both: 17–12	CHA: 94–68 (1st) TEX: 86–76 (2nd)
8/24/1993	A's–Brewers	Dickie Thon, Mark McGwire, Troy Neel, Ed Nunez, Tommie Reynolds	MIL: 52–74 (last) OAK: 51–73 (last)	Both: 4–6	MIL: 6–4 OAK: 1–9	September: MIL: 9–16 OAK: 15–13	MIL: 69–93 (last) OAK: 68–94 (last)
5/2/1994	Padres–Phillies	Pete Incaviglia, Jeff Juden	PHI: 11–14 (last) SD: 7–19 (last)	PHI: 3–7 SD: 5–5	Both: 3–7	PHI: 15–13 SD: 11–17	PHI: 54–61 (4th) SD: 47–70 (last)
5/22/1994	Marlins–Cardinals	Luis Aquino, Bernard Gilkey	FLA: 22–21 (3rd) STL: 22–18 (2nd)	FLA: 5–5 STL: 6–4	Both: 4–6	June: FLA: 12–15 STL: 13–13	FLA: 51–64 (last) STL: 53–61 (4th)
6/14/1994	Expos–Pirates	Juan Bell, Pedro Martinez, Larry Walker, Rick White, Kevin Young, Geronimo Pena	MON: 39–24 (2nd) PIT: 28–34 (4th)	MON: 8–2 PIT: 7–3	MON: 5–5 PIT: 8–2	MON: 19–8 PIT: 17–10	MON: 74–40 (1st) PIT: 53–61 (3rd)
5/11/1996	Cubs–Mets	Scott Servais, Turk Wendell, John Franco, Pete Harnish, Todd Hundley, Steve Swisher	CHN: 16–20 (4th) NYM: 15–19 (last)	Both: 4–6	CHN: 5–5 NYM: 3–7	CHN: 9–17 NYM: 11–17	CHN: 76–86 (4th) NYM: 71–91 (4th)
5/31/1996	Indians–Brewers	Albert Belle, Fernando Vina	CLE: 35–17 (1st) MIL: 23–28 (3rd)	CLE: 6–4 MIL: 3–7	CLE: 6–4 MIL: 5–5	June: CLE: 14–14 MIL: 17–11	CLE: 99–62 (1st) MIL: 80–82 (3rd)
8/12/1996	Expos–Astros	Danny Darwin, Derrick May, Moises Alou, Jeff Juden, Henry Rodriguez	HOU: 64–55 (1st) MON: 65–52 (2nd)	Both: 7–3	HOU: 4–6 MON: 5–5	HOU: 17–11 MON: 14–14	HOU: 82–80 (2nd) MON: 88–74 (2nd)
8/28/1996	Yankees–Mariners	Jeff Nelson, Paul O'Neill, Darryl Strawberry, Bobby Ayala, Chris Bosio	NYY: 74–58 (1st) SEA: 69–63 (2nd)	NYY: 4–6 SEA: 5–5	NYY: 5–5 SEA: 4–6	September: NYY: 16–11 SEA: 15–11	NYY: 92–70 (Win WS) SEA: 85–76 (2nd)
9/24/1996	Phillies–Expos	Pedro Martinez, Tim Spehr, Curt Schilling	MON: 86–71 (2nd) PHI: 69–93 (last)	Both: 5–5	MON: 2–3 PHI: 3–2	MON: 16–12 PHI: 13–13	MON: 88–74 (2nd) PHI: 67–95 (last)
5/21/1997	Pirates–Cardinals	Mark Johnson, Kevin Young	PIT: 22–22 (2nd) STL: 18–26 (3rd)	PIT: 3–7 STL: 2–8	PIT: 5–5 STL: 6–4	June: PIT: 11–16 STL: 15–13	PIT: 79–83 (2nd) STL: 73–89 (4th)
8/13/1997	Giants–Cubs	Tyler Houston, Jeff Kent	SF: 67–54 (1st) CHN: 49–72 (last)	SF: 7–3 CHN: 5–5	SF: 5–5 CHN: 4–6	SF: 16–13 CHN: 13–12	SF: 90–72 (1st) CHN: 68–94 (last)
5/19/1998	Orioles–Yankees	Armando Benitez, Tino Martinez	NYY: 29–9 (1st) BAL: 20–24 (5th)	NYY: 7–3 BAL: 3–7	NYY: 8–2 BAL: 5–5	NYY: 20–7 BAL: 11–17	NYY: 114–48 (Win WS) BAL: 79–83 (4th)

DATE	TEAMS	PARTICIPANTS	RECORD AT TIME OF BRAWL	PREVIOUS 10	NEXT 10	MONTH	SEASON FINISH
6/2/1998	Royals–Angels	Phil Nevin, Jim Pittsley, Rich Dauer, Jamie Quirk	ANA: 29–26 (2nd) KC: 21–43 (last)	Both: 5–5	ANA: 9–1 KC: 3–7	ANA: 22–6 KC: 15–13	ANA: 85–77 (2nd) KC: 72–89 (3rd)
6/28/1998	Dodgers–Pirates	Gary Sheffield, Jason Kendall	LA: 40–42 (3rd) PIT: 39–42 (5th)	LA: 6–4 PIT: 4–6	LA: 6–4 PIT: 2–8	LA: 17–10 PIT: 11–15	LA: 83–79 (3rd) PIT: 69–93 (6th)
9/11/1998	Blue Jays–Yankees	Homer Bush, Darryl Strawberry, Don Zimmer, Tim Johnson, Bill Risley	NYY: 103–42 (1st) TOR: 79–68 (3rd)	NYY: 5–5 TOR: 8–2	NYY: 4–6 TOR: 5–5	NYY: 16–11 TOR: 17–8	NYY: 114–78 (Win WS) TOR: 88–74 (3rd)
5/23/1999	Dodgers–Cardinals	Shawon Dunston, Jamie Arnold	LA: 22–21 (3rd) STL: 23–19 (3rd)	LA: 4–6 STL: 5–5	LA: 5–5 STL: 4–6	June: LA: 8–17 STL: 12–16	LA: 77–85 (3rd) STL: 75–86 (4th)
7/11/1999	Dodgers–Mariners	Frankie Rodriquez, Mark Grudz	LA: 37–47 (5th) SEA: 42–45 (3rd)	LA: 4–6 SEA: 3–7	Both: 4–6	LA: 11–18 SEA: 11–15	LA: 77–85 (3rd) SEA: 79–83 (3rd)
8/31/1999	Twins–Blue Jays	Paul Spoljaric, Christian Guzman	MIN: 56–74 (3rd) TOR: 70–64 (3rd)	Both: 5–5	MIN: 2–8 TOR: 6–4	September: MIN: 7–21 TOR: 11–14	MIN: 63–97 (last) TOR: 84–78 (3rd)
4/22/2000	White Sox–Tigers	Magglio Ordonez, Bill Simas, Doug Brocail, Robert Fick, Dean Palmer, Danny Patterson, Jeff Weaver	CHA: 11–6 (1st) DET: 4–12 (last)	CHA: 5–5 DET: 3–7	CHA: 6–4 DET: 3–7	May: CHA: 13–14 DET: 12–14	CHA: 95–67 (1st) DET: 79–83 (3rd)
8/29/2000	Red Sox–Devil Rays	Pedro Martinez, Gerald Williams	BOS: 69–60 (2nd) TB: 57–74 (5th)	BOS: 5–5 TB: 6–4	Both: 4–6	September: BOS: 16–15 TB: 9–18	BOS: 85–77 (2nd) TB: 69–92 (5th)
8/10/2001	Tigers–Royals	Jeff Weaver, Mike Sweeney	DET: 48–66 (4th) KC: 46–70 (last)	DET: 3–7 KC: 4–6	Both: 5–5	DET: 9–20 KC: 12–17	DET: 66–96 (4th) KC: 65–97 (last)
7/28/2002	Orioles–Red Sox	Derek Lowe, Gary Matthews Jr.	BAL: 48–53 (3rd) BOS: 61–42 (2nd)	BAL: 4–6 BOS: 5–5	BAL: 6–4 BOS: 5–5	August: BAL: 14–16 BOS: 12–15	BAL: 67–95 (4th) BOS: 93–69 (2nd)
6/13/2003	Reds–Phillies	Sean Casey, Carlos Silva, Larry Bowa, Jose Mesa, Jason Kendall, Julian Taverez, Marlon Anderson, Al Martin	CIN: 34–32 (4th) PHI: 34–32 (3rd)	CIN: 7–3 PHI: 4–6	CIN: 3–7 PHI: 8–2	CIN: 12–13 PHI: 16–9	CIN: 69–93 (5th) PHI: 86–76 (3rd)
7/4/2003	Indians–Twins	Jason Davis, Torii Hunter, C.C. Sabathia	CLE: 35–50 (4th) MIN: 44–41 (2nd)	CLE: 5–5 MIN: 3–7	CLE: 6–4 MIN: 3–7	CLE: 11–16 MIN: 10–16	CLE: 68–94 (4th) MIN: 90–72 (1st)
7/24/2004	Yankees–Red Sox	Alex Rodriguez, Jason Varitek, Gabe Kapler, Kenny Lofton	BOS: 53–44 (2nd) NYY: 61–35 (1st)	BOS: 3–7 NYY: 7–3	BOS: 5–5 NYY: 6–4	August: BOS: 21–7 NYY: 16–12	BOS: 98–64 (2nd) Win WS NYA: 101–61 (1st)

Appendix III

GLOSSARY AND STATISTICAL LEADERS

The following pages contain definitions and leader lists for many of the so-called advanced statistics in this book. "Advanced" in this context signifies "better," rather than "difficult." These statistics give a better picture of what is really happening on the field.

The original baseball statistics—like batting average, runs scored, runs batted in, and earned run average—leave out the key factors of context (what was happening around the player when he compiled his statistics), environment (where in time and space he compiled his statistics), and opportunity (how the way the player was used affected his statistics). The field of sabermetrics was based on finding ways to account for these three biases in the statistics.

When considering these statistics, one key phrase to keep in mind is "replacement level." A replacement-level player is one you could pick up from the end of a major league bench, off of the waiver wire, or from a AAA team. He is a fringe player, just barely hanging around the majors. Since all statistics are meaningless without context (a .300 average sounds great until you learn that the league as a whole averaged .315), many Baseball Prospectus statistics attempt to measure what a player accomplished above what could have been expected of the league-average player and the replacement-level player.

The popular perception of second- and third-generation baseball statistics seems to be that they are obscure, that they tend to make the game mysterious. This is a misperception based on the usual American tendency to be suspicious of the new. The purpose here is precisely the opposite.

Equivalent Average

Equivalent Average (EqA) is a tool that measures the total offensive performance, per out, of a player. It is scaled so that it roughly matches the historical range of batting average. A .260 EqA is league average. A .300 EqA is good in the same way a .300 batting average is good. In other words, EqA is completely intuitive. It looks just like batting average, but it contributes something entirely more useful: a summation of a player's complete offensive contribution.

EqA adjusts for numerous biases that distort player statistic. These include the league-wide offensive level, the effects of the player's home park, effects of not having to face your own team's pitchers or hitters, distortions to the league average caused by the designated hitter rule, and the difficulty level of the league. The difficulty adjustment tends to give a slight edge to players from more recent eras, and to penalize players from before the mid-1930s, prior to the widespread use of farm systems and integration.

CAREER BEST EQUIVALENT AVERAGE
(2,000 OUTS OR 500 EQUIVALENT RUNS MINIMUM)

1.	Babe Ruth	0.364	26.	Frank Robinson	0.322
2.	Ted Williams	0.363	27.	Jeff Bagwell	0.322
3.	Barry Bonds	0.355	28.	Dick Allen	0.321
4.	Frank Thomas	0.344	29.	Alex Rodriguez	0.320
5.	Lou Gehrig	0.344	30.	Joe Jackson	0.320
6.	Albert Pujols	0.338	31.	Lance Berkman	0.319
7.	Mickey Mantle	0.337	32.	Albert Belle	0.318
8.	Mark McGwire	0.334	33.	Carlos Delgado	0.318
9.	Manny Ramirez	0.333	34.	Gary Sheffield	0.318
10.	Rogers Hornsby	0.333	35.	Ken Griffey	0.318
11.	Stan Musial	0.330	36.	Mike Piazza	0.318
12.	Edgar Martinez	0.329	37.	Ralph Kiner	0.318
13.	Jason Giambi	0.328	38.	Todd Helton	0.318
14.	Jim Thome	0.328	39.	Vladimir Guerrero	0.316
15.	Jimmie Foxx	0.328	40.	Bob Abreu	0.315
16.	Joe DiMaggio	0.326	41.	Eddie Mathews	0.315
17.	Mel Ott	0.326	42.	Tris Speaker	0.315
18.	Dan Brouthers	0.325	43.	Willie McCovey	0.315
19.	Hank Greenberg	0.325	44.	Rickey Henderson	0.314
20.	Johnny Mize	0.325	45.	Chipper Jones	0.313
21.	Willie Mays	0.325	46.	Lefty O'Doul	0.312
22.	Hank Aaron	0.323	47.	Mike Schmidt	0.312
23.	Ty Cobb	0.323	48.	Wade Boggs	0.312
24.	Brian Giles	0.322	49.	Will Clark	0.312
25.	Charlie Keller	0.322	50.	Arky Vaughan	0.311

CAREER EQUIVALENT AVERAGE, BOSTON RED SOX

1.	Ted Williams	0.363	26.	Trot Nixon	0.295
2.	Manny Ramirez	0.340	27.	Dale Alexander	0.294
3.	Babe Ruth	0.338	28.	Pete Runnels	0.294
4.	Jimmie Foxx	0.328	29.	Ben Chapman	0.293
5.	Wade Boggs	0.324	30.	Carl Everett	0.292
6.	Mo Vaughn	0.319	31.	Felix Mantilla	0.292
7.	David Ortiz	0.318	32.	Carlton Fisk	0.291
8.	Jose Canseco	0.318	33.	Carney Lansford	0.291
9.	Tris Speaker	0.315	34.	Jack Clark	0.291
10.	Nomar Garciaparra	0.309	35.	Joe Cronin	0.291
11.	Fred Lynn	0.308	36.	Mike Easler	0.291
12.	Bob Johnson	0.303	37.	Ike Boone	0.290
13.	Nick Esasky	0.302	38.	Patsy Dougherty	0.290
14.	Bill Mueller	0.300	39.	Joe Harris	0.289
15.	Doc Gessler	0.300	40.	Kevin Millar	0.289
16.	Bernie Carbo	0.299	41.	Reggie Smith	0.289
17.	Dwight Evans	0.297	42.	Jake Stahl	0.287
18.	Mike Stanley	0.297	43.	Ellis Burks	0.286
19.	Earl Webb	0.296	44.	Jackie Jensen	0.286
20.	Ken Harrelson	0.296	45.	John Valentin	0.284
21.	Wally Schang	0.296	46.	Johnny Damon	0.283
22.	Carl Yastrzemski	0.295	47.	Buck Freeman	0.282
23.	Jim Rice	0.295	48.	Brian Daubach	0.281
24.	Mike Greenwell	0.295	49.	George Kell	0.281
25.	Reggie Jefferson	0.295	50.	Johnny Pesky	0.281

BEST SINGLE SEASON EQUIVALENT AVERAGE

1.	Barry Bonds	2004	0.454	26.	Jason Giambi	2000	0.373
2.	Barry Bonds	2002	0.449	27.	Rickey Henderson	1993	0.373
3.	Barry Bonds	2001	0.424	28.	Ted Williams	1954	0.373
4.	Ted Williams	1941	0.419	29.	Willie McCovey	1969	0.373
5.	Barry Bonds	2003	0.410	30.	Barry Bonds	1992	0.372
6.	Babe Ruth	1920	0.405	31.	Edgar Martinez	1995	0.372
7.	Frank Thomas	1994	0.396	32.	John Olerud	1993	0.372
8.	Babe Ruth	1923	0.395	33.	Lou Gehrig	1927	0.372
9.	Ted Williams	1957	0.395	34.	Mickey Mantle	1956	0.372
10.	Mickey Mantle	1957	0.393	35.	Mickey Mantle	1962	0.372
11.	Babe Ruth	1926	0.390	36.	Ross Barnes	1876	0.372
12.	Ted Williams	1946	0.388	37.	Arky Vaughan	1935	0.371
13.	Babe Ruth	1921	0.387	38.	Barry Bonds	1993	0.371
14.	Ted Williams	1942	0.383	39.	Lou Gehrig	1934	0.371
15.	Mark McGwire	1996	0.382	40.	Rogers Hornsby	1925	0.371
16.	Babe Ruth	1931	0.381	41.	Rogers Hornsby	1928	0.371
17.	Jeff Bagwell	1994	0.381	42.	Stan Musial	1948	0.371
18.	Babe Ruth	1924	0.380	43.	Mark McGwire	1995	0.370
19.	Jason Giambi	2001	0.380	44.	Rickey Henderson	1990	0.370
20.	Ted Williams	1947	0.380	45.	Babe Ruth	1919	0.369
21.	Babe Ruth	1927	0.379	46.	Babe Ruth	1930	0.369
22.	Mark McGwire	1998	0.379	47.	Mickey Mantle	1961	0.369
23.	Mark McGwire	2000	0.376	48.	Norm Cash	1961	0.369
24.	Rogers Hornsby	1924	0.376	49.	Ted Williams	1948	0.369
25.	Babe Ruth	1932	0.373	50.	Frank Thomas	1997	0.368

BEST SINGLE SEASON EQUIVALENT AVERAGE, BOSTON RED SOX

#	Player	Year	Avg		#	Player	Year	Avg
1.	Ted Williams	1941	0.419		26.	Carl Yastrzemski	1970	0.338
2.	Ted Williams	1957	0.395		27.	Carl Yastrzemski	1968	0.337
3.	Ted Williams	1946	0.388		28.	Tris Speaker	1912	0.337
4.	Ted Williams	1942	0.383		29.	Wade Boggs	1985	0.337
5.	Ted Williams	1947	0.380		30.	Wade Boggs	1986	0.337
6.	Ted Williams	1954	0.373		31.	Manny Ramirez	2001	0.335
7.	Babe Ruth	1919	0.369		32.	Mo Vaughn	1997	0.335
8.	Ted Williams	1948	0.369		33.	Nomar Garciaparra	1999	0.335
9.	Ted Williams	1955	0.368		34.	Babe Ruth	1918	0.334
10.	Ted Williams	1949	0.364		35.	Mo Vaughn	1998	0.334
11.	Manny Ramirez	2002	0.363		36.	Dwight Evans	1981	0.333
12.	Jimmie Foxx	1938	0.360		37.	Mike Greenwell	1988	0.333
13.	Jimmie Foxx	1939	0.358		38.	Ted Williams	1939	0.333
14.	Wade Boggs	1987	0.358		39.	Tris Speaker	1913	0.333
15.	Ted Williams	1960	0.355		40.	Dwight Evans	1987	0.332
16.	Wade Boggs	1988	0.354		41.	Mo Vaughn	1996	0.332
17.	Ted Williams	1958	0.348		42.	Dale Alexander	1932	0.330
18.	Carl Yastrzemski	1967	0.346		43.	Wade Boggs	1983	0.330
19.	Ted Williams	1956	0.345		44.	Bob Johnson	1944	0.328
20.	Fred Lynn	1979	0.342		45.	Manny Ramirez	2004	0.327
21.	Ted Williams	1940	0.342		46.	Fred Lynn	1975	0.326
22.	Nomar Garciaparra	2000	0.341		47.	Jimmie Foxx	1940	0.324
23.	Ted Williams	1950	0.341		48.	Mo Vaughn	1994	0.324
24.	Manny Ramirez	2003	0.339		49.	Tris Speaker	1914	0.324
25.	Ted Williams	1951	0.339		50.	Wade Boggs	1989	0.324

Equivalent Runs

Equivalent Runs is the counting statistic that goes with Equivalent Average, similar to the way that hits (a counting stat) and batting average (a rate stat) are related. EqR shows how many runs a player put on the scoreboard for his team, accounting for all of the same adjustments (league, park, difficulty, etc.) included in EqA. The scale is generally similar to looking at a player's runs or runs batted in, with 100 having the same cachet as it does with the traditional scoring statistics.

The EqR leader lists begin on the next page.

CAREER BEST EQUIVALENT RUNS

1.	Hank Aaron	2614	26. Robin Yount	1790
2.	Barry Bonds	2469	27. Al Kaline	1775
3.	Willie Mays	2358	28. Eddie Mathews	1775
4.	Stan Musial	2344	29. Rogers Hornsby	1769
5.	Ty Cobb	2341	30. Jimmie Foxx	1735
6.	Rickey Henderson	2301	31. Wade Boggs	1728
7.	Babe Ruth	2300	32. Mike Schmidt	1715
8.	Pete Rose	2238	33. Nap Lajoie	1702
9.	Frank Robinson	2135	34. Tim Raines	1699
10.	Carl Yastrzemski	2087	35. Frank Thomas	1695
11.	Eddie Murray	2049	36. Willie McCovey	1694
12.	Mel Ott	2037	37. Rusty Staub	1681
13.	Ted Williams	2025	38. Harold Baines	1674
14.	Tris Speaker	2012	39. Paul Waner	1665
15.	Dave Winfield	1989	40. Rod Carew	1657
16.	Rafael Palmeiro	1936	41. Fred McGriff	1656
17.	George Brett	1930	42. Tony Gwynn	1652
18.	Paul Molitor	1921	43. Cap Anson	1648
19.	Eddie Collins	1919	44. Jeff Bagwell	1647
20.	Honus Wagner	1912	45. Billy Williams	1646
21.	Mickey Mantle	1912	46. Sam Crawford	1641
22.	Reggie Jackson	1905	47. Dwight Evans	1626
23.	Lou Gehrig	1904	48. Roberto Clemente	1621
24.	Joe Morgan	1876	49. Lou Brock	1599
25.	Cal Ripken	1839	50. Andre Dawson	1594

CAREER EQUIVALENT RUNS, BOSTON RED SOX

1.	Carl Yastrzemski	2089	26. George Scott	578
2.	Ted Williams	2025	27. Freddy Parent	507
3.	Dwight Evans	1574	28. Manny Ramirez	487
4.	Jim Rice	1394	29. Buck Freeman	481
5.	Wade Boggs	1259	30. Rick Burleson	479
6.	Bobby Doerr	1076	31. Troy O'Leary	479
7.	Harry Hooper	960	32. Chick Stahl	466
8.	Dom DiMaggio	843	33. Ellis Burks	461
9.	Tris Speaker	790	34. Tony Conigliaro	461
10.	Rico Petrocelli	785	35. Jimmy Collins	444
11.	Mike Greenwell	782	36. Trot Nixon	438
12.	Mo Vaughn	777	37. Marty Barrett	437
13.	Nomar Garciaparra	736	38. Pete Runnels	423
14.	Jimmie Foxx	705	39. Heinie Wagner	418
15.	Joe Cronin	652	40. Jim Piersall	408
16.	Carlton Fisk	649	41. Jim Tabor	404
17.	Reggie Smith	633	42. Jason Varitek	403
18.	Duffy Lewis	632	43. Ira Flagstead	400
19.	Jackie Jensen	628	44. Jody Reed	399
20.	Frank Malzone	615	45. Vern Stephens	384
21.	Johnny Pesky	613	46. Hobe Ferris	383
22.	John Valentin	598	47. Rich Gedman	374
23.	Larry Gardner	582	48. Everett Scott	371
24.	Billy Goodman	580	49. Rick Miller	337
25.	Fred Lynn	579	50. Phil Todt	336

BEST SINGLE SEASON EQUIVALENT RUNS

1.	Barry Bonds	2001	190		26.	Ted Williams	1942	154
2.	Barry Bonds	2002	174		27.	Babe Ruth	1928	153
3.	Babe Ruth	1923	168		28.	Jimmie Foxx	1932	153
4.	Barry Bonds	2004	168		29.	Albert Pujols	2003	152
5.	Lou Gehrig	1927	166		30.	Babe Ruth	1931	152
6.	Babe Ruth	1921	164		31.	John Olerud	1993	152
7.	Sammy Sosa	2001	164		32.	Lou Gehrig	1930	152
8.	Babe Ruth	1927	162		33.	Lou Gehrig	1931	151
9.	Stan Musial	1948	161		34.	Babe Ruth	1930	150
10.	Mark McGwire	1998	160		35.	Frank Robinson	1966	150
11.	Babe Ruth	1920	159		36.	Rogers Hornsby	1922	150
12.	Ted Williams	1946	159		37.	Cal Ripken	1991	149
13.	Barry Bonds	1993	158		38.	Don Mattingly	1986	149
14.	Hank Aaron	1959	158		39.	Jose Canseco	1988	149
15.	Babe Ruth	1926	157		40.	Lou Gehrig	1936	149
16.	Frank Thomas	1992	157		41.	Mickey Mantle	1957	149
17.	Lou Gehrig	1934	157		42.	Ted Williams	1949	149
18.	Albert Belle	1998	156		43.	Frank Thomas	1993	148
19.	Jason Giambi	2001	156		44.	Jason Giambi	2000	148
20.	Ted Williams	1941	156		45.	Lou Gehrig	1937	148
21.	Babe Ruth	1924	155		46.	Mickey Mantle	1956	148
22.	Frank Thomas	1991	155		47.	Mickey Mantle	1961	148
23.	Ted Williams	1947	155		48.	Jeff Bagwell	1996	147
24.	Carlos Delgado	2000	154		49.	Ken Griffey	1997	147
25.	Hank Aaron	1963	154		50.	Luis Gonzalez	2001	147

BEST SINGLE SEASON EQUIVALENT RUNS, BOSTON RED SOX

1.	Ted Williams	1946	159		26.	Tris Speaker	1914	126
2.	Ted Williams	1941	156		27.	Dwight Evans	1987	124
3.	Ted Williams	1947	155		28.	Babe Ruth	1919	123
4.	Ted Williams	1942	154		29.	Fred Lynn	1979	123
5.	Ted Williams	1949	149		30.	Manny Ramirez	2004	123
6.	Jimmie Foxx	1938	145		31.	Ted Williams	1939	123
7.	Carl Yastrzemski	1967	142		32.	Jim Rice	1977	122
8.	Wade Boggs	1988	142		33.	Jim Rice	1979	122
9.	Mo Vaughn	1996	139		34.	Ted Williams	1951	121
10.	Wade Boggs	1987	139		35.	David Ortiz	2004	120
11.	Wade Boggs	1985	138		36.	Manny Ramirez	2001	120
12.	Jim Rice	1978	137		37.	Wade Boggs	1983	120
13.	Ted Williams	1948	133		38.	Mo Vaughn	1997	119
14.	Carl Yastrzemski	1970	132		39.	Nomar Garciaparra	1997	119
15.	Dwight Evans	1984	132		40.	Jimmie Foxx	1939	118
16.	Mike Greenwell	1988	132		41.	Nomar Garciaparra	1998	118
17.	Manny Ramirez	2003	131		42.	Dwight Evans	1985	116
18.	Mo Vaughn	1998	131		43.	Jimmie Foxx	1936	116
19.	Carl Yastrzemski	1968	128		44.	Rico Petrocelli	1969	116
20.	Ted Williams	1940	128		45.	Tris Speaker	1913	116
21.	Wade Boggs	1989	128		46.	Jim Rice	1983	115
22.	Ted Williams	1957	127		47.	Nomar Garciaparra	2000	115
23.	Wade Boggs	1986	127		48.	Jim Rice	1986	114
24.	Dwight Evans	1982	126		49.	Fred Lynn	1975	113
25.	Tris Speaker	1912	126		50.	Manny Ramirez	2002	113

Fielding Runs Above Replacement

Fielding Runs Above Replacement (FRAR) is a measure of how many runs a fielder saved, compared to a replacement-level fielder—roughly defined as the worst player in the league at the position who still managed to get used semi-regularly. Fielders are rated primarily by how many more plays they made than one would expect based on the statistics of the pitchers and the other fielders on the team; errors are somewhat less important, but still count. Not all positions are equal in FRAR—the difference between an average shortstop and a replacement-level shortstop is a lot bigger (about twenty runs a season) than the difference between an average-level and replacement-level first baseman. For that reason, the all-time and single-season lists are dominated by the so-called skill positions: shortstops, second basemen, catchers, center fielders, and the occasional third baseman.

CAREER BEST FIELDING RUNS ABOVE REPLACEMENT

1.	Ozzie Smith	765	26. Lance Parrish	520
2.	Cal Ripken	708	27. Al Lopez	516
3.	Rabbit Maranville	677	28. Frankie Frisch	513
4.	Honus Wagner	635	29. Gabby Hartnett	507
5.	Bill Mazeroski	633	30. Joe Tinker	500
6.	Bill Dahlen	625	31. Tony Fernandez	498
7.	Dave Concepcion	617	32. Chris Speier	496
8.	Gary Carter	608	33. Frank White	495
9.	Luis Aparicio	597	34. Alan Trammell	493
10.	Bob Boone	587	35. Mark Belanger	493
11.	Johnny Bench	584	36. Bill Dickey	491
12.	Nap Lajoie	572	37. Lave Cross	485
13.	Ivan Rodriguez	566	38. Ray Schalk	485
14.	Bobby Wallace	564	39. Dick Bartell	483
15.	Eddie Collins	555	40. Omar Vizquel	481
16.	Bid McPhee	547	41. Nellie Fox	479
17.	Yogi Berra	545	42. Roger Peckinpaugh	477
18.	Carlton Fisk	539	43. Bert Campaneris	475
19.	Tony Pena	536	44. Red Schoendienst	471
20.	Willie Mays	533	45. Barry Larkin	470
21.	Tommy Corcoran	532	46. Ryne Sandberg	468
22.	Brooks Robinson	531	47. Buddy Bell	467
23.	Roy McMillan	531	48. Charlie Gehringer	467
24.	Jim Sundberg	527	49. Luke Appling	467
25.	Tris Speaker	524	50. Bobby Doerr	465

CAREER FIELDING RUNS ABOVE REPLACEMENT, BOSTON RED SOX

1.	Bobby Doerr	466	26.	Heinie Wagner	159
2.	Carl Yastrzemski	328	27.	Marty Barrett	159
3.	Rico Petrocelli	317	28.	Jim Rice	152
4.	Rick Burleson	313	29.	Tony Pena	151
5.	Dom DiMaggio	308	30.	Rick Ferrell	150
6.	Everett Scott	297	31.	Vern Stephens	149
7.	Wade Boggs	291	32.	Jody Reed	143
8.	Frank Malzone	276	33.	Jimmy Collins	139
9.	Carlton Fisk	265	34.	Fred Lynn	135
10.	Lou Criger	261	35.	Billy Goodman	130
11.	Dwight Evans	235	36.	Larry Gardner	126
12.	John Valentin	228	37.	Doc Cramer	122
13.	Harry Hooper	220	38.	Jackie Jensen	116
14.	Tris Speaker	215	39.	Ira Flagstead	113
15.	Johnny Pesky	208	40.	Reggie Smith	105
16.	Hobe Ferris	201	41.	Duffy Lewis	104
17.	Sammy White	200	42.	Eddie Bressoud	103
18.	Rich Gedman	190	43.	Mike Greenwell	100
19.	Jim Piersall	181	44.	Skeeter Newsome	99
20.	Ted Williams	178	45.	Rick Miller	98
21.	Jason Varitek	172	46.	Tom Oliver	98
22.	Joe Cronin	167	47.	Chuck Schilling	92
23.	Nomar Garciaparra	165	48.	Hal Rhyne	91
24.	Freddy Parent	161	49.	Pete Runnels	89
25.	Bill Carrigan	159	50.	Glenn Hoffman	88

BEST SINGLE SEASON FIELDING RUNS ABOVE REPLACEMENT

1.	Orlando Cabrera	2001	62	26.	Ray Schalk	1922	55
2.	Jim Sundberg	1977	61	27.	Roger Peckinpaugh	1924	55
3.	Bucky Dent	1975	59	28.	Barry Larkin	1990	54
4.	Frankie Frisch	1927	58	29.	Bill Mazeroski	1962	54
5.	George Gibson	1909	58	30.	Bill Mazeroski	1964	54
6.	Jerry Grote	1969	58	31.	Cal Ripken	1989	54
7.	Ozzie Guillen	1988	58	32.	Chico Carrasquel	1951	54
8.	Randy Hundley	1969	58	33.	Johnny Bench	1970	54
9.	Ray Mueller	1943	58	34.	Johnny Bench	1975	54
10.	Art Fletcher	1917	57	35.	Kevin Elster	1989	54
11.	Bill Mazeroski	1966	57	36.	Lou Boudreau	1940	54
12.	Dave Concepcion	1977	57	37.	Ozzie Smith	1987	54
13.	Ozzie Smith	1985	57	38.	Rennie Stennett	1974	54
14.	Roy McMillan	1956	57	39.	Rick Burleson	1978	54
15.	Tommy Thevenow	1926	57	40.	Roy McMillan	1955	54
16.	Cal Ripken	1984	56	41.	Bill Mazeroski	1963	53
17.	Graig Nettles	1971	56	42.	Bob O'Farrell	1926	53
18.	Ivan Rodriguez	1997	56	43.	Brad Ausmus	2000	53
19.	Joe Tinker	1908	56	44.	Brooks Robinson	1967	53
20.	Mike Bordick	1999	56	45.	Chris Speier	1972	53
21.	Ozzie Smith	1980	56	46.	Dick Bartell	1932	53
22.	Rick Burleson	1979	56	47.	Dick Bartell	1934	53
23.	Cal Ripken	1986	55	48.	Everett Scott	1921	53
24.	Ivan Rodriguez	1998	55	49.	George Gibson	1910	53
25.	Joe Sewell	1925	55	50.	George McBride	1908	53

BEST SINGLE SEASON FIELDING RUNS ABOVE REPLACEMENT, BOSTON RED SOX

1.	Rick Burleson	1979	56		26.	Carlton Fisk	1976	42
2.	Rick Burleson	1978	54		27.	Topper Rigney	1926	42
3.	Everett Scott	1921	53		28.	Wade Boggs	1984	42
4.	Rick Burleson	1977	53		29.	Carlton Fisk	1978	41
5.	Rick Burleson	1980	53		30.	Joe Cronin	1938	41
6.	Heinie Wagner	1908	52		31.	Everett Scott	1918	40
7.	Bobby Doerr	1946	51		32.	Everett Scott	1920	40
8.	Lou Criger	1903	51		33.	Hal Rhyne	1931	40
9.	Rick Burleson	1975	51		34.	John Valentin	1993	40
10.	Rich Gedman	1986	50		35.	Rico Petrocelli	1970	40
11.	Rico Petrocelli	1967	49		36.	Bobby Doerr	1938	39
12.	Carlton Fisk	1977	48		37.	Dom DiMaggio	1946	39
13.	Johnny Pesky	1942	48		38.	Dom DiMaggio	1948	39
14.	Johnny Pesky	1946	47		39.	Dom DiMaggio	1949	39
15.	Rich Gedman	1985	47		40.	Jody Reed	1992	39
16.	Dom DiMaggio	1942	46		41.	Lou Criger	1905	39
17.	Eddie Bressoud	1962	45		42.	Tony Pena	1993	39
18.	Jim Piersall	1956	44		43.	Tris Speaker	1909	39
19.	John Valentin	1998	44		44.	Vern Stephens	1948	39
20.	Lou Criger	1904	44		45.	Hobe Ferris	1905	38
21.	Bobby Doerr	1947	43		46.	Jimmy Collins	1904	38
22.	Chuck Schilling	1961	43		47.	Rick Ferrell	1935	38
23.	Everett Scott	1917	43		48.	Sammy White	1953	38
24.	Bobby Doerr	1942	42		49.	Skeeter Newsome	1944	38
25.	Bobby Doerr	1943	42		50.	Tony Pena	1991	38

Fielding Runs Above Average

Fielding Runs Above Average (FRAA) are similar to FRAR, except that the player is being compared to an average player at his position. This is a more stringent standard than FRAR; a fielder may be above replacement level yet still be below average.

CAREER BEST FIELDING RUNS ABOVE AVERAGE

1.	Ozzie Smith	271	26.	Gary Gaetti	134
2.	Bill Mazeroski	266	27.	Yogi Berra	134
3.	Ivan Rodriguez	184	28.	Marty Marion	133
4.	Nap Lajole	172	29.	Andruw Jones	132
5.	Dave Concepcion	170	30.	Frankie Frisch	132
6.	Bid McPhee	167	31.	Gary Carter	132
7.	Honus Wagner	167	32.	Tim Wallach	132
8.	Buddy Bell	160	33.	Bobby Wallace	131
9.	Johnny Bench	160	34.	Willie Mays	131
10.	Cal Ripken	159	35.	Red Schoendienst	130
11.	Lou Criger	158	36.	Steve Garvey	130
12.	Bill Dahlen	155	37.	Jesse Barfield	129
13.	Rabbit Maranville	154	38.	Tris Speaker	129
14.	Curt Flood	153	39.	Bobby Grich	126
15.	Brooks Robinson	152	40.	Rick Burleson	124
16.	Lave Cross	146	41.	George McBride	123
17.	Joe Tinker	145	42.	Tony Fernandez	123
18.	Lou Boudreau	145	43.	Dal Maxvill	122
19.	Mark Belanger	145	44.	Paul Blair	120
20.	Clete Boyer	143	45.	Everett Scott	119
21.	Mike Schmidt	142	46.	Phil Rizzuto	117
22.	Roy McMillan	139	47.	Frank White	116
23.	Bobby Doorr	137	48.	Buck Ewing	115
24.	Willie Kamm	136	49.	Heinie Groh	115
25.	Pete O'Brien	135	50.	Jimmy Collins	115

CAREER FIELDING RUNS ABOVE AVERAGE, BOSTON RED SOX

1.	Bobby Doerr	136	26.	Hick Cady	24
2.	Lou Criger	120	27.	Hobe Ferris	24
3.	Dom DiMaggio	111	28.	Carl Mays	23
4.	Rick Burleson	111	29.	Tom Brunansky	23
5.	Frank Malzone	98	30.	Bob Stanley	21
6.	Harry Hooper	89	31.	Scott Fletcher	21
7.	Wade Boggs	86	32.	Tom Brewer	21
8.	Everett Scott	84	33.	Darren Lewis	20
9.	Carl Yastrzemski	82	34.	Doc Cramer	20
10.	Dwight Evans	68	35.	Roxy Walters	19
11.	Rico Petrocelli	68	36.	Fred Lynn	18
12.	Jim Piersall	67	37.	Sam Agnew	18
13.	John Valentin	60	38.	Bill Carrigan	17
14.	Tris Speaker	60	39.	Candy Lachance	16
15.	Stuffy McInnis	41	40.	Jody Reed	16
16.	Jimmy Collins	40	41.	Johnny Damon	16
17.	Johnny Pesky	35	42.	Eddie Lake	15
18.	Phil Todt	35	43.	Hal Rhyne	15
19.	Tony Pena	35	44.	Ben Chapman	14
20.	Carlton Fisk	34	45.	Ernie Shore	14
21.	Rick Ferrell	32	46.	Pinch Thomas	14
22.	Vern Stephens	29	47.	Cecil Cooper	13
23.	Jackie Jensen	28	48.	Darren Bragg	13
24.	Dick Hoblitzel	26	49.	Derek Lowe	13
25.	Tom Oliver	26	50.	Joe Wood	13

BEST SINGLE SEASON FIELDING RUNS ABOVE AVERAGE

1.	Graig Nettles	1971	35		26.	Bill Mazeroski	1964	26
2.	Jerry Grote	1969	33		27.	Dave Concepcion	1977	26
3.	Brooks Robinson	1967	31		28.	Hughie Jennings	1895	26
4.	Frankie Frisch	1927	31		29.	Joe Vosmik	1932	26
5.	Glenn Hubbard	1985	30		30.	Johnny Bench	1975	26
6.	Jim Sundberg	1977	29		31.	Kevin Elster	1989	26
7.	Orlando Cabrera	2001	29		32.	Lave Cross	1895	26
8.	Ossie Vitt	1916	29		33.	Ozzie Smith	1985	26
9.	Bill Mazeroski	1963	28		34.	Pop Snyder	1884	26
10.	Bill Mazeroski	1966	28		35.	Ray Mueller	1943	26
11.	Darin Erstad	2002	28		36.	Rennie Stennett	1975	26
12.	Hughie Critz	1933	28		37.	Rick Burleson	1979	26
13.	Jesse Barfield	1985	28		38.	Tommy Thevenow	1926	26
14.	Lou Criger	1903	28		39.	Bill Mazeroski	1962	25
15.	Roger Connor	1890	28		40.	Billy Shindle	1888	25
16.	Tommy McCarthy	1888	28		41.	Chico Carrasquel	1951	25
17.	Art Fletcher	1917	27		42.	Curt Flood	1962	25
18.	Bill Holbert	1883	27		43.	Eddie Collins	1910	25
19.	Bucky Dent	1975	27		44.	Harlond Clift	1937	25
20.	Clete Boyer	1962	27		45.	Mike Bordick	1999	25
21.	Ozzie Guillen	1988	27		46.	Rick Burleson	1978	25
22.	Rennie Stennett	1974	27		47.	Tom Daly	1887	25
23.	Roy McMillan	1956	27		48.	Art Fletcher	1918	24
24.	Tim Wallach	1984	27		49.	Bill Holbert	1884	24
25.	Vinny Castilla	1996	27		50.	Billy Moran	1962	24

BEST SINGLE SEASON FIELDING RUNS ABOVE AVERAGE, BOSTON RED SOX

1.	Lou Criger	1903	28		26.	Dwight Evans	1975	17
2.	Rick Burleson	1979	26		27.	Jimmy Collins	1904	17
3.	Rick Burleson	1978	25		28.	Johnny Pesky	1946	17
4.	Bobby Doerr	1946	24		29.	Bobby Doerr	1942	16
5.	Dom DiMaggio	1942	24		30.	Dom DiMaggio	1948	16
6.	John Valentin	1998	24		31.	Rich Gedman	1985	16
7.	Everett Scott	1921	22		32.	Tris Speaker	1912	16
8.	Jim Piersall	1956	22		33.	Billy Werber	1934	15
9.	Rick Burleson	1977	22		34.	Bobby Doerr	1939	15
10.	Rick Burleson	1980	22		35.	Bobby Doerr	1943	15
11.	Heinie Wagner	1908	21		36.	Chuck Schilling	1961	15
12.	Lou Criger	1904	21		37.	Everett Scott	1918	15
13.	Rico Petrocelli	1967	21		38.	Frank Malzone	1957	15
14.	Wade Boggs	1984	21		39.	Harry Hooper	1915	15
15.	Rich Gedman	1986	20		40.	Phil Todt	1927	15
16.	Rick Burleson	1975	20		41.	Tony Pena	1993	15
17.	Dom DiMaggio	1946	19		42.	Tris Speaker	1914	15
18.	Lou Criger	1901	19		43.	Wade Boggs	1985	15
19.	Dom DiMaggio	1949	18		44.	Bobby Doerr	1938	14
20.	Jim Piersall	1953	18		45.	Carl Yastrzemski	1966	14
21.	Johnny Pesky	1942	18		46.	Carl Yastrzemski	1975	14
22.	Tris Speaker	1909	18		47.	Carl Yastrzemski	1977	14
23.	Bobby Doerr	1947	17		48.	Doc Cramer	1938	14
24.	Dom DiMaggio	1947	17		49.	Dwight Evans	1974	14
25.	Dom DiMaggio	1950	17		50.	Eddie Bressoud	1962	14

310

Pitching Runs Above Replacement

Pitching Runs Above Replacement (PRAR) are the number of runs a pitcher saved his team compared to a replacement-level pitcher. One big difference between PRAR and other systems is that PRAR adjusts for the defense behind him. Jim Palmer, for instance, was an outstanding pitcher who performed at an even higher level thanks to having defenders like Brooks Robinson, Mark Belanger, Bobby Grich, and Paul Blair playing behind him for most of his career. Pitchers from the nineteenth and early twentieth centuries relied on their defenses to a much greater extent than the pitchers of today; part of the reason they could throw 300, 400, or more innings was that they often just lobbed it in and let the defense do the work. Due to these defensive and difficulty adjustments, the lists are not dominated by pre-1920 pitchers.

CAREER BEST PITCHING RUNS ABOVE REPLACEMENT

1.	Walter Johnson	1737	26. Frank Tanana	1074
2.	Roger Clemens	1712	27. Ted Lyons	1062
3.	Cy Young	1668	28. Jim Palmer	1061
4.	Warren Spahn	1651	29. Jim Bunning	1043
5.	Greg Maddux	1504	30. Rick Reuschel	1039
6.	Tom Seaver	1495	31. Mike Mussina	1036
7.	Phil Niekro	1476	32. Carl Hubbell	1027
8.	Gaylord Perry	1446	33. Chuck Finley	1023
9.	Robin Roberts	1435	34. Don Drysdale	1022
10.	Nolan Ryan	1429	35. Curt Schilling	1020
11.	Bert Blyleven	1422	36. Jim Kaat	1018
12.	Steve Carlton	1403	37. Bob Friend	1012
13.	Pete Alexander	1380	38. Hal Newhouser	1005
14.	Don Sutton	1317	39. Kid Nichols	1003
15.	Randy Johnson	1301	40. Jerry Koosman	998
16.	Lefty Grove	1297	41. Juan Marichal	998
17.	Fergie Jenkins	1282	42. Billy Pierce	991
18.	Tom Glavine	1218	43. Red Ruffing	986
19.	Bob Gibson	1210	44. Luis Tiant	981
20.	Dennis Eckersley	1182	45. Pedro Martinez	974
21.	Early Wynn	1151	46. John Smoltz	960
22.	Bob Feller	1141	47. Charlie Hough	956
23.	Tommy John	1129	48. Dutch Leonard	952
24.	Christy Mathewson	1087	49. David Cone	944
25.	Kevin Brown	1086	50. Whitey Ford	939

CAREER PITCHING RUNS ABOVE REPLACEMENT, BOSTON RED SOX

1.	Roger Clemens	1074	26.	Ray Culp	261
2.	Cy Young	652	27.	Willard Nixon	259
3.	Pedro Martinez	637	28.	Babe Ruth	251
4.	Bob Stanley	551	29.	Oil Can Boyd	251
5.	Mel Parnell	541	30.	Wes Ferrell	251
6.	Tim Wakefield	537	31.	Ray Collins	237
7.	Lefty Grove	533	32.	Mickey McDermott	231
8.	Luis Tiant	515	33.	Bill Dinneen	230
9.	Ellis Kinder	474	34.	Danny MacFayden	226
10.	Frank Sullivan	459	35.	Jim Lonborg	225
11.	Joe Dobson	455	36.	Jack Quinn	222
12.	Bill Monbouquette	445	37.	Earl Wilson	219
13.	Tex Hughson	415	38.	Carl Mays	214
14.	Derek Lowe	408	39.	Greg Harris	212
15.	Tom Brewer	368	40.	Dave Ferriss	207
16.	Bruce Hurst	362	41.	Red Ruffing	200
17.	Bill Lee	345	42.	Tom Gordon	198
18.	Dennis Eckersley	344	43.	Herb Pennock	188
19.	Dick Radatz	324	44.	Aaron Sele	183
20.	Ike Delock	323	45.	Mike Fornieles	181
21.	Joe Wood	318	46.	Jack Russell	180
22.	Dutch Leonard	309	47.	Bob Ojeda	179
23.	Fritz Ostermueller	286	48.	Sonny Siebert	178
24.	Jack Wilson	274	49.	Mike Torrez	173
25.	Howard Ehmke	267	50.	Danny Darwin	172

BEST SINGLE SEASON PITCHING RUNS ABOVE REPLACEMENT

1.	Bob Feller	1946	148	26.	Mel Parnell	1949	122
2.	Steve Carlton	1972	148	27.	Pete Alexander	1915	122
3.	Walter Johnson	1913	146	28.	Cy Young	1893	121
4.	John Clarkson	1889	143	29.	Tom Seaver	1971	121
5.	Pud Galvin	1884	137	30.	Walter Johnson	1914	121
6.	Gaylord Perry	1972	135	31.	Pedro Martinez	2000	120
7.	Wilbur Wood	1971	134	32.	Randy Johnson	2002	120
8.	Robin Roberts	1953	133	33.	Fergie Jenkins	1971	119
9.	Sandy Koufax	1966	133	34.	Pete Alexander	1916	119
10.	Red Faber	1921	132	35.	Thornton Lee	1941	119
11.	Bob Feller	1940	131	36.	Sandy Koufax	1963	118
12.	Roger Clemens	1997	131	37.	Walter Johnson	1916	118
13.	Amos Rusie	1894	129	38.	Warren Spahn	1947	118
14.	Walter Johnson	1912	128	39.	Bert Blyleven	1973	117
15.	Robin Roberts	1954	127	40.	Bob Gibson	1969	117
16.	Bob Gibson	1968	126	41.	Denny McLain	1968	117
17.	Hal Newhouser	1946	126	42.	Ed Walsh	1908	117
18.	Amos Rusie	1893	125	43.	Hal Newhouser	1945	117
19.	Pete Alexander	1920	125	44.	Jack Chesbro	1904	117
20.	John Clarkson	1887	124	45.	Randy Johnson	2004	117
21.	Dizzy Trout	1944	123	46.	Robin Roberts	1952	117
22.	Juan Marichal	1965	123	47.	Roger Clemens	1987	117
23.	Christy Mathewson	1908	122	48.	Vida Blue	1971	117
24.	Dean Chance	1964	122	49.	Wilbur Wood	1972	117
25.	Dwight Gooden	1985	122	50.	Bob Feller	1941	116

BEST SINGLE SEASON PITCHING RUNS ABOVE REPLACEMENT, BOSTON RED SOX

1.	Mel Parnell	1949	122	26.	Babe Ruth	1916	92
2.	Pedro Martinez	2000	120	27.	Dick Radatz	1963	91
3.	Roger Clemens	1987	117	28.	Wes Ferrell	1936	90
4.	Pedro Martinez	1999	116	29.	Dennis Eckersley	1979	89
5.	Lefty Grove	1936	110	30.	Dutch Leonard	1914	89
6.	Roger Clemens	1990	110	31.	Frank Sullivan	1955	89
7.	Cy Young	1901	109	32.	Pedro Martinez	2002	89
8.	Roger Clemens	1992	109	33.	Cy Young	1908	88
9.	Roger Clemens	1986	108	34.	Howard Ehmke	1923	88
10.	Lefty Grove	1935	107	35.	Joe Wood	1912	88
11.	Wes Ferrell	1935	107	36.	Sad Sam Jones	1921	88
12.	Cy Young	1902	106	37.	Cy Young	1904	87
13.	Derek Lowe	2002	106	38.	Bill Lee	1973	86
14.	Roger Clemens	1991	106	39.	Danny Darwin	1993	86
15.	Dick Radatz	1964	104	40.	Mel Parnell	1950	86
16.	Luis Tiant	1974	104	41.	Pedro Martinez	2003	86
17.	Lefty Grove	1937	103	42.	Tim Wakefield	1995	86
18.	Howard Ehmke	1924	101	43.	Oil Can Boyd	1985	85
19.	Curt Schilling	2004	100	44.	Tom Brewer	1956	85
20.	Roger Clemens	1988	98	45.	Cy Young	1905	84
21.	Pedro Martinez	1998	97	46.	Dennis Eckersley	1978	84
22.	Roger Clemens	1996	97	47.	Bill Dinneen	1902	83
23.	Ellis Kinder	1949	95	48.	Frank Viola	1992	83
24.	Frank Sullivan	1957	95	49.	Luis Tiant	1976	83
25.	Tex Hughson	1946	95	50.	Roger Clemens	1989	83

Wins Above Replacement Player

Wins Above Replacement Player (WARP) is a statistic that combines the batting, fielding, and pitching statistics into a single overall rating. It measures exactly what it says it does: the number of wins a given player added to his team's record over the course of a season or career. This is derived by figuring the difference between how many games an otherwise average team would win by having this player on their team compared to how many wins they would have using a replacement-level player. Note that the replacement-level player used here is a bad hitter, a bad fielder, and a bad pitcher; he's a bit worse than the "replacement level" assumed by most other methodologies.

CAREER WINS ABOVE REPLACEMENT PLAYER

1.	Babe Ruth	224.6	26. Tom Seaver	147.0
2.	Barry Bonds	212.4	27. Wade Boggs	145.9
3.	Willie Mays	208.6	28. Lou Gehrig	145.4
4.	Hank Aaron	199.6	29. Pete Alexander	144.8
5.	Ty Cobb	191.3	30. Carl Yastrzemski	143.4
6.	Walter Johnson	189.6	31. Phil Niekro	138.8
7.	Stan Musial	188.1	32. Bert Blyleven	137.1
8.	Tris Speaker	182.2	33. Jimmie Foxx	135.4
9.	Honus Wagner	180.7	34. Gaylord Perry	134.1
10.	Roger Clemens	178.3	35. Eddie Murray	133.3
11.	Cy Young	176.0	36. Robin Roberts	132.8
12.	Eddie Collins	172.2	37. George Brett	131.7
13.	Ted Williams	169.3	38. Rafael Palmeiro	131.3
14.	Rickey Henderson	169.2	39. Eddie Mathews	130.4
15.	Mel Ott	167.6	40. Steve Carlton	130.2
16.	Cal Ripken	162.5	41. Robin Yount	129.5
17.	Nap Lajoie	161.7	42. Johnny Bench	128.2
18.	Warren Spahn	161.7	43. Ozzie Smith	127.7
19.	Joe Morgan	158.2	44. Randy Johnson	127.5
20.	Frank Robinson	157.3	45. Paul Molitor	127.4
21.	Greg Maddux	156.2	46. Lefty Grove	126.9
22.	Mickey Mantle	155.6	47. Roberto Alomar	126.6
23.	Rogers Hornsby	150.1	48. Charlie Gehringer	125.9
24.	Mike Schmidt	150.0	49. Cap Anson	125.1
25.	Pete Rose	148.2	50. Dave Winfield	124.9

CAREER WINS ABOVE REPLACEMENT PLAYER, BOSTON RED SOX

1.	Ted Williams	169.4	26. Luis Tiant	49.5
2.	Carl Yastrzemski	143.4	27. Fred Lynn	47.6
3.	Roger Clemens	112.7	28. Mo Vaughn	45.5
4.	Dwight Evans	110.1	29. Ellis Kinder	45.1
5.	Wade Boggs	109.8	30. Frank Malzone	44.4
6.	Bobby Doerr	99.2	31. Rick Burleson	44.4
7.	Jim Rice	88.9	32. Derek Lowe	44.1
8.	Dom DiMaggio	72.2	33. Jackie Jensen	42.9
9.	Tris Speaker	72.1	34. Reggie Smith	42.2
10.	Cy Young	67.9	35. Frank Sullivan	41.1
11.	Pedro Martinez	67.8	36. Joe Dobson	40.7
12.	Harry Hooper	65.2	37. Tex Hughson	37.8
13.	Rico Petrocelli	63.5	38. Joe Wood	37.3
14.	Bob Stanley	61.3	39. Larry Gardner	36.3
15.	Carlton Fisk	60.9	40. Bill Monbouquette	36.1
16.	Nomar Garciaparra	60.0	41. Bruce Hurst	36.0
17.	John Valentin	54.0	42. Jimmy Collins	35.7
18.	Lefty Grove	53.3	43. Duffy Lewis	35.2
19.	Tim Wakefield	52.7	44. Bill Lee	34.9
20.	Joe Cronin	51.8	45. Billy Goodman	34.9
21.	Mike Greenwell	51.3	46. Tom Brewer	34.9
22.	Jimmie Foxx	51.0	47. Jason Varitek	34.8
23.	Johnny Pesky	50.9	48. Dennis Eckersley	34.2
24.	Mel Parnell	50.4	49. Manny Ramirez	33.8
25.	Babe Ruth	49.9	50. Vern Stephens	33.7

BEST SINGLE SEASON WINS ABOVE REPLACEMENT PLAYER

#	Player	Year	WAR	#	Player	Year	WAR
1.	Walter Johnson	1913	17.9	26.	Alex Rodriguez	2000	14.4
2.	Pud Galvin	1884	17.6	27.	Mickey Mantle	1957	14.4
3.	Babe Ruth	1923	17.2	28.	Walter Johnson	1918	14.4
4.	John Clarkson	1889	16.8	29.	Willie Mays	1955	14.2
5.	Jim Devlin	1876	16.7	30.	Babe Ruth	1924	14.1
6.	John Clarkson	1887	16.1	31.	Charles Radbourn	1884	14.1
7.	Amos Rusie	1894	16.0	32.	Christy Mathewson	1908	14.1
8.	Cal Ripken	1991	15.6	33.	Lou Gehrig	1927	14.1
9.	Barry Bonds	2001	15.4	34.	Red Faber	1921	14.1
10.	Steve Carlton	1972	15.4	35.	Alex Rodriguez	2001	14.0
11.	Babe Ruth	1921	15.3	36.	Honus Wagner	1908	14.0
12.	Walter Johnson	1912	15.3	37.	Amos Rusie	1893	13.9
13.	Rogers Hornsby	1924	15.2	38.	Cal Ripken	1984	13.9
14.	Barry Bonds	2004	15.1	39.	Cy Young	1893	13.9
15.	Bob Feller	1946	15.0	40.	Pete Alexander	1916	13.9
16.	Ted Williams	1942	15.0	41.	Walter Johnson	1914	13.9
17.	Ted Williams	1946	15.0	42.	Walter Johnson	1919	13.9
18.	Babe Ruth	1920	14.9	43.	Willie Mays	1954	13.9
19.	Roger Clemens	1997	14.8	44.	Alex Rodriguez	1996	13.8
20.	Arky Vaughan	1935	14.7	45.	Barry Bonds	1993	13.8
21.	Babe Ruth	1927	14.7	46.	Dwight Gooden	1985	13.8
22.	Mickey Mantle	1956	14.7	47.	Ed Walsh	1908	13.8
23.	Barry Bonds	2002	14.6	48.	Ernie Banks	1959	13.8
24.	Dizzy Trout	1944	14.0	49.	Pete Alexander	1915	13.8
25.	Pete Alexander	1920	14.6	50.	Silver King	1888	13.8

BEST SINGLE SEASON WINS ABOVE REPLACEMENT PLAYER, BOSTON RED SOX

#	Player	Year	WAR	#	Player	Year	WAR
1.	Ted Williams	1942	15.0	26.	Derek Lowe	2002	11.3
2.	Ted Williams	1946	15.0	27.	Roger Clemens	1992	11.3
3.	Pedro Martinez	2000	13.7	28.	Wade Boggs	1983	11.3
4.	Ted Williams	1941	13.7	29.	Babe Ruth	1916	11.2
5.	Babe Ruth	1919	13.6	30.	Fred Lynn	1979	11.2
6.	Wes Ferrell	1935	13.5	31.	Nomar Garciaparra	2000	11.2
7.	Wade Boggs	1985	13.2	32.	Carlton Fisk	1977	11.1
8.	Wade Boggs	1987	13.0	33.	Roger Clemens	1991	11.1
9.	Ted Williams	1947	12.9	34.	Ted Williams	1948	11.1
10.	Pedro Martinez	1999	12.8	35.	Cy Young	1902	11.0
11.	Tris Speaker	1912	12.8	36.	Rico Petrocelli	1969	11.0
12.	Cy Young	1901	12.7	37.	Dick Radatz	1964	10.9
13.	Ted Williams	1949	12.6	38.	Joe Cronin	1938	10.9
14.	Wade Boggs	1988	12.4	39.	Johnny Pesky	1946	10.9
15.	Carl Yastrzemski	1967	12.3	40.	Lefty Grove	1935	10.9
16.	Roger Clemens	1987	12.2	41.	Nomar Garciaparra	1999	10.9
17.	Roger Clemens	1990	12.2	42.	Ted Williams	1951	10.8
18.	Tris Speaker	1914	12.1	43.	Lefty Grove	1937	10.7
19.	Mel Parnell	1949	12.0	44.	Ted Williams	1957	10.7
20.	Wade Boggs	1986	11.8	45.	Wade Boggs	1984	10.7
21.	Lefty Grove	1936	11.6	46.	Jim Rice	1978	10.6
22.	Wade Boggs	1989	11.6	47.	Dwight Evans	1981	10.4
23.	Joe Wood	1912	11.4	48.	Mike Greenwell	1988	10.4
24.	Roger Clemens	1986	11.4	49.	Ted Williams	1940	10.4
25.	Carl Yastrzemski	1968	11.3	50.	Babe Ruth	1918	10.2

Value Over Replacement Player

Known as VORP, Value Over Replacement Player calculates the total number of runs a player was worth to a team compared to a theoretical "replacement level" player—a player in the high minors, on the bench, or on waivers. VORP's main advantage is this comparison to a readily available "man on the street." Not only are league-average players scarce and expensive, the calculation of the league average is easily skewed by increased playing time granted to the better players. By quantifying each player's performance in runs over the replacement-level baseline, VORP reveals just how much a team would lose if the player wasn't available.

CAREER VORP, 1901–2004

1.	Babe Ruth	1564.4	26.	George Brett	757.1
2.	Barry Bonds	1406.1	27.	Rafael Palmeiro	751.9
3.	Ty Cobb	1396.3	28.	Eddie Mathews	748.8
4.	Stan Musial	1277.0	29.	Harry Heilmann	746.0
5.	Lou Gehrig	1246.3	30.	Carl Yastrzemski	722.9
6.	Rogers Hornsby	1234.2	31.	Alex Rodriguez	722.7
7.	Ted Williams	1205.0	32.	Eddie Murray	718.8
8.	Hank Aaron	1192.1	33.	Ken Griffey Jr.	718.1
9.	Willie Mays	1110.2	34.	Sam Crawford	714.8
10.	Tris Speaker	1105.0	35.	Joe DiMaggio	709.5
11.	Eddie Collins	1080.2	36.	Roberto Alomar	709.3
12.	Jimmie Foxx	1071.0	37.	Paul Molitor	703.0
13.	Honus Wagner	1037.9	38.	Nap Lajoie	701.5
14.	Mel Ott	934.1	39.	Robin Yount	693.9
15.	Mickey Mantle	911.1	40.	Paul Waner	689.0
16.	Frank Robinson	907.1	41.	Rod Carew	687.3
17.	Charlie Gehringer	892.0	42.	Joe Cronin	678.4
18.	Joe Morgan	876.7	43.	Edgar Martinez	670.1
19.	Frank Thomas	806.4	44.	Luke Appling	666.5
20.	Rickey Henderson	800.4	45.	Ernie Banks	660.6
21.	Jeff Bagwell	787.6	46.	Al Simmons	651.4
22.	Cal Ripken Jr.	776.3	47.	Dave Winfield	646.2
23.	Pete Rose	769.5	48.	Tony Gwynn	645.9
24.	Mike Schmidt	768.2	49.	Craig Biggio	644.5
25.	Wade Boggs	757.2	50.	Billy Williams	638.3

SINGLE SEASON VORP, 1901–2004

1.	Babe Ruth	1921	New York Yankees	154.8
2.	Rogers Hornsby	1922	St. Louis Cardinals	146.5
3.	Lou Gehrig	1927	New York Yankees	142.4
4.	Barry Bonds	2001	San Francisco Giants	140.7
5.	Babe Ruth	1923	New York Yankees	137.0
6.	Babe Ruth	1924	New York Yankees	135.0
7.	Babe Ruth	1920	New York Yankees	131.2
8.	George Sisler	1920	St. Louis Browns	130.1
9.	Babe Ruth	1927	New York Yankees	127.8
10.	Barry Bonds	2002	San Francisco Giants	127.7
11.	Rogers Hornsby	1929	Chicago Cubs	127.6
12.	Ty Cobb	1911	Detroit Tigers	125.2
13.	Barry Bonds	2004	San Francisco Giants	125.2
14.	Jimmie Foxx	1932	Philadelphia Athletics	123.1
15.	Babe Ruth	1926	New York Yankees	122.5
16.	Rogers Hornsby	1925	St. Louis Cardinals	118.7
17.	Babe Herman	1930	Brooklyn Robins	116.6
18.	Nap Lajoie	1901	Philadelphia Athletics	116.4
19.	Rogers Hornsby	1924	St. Louis Cardinals	116.4
20.	Ted Williams	1941	Boston Red Sox	115.7
21.	Jimmie Foxx	1933	Philadelphia Athletics	114.5
22.	Stan Musial	1948	St. Louis Cardinals	114.3
23.	Rogers Hornsby	1921	St. Louis Cardinals	113.3
24.	Sammy Sosa	2001	Chicago Cubs	112.4
25.	Lou Gehrig	1936	New York Yankees	112.2
26.	Lou Gehrig	1934	New York Yankees	111.9
27.	Lou Gehrig	1930	New York Yankees	111.3
28.	Barry Bonds	1993	San Francisco Giants	110.2
29.	Ty Cobb	1917	Detroit Tigers	110.0
30.	Mickey Mantle	1956	New York Yankees	109.8
31.	Hack Wilson	1930	Chicago Cubs	109.4
32.	Rogers Hornsby	1928	Boston Braves	106.6
33.	Chuck Klein	1930	Philadelphia Phillies	106.4
34.	Joe Jackson	1911	Cleveland Naps	106.4
35.	Jimmie Foxx	1938	Boston Red Sox	106.3
36.	Carlos Delgado	2000	Toronto Blue Jays	106.0
37.	Ted Williams	1942	Boston Red Sox	106.0
38.	Ted Williams	1949	Boston Red Sox	105.7
39.	Tris Speaker	1912	Boston Red Sox	105.4
40.	Alex Rodriguez	2001	Texas Rangers	105.2
41.	Derek Jeter	1999	New York Yankees	105.2
42.	Babe Ruth	1931	New York Yankees	104.5
43.	Babe Ruth	1928	New York Yankees	104.0
44.	Bill Terry	1930	New York Giants	103.9
45.	Charlie Gehringer	1936	Detroit Tigers	103.5
46.	Joe Jackson	1912	Cleveland Naps	103.4
47.	Mark McGwire	1998	St. Louis Cardinals	102.8
48.	Chipper Jones	1999	Atlanta Braves	102.7
49.	Ted Williams	1946	Boston Red Sox	102.6
50.	Lou Gehrig	1937	New York Yankees	102.0

CAREER VORP, BOSTON RED SOX

1.	Ted Williams	1205.0	26.	Larry Gardner	191.3
2.	Carl Yastrzemski	722.9	27.	Pete Runnels	190.2
3.	Wade Boggs	630.6	28.	Freddy Parent	186.3
4.	Jim Rice	561.3	29.	Buck Freeman	186.0
5.	Dwight Evans	531.6	30.	Rick Burleson	168.8
6.	Bobby Doerr	480.5	31.	Chick Stahl	157.0
7.	Tris Speaker	450.2	32.	Duffy Lewis	156.0
8.	Nomar Garciaparra	424.1	33.	Babe Ruth	150.0
9.	Jimmie Foxx	409.1	34.	Frank Malzone	133.1
10.	Joe Cronin	357.9	35.	Heinie Wagner	117.0
11.	Mo Vaughn	350.2	36.	Eddie Bressoud	117.0
12.	Mike Greenwell	266.8	37.	Ellis Burks	116.7
13.	Rico Petrocelli	253.9	38.	Trot Nixon	116.0
14.	Johnny Pesky	245.6	39.	George Scott	114.3
15.	Harry Hooper	239.8	40.	Tony Conigliaro	113.3
16.	Manny Ramirez	239.3	41.	Billy Werber	112.9
17.	Carlton Fisk	238.6	42.	Jason Varitek	110.5
18.	Fred Lynn	236.9	43.	Mike Andrews	108.7
19.	Dom DiMaggio	226.6	44.	Jody Reed	105.9
20.	John Valentin	219.8	45.	Jake Stahl	104.6
21.	Jackie Jensen	218.7	46.	Marty Barrett	101.6
22.	Jimmy Collins	200.2	47.	Johnny Damon	98.7
23.	Billy Goodman	198.8	48.	Roy Johnson	97.7
24.	Reggie Smith	196.1	49.	Jim Tabor	92.8
25.	Vern Stephens	196.1	50.	Rick Ferrell	88.1

SINGLE SEASON VORP, BOSTON RED SOX

1.	Ted Williams	1941	115.7	26.	Jim Rice	1979	72.3
2.	Jimmie Foxx	1938	106.3	27.	Ted Williams	1940	72.2
3.	Ted Williams	1942	106.0	28.	Nomar Garciaparra	1998	71.8
4.	Ted Williams	1949	105.7	29.	Jimmie Foxx	1939	71.7
5.	Tris Speaker	1912	105.4	30.	Mike Greenwell	1988	71.6
6.	Ted Williams	1946	102.6	31.	Vern Stephens	1949	71.3
7.	Ted Williams	1947	97.5	32.	Mo Vaughn	1998	70.3
8.	Babe Ruth	1919	90.5	33.	Jim Rice	1977	69.6
9.	Jimmie Foxx	1936	87.6	34.	John Valentin	1995	69.4
10.	Ted Williams	1957	87.3	35.	Wade Boggs	1983	68.9
11.	Wade Boggs	1988	86.3	36.	Ted Williams	1951	68.2
12.	Wade Boggs	1987	84.5	37.	Wade Boggs	1986	68.1
13.	Nomar Garciaparra	2000	83.4	38.	Manny Ramirez	2003	66.5
14.	Ted Williams	1939	82.8	39.	Dwight Evans	1982	66.3
15.	Carl Yastrzemski	1970	81.3	40.	Nomar Garciaparra	1997	66.2
16.	Wade Boggs	1985	81.3	41.	Jimmy Collins	1901	64.1
17.	Tris Speaker	1913	80.9	42.	Dwight Evans	1984	62.6
18.	Ted Williams	1948	80.9	43.	Dwight Evans	1987	61.9
19.	Carl Yastrzemski	1967	80.5	44.	Nomar Garciaparra	2002	61.6
20.	Rico Petrocelli	1969	79.6	45.	Tris Speaker	1914	61.6
21.	Mo Vaughn	1996	78.7	46.	Joe Cronin	1937	61.2
22.	Nomar Garciaparra	1999	76.9	47.	Wade Boggs	1989	61.2
23.	Jim Rice	1978	76.9	48.	Buck Freeman	1901	60.9
24.	Fred Lynn	1979	75.7	49.	Jimmie Foxx	1940	60.7
25.	Joe Cronin	1938	75.0	50.	Billy Werber	1934	60.3

Marginal Lineup Value Rate

Referred to as MLVr, Marginal Lineup Value Rate is the number of runs each player is worth per game if he were placed in a lineup consisting of only league-average players. While batting average, on-base percentage, and slugging percentage all reveal how much a player is worth per at-bat, they do not take into account how his performance affects the rest of the lineup. A player with a higher on-base percentage gives more plate appearances to his teammates—by helping the lineup turn over—and consequently to himself. MLVr better captures this compounding effect.

SINGLE SEASON MLVr, BOSTON RED SOX

1.	Ted Williams	1953	1.055	26.	Phil Plantier	1991	0.478
2.	Ted Williams	1941	0.873	27.	Nomar Garciaparra	2000	0.478
3.	Ted Williams	1957	0.802	28.	Ted Williams	1940	0.475
4.	Ted Williams	1955	0.694	29.	Ted Williams	1939	0.459
5.	Ted Williams	1942	0.657	30.	Babe Ruth	1915	0.45
6.	Jimmie Foxx	1939	0.656	31.	Dale Alexander	1932	0.439
7.	Ted Williams	1946	0.649	32.	Babe Ruth	1918	0.437
8.	Jimmie Foxx	1938	0.641	33.	Nomar Garciaparra	1999	0.437
9.	Babe Ruth	1919	0.614	34.	Ted Williams	1951	0.433
10.	Ted Williams	1949	0.614	35.	Wade Boggs	1988	0.431
11.	Ted Williams	1948	0.611	36.	Rico Petrocelli	1969	0.417
12.	Ted Williams	1947	0.61	37.	Bob Johnson	1944	0.417
13.	Ted Williams	1954	0.61	38.	Tris Speaker	1914	0.416
14.	Manny Ramirez	2002	0.573	39.	Manny Ramirez	2003	0.411
15.	Tris Speaker	1912	0.554	40.	Fred Lynn	1975	0.399
16.	Ted Williams	1960	0.542	41.	Manny Ramirez	2001	0.395
17.	Ted Williams	1956	0.527	42.	Mo Vaughn	1998	0.395
18.	Carl Yastrzemski	1967	0.511	43.	Bobby Doerr	1944	0.383
19.	Wade Boggs	1987	0.511	44.	Jim Rice	1978	0.38
20.	Ted Williams	1950	0.51	45.	Wade Boggs	1986	0.378
21.	Carl Yastrzemski	1970	0.494	46.	Jim Rice	1979	0.376
22.	Fred Lynn	1979	0.494	47.	Manny Ramirez	2004	0.372
23.	Ted Williams	1958	0.487	48.	Wade Boggs	1985	0.372
24.	Jimmie Foxx	1936	0.481	49.	Mo Vaughn	1996	0.366
25.	Tris Speaker	1913	0.48	50.	Mike Greenwell	1988	0.366

SINGLE SEASON MLVr

	NAME	YEAR	TEAM	MLVr
1.	Ted Williams	1953	Boston Red Sox	.105
2.	Barry Bonds	2002	San Francisco Giants	.962
3.	Babe Ruth	1920	New York Yankees	.948
4.	Babe Ruth	1921	New York Yankees	.944
5.	Barry Bonds	2004	San Francisco Giants	.930
6.	Barry Bonds	2001	San Francisco Giants	.918
7.	Babe Ruth	1923	New York Yankees	.888
8.	Ted Williams	1941	Boston Red Sox	.873
9.	Rogers Hornsby	1925	St. Louis Cardinals	.836
10.	Rogers Hornsby	1924	St. Louis Cardinals	.828
11.	Lou Gehrig	1927	New York Yankees	.818
12.	Babe Ruth	1926	New York Yankees	.812
13.	Babe Ruth	1924	New York Yankees	.812
14.	Babe Ruth	1927	New York Yankees	.809
15.	Ted Williams	1957	Boston Red Sox	.802
16.	Rogers Hornsby	1922	St. Louis Cardinals	.790
17.	Barry Bonds	2003	San Francisco Giants	.780
18.	Oscar Gamble	1979	New York Yankees	.768
19.	Jeff Bagwell	1994	Houston Astros	.760
20.	Babe Ruth	1931	New York Yankees	.757
21.	Babe Ruth	1930	New York Yankees	.752
22.	Lou Gehrig	1930	New York Yankees	.748
23.	Jimmie Foxx	1932	Philadelphia Athletics	.745
24.	Lou Gehrig	1934	New York Yankees	.724
25.	Frank Thomas	1994	Chicago White Sox	.722
26.	Bob Hazle	1957	Milwaukee Braves	.717
27.	Mickey Mantle	1957	New York Yankees	.708
28.	Nap Lajoie	1901	Philadelphia Athletics	.707
29.	Mickey Mantle	1956	New York Yankees	.699
30.	Mark McGwire	1993	St. Louis Cardinals	.695
31.	Ted Williams	1955	Boston Red Sox	.694
32.	Stan Musial	1948	St. Louis Cardinals	.691
33.	Harry Heilmann	1923	Detroit Tigers	.682
34.	Rogers Hornsby	1928	Boston Braves	.680
35.	Ty Cobb	1911	Detroit Tigers	.677
36.	Gates Brown	1968	Detroit Tigers	.675
37.	Lou Gehrig	1936	New York Yankees	.672
38.	Jimmie Foxx	1933	Philadelphia Athletics	.671
39.	Mark McGwire	1998	St. Louis Cardinals	.671
40.	Mark McGwire	2000	St. Louis Cardinals	.668
41.	George Brett	1980	Kansas City Royals	.666
42.	Joe DiMaggio	1939	New York Yankees	.659
43.	Ted Williams	1942	Boston Red Sox	.657
44.	Jimmie Foxx	1939	Boston Red Sox	.656
45.	Sammy Sosa	2001	Chicago Cubs	.655
46.	Norm Cash	1961	Detroit Tigers	.654
47.	Al Simmons	1930	Philadelphia Athletics	.650
48.	Babe Ruth	1928	New York Yankees	.650
49.	Rogers Hornsby	1929	Chicago Cubs	.650
50.	Ted Williams	1946	Boston Red Sox	.649

Support Neutral Lineup-Adjusted Value Above Replacement

Support Neutral Lineup-Adjusted Value Above Replacement (SNLVAR) measures how many wins a pitcher is worth over a replacement-level pitcher. SNLVAR is superior to a pitcher's win-loss record because it is adjusted for disparities such as run support, park factors, and quality of opponent. In other words, the individual pitcher's contribution to the bottom line is separated from the background noise of his environment.

CAREER SNLVAR, 1972–2004

1.	Roger Clemens	136.0	26.	Dwight Gooden	66.8
2.	Greg Maddux	122.9	27.	Dave Stieb	65.0
3.	Nolan Ryan	112.6	28.	Jimmy Key	64.7
4.	Tom Glavine	97.8	29.	Steve Rogers	64.6
5.	Randy Johnson	97.8	30.	Gaylord Perry	64.6
6.	Bert Blyleven	93.3	31.	Tommy John	63.1
7.	Kevin Brown	92.1	32.	David Wells	62.3
8.	Don Sutton	91.4	33.	Jamie Moyer	62.2
9.	Tom Seaver	88.3	34.	John Smoltz	61.4
10.	Mike Mussina	83.5	35.	Al Leiter	59.7
11.	Pedro Martinez	82.1	36.	Vida Blue	59.0
12.	Dennis Martinez	79.2	37.	Jerry Reuss	57.8
13.	Steve Carlton	78.1	38.	Frank Viola	56.9
14.	Curt Schilling	77.8	39.	Ron Guidry	56.7
15.	David Cone	76.4	40.	Fernando Valenzuela	56.3
16.	Frank Tanana	76.2	41.	Andy Benes	55.9
17.	Rick Reuschel	75.5	42.	Tom Candiotti	55.2
18.	Jim Palmer	75.1	43.	Doug Drabek	55.0
19.	Orel Hershiser	74.4	44.	Burt Hooton	53.9
20.	Kevin Appier	71.4	45.	Mark Langston	53.7
21.	Chuck Finley	71.1	46.	Doyle Alexander	53.0
22.	Phil Niekro	70.7	47.	Charlie Hough	52.3
23.	Bob Welch	69.0	48.	John Candelaria	51.9
24.	Bret Saberhagen	68.5	49.	Jerry Koosman	51.7
25.	Jack Morris	67.5	50.	John Burkett	51.2

SINGLE SEASON SNLVAR, 1972–2004

RANK	NAME	TEAM	YEAR	SNLVAR
1.	Dwight Gooden	New York Mets	1985	12.7
2.	Roger Clemens	Toronto Blue Jays	1997	12.3
3.	Pedro Martinez	Boston Red Sox	2000	11.5
4.	Tom Seaver	New York Mets	1973	11.4
5.	Steve Carlton	Philadelphia Phillies	1972	11.3
6.	Andy Messersmith	Los Angeles Dodgers	1975	10.9
7.	Jim Palmer	Baltimore Orioles	1975	10.8
8.	Randy Johnson	Arizona Diamondbacks	1999	10.7
9.	Greg Maddux	Atlanta Braves	1995	10.7
10.	Ron Guidry	New York Yankees	1978	10.4
11.	Gaylord Perry	Cleveland Indians	1972	10.4
12.	John Tudor	St. Louis Cardinals	1985	10.3
13.	Mike Scott	Houston Astros	1986	10.1
14.	Kevin Brown	Florida Marlins	1996	10.1
15.	Pedro Martinez	Boston Red Sox	1999	10.0
16.	Greg Maddux	Atlanta Braves	1997	10.0
17.	Jim Palmer	Baltimore Orioles	1973	10.0
18.	Tom Seaver	New York Mets	1975	9.9
19.	Jim Palmer	Baltimore Orioles	1977	9.8
20.	Randy Johnson	Arizona Diamondbacks	2000	9.7
21.	Phil Niekro	Atlanta Braves	1974	9.7
22.	Randy Johnson	Arizona Diamondbacks	2001	9.7
23.	Tom Seaver	New York Mets/Cincinnati Reds	1977	9.6
24.	Johan Santana	Minnesota Twins	2004	9.5
25.	Greg Maddux	Atlanta Braves	1994	9.5
26.	Jose Rijo	Cincinnati Reds	1993	9.4
27.	Greg Maddux	Atlanta Braves	1993	9.4
28.	Randy Johnson	Arizona Diamondbacks	2002	9.3
29.	Gaylord Perry	Cleveland Indians	1974	9.3
30.	Pedro Martinez	Montreal Expos	1997	9.3
31.	Greg Maddux	Atlanta Braves	1998	9.3
32.	Mike Norris	Oakland Athletics	1980	9.3
33.	Kevin Appier	Kansas City Royals	1993	9.2
34.	Kevin Brown	San Diego Padres	1998	9.2
35.	Catfish Hunter	Oakland Athletics	1974	9.2
36.	Roger Clemens	Boston Red Sox	1987	9.2
37.	Catfish Hunter	New York Yankees	1975	9.2
38.	Curt Schilling	Arizona Diamondbacks	2001	9.2
39.	Kevin Brown	Los Angeles Dodgers	2000	9.2
40.	Roger Clemens	Boston Red Sox	1990	9.1
41.	Roger Clemens	Boston Red Sox	1986	9.1
42.	Bret Saberhagen	Kansas City Royals	1989	9.1
43.	Orel Hershiser	Los Angeles Dodgers	1988	9.0
44.	J. R. Richard	Houston Astros	1979	8.9
45.	Tom Glavine	Atlanta Braves	1998	8.9
46.	Roger Clemens	Toronto Blue Jays	1998	8.9
47.	Mike Hampton	Houston Astros	1999	8.9
48.	Joe Niekro	Houston Astros	1982	8.9
49.	Nolan Ryan	California Angels	1973	8.9
50.	Don Sutton	Los Angeles Dodgers	1973	8.9

CAREER SNLVAR, BOSTON RED SOX

1. Roger Clemens 81.7
2. Pedro Martinez 57.2
3. Luis Tiant 35.2
4. Tim Wakefield 28.7
5. Bruce Hurst 24.0
6. Dennis Eckersley 22.3
7. Bill Lee 15.4
8. Derek Lowe 14.9
9. Oil Can Boyd 14.5
10. Aaron Sele 12.5
11. Mike Boddicker 11.8
12. Frank Viola 11.5
13. Bob Ojeda 10.9
14. Mike Torrez 10.8
15. Bret Saberhagen 10.2
16. Danny Darwin 9.7
17. John Tudor 9.4
18. Rick Wise 8.9
19. Bob Stanley 7.8
20. Curt Schilling 7.7
21. Tom Gordon 7.5
22. Al Nipper 7.5
23. Joe Hesketh 6.9
24. Roger Moret 6.6
25. John Dopson 6.2

SINGLE SEASON SNLVAR, BOSTON RED SOX

1. Roger Clemens 81.7
2. Pedro Martinez 57.2
3. Luis Tiant 35.2
4. Tim Wakefield 28.7
5. Bruce Hurst 24.0
6. Dennis Eckersley 22.3
7. Bill Lee 15.4
8. Derek Lowe 14.9
9. Oil Can Boyd 14.5
10. Aaron Sele 12.5
11. Mike Boddicker 11.8
12. Frank Viola 11.5
13. Bob Ojeda 10.9
14. Mike Torrez 10.8
15. Bret Saberhagen 10.2
16. Danny Darwin 9.7
17. John Tudor 9.4
18. Rick Wise 8.9
19. Bob Stanley 7.8
20. Curt Schilling 7.7
21. Tom Gordon 7.5
22. Al Nipper 7.5
23. Joe Hesketh 6.9
24. Roger Moret 6.6
25. John Dopson 6.2

Win Expectation—
Adjusted for Replacement Level and Lineup

"Win Expectation—Adjusted for Replacement Level and Lineup" (WXRL) is used for relief pitchers. WXRL is very similar to SNLVAR, but adjusts for the context of each reliever's appearances. WXRL is superior to conventional pitching measures of relievers, such as saves, because it corrects for relievers who are used in important and difficult situations as opposed to mop-up time. It also takes note if there are runners on base when a reliever enters the game or runners on base when they leave. Say an average pitcher converts 80 percent of save opportunities. If Eric Gagne was a perfect 50-for-50 (100 percent), then an average pitcher would convert 80 percent, or 40 saves. If all the blown saves turn into losses, then that's 10 wins that Gagne earned beyond what an average pitcher would do. That's the gist of WXRL.

CAREER WXRL, 1972–2004

1.	Rich Gossage	54.0	26.	Greg Minton	28.1
2.	Trevor Hoffman	50.0	27.	Rod Beck	27.4
3.	Mariano Rivera	48.5	28.	Tug McGraw	27.1
4.	Lee Smith	47.5	29.	Roberto Hernandez	26.6
5.	John Franco	45.0	30.	Mike Stanton	26.6
6.	Rollie Fingers	40.0	31.	Todd Worrell	26.4
7.	Randy Myers	39.0	32.	Dave Righetti	26.0
8.	Troy Percival	38.3	33.	Jeff Shaw	25.9
9.	Armando Benitez	37.7	34.	Tom Gordon	25.9
10.	Bruce Sutter	37.6	35.	Steve Bedrosian	25.3
11.	Tom Henke	36.9	36.	Eric Gagne	25.2
12.	John Wetteland	35.3	37.	Mike Henneman	24.9
13.	Dennis Eckersley	35.3	38.	Jeff Brantley	24.0
14.	Keith Foulke	34.8	39.	Dave Smith	23.2
15.	Mike Jackson	34.0	40.	Bob Wickman	23.0
16.	Dan Quisenberry	33.9	41.	Rick Aguilera	22.7
17.	Jesse Orosco	33.6	42.	Willie Hernandez	22.6
18.	Doug Jones	33.1	43.	Mike Marshall	22.5
19.	Robb Nen	32.0	44.	Roger McDowell	22.3
20.	Billy Wagner	31.6	45.	John Smoltz	22.0
21.	Jeff Reardon	31.4	46.	Gene Garber	21.9
22.	Kent Tekulve	30.7	47.	Ugueth Urbina	21.8
23.	Jose Mesa	29.7	48.	Tippy Martinez	21.6
24.	Todd Jones	29.3	49.	Mark Wohlers	21.1
25.	Jeff Montgomery	28.8	50.	Terry Forster	21.0

SINGLE SEASON WXRL, 1972–2004

RANK	NAME	TEAM	YEAR	WXRL
1.	John Hiller	Detroit Tigers	1973	9.6
2.	Eric Gagne	Los Angeles Dodgers	2003	9.3
3.	Willie Hernandez	Detroit Tigers	1984	9.2
4.	Troy Percival	California Angels	1996	8.4
5.	Trevor Hoffman	San Diego Padres	1998	8.3
6.	Eric Gagne	Los Angeles Dodgers	2002	8.2
7.	Keith Foulke	Chicago White Sox	2000	8.2
8.	Dan Quisenberry	Kansas City Royals	1980	8.2
9.	Brad Lidge	Houston Astros	2004	8.1
10.	Rich Gossage	Pittsburgh Pirates	1977	8.1
11.	Eric Gagne	Los Angeles Dodgers	2004	8.0
12.	Doug Corbett	Minnesota Twins	1980	7.9
13.	Aurelio Lopez	Detroit Tigers	1979	7.9
14.	Trevor Hoffman	San Diego Padres	1996	7.7
15.	Joe Nathan	Minnesota Twins	2004	7.7
16.	Bruce Sutter	St. Louis Cardinals	1984	7.7
17.	Tug McGraw	New York Mets	1972	7.7
18.	Rich Gossage	Chicago White Sox	1975	7.6
19.	Bruce Sutter	Chicago Cubs	1977	7.6
20.	Rod Beck	San Francisco Giants	1993	7.5
21.	Mariano Rivera	New York Yankees	2004	7.4
22.	Jim Kern	Texas Rangers	1979	7.4
23.	Randy Myers	Baltimore Orioles	1997	7.3
24.	Derek Lowe	Boston Red Sox	2000	7.3
25.	Greg Minton	San Francisco Giants	1982	7.3
26.	Tom Gordon	Boston Red Sox	1998	7.2
27.	Jose Mesa	Cleveland Indians	1995	7.2
28.	Billy Wagner	Houston Astros	1999	7.1
29.	John Wetteland	Montreal Expos	1993	7.1
30.	John Smoltz	Atlanta Braves	2002	7.1
31.	Dan Quisenberry	Kansas City Royals	1983	7.1
32.	John Smoltz	Atlanta Braves	2004	7.0
33.	Mariano Rivera	New York Yankees	1996	6.9
34.	Rich Gossage	New York Yankees	1982	6.9
35.	Jeff Montgomery	Kansas City Royals	1993	6.8
36.	Dennis Eckersley	Oakland Athletics	1990	6.8
37.	Keith Foulke	Oakland Athletics	2003	6.8
38.	Dan Quisenberry	Kansas City Royals	1984	6.7
39.	Tom Burgmeier	Boston Red Sox	1980	6.6
40.	Billy Wagner	Houston Astros	2003	6.5
41.	Bryan Harvey	Florida Marlins	1993	6.5
42.	Jeff Shaw	Cincinnati Reds	1997	6.5
43.	Bill Campbell	Boston Red Sox	1977	6.5
44.	Billy Koch	Oakland Athletics	2002	6.5
45.	Trevor Hoffman	San Diego Padres	1999	6.5
46.	Kent Tekulve	Pittsburgh Pirates	1979	6.5
47.	Tom Gordon	New York Yankees	2004	6.4
48.	Rich Gossage	New York Yankees	1980	6.4
49.	Mark Davis	San Diego Padres	1989	6.4
50.	Dennis Eckersley	Oakland Athletics	1992	6.4

CAREER WXRL, BOSTON RED SOX

RANK	PITCHER	WXRL
1.	Bob Stanley	19.8
2.	Derek Lowe	14.5
3.	Tom Burgmeier	9.7
4.	Tom Gordon	8.7
5.	Rich Garces	7.7
6.	Dick Drago	7.2
7.	Greg Harris	7.1
8.	Rheal Cormier	5.6
9.	Bill Campbell	5.6
10.	Mike Timlin	5.5
11.	Alan Embree	4.6
12.	Ken Ryan	4.5
13.	Keith Foulke	4.4
14.	Lee Smith	4.4
15.	Tim Wakefield	4.3
16.	Mark Clear	4.3
17.	Rod Beck	4.2
18.	Stan Belinda	4.2
19.	Jeff Reardon	3.7
20.	Tony Fossas	3.6
21.	Calvin Schiraldi	3.5
22.	Jeff Gray	3.4
23.	Ugueth Urbina	3.3
24.	Heathcliff Slocumb	2.7
25.	Bill Lee	2.6

SINGLE SEASON WXRL, BOSTON RED SOX

1.	Derek Lowe	2000	7.3
2.	Tom Gordon	1998	7.2
3.	Tom Burgmeier	1980	6.6
4.	Bill Campbell	1977	6.5
5.	Bob Stanley	1983	5.7
6.	Bob Stanley	1982	5.0
7.	Derek Lowe	1999	4.9
8.	Keith Foulke	2004	4.4
9.	Stan Belinda	1995	4.1
10.	Ken Ryan	1994	3.2
11.	Rich Garces	2000	3.0
12.	Lee Smith	1988	3.0
13.	Tom Burgmeier	1982	3.0
14.	Rob Murphy	1989	2.9
15.	Calvin Schiraldi	1986	2.9
16.	Bob Stanley	1980	2.9
17.	Mike Timlin	2003	2.8
18.	Mike Timlin	2004	2.7
19.	Heathcliff Slocumb	1996	2.7
20.	Rich Garces	2001	2.6
21.	Jeff Reardon	1991	2.6
22.	Greg Harris	1993	2.6
23.	Dick Drago	1979	2.6
24.	Mark Clear	1982	2.5
25.	Byung-Hyun Kim	2003	2.3

Pitcher Abuse Points Cubed

Pitcher Abuse Points Cubed (PAP[3]) measures the typical short-term decline in pitching performance following a high-pitch outing. As pitchers accumulate PAP[3], the likelihood that they will succumb to injury or have a bad outing increases because of the fatigue of high-pitch-count outings. If pitchers had an odometer on their arms, it would look like this. The pitchers below have been worked longer and harder than any others.

CAREER PAP[3], 1972–2004

1.	Randy Johnson	6783788	26.	Ramon Martinez	547570
2.	Roger Clemens	6438242	27.	Curt Schilling	509470
3.	David Cone	3525453	28.	Jack Morris	507931
4.	Chuck Finley	2939831	29.	Steve Rogers	483695
5.	Mark Langston	2253771	30.	Dan Warthen	428366
6.	Bobby Witt	2124344	31.	Wilson Alvarez	420250
7.	Nolan Ryan	1697045	32.	Erik Hanson	414261
8.	Livan Hernandez	1682244	33.	Matt Young	383436
9.	Charlie Hough	1573595	34.	Rick Sutcliffe	381881
10.	Tim Wakefield	1297111	35.	Mike Harkey	374024
11.	Jack McDowell	1222691	36.	John Farrell	363292
12.	Tom Candiotti	1171471	37.	Tom Gordon	356371
13.	Dave Stewart	1103797	38.	Jose Dejesus	352449
14.	Frank Tanana	941419	39.	Bruce Hurst	349087
15.	Mark Gubicza	897014	40.	Jay Tibbs	341112
16.	Cal Eldred	851919	41.	Mike Mussina	329504
17.	Mike Moore	802953	42.	Don Carman	328968
18.	Kevin Gross	724269	43.	Mike Boddicker	327591
19.	Alex Fernandez	713514	44.	Bob Welch	324147
20.	Pete Harnisch	691711	45.	Rick Helling	321977
21.	Tim Belcher	685992	46.	Andy Benes	318517
22.	Pedro Martinez	654651	47.	Mike Witt	317074
23.	Fernando Valenzuela	654612	48.	Tommy Greene	316619
24.	Orel Hershiser	602230	49.	Kevin Brown	314419
25.	Greg Maddux	574260	50.	Bob Milacki	312861

SINGLE SEASON PAP³, 1972–2004

RANK	NAME	TEAM	YEAR	PAP³
1.	Nolan Ryan	Texas Rangers	1989	1268012
2.	Randy Johnson	Seattle Mariners	1993	1266521
3.	Roger Clemens	Boston Red Sox	1988	1254755
4.	Charlie Hough	Texas Rangers	1988	1225997
5.	Randy Johnson	Seattle Mariners	1992	1099231
6.	Roger Clemens	Boston Red Sox	1996	1068743
7.	David Cone	New York Mets/Toronto Blue Jays	1992	1027019
8.	Roger Clemens	Boston Red Sox	1989	1011983
9.	Livan Hernandez	Florida Marlins	1998	908677
10.	Cal Eldred	Milwaukee Brewers	1993	851919
11.	Mark Langston	Seattle Mariners	1988	847874
12.	Randy Johnson	Seattle Mariners	1995	789370
13.	Randy Johnson	Seattle Mariners	1997	788875
14.	Bobby Witt	Texas Rangers	1988	783750
15.	Mark Langston	Seattle Mariners/Montreal Expos	1989	752246
16.	Randy Johnson	Seattle Mariners	1994	709156
17.	Randy Johnson	Seattle Mariners/Houston Astros	1998	708837
18.	Roger Clemens	Boston Red Sox	1992	653525
19.	David Cone	Kansas City Royals	1993	645985
20.	David Cone	Toronto Blue Jays/New York Yankees	1995	628581
21.	Randy Johnson	Seattle Mariners	1990	628542
22.	Orel Hershiser	Los Angeles Dodgers	1989	602230
23.	Chuck Finley	California Angels	1990	596249
24.	Bobby Witt	Texas Rangers	1990	578769
25.	Greg Maddux	Chicago Cubs	1988	574260
26.	Roger Clemens	Boston Red Sox	1991	555991
27.	Mark Gubicza	Kansas City Royals	1988	554984
28.	Roger Clemens	Toronto Blue Jays	1998	551375
29.	Chuck Finley	California Angels	1993	550847
30.	Ramon Martinez	Los Angeles Dodgers	1990	547570
31.	Frank Tanana	Detroit Tigers	1989	513735
32.	Roger Clemens	Boston Red Sox	1990	509887
33.	Curt Schilling	Philadelphia Phillies	1998	509470
34.	Jack Morris	Detroit Tigers	1988	507931
35.	Roger Clemens	Toronto Blue Jays	1997	501807
36.	Tim Wakefield	Pittsburgh Pirates	1993	493648
37.	Dave Stewart	Oakland Athletics	1988	488925
38.	Steve Rogers	Montreal Expos	1975	483695
39.	Tom Candiotti	Cleveland Indians	1988	481904
40.	Jack McDowell	New York Yankees	1995	465501
41.	Mike Moore	Oakland Athletics	1991	463149
42.	Bobby Witt	Texas Rangers	1989	451764
43.	David Cone	New York Mets	1991	447392
44.	Chuck Finley	California Angels	1991	443401
45.	Randy Johnson	Arizona Diamondbacks	2000	440055
46.	Nolan Ryan	Texas Rangers	1990	429033
47.	Dan Warthen	Montreal Expos	1975	428366
48.	Frank Tanana	Detroit Tigers	1991	427684
49.	David Cone	New York Mets	1989	424756
50.	Wilson Alvarez	Chicago White Sox	1993	420250

CAREER PAP³, 1972–2004, BOSTON RED SOX

RANK	PITCHER	PAP³
1.	Roger Clemens	5761958
2.	Tim Wakefield	1056052
3.	Pedro Martinez	624737
4.	Mike Boddicker	522481
5.	Tom Gordon	450766
6.	Aaron Sele	366834
7.	Bruce Hurst	349087
8.	Frank Viola	280765
9.	Jeff Sellers	248293
10.	Wes Gardner	218275
11.	Danny Darwin	188674
12.	Erik Hanson	137825
13.	Tom Bolton	109583
14.	Greg Harris	107611
15.	Oil Can Boyd	99359
16.	John Dopson	87774
17.	Mike Smithson	69631
18.	Curt Schilling	64636
19.	Matt Young	46872
20.	Mike Gardiner	46679
21.	Nate Minchey	46341
22.	Derek Lowe	33510
23.	Joe Hesketh	26662
24.	Bronson Arroyo	19979
25.	Kevin Morton	17605

SINGLE SEASON PAP³, 1972–2004, BOSTON RED SOX

	PITCHER	YEAR	PAP³
1.	Roger Clemens	1988	1254755
2.	Roger Clemens	1996	1068743
3.	Roger Clemens	1989	1011983
4.	Roger Clemens	1992	653525
5.	Roger Clemens	1991	555991
6.	Roger Clemens	1990	509887
7.	Tim Wakefield	1996	404046
8.	Tim Wakefield	1997	399417
9.	Tom Gordon	1996	356371
10.	Bruce Hurst	1988	349087
11.	Roger Clemens	1994	330176
12.	Mike Boddicker	1990	327591
13.	Pedro Martinez	1998	311011
14.	Roger Clemens	1993	273344
15.	Jeff Sellers	1988	248293
16.	Pedro Martinez	2000	196478
17.	Aaron Sele	1994	182308
18.	Tim Wakefield	1995	180890
19.	Mike Boddicker	1989	179435
20.	Wes Gardner	1989	176605
21.	Frank Viola	1992	143752
22.	Erik Hanson	1995	137825
23.	Frank Viola	1993	137013
24.	Danny Darwin	1992	108315
25.	Greg Harris	1990	104655

Expected Win-Loss

Expected Win-Loss estimates a pitcher's win-loss record based on his innings pitched and runs allowed in each outing. Because run support and bullpen performance have such high influence on a pitcher's record, expected win-loss approximates a pitcher's win-loss record as if he received average run and bullpen support in each of his outings.

CAREER EXPECTED W-L, 1972–2004
(BY WINNING PERCENTAGE, MINIMUM 100 DECISIONS)

	PITCHER	W	L	WIN-PERC
1.	Jim Palmer	194.6	106.6	0.646
2.	Pedro Martinez	153.9	85.4	0.643
3.	Andy Messersmith	96.0	56.7	0.629
4.	J. R. Richard	105.1	65.6	0.616
5.	Catfish Hunter	124.1	78.0	0.614
6.	Greg Maddux	282.1	177.7	0.613
7.	Tom Seaver	226.6	144.9	0.610
8.	Ron Guidry	154.3	101.0	0.604
9.	Nolan Ryan	324.6	214.4	0.602
10.	Doug Rau	81.4	54.2	0.601
11.	John Candelaria	155.8	104.4	0.599
12.	Roger Clemens	295.7	198.2	0.599
13.	John Tudor	114.2	78.4	0.593
14.	Randy Johnson	218.0	150.4	0.592
15.	Gaylord Perry	194.3	134.2	0.591
16.	Curt Schilling	171.7	118.6	0.591
17.	Jon Matlack	146.2	101.1	0.591
18.	Don Sutton	246.8	173.1	0.588
19.	Dave Dravecky	61.4	43.2	0.587
20.	Don Gullett	67.8	47.8	0.586
21.	Steve Rogers	181.7	128.2	0.586
22.	Sid Fernandez	120.6	85.6	0.585
23.	Bert Blyleven	288.0	205.4	0.584
24.	Bret Saberhagen	161.7	116.7	0.581
25.	Tim Hudson	80.8	58.4	0.581

CAREER EXPECTED W-L, 1972–2004 (BY WINS)

	PITCHER	W	L	WIN-PERC
1.	Nolan Ryan	324.6	214.4	0.602
2.	Roger Clemens	295.7	198.2	0.599
3.	Bert Blyleven	288.0	205.4	0.584
4.	Greg Maddux	282.1	177.7	0.613
5.	Steve Carlton	250.5	181.1	0.580
6.	Frank Tanana	247.3	220.7	0.528
7.	Don Sutton	246.8	173.1	0.588
8.	Phil Niekro	240.5	200.7	0.545
9.	Tom Glavine	235.1	183.9	0.561
10.	Rick Reuschel	227.5	168.3	0.575
11.	Dennis Martinez	227.3	196.9	0.536
12.	Tom Seaver	226.6	144.9	0.610
13.	Jack Morris	219.7	203.4	0.519
14.	Randy Johnson	218.0	150.4	0.592
15.	Kevin Brown	203.4	147.8	0.579
16.	Jerry Reuss	200.6	166.8	0.546
17.	Jim Palmer	194.6	106.6	0.646
18.	Gaylord Perry	194.3	134.2	0.591
19.	Tommy John	194.1	155.6	0.555
20.	Orel Hershiser	193.0	151.4	0.560
21.	Bob Welch	191.8	146.6	0.566
22.	Vida Blue	186.6	136.9	0.577
23.	Chuck Finley	183.7	167.4	0.523
24.	Fernando Valenzuela	182.4	144.3	0.558
25.	Steve Rogers	181.7	128.2	0.586

SINGLE SEASON EXPECTED W-L, 1972–2004
(MINIMUM 10 DECISIONS, BY WINNING PERCENTAGE)

	PITCHER	YEAR	TEAM	W	L	WIN-PERC
1.	Greg Maddux	1995	Atlanta Braves	19.0	3.8	0.832
2.	Dwight Gooden	1985	New York Mets	24.0	5.4	0.814
3.	Cal Eldred	1992	Milwaukee Brewers	8.4	2.2	0.793
4.	Greg Maddux	1994	Atlanta Braves	17.0	4.4	0.790
5.	Ron Guidry	1978	New York Yankees	23.0	6.2	0.788
6.	Luis Tiant	1972	Boston Red Sox	12.0	3.4	0.784
7.	Steve Rogers	1973	Montreal Expos	11.0	3.0	0.781
8.	Nolan Ryan	1981	Houston Astros	13.0	3.7	0.773
9.	Pedro Martinez	2000	Boston Red Sox	17.0	5.4	0.765
10.	Steve Carlton	1972	Philadelphia Phillies	27.0	8.4	0.762
11.	Danny Darwin	1990	Houston Astros	9.6	3.0	0.760
12.	Roger Nelson	1972	Kansas City Royals	12.0	3.7	0.755
13.	Roger Clemens	1997	Toronto Blue Jays	21.0	7.2	0.744
14.	Jim Palmer	1972	Baltimore Orioles	22.0	7.5	0.743
15.	John Candelaria	1977	Pittsburgh Pirates	18.0	6.4	0.741
16.	Catfish Hunter	1972	Oakland Athletics	22.0	7.6	0.741
17.	Steve McCatty	1981	Oakland Athletics	14.0	4.8	0.741
18.	Roger Clemens	1990	Boston Red Sox	18.0	6.4	0.739
19.	Gaylord Perry	1972	Cleveland Indians	24.0	8.4	0.737
20.	Pedro Martinez	2003	Boston Red Sox	15.0	5.2	0.736
21.	John Tudor	1985	St. Louis Cardinals	21.0	7.6	0.735
22.	Pedro Martinez	1997	Montreal Expos	19.0	6.9	0.734
23.	Tom Seaver	1973	New York Mets	22.0	7.9	0.734
24.	Dave Righetti	1981	New York Yankees	8.2	3.0	0.734
25.	Greg Maddux	1997	Atlanta Braves	18.0	6.5	0.733

SINGLE SEASON EXPECTED W-L, 1972–2004 (BY TOTAL WINS)

	PITCHER	YEAR	TEAM	W	L	WIN-PERC
1.	Steve Carlton	1972	Philadelphia Phillies	26.8	8.4	0.762
2.	Wilbur Wood	1972	Chicago White Sox	26.6	13.5	0.664
3.	Fergie Jenkins	1974	Texas Rangers	24.5	11.9	0.673
4.	Mickey Lolich	1972	Detroit Tigers	24.5	10.4	0.701
5.	Jim Palmer	1975	Baltimore Orioles	23.7	8.9	0.726
6.	Andy Messersmith	1975	Los Angeles Dodgers	23.7	9.9	0.706
7.	Dwight Gooden	1985	New York Mets	23.7	5.4	0.814
8.	Gaylord Perry	1972	Cleveland Indians	23.6	8.4	0.737
9.	Bert Blyleven	1973	Minnesota Twins	23.5	11.3	0.676
10.	Gaylord Perry	1974	Cleveland Indians	23.4	8.7	0.728
11.	Catfish Hunter	1974	Oakland Athletics	23.4	10.6	0.688
12.	Ron Guidry	1978	New York Yankees	23.1	6.2	0.788
13.	Catfish Hunter	1975	New York Yankees	23.1	11.3	0.672
14.	Jim Palmer	1976	Baltimore Orioles	22.6	10.8	0.677
15.	Nolan Ryan	1972	California Angels	22.3	8.7	0.721
16.	Randy Jones	1976	San Diego Padres	22.3	11.7	0.656
17.	Nolan Ryan	1973	California Angels	22.2	11.5	0.658
18.	Jim Palmer	1973	Baltimore Orioles	22.2	8.8	0.716
19.	Jim Palmer	1978	Baltimore Orioles	22.2	10.0	0.690
20.	Phil Niekro	1974	Atlanta Braves	22.0	9.6	0.696
21.	Steve Carlton	1980	Philadelphia Phillies	21.9	9.5	0.699
22.	Vida Blue	1976	Oakland Athletics	21.9	9.3	0.702
23.	Catfish Hunter	1972	Oakland Athletics	21.8	7.6	0.741
24.	Tom Seaver	1973	New York Mets	21.8	7.9	0.734
25.	Gaylord Perry	1973	Cleveland Indians	21.8	14.5	0.600

CAREER EXPECTED W-L, BOSTON RED SOX (BY WINNING PERCENTAGE)

1.	Pedro Martinez	99.3	49.4	.668
2.	Luis Tiant	112.7	72.2	.610
3.	Roger Clemens	184.1	119.1	.607
4.	Roger Moret	23.9	16.7	.589
5.	Mike Boddicker	32.9	25.4	.565
6.	Marty Pattin	29.4	22.9	.562
7.	Frank Viola	29.0	22.6	.561
8.	Bret Saberhagen	21.5	18.3	.540
9.	Fergie Jenkins	23.1	19.8	.539
10.	Bill Lee	68.3	58.8	.537
11.	Dennis Eckersley	80.2	70.7	.532
12.	John Curtis	21.2	18.8	.530
13.	Rick Wise	40.0	35.7	.529
14.	Steve Renko	18.7	17.8	.513
15.	Danny Darwin	27.7	26.6	.510

SINGLE SEASON EXPECTED W-L, BOSTON RED SOX (BY WINS)

1. Roger Clemens	184.1	119.1	.607
2. Luis Tiant	112.7	72.2	.610
3. Pedro Martinez	99.3	49.4	.668
4. Bruce Hurst	83.1	80.5	.508
5. Tim Wakefield	81.9	103.6	.442
6. Dennis Eckersley	80.2	70.7	.532
7. Bill Lee	68.3	58.8	.537
8. Oil Can Boyd	56.8	57.4	.497
9. Mike Torrez	53.6	62.4	.462
10. Rick Wise	40.0	35.7	.529
11. Bob Ojeda	39.2	41.5	.486
12. Derek Lowe	38.7	41.1	.485
13. Al Nipper	34.9	45.3	.435
14. Aaron Sele	34.4	40.6	.459
15. John Tudor	34.1	34.8	.495

Park Adjusted Defensive Efficiency

Park Adjusted Defensive Efficiency (PADE) measures the percentage of balls in play a defense converted into outs above the average team (given their park). While fielding statistics like range factor, fielding percentage, and FRAA measure individual players, PADE reveals the overall team defensive quality in the purest way possible—by measuring how well they turn balls in play into outs. If you want to find the greatest defensive units of all time, this is where to look.

SINGLE SEASON PADE, 1972–2004

	TEAM	YEAR	PADE
1.	Los Angeles Dodgers	1973	6.47
2.	Boston Red Sox	1993	6.42
3.	Boston Red Sox	2000	6.24
4.	Los Angeles Dodgers	1975	5.78
5.	Colorado Rockies	2001	5.43
6.	Boston Red Sox	2002	5.30
7.	Baltimore Orioles	1973	5.20
8.	Colorado Rockies	2000	5.06
9.	Colorado Rockies	1996	4.98
10.	Atlanta Braves	1993	4.88
11.	Boston Red Sox	1998	4.80
12.	Anaheim Angels	2002	4.65
13.	Baltimore Orioles	1972	4.56
14.	Los Angeles Dodgers	1974	4.44
15.	Colorado Rockies	1995	4.42
16.	Boston Red Sox	1999	4.26
17.	Baltimore Orioles	1995	4.21
18.	Atlanta Braves	1992	3.78
19.	Minnesota Twins	2001	3.62
20.	Cleveland Indians	1999	3.57
21.	Kansas City Royals	2001	3.54
22.	Toronto Blue Jays	1991	3.53
23.	Chicago White Sox	1991	3.43
24.	New York Mets	1999	3.35
25.	Boston Red Sox	1994	3.27
26.	New York Yankees	1976	3.25
27.	Chicago Cubs	1992	3.18
28.	Cincinnati Reds	1988	3.15
29.	Montreal Expos	1977	3.11
30.	Boston Red Sox	1975	3.03
31.	Cincinnati Reds	1999	3.02
32.	Colorado Rockies	2002	2.97
33.	Minnesota Twins	2002	2.97
34.	Chicago Cubs	1991	2.89
35.	Toronto Blue Jays	1983	2.88
36.	Atlanta Braves	2002	2.86
37.	Detroit Tigers	1981	2.85
38.	Florida Marlins	1994	2.85
39.	Kansas City Royals	1981	2.81
40.	Toronto Blue Jays	1982	2.77
41.	Atlanta Braves	1994	2.76
42.	Kansas City Royals	2002	2.75
43.	Minnesota Twins	1991	2.73
44.	Pittsburgh Pirates	1984	2.72
45.	Atlanta Braves	1974	2.71
46.	Seattle Mariners	2001	2.65
47.	Boston Red Sox	1995	2.63
48.	St. Louis Cardinals	1982	2.63
49.	Kansas City Royals	1982	2.62
50.	Milwaukee Brewers	1997	2.61

—JAMES CLICK, CLAY DAVENPORT, KEITH WOOLNER

NOTES

Chapter 1. The Banality of Incompetence

1. Frederick Lewis Allen, *Only Yesterday* (New York: HarperCollins, 2000), p. 132; John M. Barry, *The Great Influenza* (New York: Viking Penguin, 2004), p. 397.
2. Glenn Stout and Richard Johnson, *Red Sox Century* (Boston: Houghton Mifflin, 2004), pp. 146–147.
3. Glenn Stout, *Impossible Dreams: A Red Sox Collection* (Boston: Houghton Mifflin, 2003), p. 111.
4. *Baseball Magazine*, January, 1946.
5. Bob Hoie in *Total Baseball: The Ultimate Baseball* (8th ed.), edited by John Thorn, Bill Deane, Phil Birnbaum, et al. (Sportclassic Books, 2004), p. 497.
6. Stout and Johnson, *Red Sox Century*, p. 234.
7. Howard Bryant, *Shut Out* (Boston: Beacon Press, 2003), p. 41.
8. Stout and Johnson, *Red Sox Century*, p. 241.
9. Jules Tygiel, *Baseball's Great Experiment* (New York: Oxford University Press, 1997), p. 329.
10. James A. Riley, *The Biographical Encyclopedia of the Negro Baseball Leagues* (New York: Carroll & Graf Publishers, 2002), pp. 217–218.
11. Carl Yastrzemski and Gerald Eskenazi, *Yaz: Baseball, the Wall, and Me* (New York: Warner Books, 1991), p. 80.
12. *The Sporting News*, June 8, 1960, p. 7.
13. Howard Bryant, *Shut Out*, p. 25.
14. Stout and Johnson, *Red Sox Century*, p. 312.
15. Al Hirshberg, *What's the Matter with the Red Sox*, p. 143.
16. Bryant, *Shut Out*, p. 64.
17. Stout and Johnson, *Red Sox Century*, p. 435.
18. Compiled by Baseball Prospectus.

Dan Duquette: Failed Epstein Prototype

1. http://espn.go.com/mlb/news/2002/0228/1342318.html
2. http://www.s-t.com/daily/10-99/10-14-99/d03sp006.htm
3. http://www.bizforward.com/bos/issues/2001-12/twenty20/
4. Minimum two seasons.
5. Duquette is fourth behind Theo Epstein (.595), Joe Cronin (.550), and Haywood Sullivan (.545).
6. David Neft, Michael Neft, Bob Carroll, and Richard Cohen, *The Boston Red Sox Fan Book* (New York: St. Martin's Press, 2005), p. 62.
7. http://www.baseball-reference.com/h/hansoer01.shtml
8. http://www.baseball-reference.com/o/o'leatr01.shtml
9. http://www.baseball-reference.com/postseason/1995_ALDS1.shtml
10. Baseball America, *Draft Almanac*, pp. 326, 340, 353, 366, 378, and 389.
11. http://www.baseball-reference.com/c/carrahe01.shtml
12. http://www.baseball-reference.com/f/floribr01.shtml
13. http://www.baseball-reference.com/b/bicheda01.shtml
14. The eight teams being the Cardinals, Expos, Mariners, Mets, Phillies, Rangers, Reds, and Twins.
15. http://www.southcoasttoday.com/daily/03-98/03-03-98/d01sp127.htm and http://www.southcoasttoday.com/daily/03-98/03-12-98/d01sp138.htm
16. http://slate.msn.com/id/84318/
17. http://sports.espn.go.com/gammons/s/2001/0206/1066218.html
18. http://www.usatoday.com/sports/bbw/2001-07-25/2001-07-25-cover.htm

Chapter 3. The A-Rod Advantage

1. Rodriguez would have had the option to become a free agent after the 2007 season under the terms of his original deal with Texas. Because Rodriguez's original contract was so large, guaranteeing him $25 million in 2006 and $27 million in 2007, it is questionable how much this extra flexibility would have been worth to him. Even if Rodriguez had posted outstanding numbers in 2004 and 2005, thereby increasing his market value, he would have been hard-pressed to receive an offer as great as $25–$27 million per season, as no player in baseball history had been promised such a large annual salary.
2. That the union has the right to reject certain contract restructurings, with or without the player's consent, is not in much debate. The Red Sox and the commissioner's office would argue, however, that the restructuring would in fact be beneficial to Rodriguez because of the additional marketing rights and guarantees provided.

3. Without the commissioner's waiver, this behavior would have been considered tampering, and forbidden by the Collective Bargaining Agreement.

4. Larry Lucchino, Red Sox press release, December 17, 2003.

5. Larry Lucchino, Red Sox press release, December 18, 2003.

6. It is my belief that the Players Association believed that its hard-line position was likely to result in further negotiations between the respective parties that would have sent Rodriguez to Boston under terms it considered more favorable, rather than triggering a sequence of events that collapsed the deal entirely. That is, if the Players Association had been presented with a choice between accepting the initial deal as is, and rejecting any Rodriguez-to-Boston deal, it might have proceeded differently.

7. For example, Chris Stynes, Robert Fick, and Darren Oliver are players who had WARP scores close to 0 in 2004; each of these players was released unconditionally during the course of the season.

8. Red Sox press release, December 23, 2003.

Chapter 4. Squeezing the Merchandise

1. All projections from *Baseball Prospectus 2004*.

2. In 2004, Millar would hit 27 doubles at Fenway, nine on the road. His two-year total is 45/21. Home batting average is .318, road .253.

3. http://sports.espn.go.com/mlb/gammons/story?id=1782139

4. Isolated power (ISO) is slugging percentage minus batting average.

5. Marginal lineup value (MLVr) is an estimate of the additional number of runs a given player will contribute to a lineup that otherwise consists of average offensive performers. In its rate form, this is stated as the additional runs per game.

6. *The 2005 ESPN Baseball Encyclopedia,* edited by Pete Palmer and Gary Gillette (New York: Sterling Publishing, 2005).

Chapter 5. Varieties of Relief

1. Bill James, *The Baseball Book 1991*, (New York: Villard, 1991) p. 362.

2. Bill James, *The New Bill James Historical Baseball Abstract* (New York: Simon and Schuster, 2003). Emphasis in the original.

3. http://www.baseballprospectus.com/article.php?articleid=648

4. http://www.bostondirtdogs.com/2003/barks_and_bites_2003_1.htm

5. http://www2.ocregister.com/ocrweb/ocr/article.do?id=34500&section= SPORTS&subsection=SPORTS_COLUMNS&year=2003&month=4&day=12

6. *Boston Herald,* July 29, 2003.

Chapter 9. The Caveman Cleans Up

1. Steve Krasner, *Providence Journal*, Feb. 26, 2004.

2. Michael Lewis, *Moneyball* (New York: W.W. Norton 2004), p. 129.

3. http://www.sptimes.com/2003/10/11/Sports/ALCS__Damon_s_head_cl.shtml

4. Sean McAdam, *Providence Journal*, March 11, 2004.

5. Ibid.

6. Bob Hohler, *The Boston Globe*, March 11, 2004.

Chapter 14. Brothers of the Mind Game

1. Michael Lewis, *Moneyball* (New York: W.W. Norton, 2004), p. xiii.

Chapter 15. Basebrawl

1. *The New York Times*, June 17, 1925, p. 17; Bill James, *The New Bill James Historical Baseball Abstract* (New York: Simon and Schuster, 2003), p. 486.

2. *Chicago Tribune*, September 23, 1974, p. C2; David H. Nathan, *The McFarland Baseball Quotations Dictionary* (Jefferson, North Carolina: McFarland & Co., 2000), p. 14.

3. Stewart O' Nan and Stephen King, *Faithful* (New York: Scribner, 2004), p. 227.

4. *The Boston Globe*, July 25, 2004, p. D1.

5. Baseball Prospectus Radio, November 28, 2004.

6. John Dewan and Don Zminda, eds., *Stats 1993 Baseball Scoreboard* (STATS, Inc., 1993), pp. 84–85.

7. All before/after records from www.retrosheet.org.

8. *The Washington Post*, July 21, 1932, p. 9.

9. John Drebinger, *The New York Times*, May 31, 1938, p. 23.

10. Joseph Durso, *The New York Times*, August 2, 1973, p. 43.

11. Peter Gammons, *Beyond the Sixth Game* (New York: Penguin Group, 1986), pp. 49–50.

12. Parton Keese, *The New York Times*, May 21, 1976, p. 46.

13. http://p086.ezboard.com/fsonsofsamhornfrm14.showMessage?topicID=21.topic

Draft-Wise but Career-Foolish

1. Figures drawn from *USA Today*.

Chapter 16. Nomargate

1. This point was made particularly well by the online analyst known simply as Tangotiger, and cited in this instance through his comments at www.robneyer.com/UER.html. For more of Tangotiger's work and analysis, which I can't recommend highly enough, you should surf over to www.tangotiger.net.

2. For more of Garciaparra's career data, defensive and offensive, you can check out his player card at our Web site, http://www.baseballprospectus.com/dt/garcino01.shtml.

3. WARP1 is Clay Davenport's metric Wins Above Replacement Player, level 1. It makes adjustments only within that season, and counts a player's defensive contribution. FRAR is Clay's Fielding Runs Above Replacement. For more on BP metrics, you can check out http://www.baseballprospectus.com/statistics/.

4. He didn't quite make it, getting to a VORP rate of .266, still an improvement on his 2004 production as an Expo.

5. Joe Sheehan, *Prospectus Today,* "Getting Separation," August 1; http://www.baseballprospectus.com/article.php?articleid=3294.

6. This Baseball Prospectus commentator, in fact. Chris Kahrl, "Transaction Analysis," August 1; http://www.baseballprospectus.com/article.php?article id=3294. Regardless of my feelings about the deal, I still feel this was a situation that could have been deflated by better communication, but the Red Sox wanted certainty, and I have to grant that Nomar couldn't provide that.

Chapter 17. Invulnerable

1. How to determine the odds of a particular team winning x out of y games:

Each team is assigned a particular winning percentage (w), the likelihood that they will win any particular game. Usually this is simply their winning percentage from the end of the season, but it can also be the estimated winning percentage based on runs scored and runs allowed. (Although, after about game 140, the real winning percentage is a slightly more accurate predictor than estimated, as per Clay Davenport's research.)

The odds that a team with a winning percentage w will win any x number of games in a row are simply w^x. Conversely, the odds that they will lose any y number of games in a row are $(1 - w)^y$. This is a binomial distribution, but a very simple one.

If, however, the goal is to determine if a team will win *at least* two of three games, the formula becomes more complex because more situations meet the standards for success. For example, if the team wins all three games, wins the first two, wins the second two, or wins the first and last games, all three situations must be counted. The odds of the team winning exactly two of the three games—$w^3*(1 - w)$—must be added to the odds that they will win all three—w^3. But since there are three ways in which the team can win two out of three games, that result has to be multiplied by three. Approaching the Red Sox's twenty-two wins in twenty-five games, the equations can become enormous.

However, the key to the puzzle is Pascal's Triangle, a tool that reveals the binomial coefficient by which each result must be multiplied—three, in the case above. Essentially, the triangle shows how many different ways the final counted result can be achieved by different distributions of the binomial choice. There are three different ways the team can win two games and lose one, but only *one* way in which they can win all three. This is also referred to as "x choose y"—essentially, if one is faced with the decision to choose y games out of x total games, how many possible combinations add up to y.

While Pascal's Triangle can be constructed by adding the two numbers immediately above, there is a shortcut: If n is the total number of games and v is the total number of wins, the formula is: n! / (v! * (n – v)!). In this example, because the numbers are so small, the math is quite simple:

$$3! / (2! * (3 - 2)!)$$
$$6 / (2 * 1) = 3$$

Back to the Red Sox's case, the odds that a team will win at least 22 of 25 games is the sum of the odds that they will win *exactly* 22, 23, 24, and 25 of the 25 games. In this situation, the binomial coefficients are 2300, 300, 25, and, of course, 1. Thus, the odds that a team with a winning percentage w will win at least 22 of 25 games is:

$$2300 * w^{22} * (1 - w)^3 + 300 * w^{23} * (1 - w)^2 + 25 * w^{24} * (1 - w) + w^{25}$$

where w is the team's winning percentage for the season.

Chapter 18. Cracking the Rivera Code

1. In the World Series, Boston faced off against one of the NL's most control-based staffs: the St. Louis Cardinals. While only Matt Morris would qualify as a control pitcher for the purposes of this study (fewer than 3.0 BB/9 and 6.0 K/9), the rest of the Cardinal staff was very close to those numbers on the season with only Chris Carpenter averaging more than 6.22 K/9. As expected, the Red Sox scored 6.0 runs per game in the World Series, almost exactly what they averaged against control pitchers all year long (6.23 runs).

Pedro, Without Qualification

1. See http://www.baseballprospectus.com/article.php?articleid=2753 and http://www.baseballprospectus.com/article.php?articleid=2846.

Chapter 21. Insult and Injury

1. http://www.boston.com/sports/baseball/redsox/articles/2005/04/28/piniella_keeps_swinging?mode=PF

Chapter 25. Beat the Yankees, Be the Yankees

1. http://news-press.com/apps/pbcs.dll/article?AID=/20050219/SPORTS/502190471/1012/SPORTS02
2. http://sports.espn.go.com/mlb/columns/story?id=1992775
3. http://bostondirtdogs.boston.com/Headline_Archives/Daily_Headlines_December_2004.html

ABOUT THE AUTHORS

Jim Baker has been a Baseball Prospectus author since May 2004. Prior to that, he was a columnist for ESPN.com's "MLB Insider." He contributed to *The New Bill James Historical Baseball Abstract*. He resides in Austin, Texas.

Will Carroll is the author of the books *Saving the Pitcher* and *The Juice*. He writes the highly acclaimed, first-ever injuries column "Under the Knife," for Baseball Prospectus, as well as contributes to *The New York Times, Slate,* and MLB.com. He lives in Indianapolis, where he's waiting to write a book about the Cubs' next championship.

James Click spends most days in San Francisco, thanking his girlfriend, Ace, for convincing him to come to California and follow the Oakland A's rather than the Mets. His history degree from Yale turns out to have little practical application to either his day job as a tech consultant or his work at Baseball Prospectus.

Clifford J. Corcoran is the co-author of Bronx Banter, a blog about the New York Yankees, on BaseballToaster.com. His music criticism has appeared in *Alternative Press* and *Ray Gun* magazines and can be found online at TrouserPress.com. His earlier baseball writing can be found on the now-dormant Clifford's Big Red Blog. This is his first involvement with the Baseball Prospectus people. He lives in New Jersey with a lovely veterinarian and the world's healthiest cat.

Clay Davenport is a meteorologist living in Bowie, Maryland, with his wife, Susan.

Steven Goldman is the creator of the long-running "Pinstriped Bible" column at www.yesnetwork.com, the "You Could Look It Up" column for baseballprospectus.com, a contributor to the Baseball Prospectus annual book, and the author of the biography *Forging Genius: The Making of Casey Stengel*. His work has also been published in *Yankees Magazine*, *The New York Sun*, and seen on Web sites too numerous to mention. Steven lives in New Jersey with his wife, Stefanie; daughter, Sarah; and, as of recently, his son Clemens.

Jay Jaffe is the founder of the Futility Infielder Web site (www.futility infielder.com), one of the oldest baseball blogs, an author of Baseball Prospectus, and a stathead since the day he discovered that fractions were merely batting averages in disguise. He is a graduate of Brown University and works as a graphic designer in New York City. He would like to thank his family and friends, who have endured and encouraged his years of ranting about baseball, and would especially like to thank his lovely bride, Andra, for her undying support for all of his writing endeavors.

Rany Jazayerli is a founding author of Baseball Prospectus, as well as a dermatologist in private practice in the Chicago suburbs. He lives with his wife, Belsam; his daughter, Cedra; and his newborn daughter, Jenna. He's thrilled that the Red Sox won the World Series last year, and would now like them to roll over for all the other teams that have suffered, with much less fanfare, for just as long.

Chris Kahrl is a University of Chicago grad, publishing professional, and founding member of Baseball Prospectus, for which she writes the popular "Trades Analysis" column. Chris lives in the Washington, D.C., area.

Jason Karegeannes got his B.A. in history at the University of Wisconsin and is currently a sports management master's student at the University of Texas–Austin. In addition to his responsibilities as an intern and author with Baseball Prospectus, he also moonlights as an associate scout for a National League team. When not watching baseball, studying, or scouting, he sops up his remaining time reading as many books as he possibly can and enjoying the added sun that his move from Wisconsin to Texas has provided.

Jonah Keri is an author and editor of Baseball Prospectus. His writing includes the weekly "Prospectus Game of the Week" column. His "Prospectus Q&A" feature includes interviews with the best and brightest names in baseball. He's served as co-editor of the Baseball Prospectus annual book, the Baseball Prospectus Web site (www.baseballprospectus. com), and other Baseball Prospectus–related publications. He also works as a stock market writer for *Investor's Business Daily*.

Ben Murphy does Web site design and database management for Baseball Prospectus. He recently earned his bachelor's degree from the University of North Carolina at Chapel Hill in mathematical decision sciences and will attend graduate school at UNC to get his master's in operations research. Ben is engaged to be married to Kristen Kirby in June 2006.

Doug Pappas was an author of Baseball Prospectus, and the chairman of SABR's Business of Baseball Committee. The foremost interpreter of baseball's byzantine economic machinations, Doug worked as a lawyer when not acting as a gadfly to the likes of Bud Selig. Doug passed away in May 2004. He is sorely missed.

Dave Pease lives in San Diego and works for a wireless communications company. He enjoys hot weather, power tools, The Mars Volta, genuine Honda engineering, and remembering the Padres' Taco Bell uniforms.

Dayn Perry is a regular contributor to Baseball Prospectus and FOXSports.com. He has also written about baseball for publications like ESPN.com, *The Miami Herald*, *Washington Monthly*, *Reason Magazine*, *The Washington Times*, *The Montreal Gazette* and the *St. Petersburg Times*. His first book, *The Winners*, the story of great baseball teams in the contemporary era, will be published in March 2006. A Mississippi native, he now lives in Chicago.

Joe Sheehan is a displaced New Yorker living outside of Los Angeles with his wife, Sophia, and their two cats. In addition to his work on the Baseball Prospectus annual book, he writes a column for BP's Web site and makes regular appearances on ESPNEWS's "Hot List."

Nate Silver attended the University of Chicago, home of the first atomic bomb and first Heisman Trophy winner, and has been stuck in the Second City ever since. A lifelong Tiger and Cub fan, Nate consoles himself by playing poker, watching *Law & Order* reruns, and visiting the city's innumerable restaurants and watering holes. Nate is the executive vice president of BP's parent company, Prospectus Entertainment Ventures, LLC.

Paul A. Swydan is both a contributor and marketer for Baseball Prospectus. He also works in the Colorado Rockies' ticketing department and is a founding partner of Standing Room Only Public Relations. Paul has earned a BSBA in marketing from Boston University and an MBA in sports management from the University of Denver. He resides in Centennial, Colorado, with his fiancée, Summer, whom he will wed this July.

Keith Woolner holds a master's degree from Stanford University in decision analysis, and bachelor's degrees from MIT in mathematics, computer science, and management science. He lives and works in Cary, North Carolina.

Derek Zumsteg is a Seattle baseball writer. He's written for Baseball Prospectus, a bunch of newspapers, and his first book is scheduled to be published in spring of next year, so please check Amazon obsessively. Derek's a long-suffering fan of the Seattle Mariners, who haven't won so much as a league championship.

INDEX

Note: Page numbers in *italics* indicate photographs.